DALLAS THROUGH A LOST LENS

1939 - 1954 · THE PHOTOGRAPHY OF CONNELL R. MILLER SR.

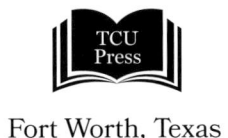

TCU Press

Fort Worth, Texas

DALLAS THROUGH A LOST LENS

1939 - 1954 ▪ THE PHOTOGRAPHY OF CONNELL R. MILLER SR.

EDITED BY CONNELL R. MILLER JR.

Library of Congress Control Number: 2024044622

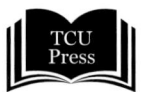

TCU Box 298300
Fort Worth, Texas 76129
www.tcupress.com

Design by Bill Brammer

I dedicate this book to my father. Thank you, Dad, for all the wonderful images you left. They serve not only as a tribute to your skill as a photographer, but more importantly to your perseverance in recording and preserving so many facets of life in our hometown of Dallas.

Thanks also to my wife, Judy, who has never complained about the sometimes inordinate amount of time I have spent huddled over my computer and scanner to create this photobook.

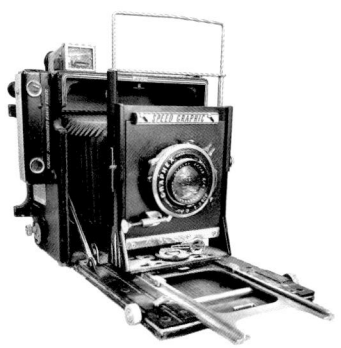

ABOVE: This is a photo of the original Graflex 4x5 "Speed Graphic" camera my father used to take most of the images in this book. "Speedo" (as Dad and I called it) is now happily retired and living quietly on a shelf in my home office.

CONTENTS

Introduction
by Connell R. Miller Jr. **1**

INTRODUCTION

by Connell R. Miller Jr.

"I've got the camera, so get dressed, tell your mom goodbye, and hop in the car!" In the early 1950s, unless there was a ball game or planned fishing trip with schoolmates, this would be a welcome weekend morning wake-up call. It meant the three of us—Dad, me, and his large-format, Speed Graphic press-type camera—were heading out for a day of taking photos around what at the time was a growing city of 430,000. Dallas then was a little larger than the size of Arlington in 2023—way before it would become the sprawling city of 1.4 million anchoring the eastern side of the Dallas–Fort Worth Metroplex.

It was always fun to look for adventure in his car—a big Cadillac festooned with an array of antennas connected to various "gizmos" inside, all for the purpose of helping us find that fire, car wreck, event, or other gathering of folks that could give us some nice images. The first piece of gear I remember was the car telephone, an early development by the engineers at Ma Bell, that he had installed in the early 1950s. It was mounted on the transmission tunnel and featured a corded handset the same size as a home phone but with a turn-to-talk, let-go-to-listen switch. To initiate a call, Dad would turn the spring-loaded switch that summoned an operator, who would then take the desired number and dial it for him. A large case of (pre-transistor) tube-powered equipment in the trunk provided power for the phone.

Next came the radio that covered the police and fire department bands, which was mounted under the dash. Another addition was the Appleton spotlight that was useful when looking for addresses or objects at night, and a few of his photos were even made using its light rather than a flashbulb.

In this digital, automatic-everything camera world of today, most people do not realize the many steps that were necessary to capture an image with a film camera, such as the one used to take the images for this book. The process involved manually setting the lens aperture (usually by guess or, if there was time, after taking a reading with a hand-held light meter), adjusting the shutter speed, and focusing on the subject. This all had to be done before clicking the shutter release to take the one photograph that hopefully captured what the photographer saw.

The talent shown by these early photographers to quickly coordinate composition while manipulating settings has been replaced, for the most part, by the technology found in today's modern cameras. With their automatic focus and ability to select the best f-stop and/or shutter speed, it allows photographers now to concentrate less on getting that one great image by banging off dozens of shots, knowing they will find at least one good "keeper" when they download their images to the computer.

The next step in the picture taking process was to bring a negative's image to life so a resulting print could be enjoyed, framed, and hung on the wall, or reproduced in the pages of a book. Let's quickly go through the process that began after we returned from our photographic session with the camera.

The 4 x 5 negatives were unloaded from the film holders in our well-equipped home darkroom and their trip towards a finished print began. First, they went into a tray with developer solution, then one with stop bath, followed by a dip in the fixer tray before finally washing them in water. When dry, the negatives would be inserted into the Beseler enlarger where, after any necessary corrections such as cropping, burning, or dodging was performed, the image was projected onto a sheet of photographic paper, usually an 8 x 10. After processing, the new print was then deposited in the large, floor-standing print washer. The final step in our darkroom sojourn was to send the now damp print on a circuit through the big drum print dryer. Whew!

Dad wasn't working for a newspaper or magazine, and he rarely sold an image for publication. His passion and love for the medium he worked in was more in the spirit of the true artist: to take a subject, whether at a planned event or spontaneously on the street, and click the shutter to capture it. Today, his output of black and white images provides us with perfect examples of the genre known as "street photography."

His interest in and dedication to his lens work began shortly after Dad graduated from high school in 1936. Aboard a tramp steamer bound for Europe, he earned extra money doing some work with the crew during the journey that allowed him to buy a nice, new Contax 35mm camera in Germany. While there, he attended the Olympic Games in Berlin, bringing home many unprocessed rolls of film (unfortunately, those negatives have disappeared over the years).

After talking my grandparents into letting him set up a small darkroom in their home, Dad soon became proficient in the post-shooting, developing, and printing process.

By 1939, however, he had adopted his trademark large-format Speed Graphic press-type camera, preferring the very sharp enlargements the 4 x 5 negatives would give him over those images taken on small 35mm film. While photographing whatever he found of interest around town, he was able to pay for his film and darkroom supplies by taking before and after pics for several body shops around Dallas, as well as shooting fraternity and sorority events at Southern Methodist University (SMU), where he was a student.

In 1942, he put his photography temporarily on hold to serve as an officer in the U.S. Navy. His ship, the USS *Crosby*, was a destroyer that usually carried troops as it dodged enemy planes, ships, and submarines in the South Pacific. After leaving active duty and going into the naval reserve, he finished his business degree while working at his family's company, which manufactured most of the duffel bags for the servicemen and servicewomen in World War II.

Dad was fortunately blessed with a coalescence of the right and left sides of his brain. On one side, he was a businessman: an executive vice president of his family's Dallas-based Texas Textile Mills, with milling and manufacturing facilities across the state. He was also active in several civic organizations, a member of the Citizen's Traffic Commission, a Mason and Shriner, and a longtime member and past president of the Bonehead Club.

The creative side was where he had fun. Besides the photography, he was a cartoonist, an amateur architect, and a musician who played the organ, piano, accordion, sax, and guitar. He had two professional-quality tape recorders, and occasionally we would set up microphones and record various musical groups in our game room. One I remember well was the Cell Block Seven, a popular Dixieland band comprised of young SMU students led by Ed Burnet, a future NFL wide receiver with the Pittsburg Steelers and the second version of the Dallas Texans. He became a country singer and was well-known in later years as owner of The Levee on Mockingbird Lane as well as Dallas's most popular recording studio, Sumet-Bernet Sound Studios.

My father was also an ardent auto enthusiast and writer, with articles and his photographs appearing in several automotive publications. As an avid race photographer since the late 1930s, when sports car racing was taking hold in Texas in the early 1950s, he became the photographer for the Texas region of the Sports Car Club of America (SCCA). One of our family's longtime good friends from those early race years was a young man whose usual driving attire was a pair of old and wrinkled bib overalls. The rumpled black hat he donned when the helmet came off between heat races would later become a part of his world-recognized logo. His name was Carroll Shelby.

In 1952, Dad had less time to devote to his photography. He and his younger brother, Giles, seeing as how college games packed over sixty thousand fans into the Cotton Bowl on any given Saturday, purchased an NFL team, the New York Yanks, and brought professional football to the rabid pigskin fans of Texas with the Dallas Texans. (Lamar Hunt would have the second version Texans several years later, before he moved the team to Kansas City and re-named them the Chiefs.) We soon found out, though, that the pro-side of the sport was not of much interest to the denizens of North Texas, as 18,700 was the largest crowd passing through the turnstiles at any of our home games in the Cotton Bowl. By 1953, we were no longer owners of an NFL team, and what was left of the Dallas Texans became players for Carroll Rosenbloom and his new Baltimore Colts. Our failed venture remains in the record book as the last team to go bankrupt in the NFL.

With football team ownership now in the past, Dad was back behind the lens in 1953. However, his world as a husband, father, businessman, and photographer would end on Thanksgiving Day in 1954 at the young age of thirty-six in a car accident at Walnut Hill Lane and Central Expressway.

Fortunately, his collection of seventy-to-eighty-five-year-old negatives are safe, with many still in pristine condition—though some had suffered various degrees of degradation over the years and needed restoration. With several photographers agreeing with me that these images of an earlier time in the life of our city and its people at work and play just begged to be published, I began the task to scan, perform any needed restoration, catalog, save, and upload these negatives into the digital world several years ago.

The business world was Dad's living, and even with his interests and abilities in so many different areas, I firmly believe he was happiest with a camera in his hand—photographing the city and its people. Always embracing new technology as it entered the marketplace, if he were still alive today, I'm sure he would be out shooting with a new Nikon, Canon, Mamiya, or Hasselblad digital camera. However, I'd be willing to bet that trusty old Speed Graphic press camera (which now rests in well-deserved retirement on a shelf in my office!) would still be in his camera bag and making an occasional appearance somewhere on the streets of Big D, with him fiddling with the settings, squinting through the viewfinder, clicking the shutter, and making plans that evening to bring the results to life in the darkroom.

Downtown Dallas

———

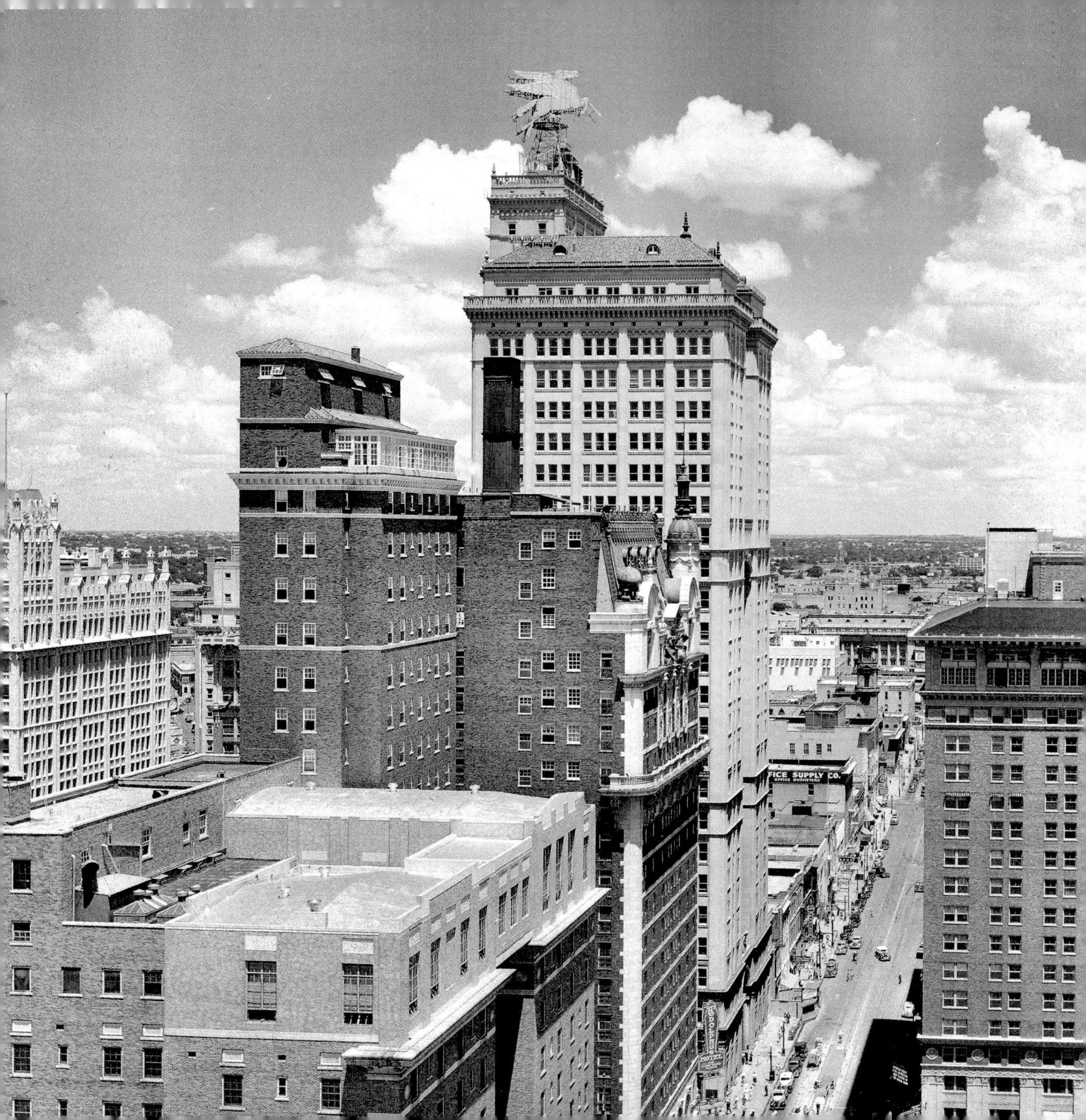

In writing about my old hometown of Dallas, I sometimes refer to it as a wonderful, "small" big city. That's the way I remember it growing up in the 1940s and 1950s, and to some extent into the 1960s. Back then, it was easy to get around and with little congestion. A person could usually get to the downtown core quickly and easily from any direction. That doesn't seem to hold true anymore today, with the increased traffic, myriad number of highways and toll roads, loops, and a High Five Interchange. Wow! I'm thankful for Mapsco as well as my GPS-enabled cellphone.

Many of the old buildings I used as navigational landmarks are gone now, but my compliments to the planners/developers/architects for a few of their modern and beautiful replacements.

———

RIGHT: A tale of two distinct eras. Quite a contrast between the old building on the left and the shiny new skyscraper to its right. 1953.

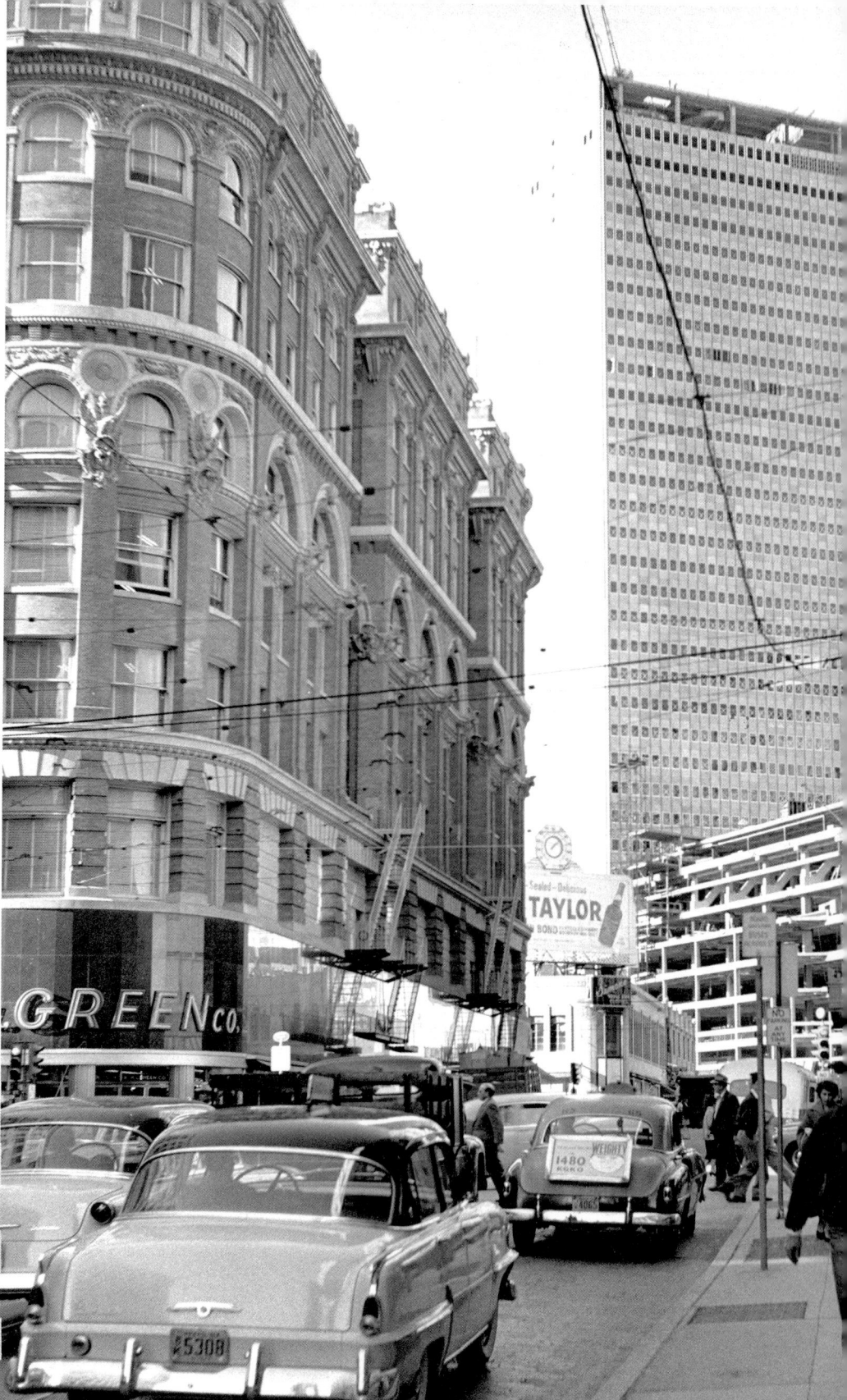

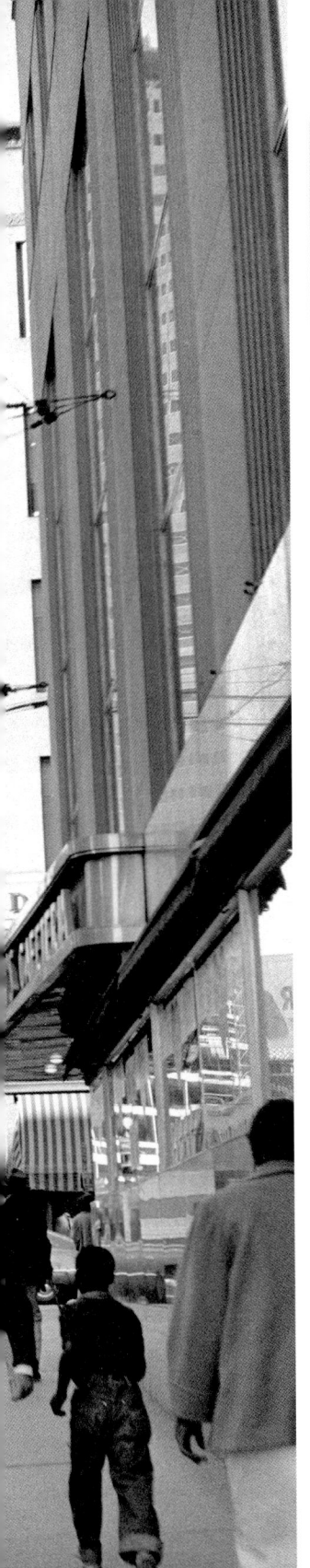

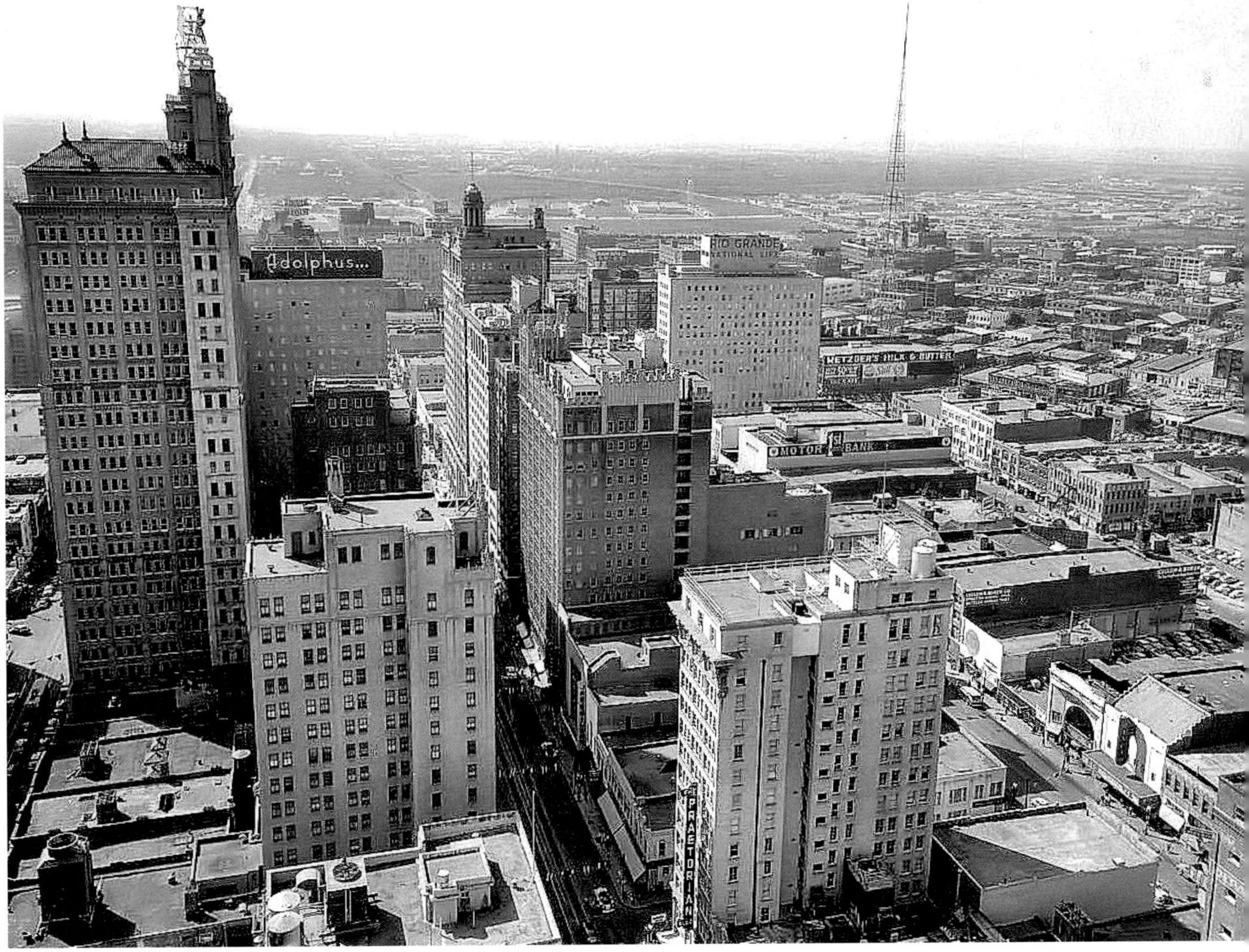

ABOVE: View of downtown Dallas. 1953.

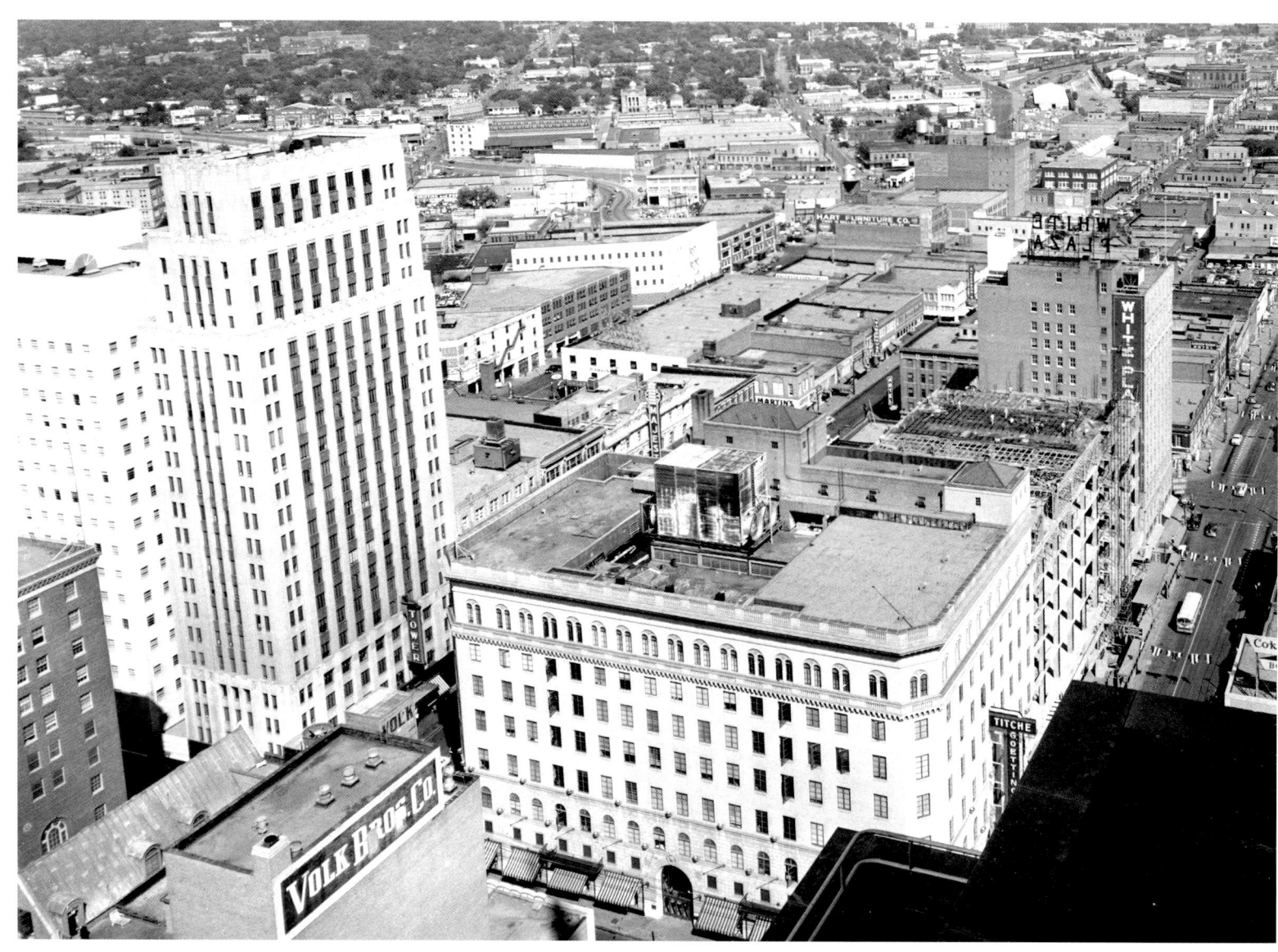

ABOVE: Downtown Dallas. 1953.

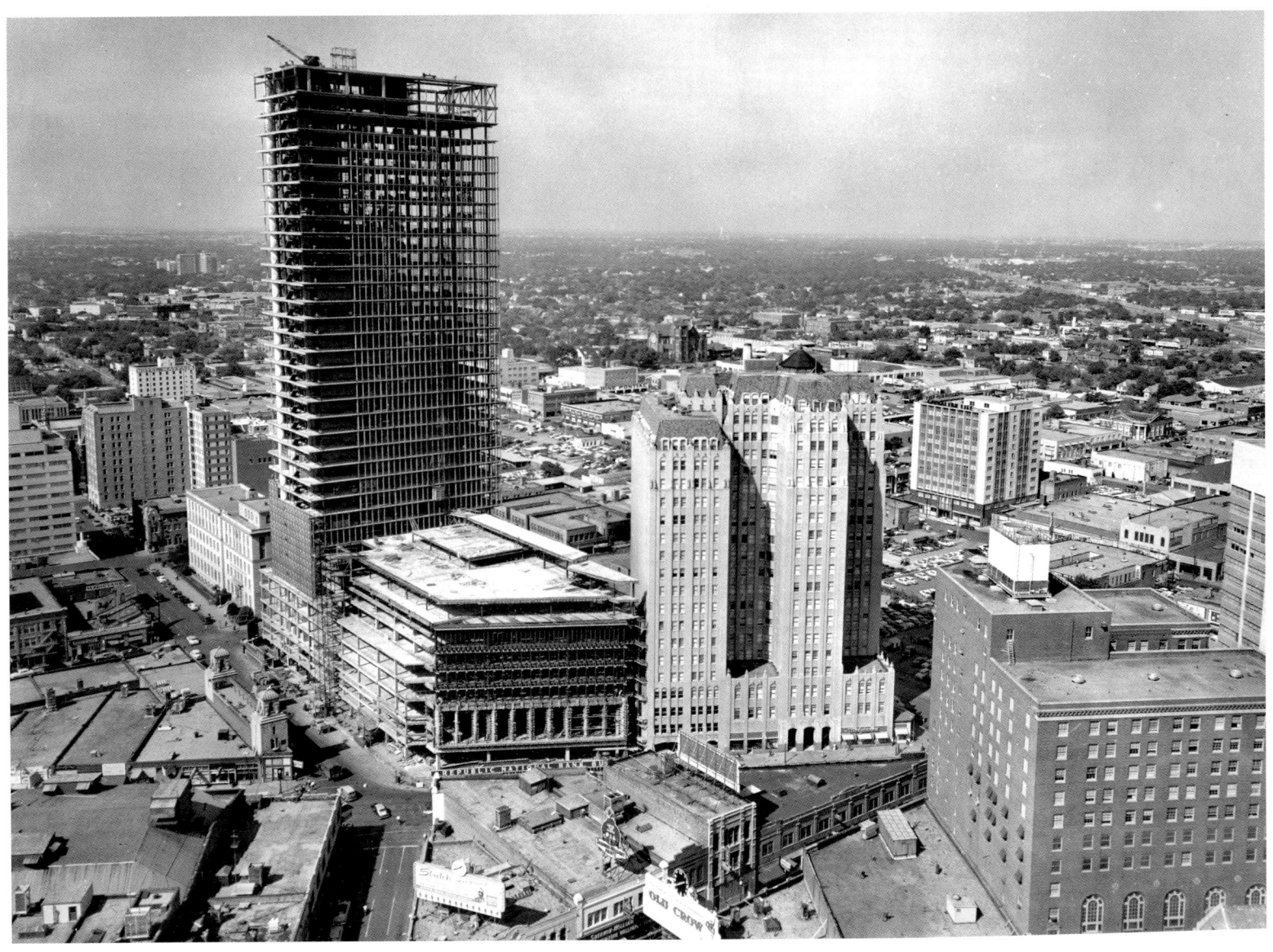

ABOVE: The Republic National Bank on Ervay Street opened in December 1954. A fire in a closet due to spontaneous combustion with oily rags threatened to halt construction for a time but was quickly brought under control. 1953.

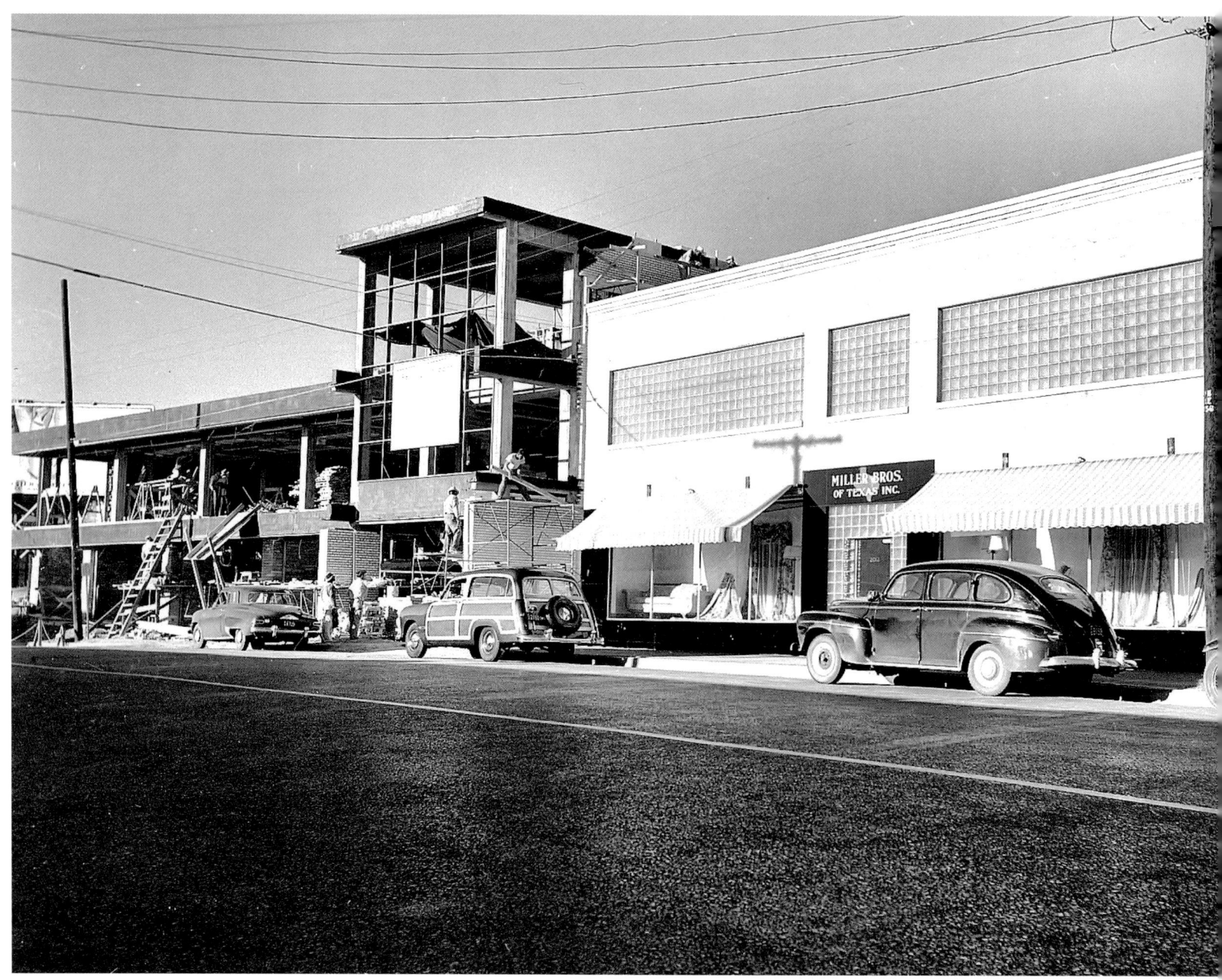

ABOVE: George Dahl building under construction on Akard Street. Dahl was the world-renowned architect that designed the Art Deco structures on the Texas State Fairgrounds. The building next to it, Miller Bros., was the showroom for fabrics and wearing apparel produced by our family's Texas Textile Mills and Conro Manufacturing. 1948.

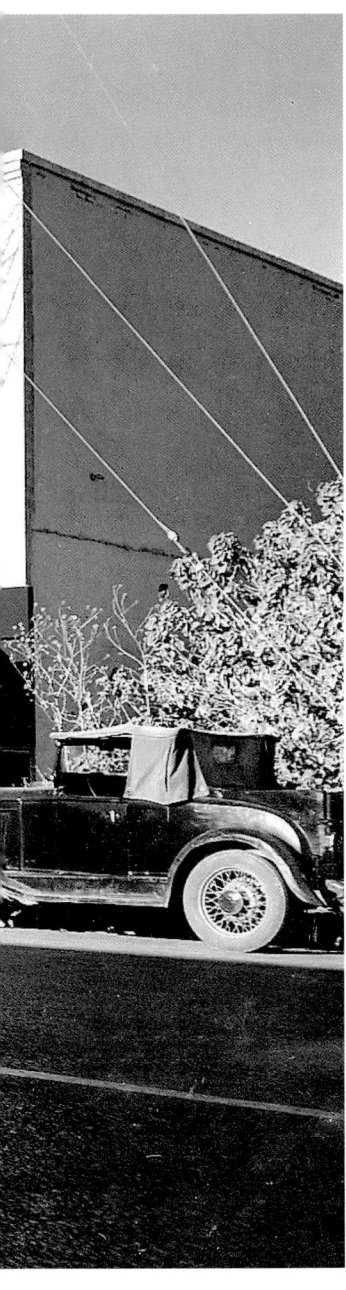

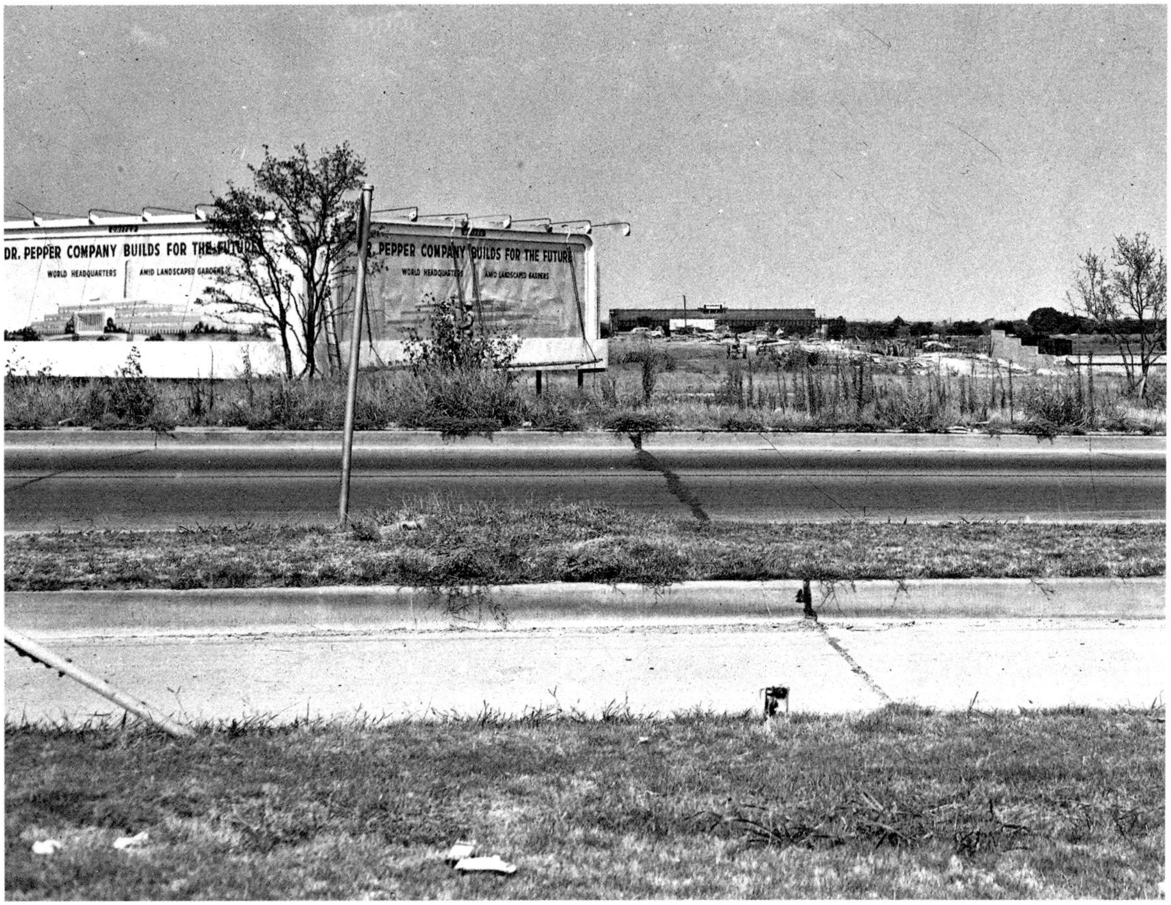

ABOVE: The location for Dr Pepper's new headquarters-to-be on Mockingbird. We can't forget the big sign that showed the drink was good at: "10 . . . 2 . . . and 4!" 1946.

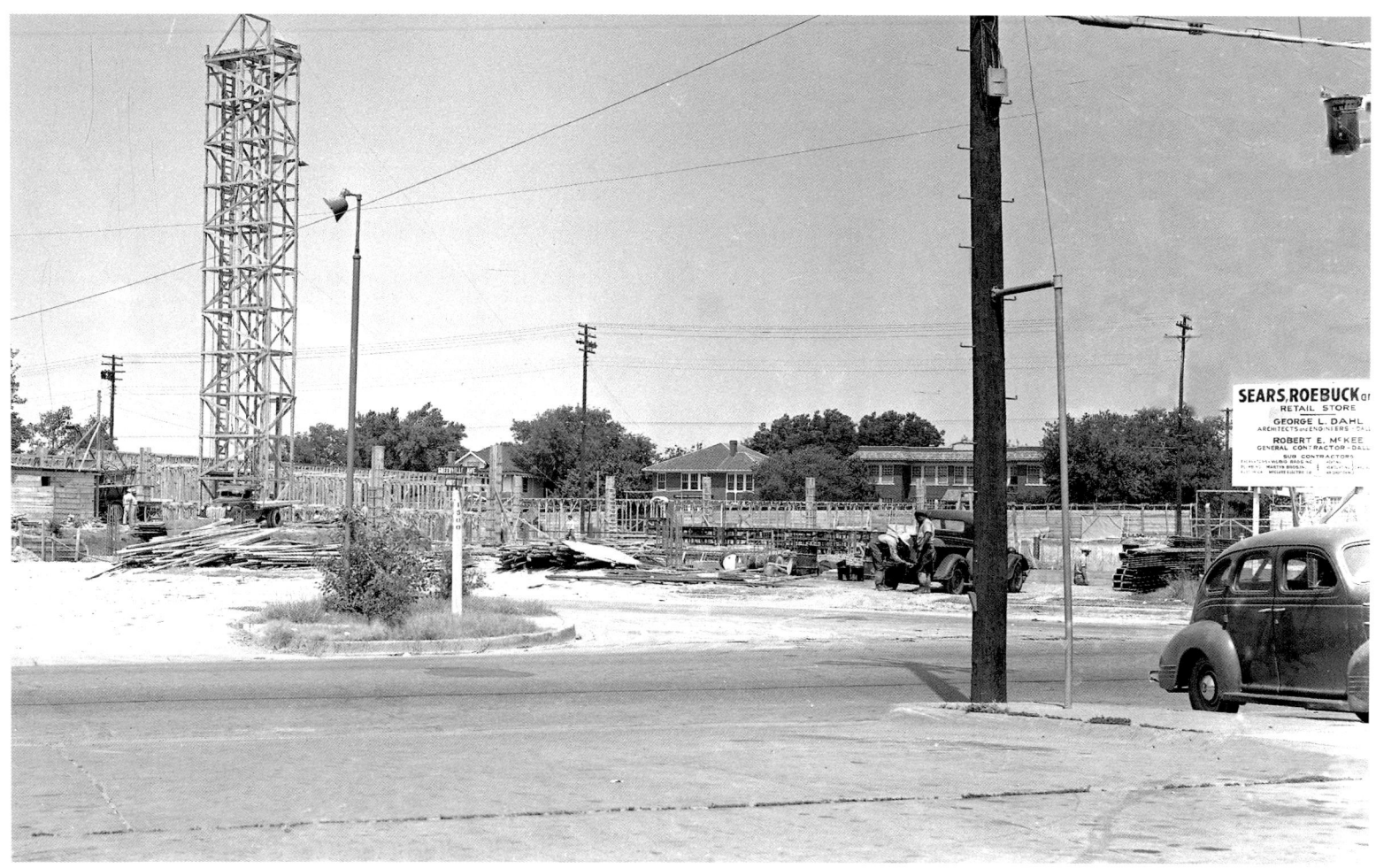

ABOVE: The Sears & Roebuck store under construction on Ross Avenue in Dallas. It opened in 1947, closed in 1993, and has since been demolished. Ca. 1946.

OPPOSITE: Workers constructing the Miller Bros. building on Akard. 1947.

PAGES 14-15: Akard Street was one of the busier streets in Dallas and remains so today. Progress has seen most of its old one- and two-story buildings razed and replaced with structures such as the fourteen-story headquarters of JPMorgan Chase. 1947.

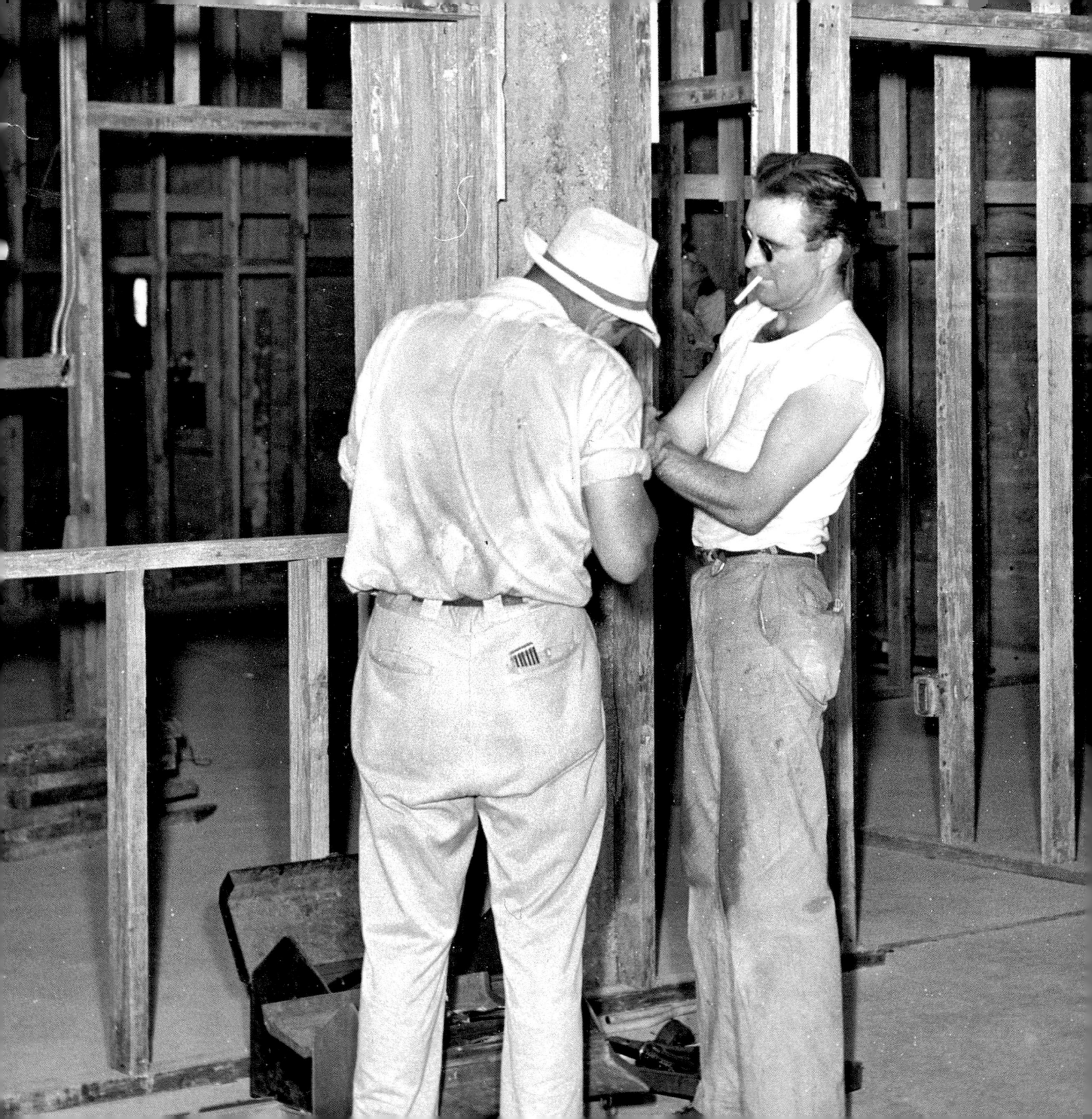

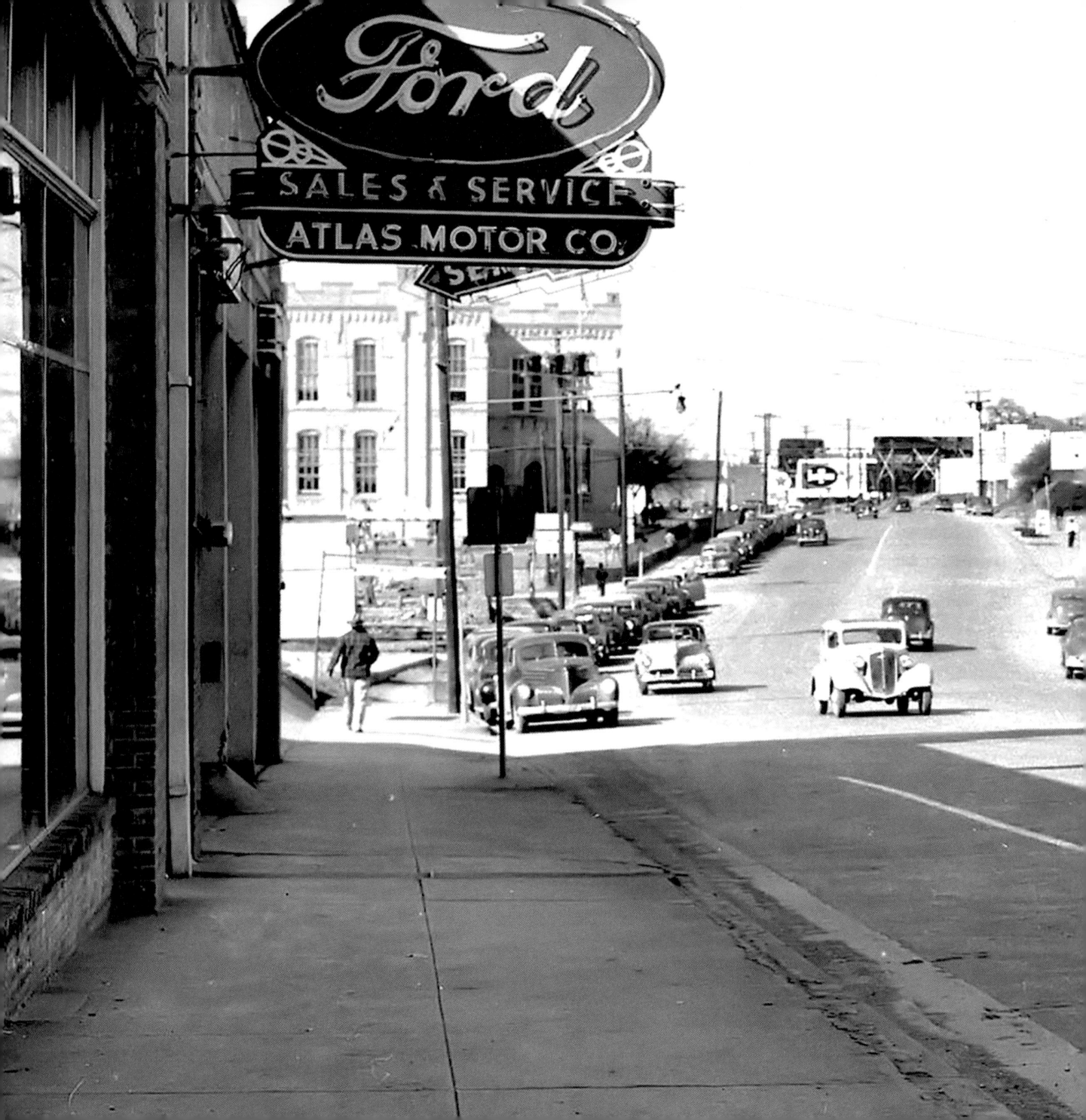

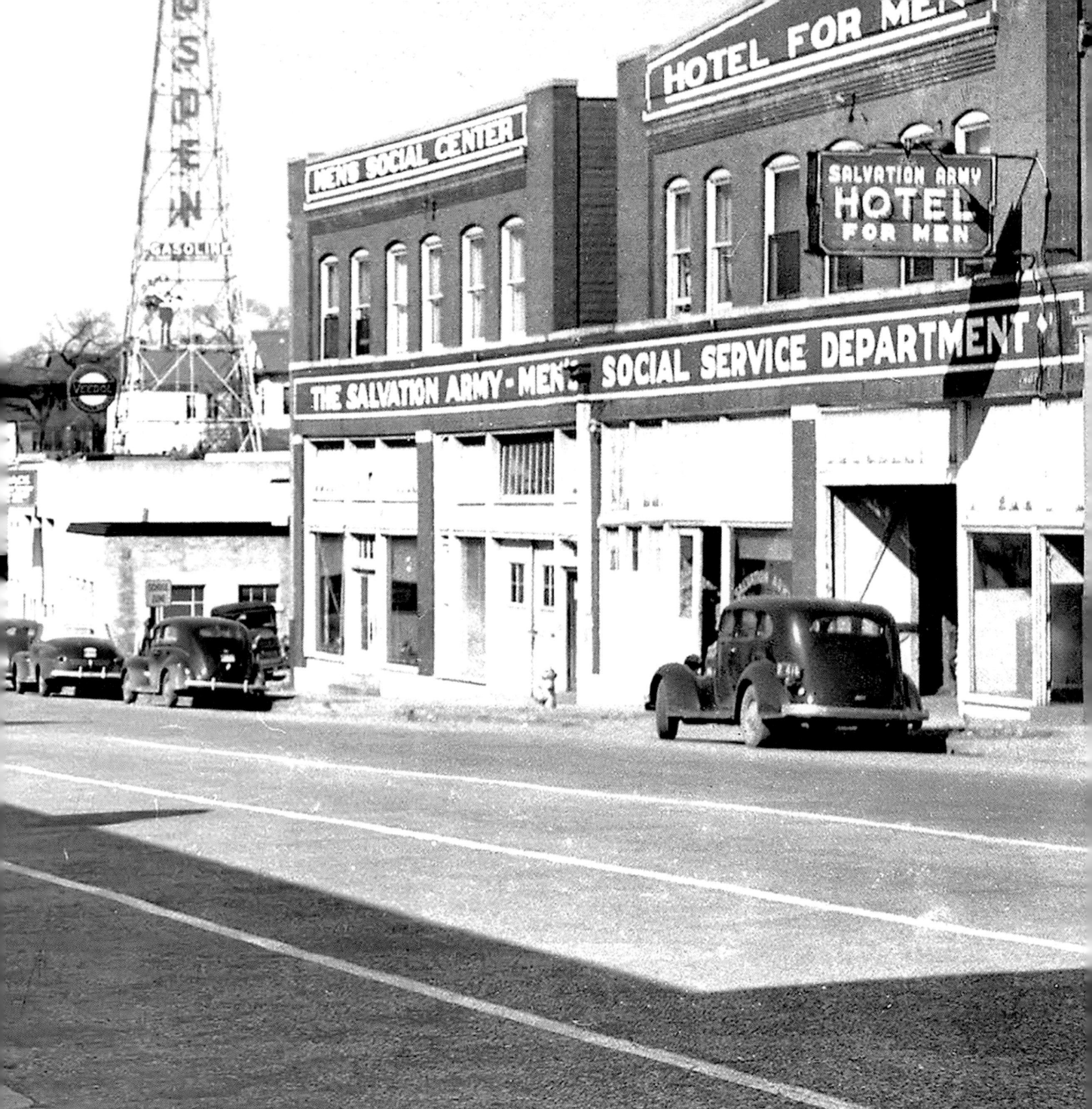

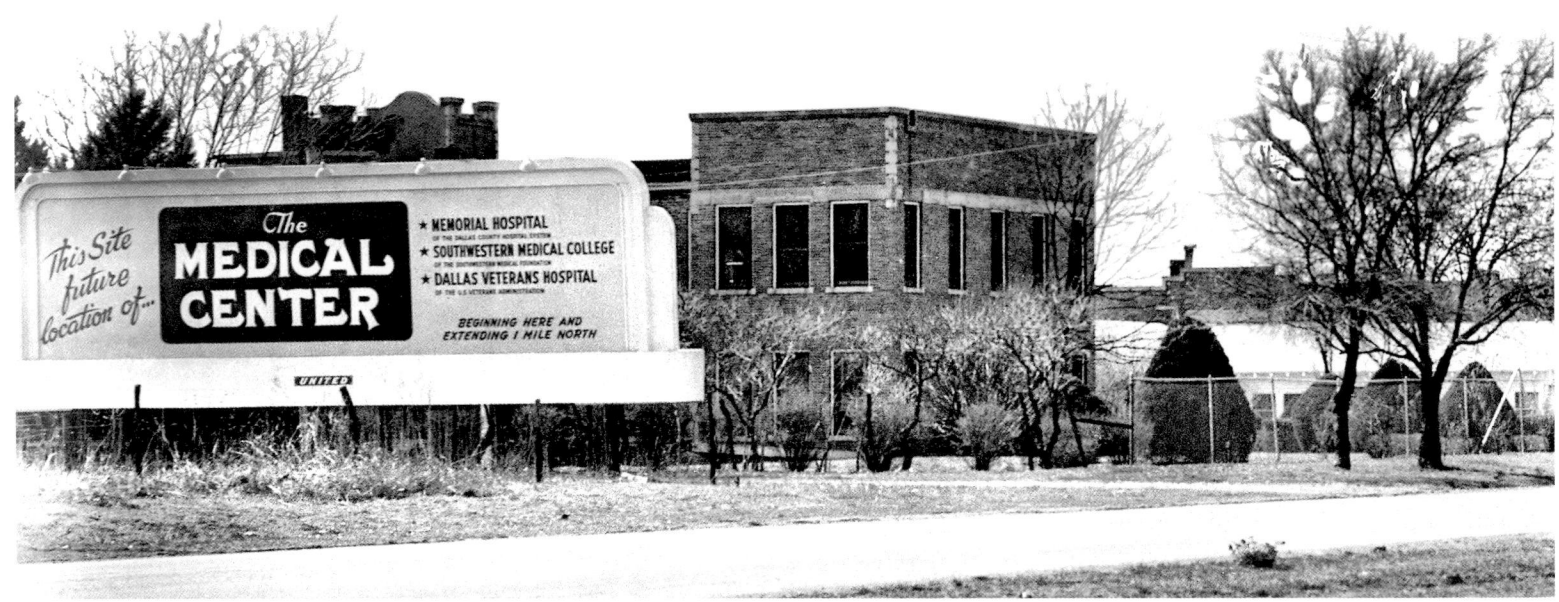

ABOVE: Sign showing the location on Harry Hines Boulevard for Dallas's new Medical Center, including the Southwestern Medical College, Memorial Hospital, and VA Hospital. 1946.

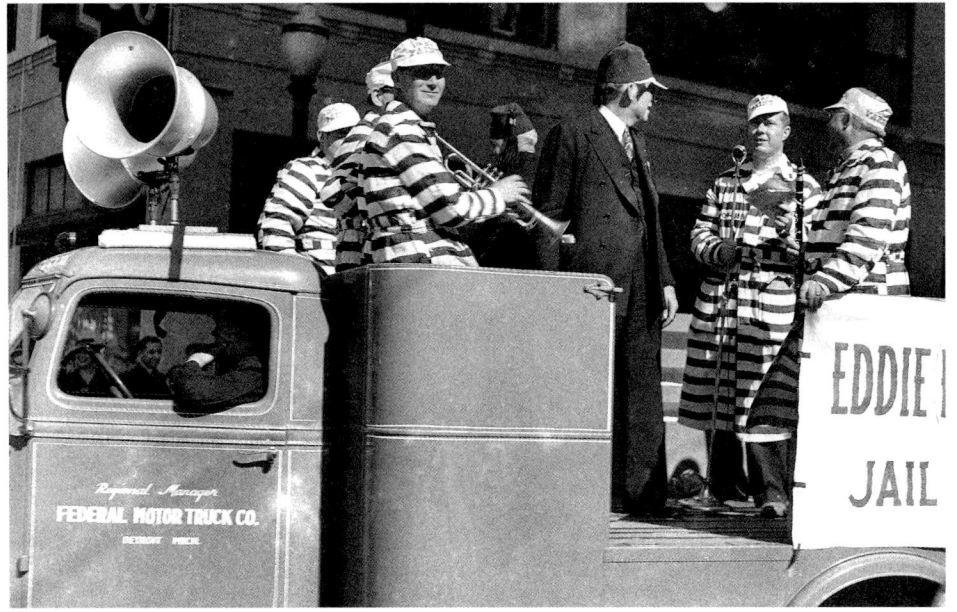

LEFT: Shriner Parade band. 1942.

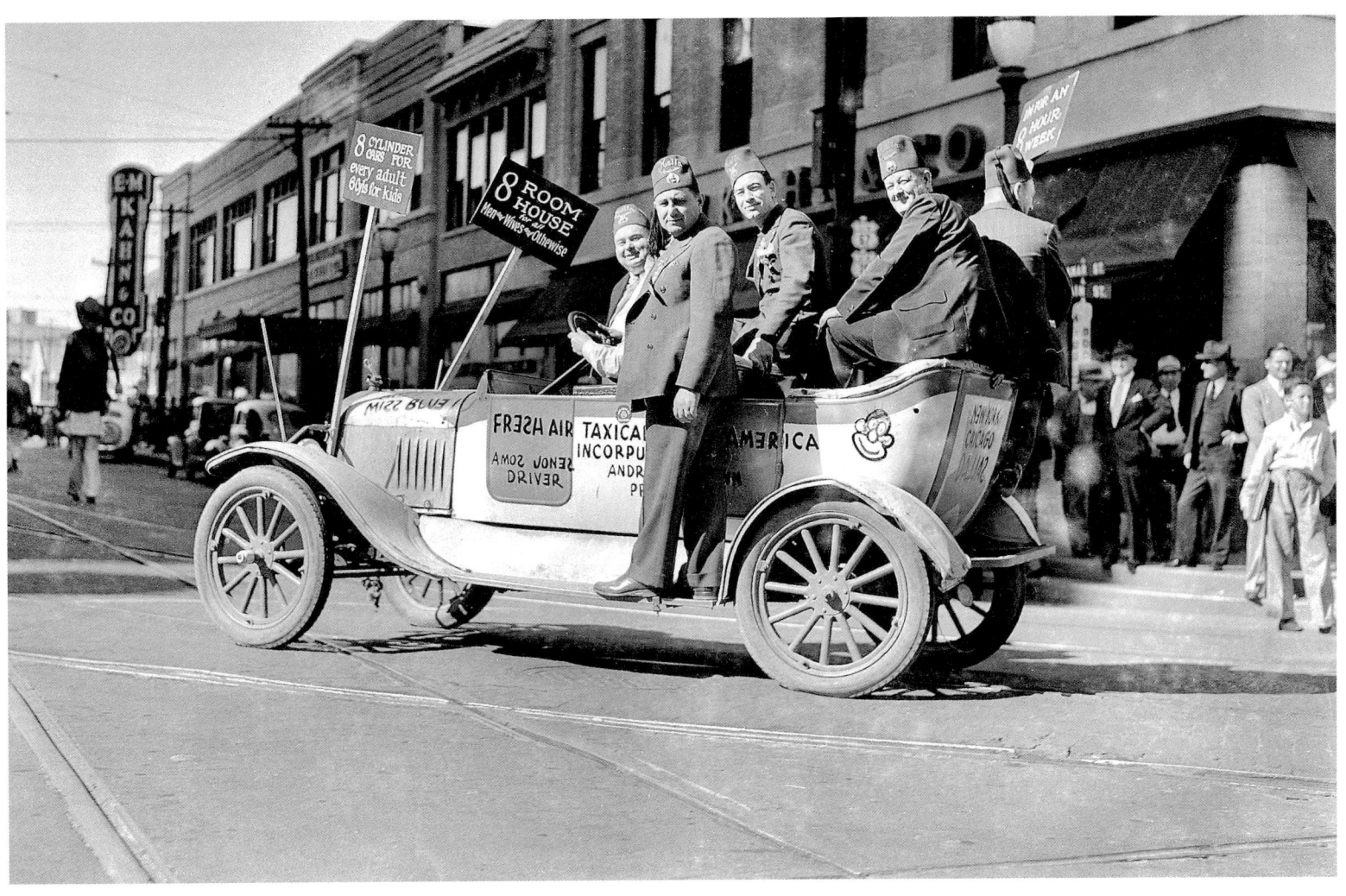

ABOVE: Shriner Parade in downtown Dallas. 1942.

Aerial Photos

___

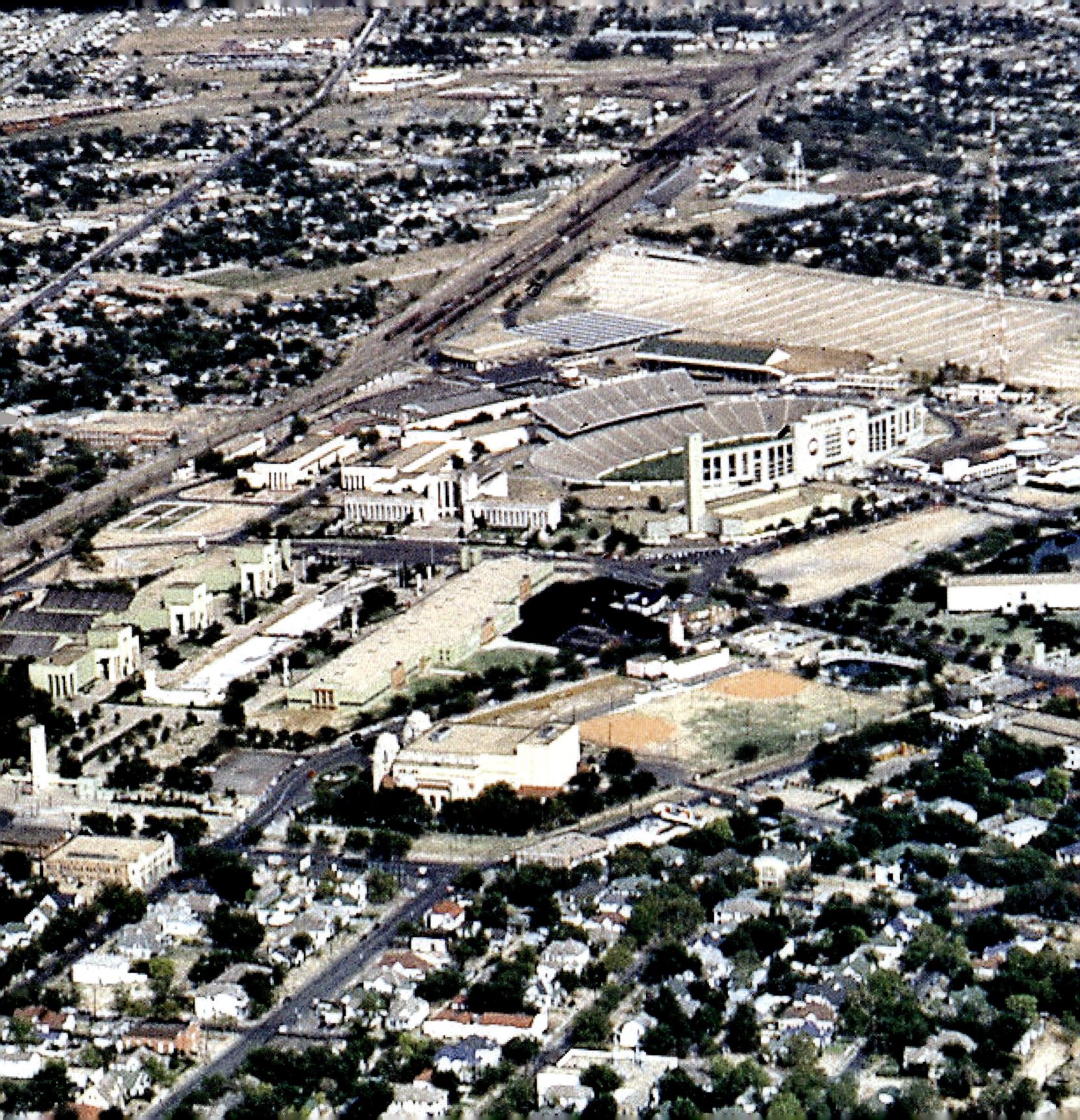

Dad had taken some flying lessons in the 1930s, while he was still a teenager, and loved it. That is, until my grandfather found out and made him stop. He never took it up again, but with having friends that were pilots, his love of shooting from the sky was never a problem.

———

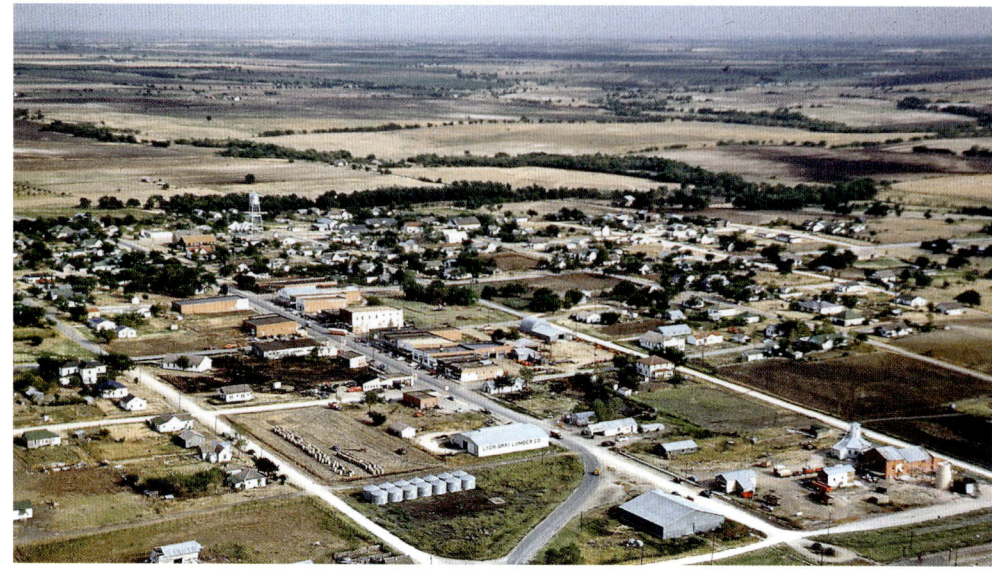

ABOVE (RIGHT): Frisco, Texas. 1952.

RIGHT: McKinney, Texas. The plant in background is Texas Textile Mills (TTM). TTM was founded by my grandfather, Clarence Miller, and was the largest cotton milling operation west of the Mississippi. After selling our mill near Love Field to Johnson & Johnson, McKinney became the flagship mill of the several we had in Texas and Oklahoma. 1952.

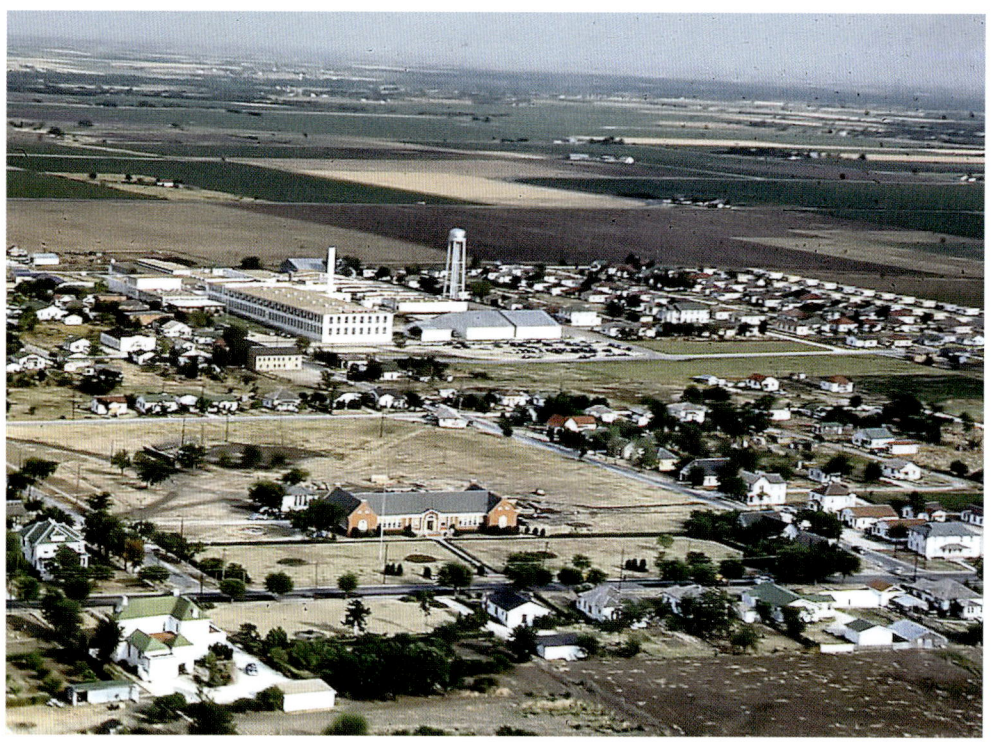

RIGHT: This is the 5100 Block of Swiss Avenue in Dallas, and the large white house on the left was Dad's parents' home at 5112. My mother and I lived there with my grandparents for two years while my dad was on active duty at sea as a naval officer aboard the USS *Crosby*. 1941.

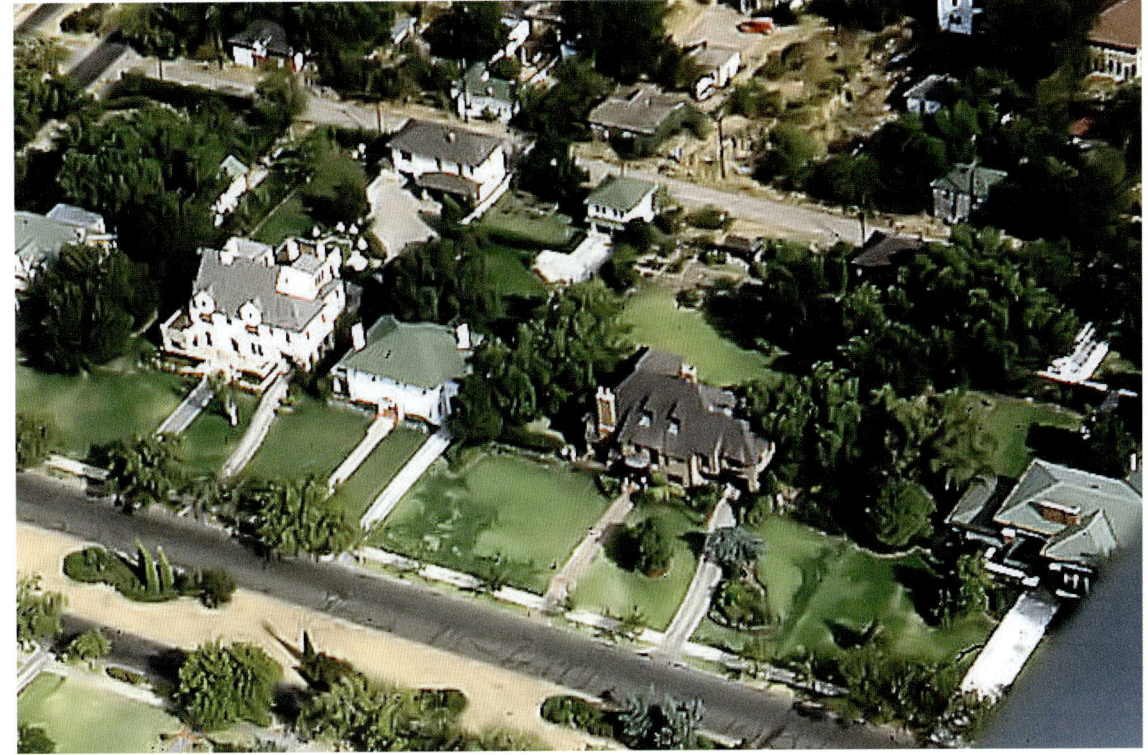

RIGHT: Crescent Oaks from the air. That is Lake Dallas to the right. 1948.

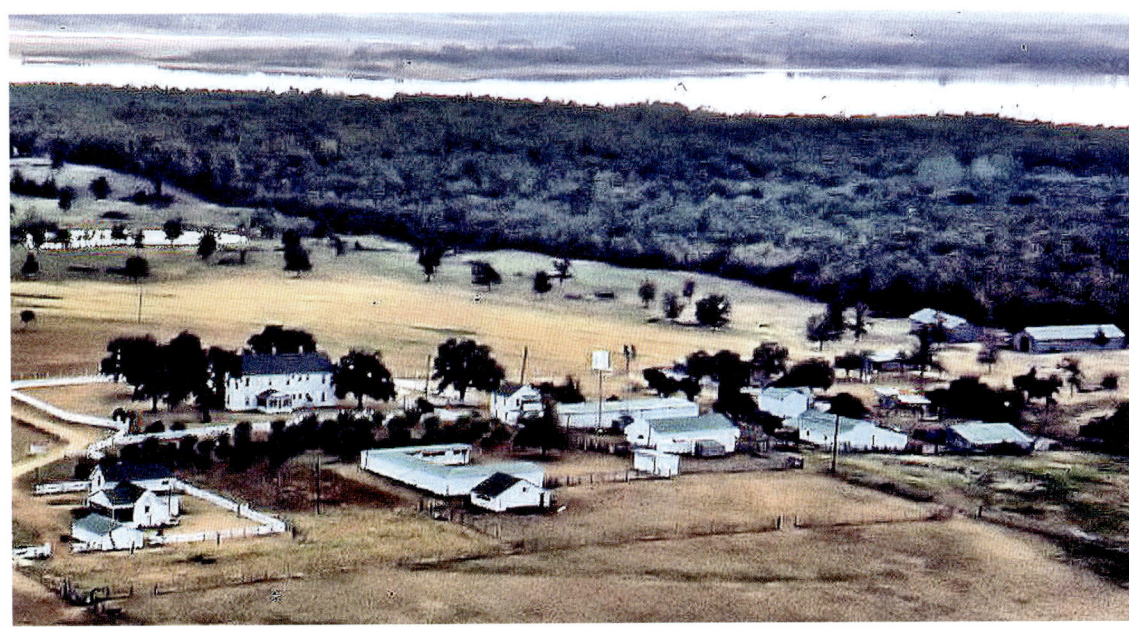

Around Town

———

OPPOSITE: In the early 1940s, the American Federation of Labor tried unsuccessfully to unionize
Sivils Drive-In's employees. This union representative was stationed in the Sivils parking lot and told Dad—
politely, it seems—where to go with his camera as a "curb hopper" looks on in amusement. Early 1940s.

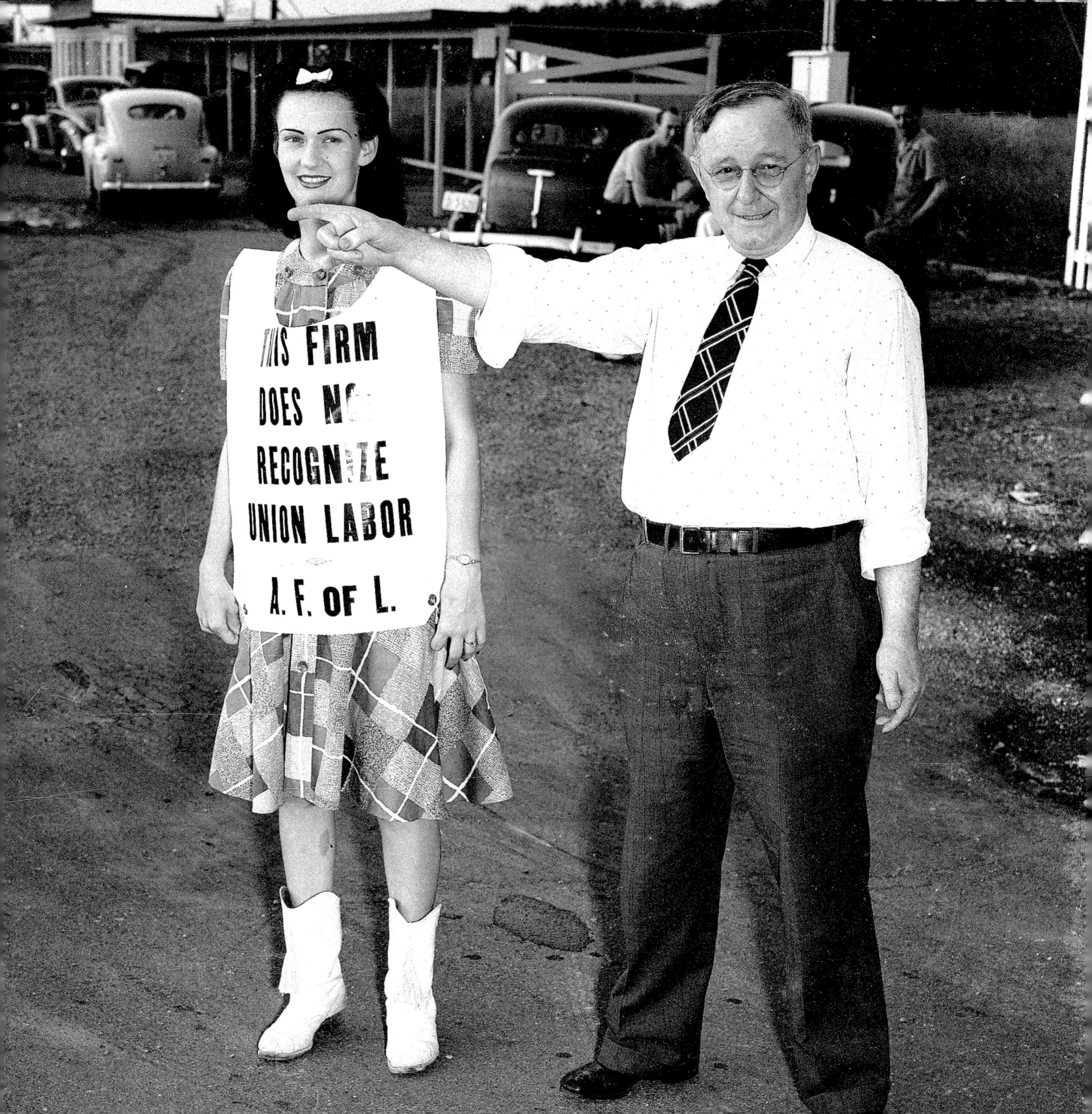

THIS FIRM
DOES NOT
RECOGNIZE
UNION LABOR

A. F. of L.

Dallas was really coming alive during the immediate pre- and post-WWII period, as it quickly notched its place as the banking, cattle, and cotton center of the South. It was nirvana to a photographer like Dad, whose love of candidly shooting his city's growth allowed us a peek into the relaxation and fun side of life there—from swimming, outdoor picnics, and sail-boating on White Rock Lake to the eateries, nightclubs, and orchestras in its stately hotels.

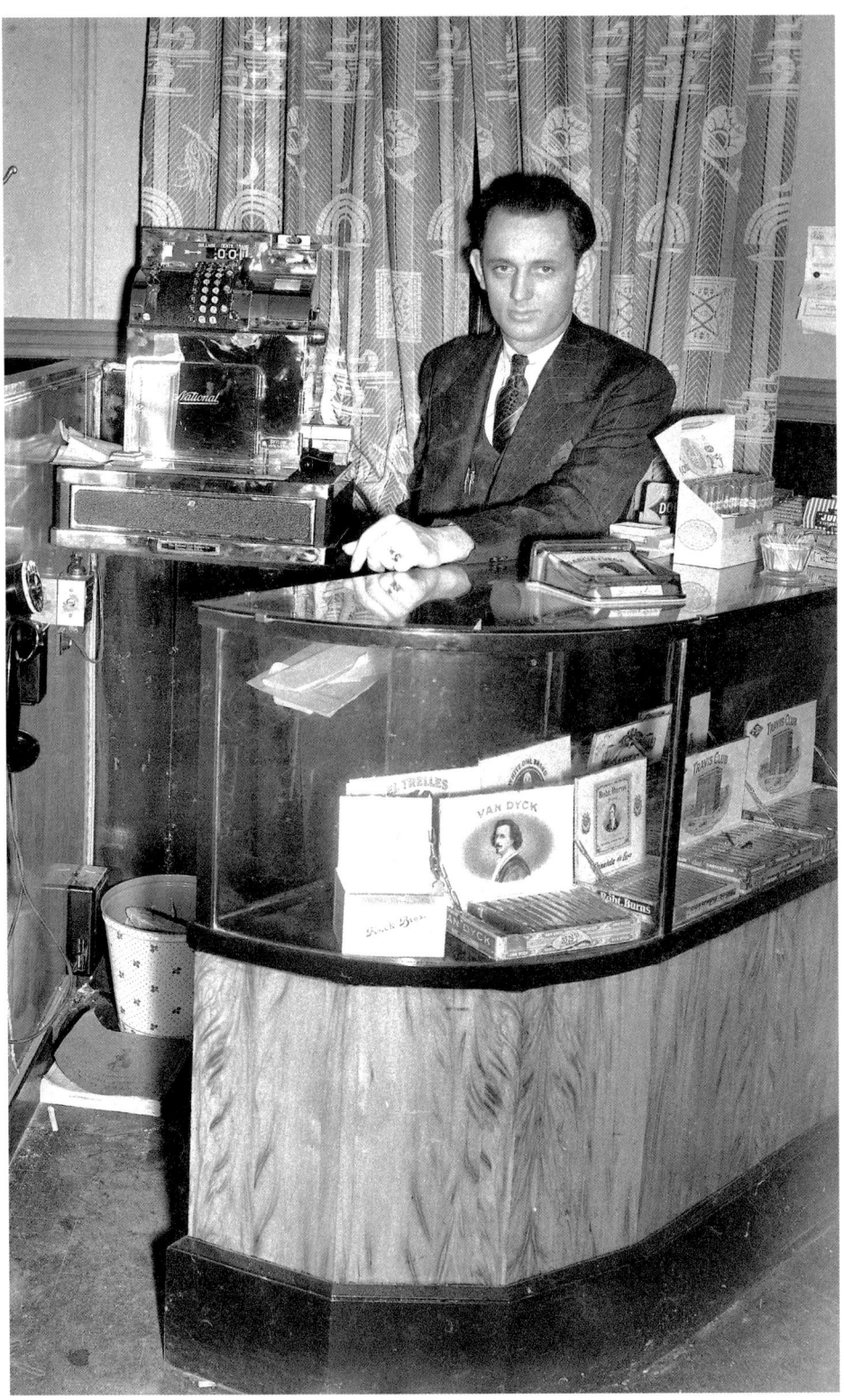

RIGHT: Benny's café. 1940s.

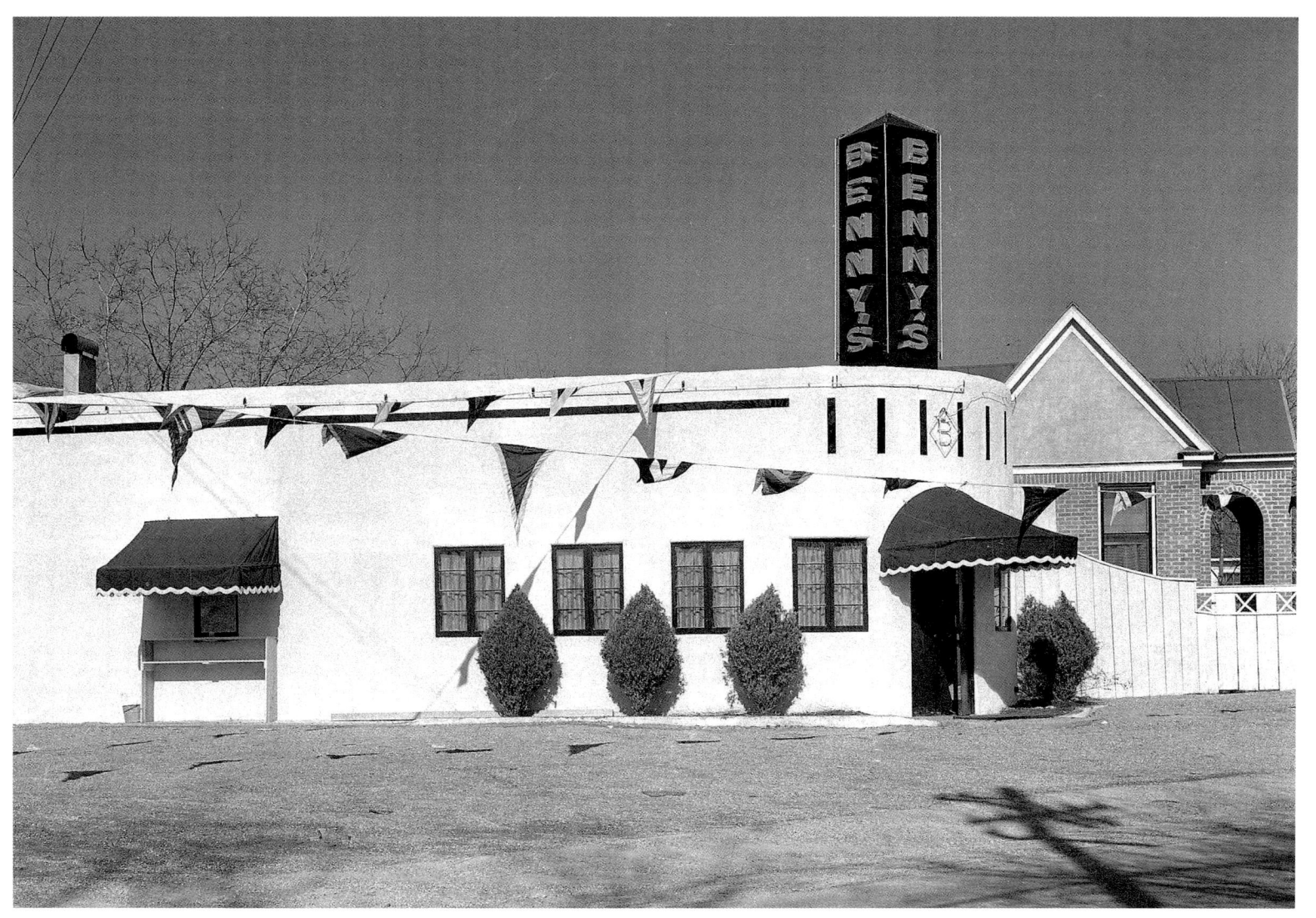

ABOVE: Benny's café. 1940s.

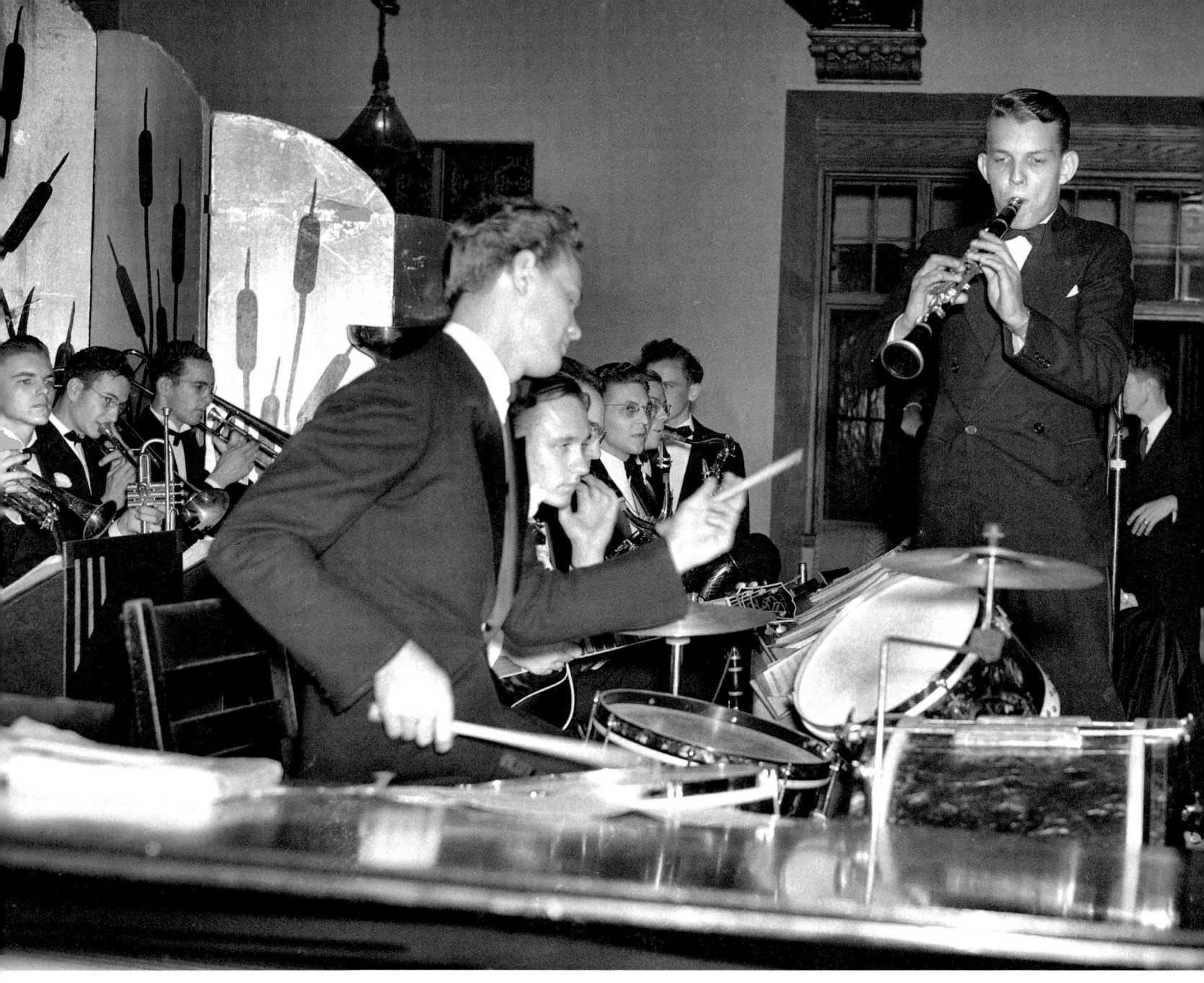

ABOVE: Baker Hotel Orchestra. 1940.

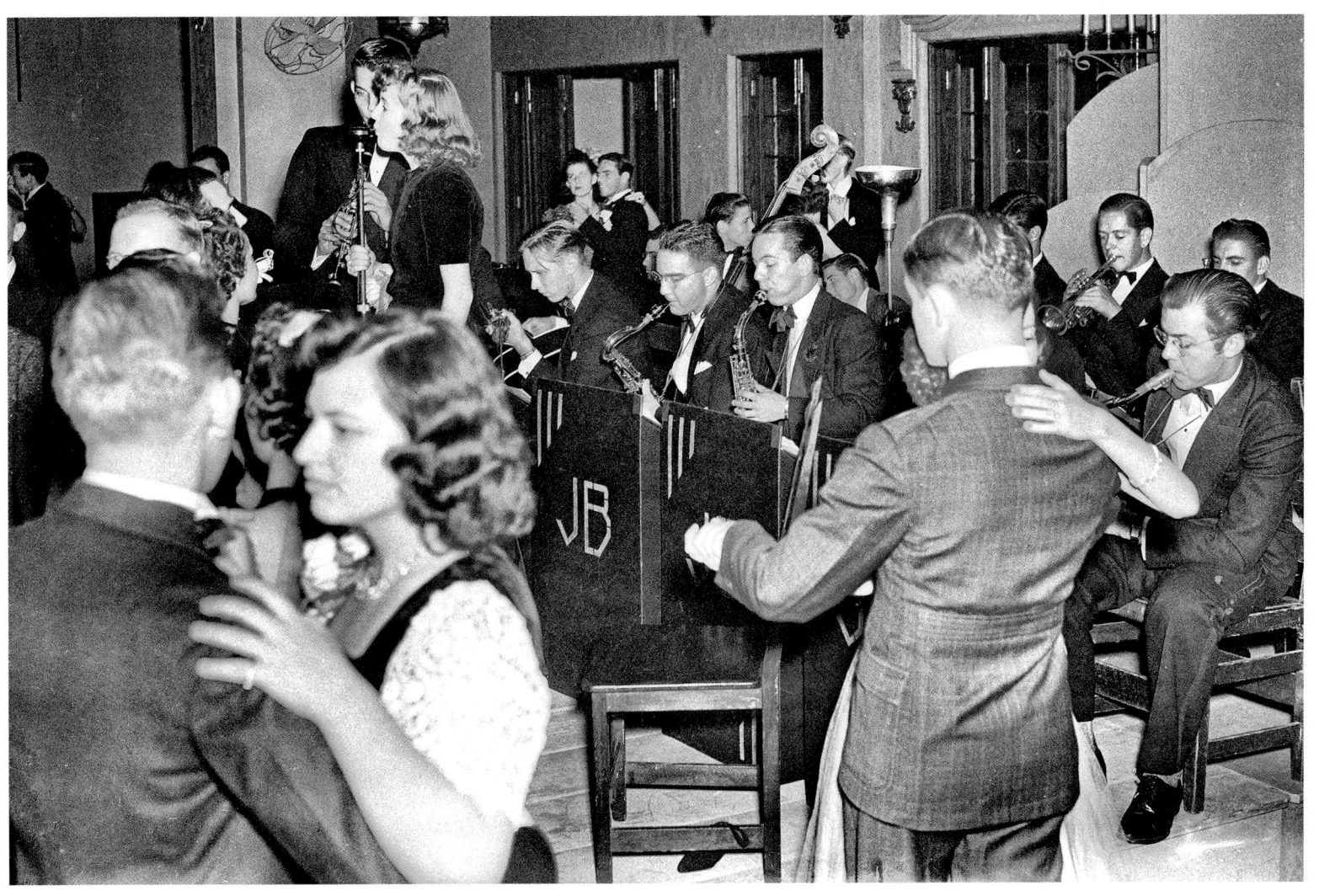

ABOVE: Dancing to the Baker Hotel Orchestra located in downtown Dallas (on the corner of Commerce and Akard Street) across the street from the Adolphus. It imploded in 1980 to make room for the Whitacre Tower. 1940.

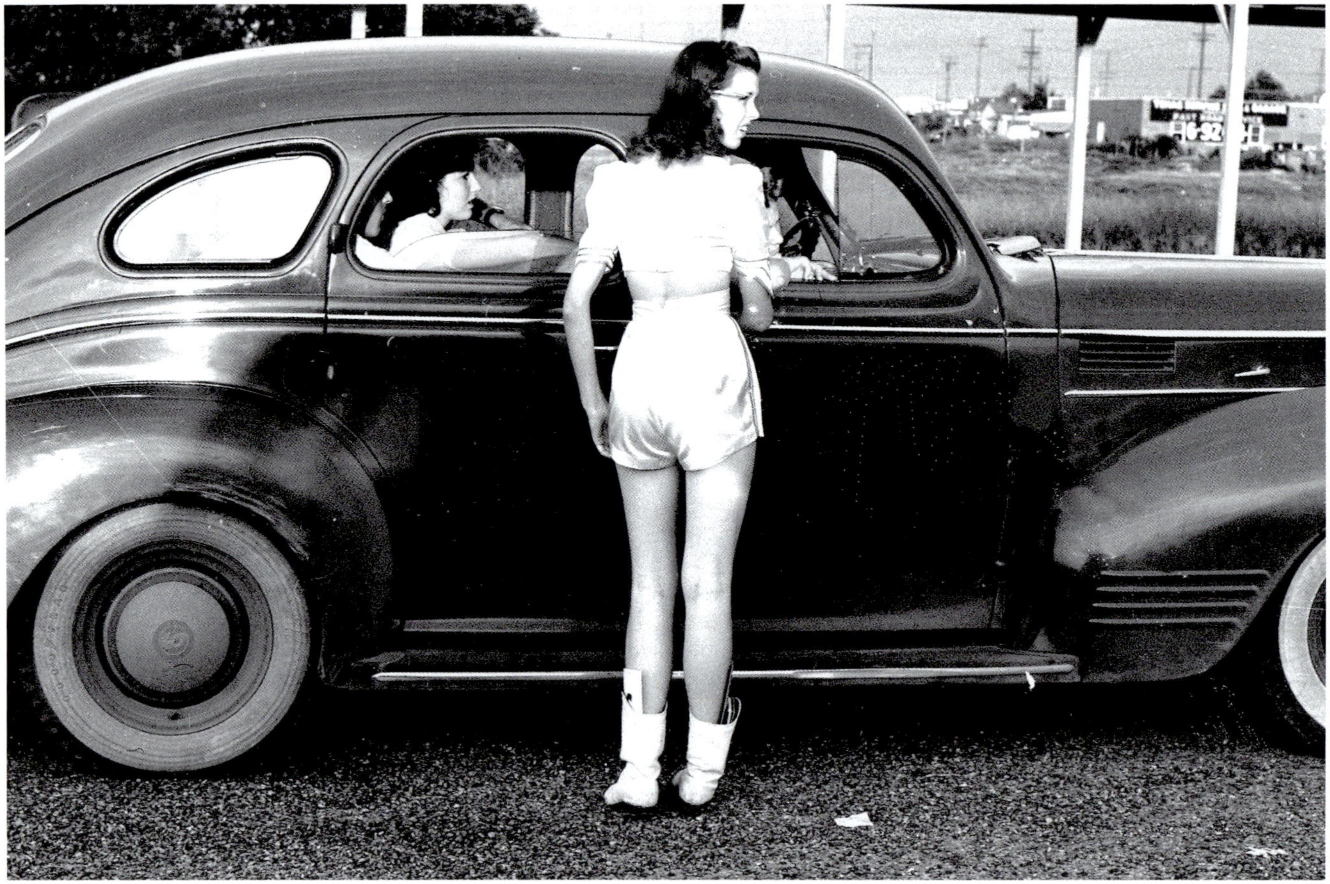

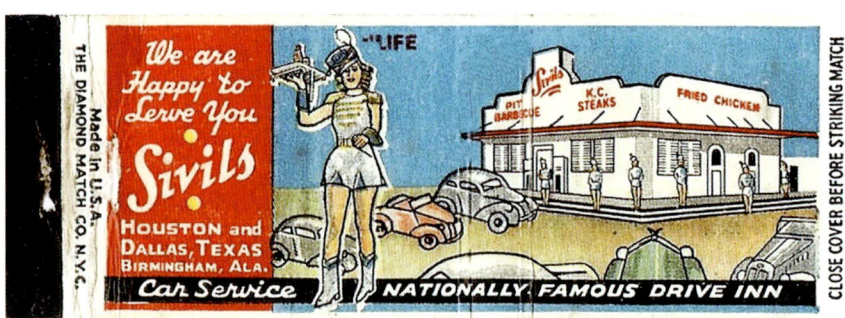

ABOVE: In 1940, Sivils Drive-In opened in Oak Cliff at the intersection of West Davis and Fort Worth Avenue. It was owned by J. D. and Louise Sivils. Featured once in a *Life* magazine article, the drive-in was for years the place to stop for cold beer and the best hamburgers—all served by "curb hoppers," the name Mrs. Sivils used instead of "carhops." For younger folks, it also was the prime place to cruise through in the evening, hoping to meet someone of the opposite sex. Sivils closed its doors in 1967. 1940s.

RIGHT: Matchbook cover for Sivils Drive-In. 1940s.

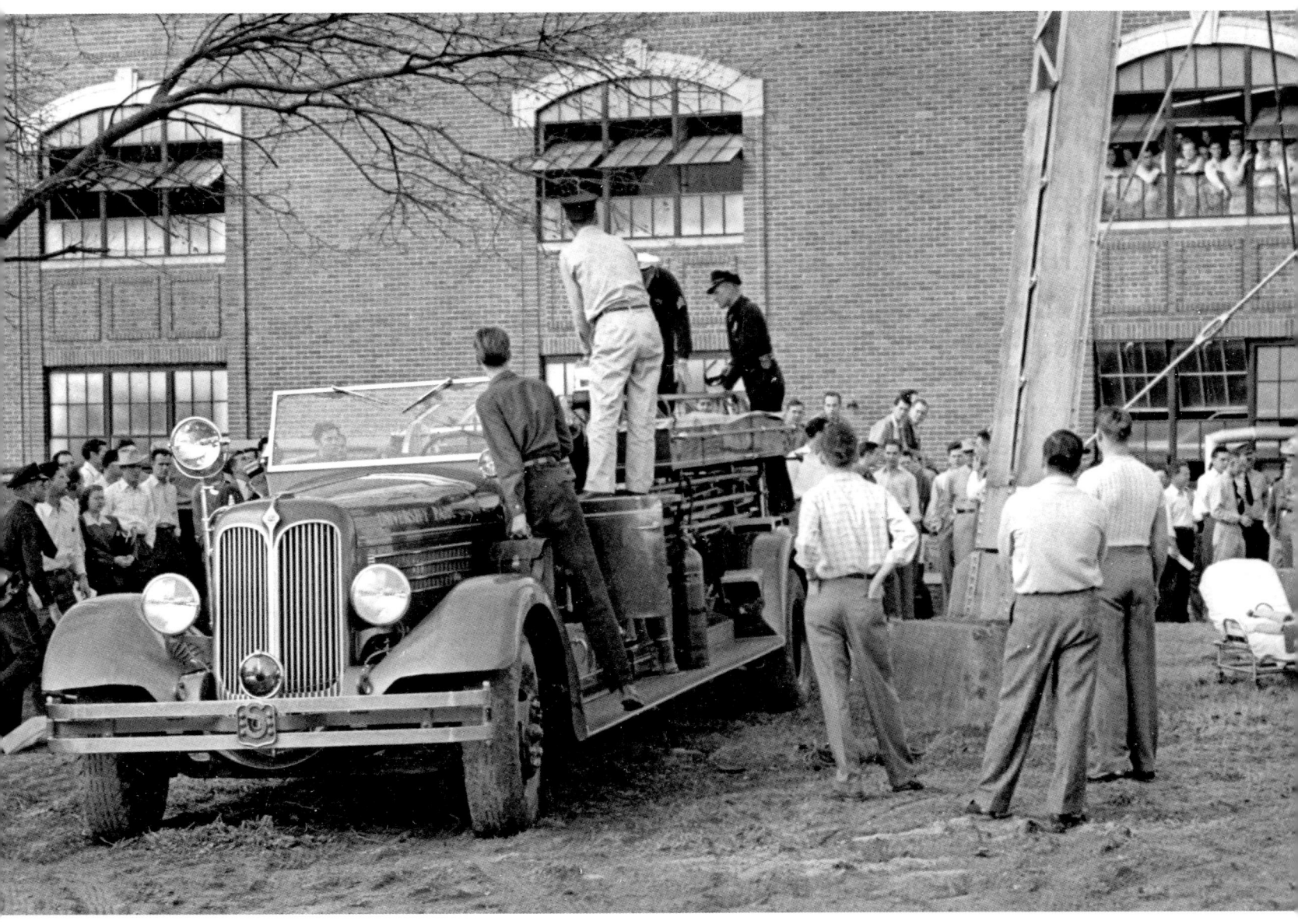

ABOVE: University Park fire truck. Late 1940s.

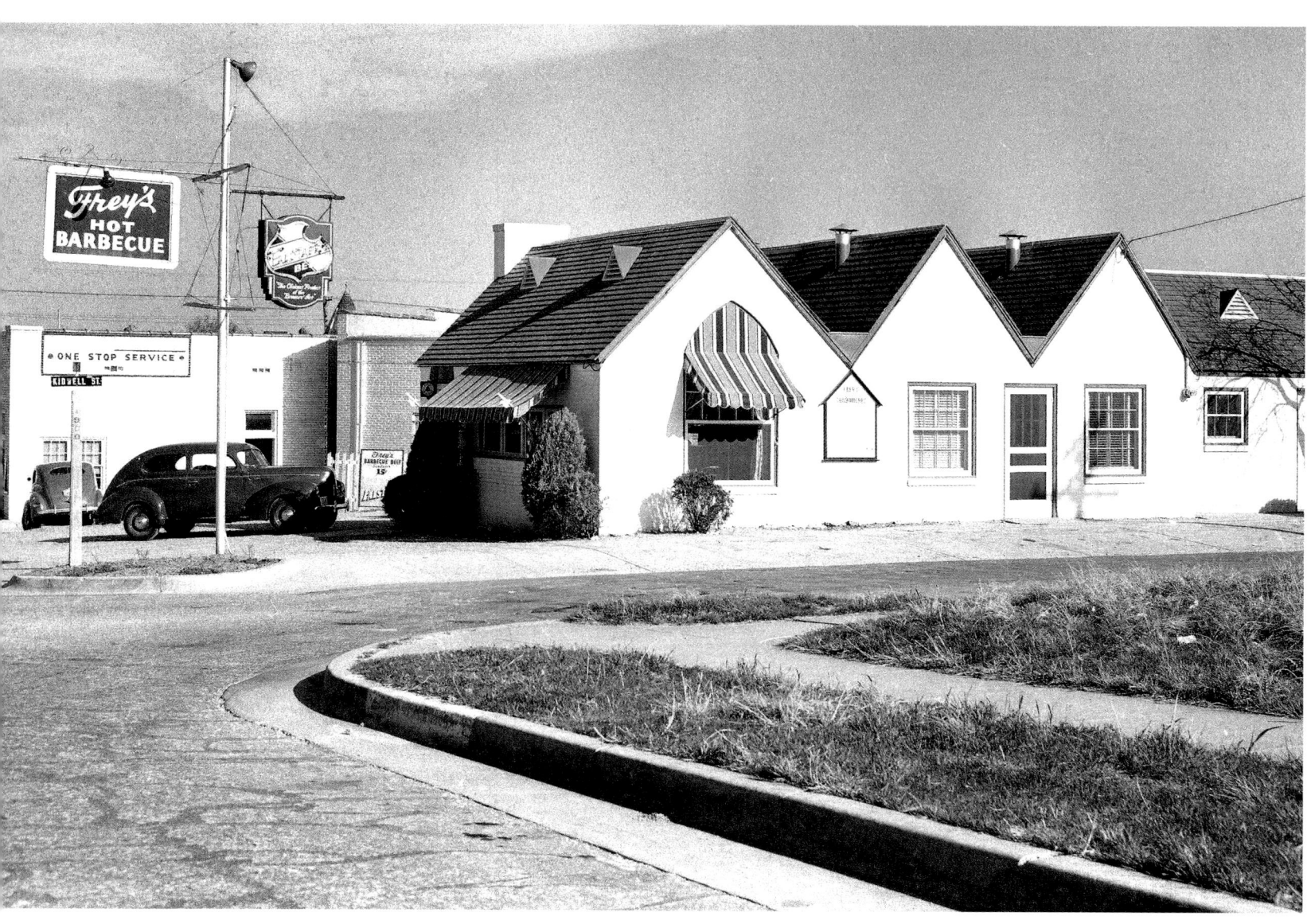

ABOVE: Frey's Barbecue in Dallas,
located off of Kidwell Street. Early 1940s.

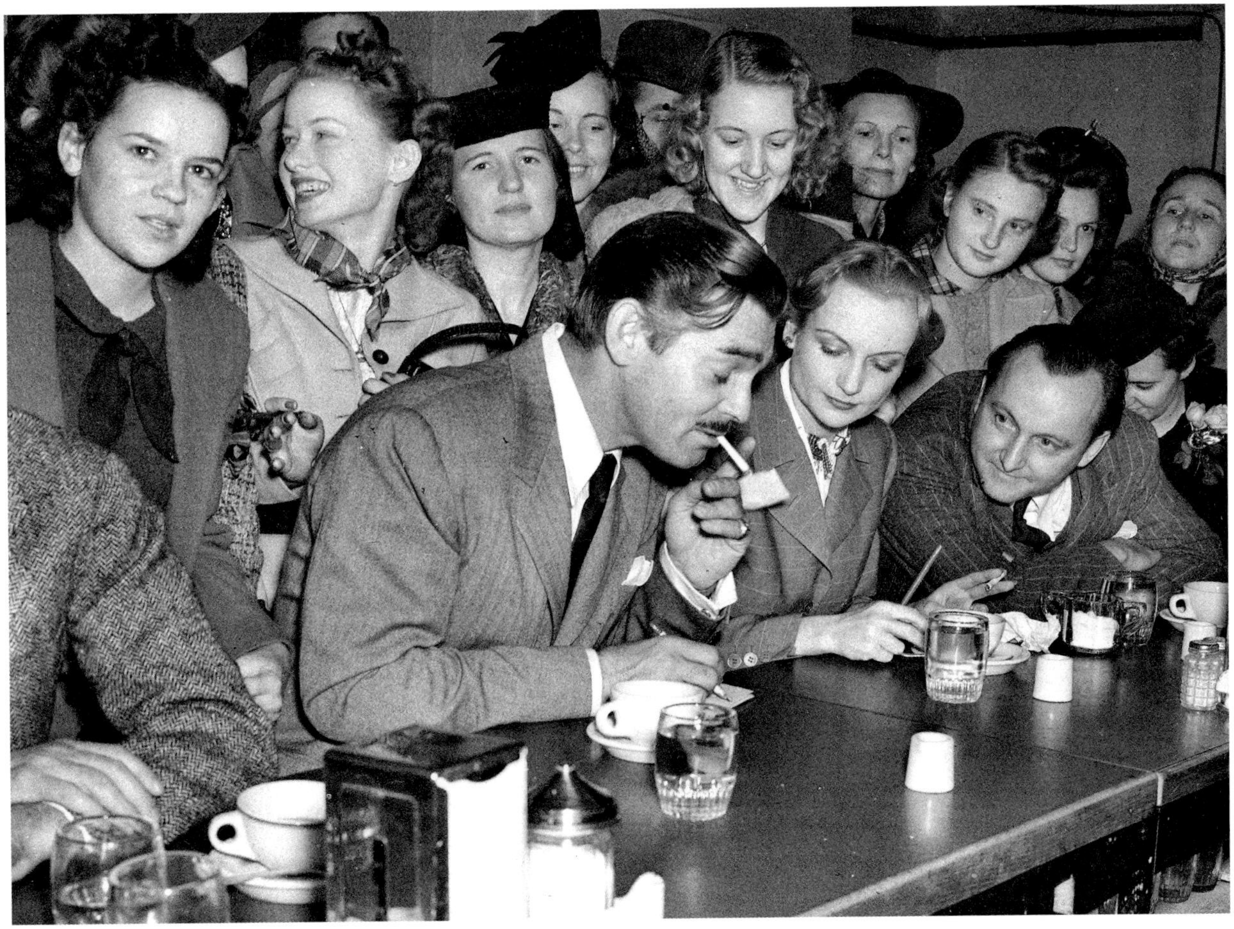

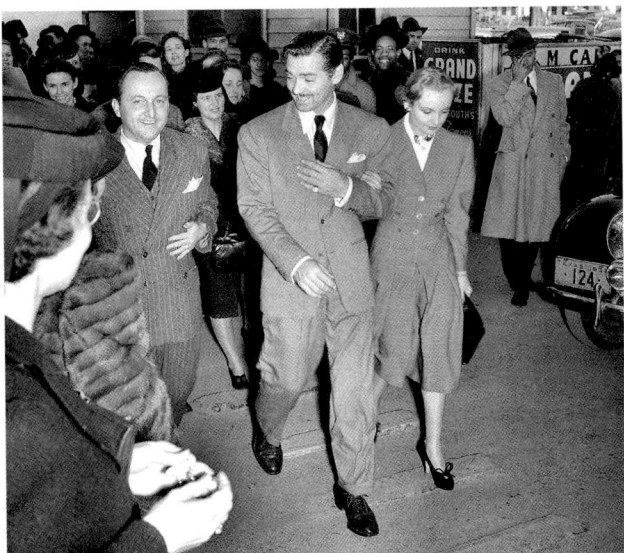

ABOVE: Clark Gable, his new wife, actress Carole Lombard, and Gable's long-time friend and publicist, Otto Winkler, were flying from Los Angeles to attend the premiere of *Gone with the Wind* in Atlanta the next day. Their flight made a stop at Dallas Love Field, where Dad took these. Gable and Lombard's star power is evident by the crush of adoring fans during their quick visit to the airport's café while the plane was being refueled. In 1942, Lombard and Winkler would perish in a plane crash as they toured promoting the sale of war bonds. December 14, 1939.

LEFT: Clark Gable, his wife, and publicist. Their dress and smiles belie a normal passenger's decorum and appearance after a long flight from Los Angeles aboard a slow and noisy propeller-driven airplane. 1939.

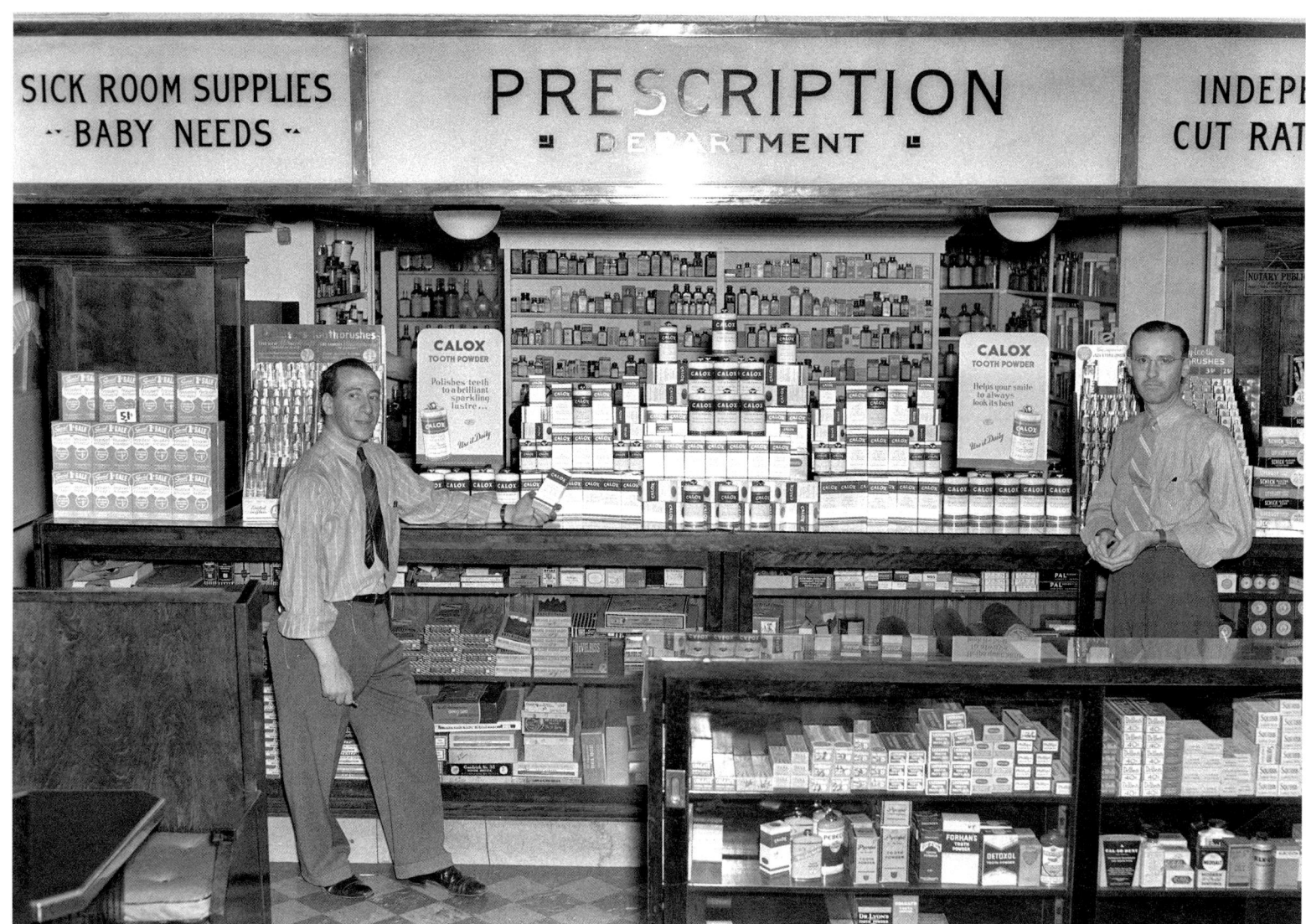

ABOVE: Harris Service Drugstore on Gaston Avenue in Dallas. Early 1940s.

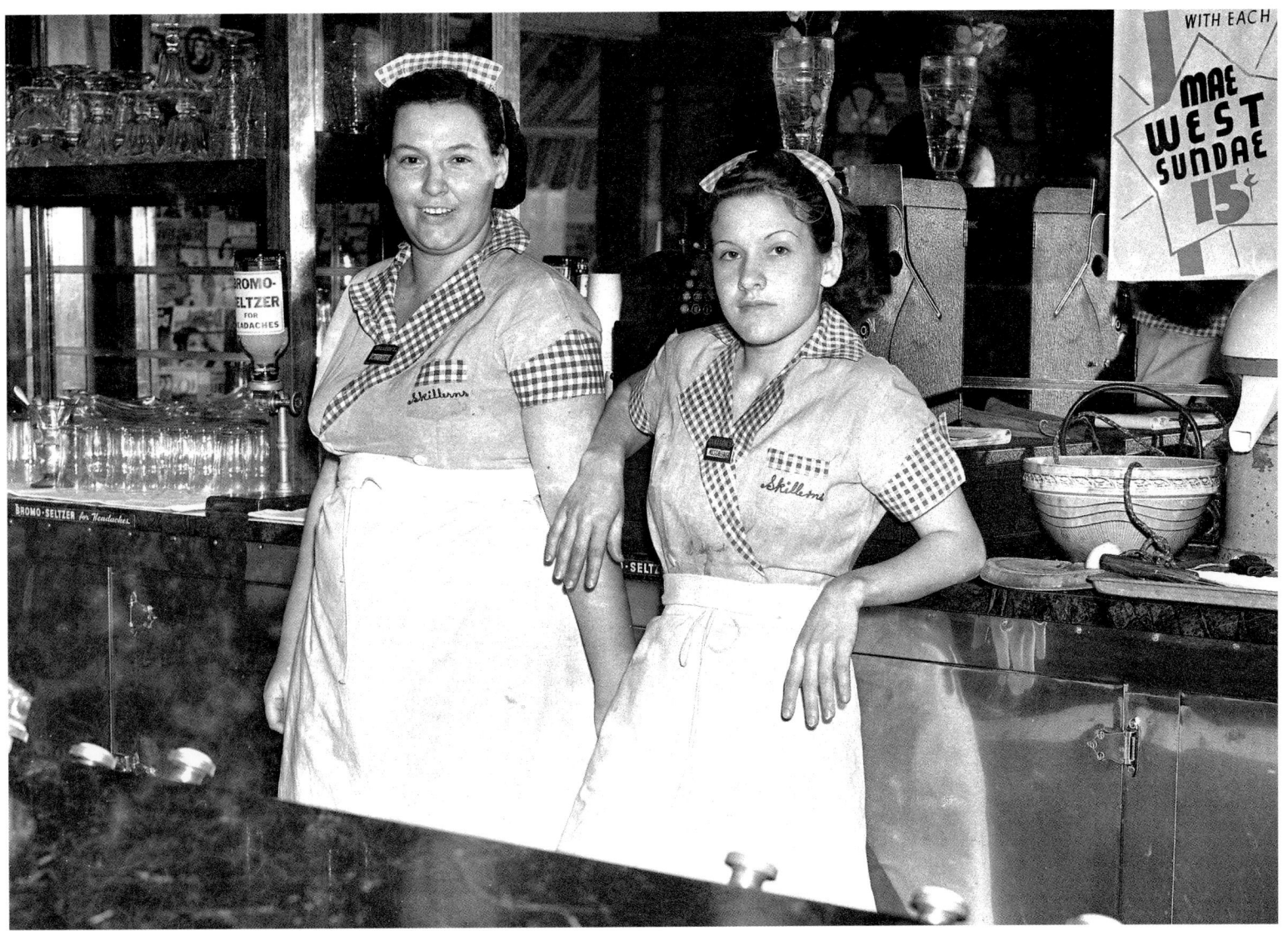

ABOVE: Freddie Galleher, the young woman on the right, standing near the soda fountain with another employee at Skillern's Drugstore in Lakewood Shopping Center. 1940.

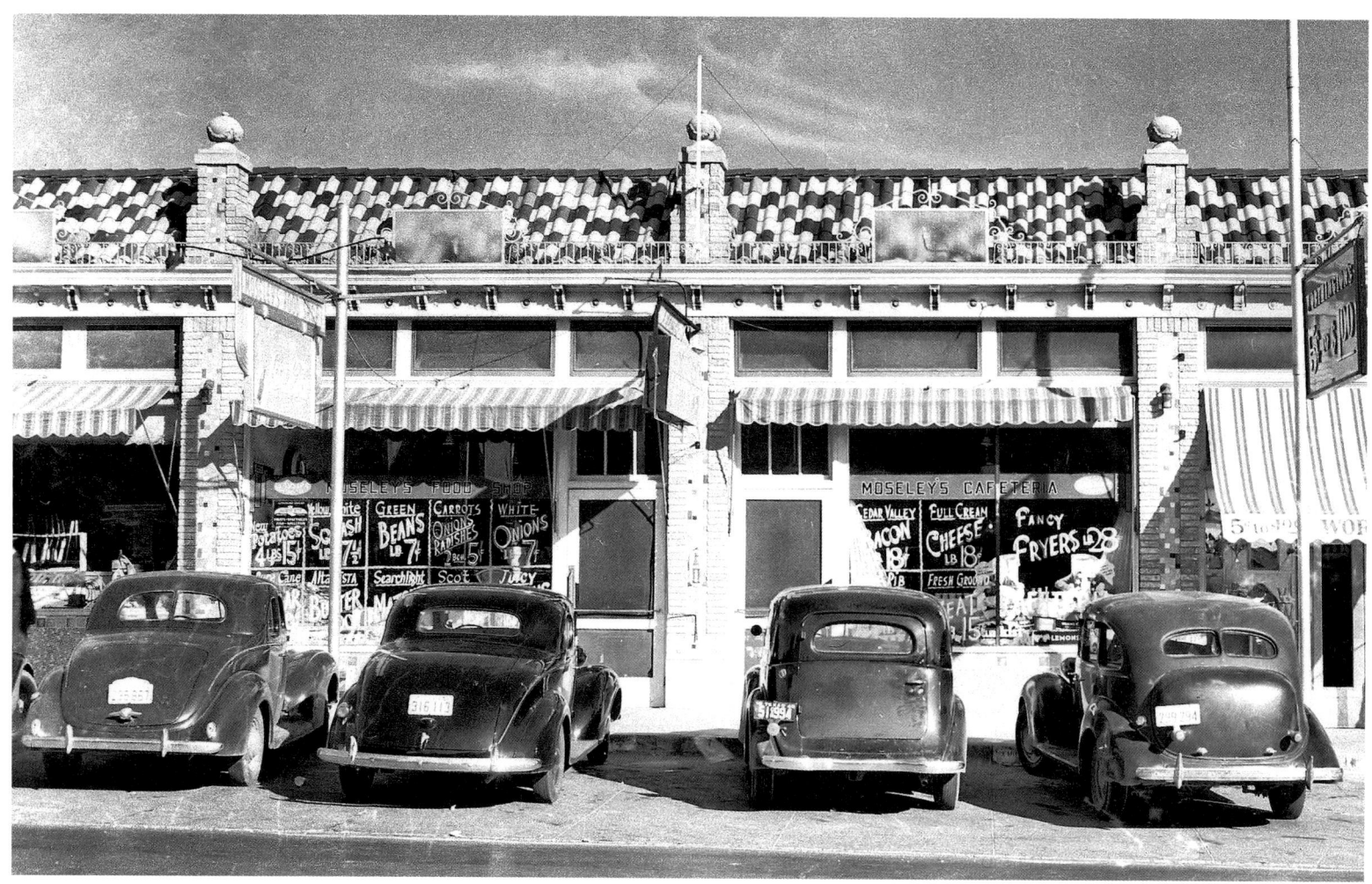

ABOVE: Moseley's Cafeteria. 1940.

OPPOSITE: Child actor Larry Simms, appearing here to be about six or seven, was best known to moviegoers for his role as Baby Dumplin' Bumstead in *Blondie*, the comedy film series spanning over twenty-eight films. He also played the oldest child of George Bailey (Jimmy Stewart) in the 1946 classic, *It's a Wonderful Life*. Nattily uniformed Simms listening to the shortwave radio in Dad's home office. Early 1940s.

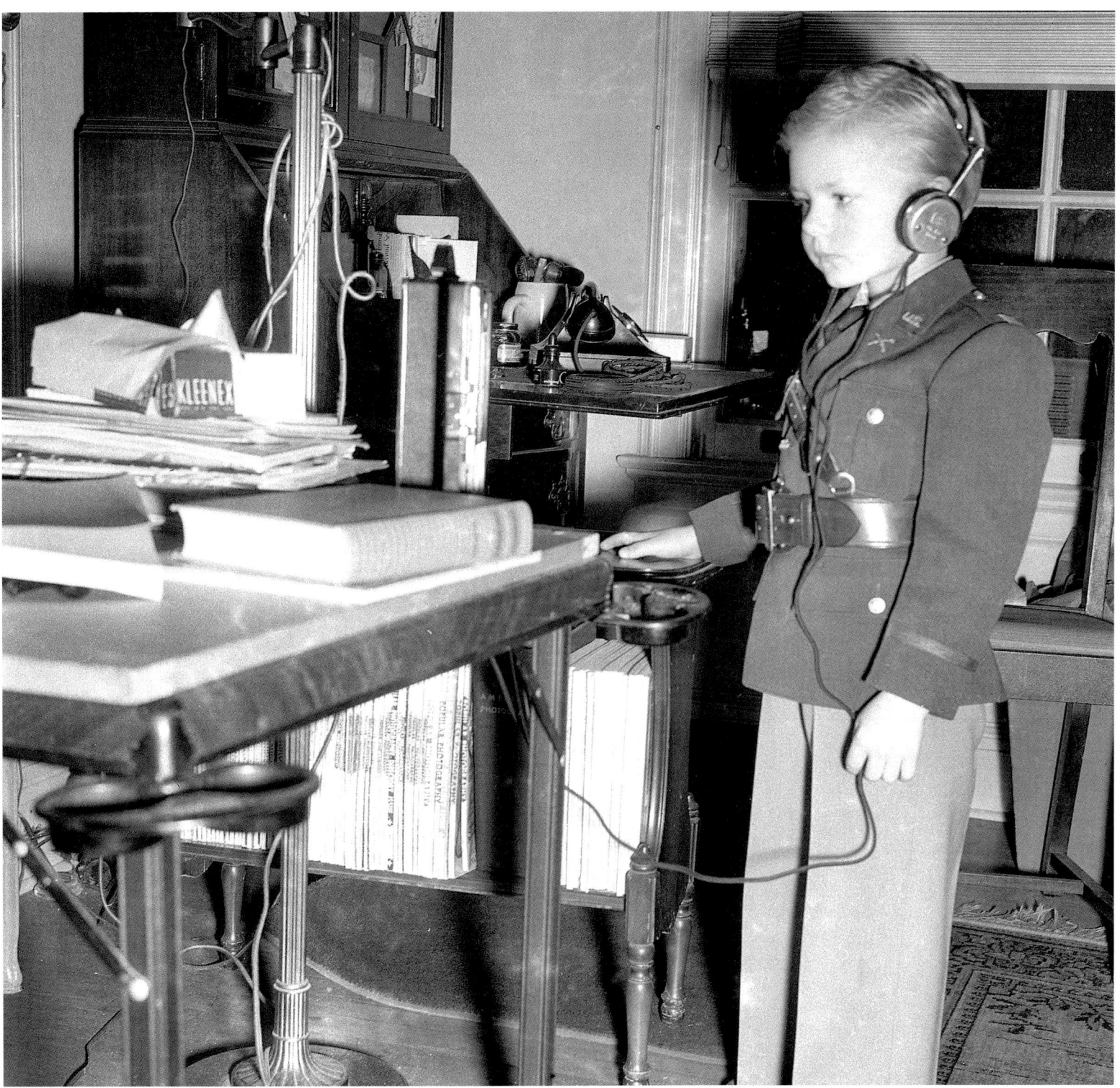

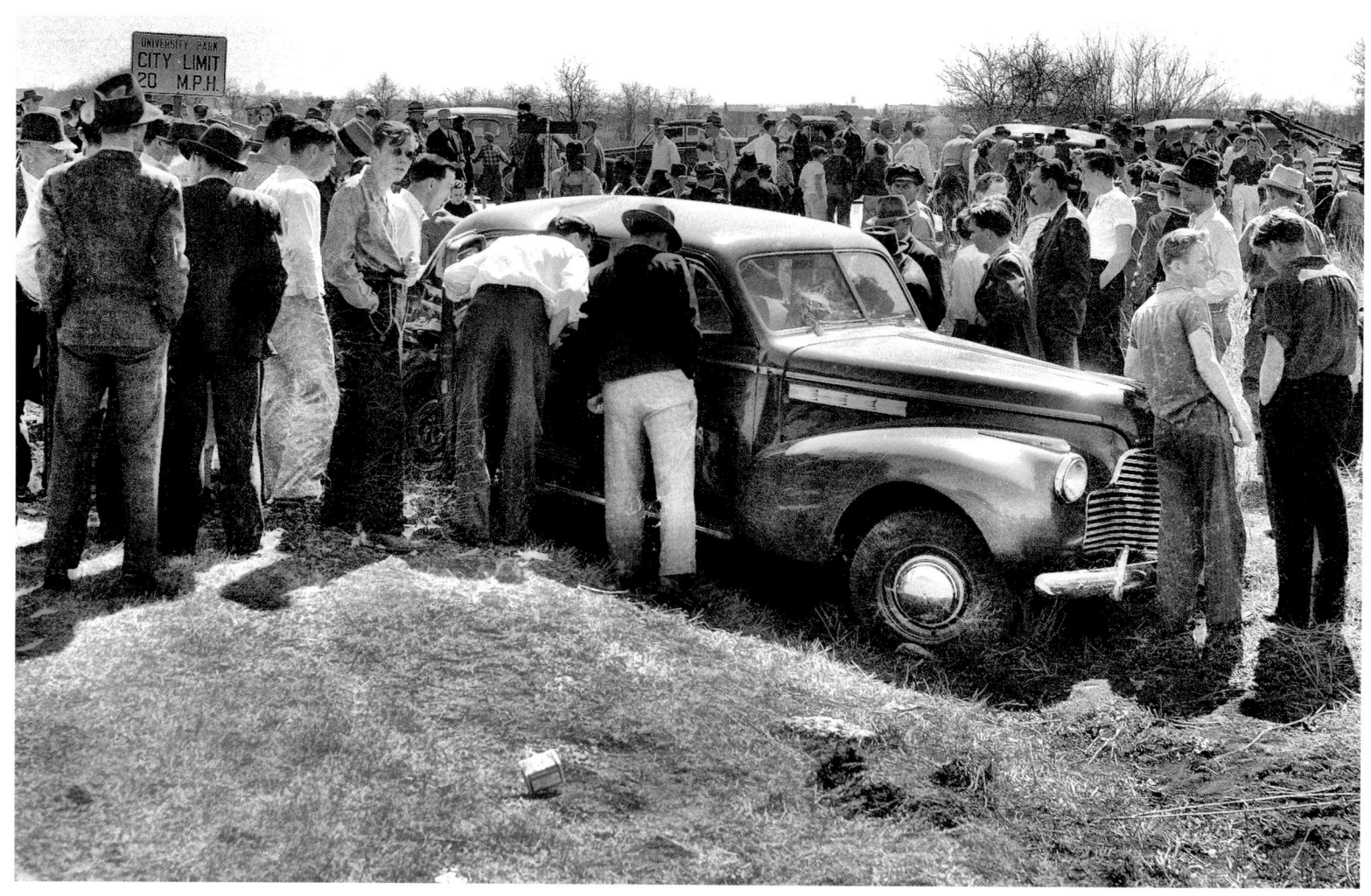

ABOVE: Large crowd gathers after a car accident.
Notice University Park's 20 mph speed limit sign.
Early 1940s.

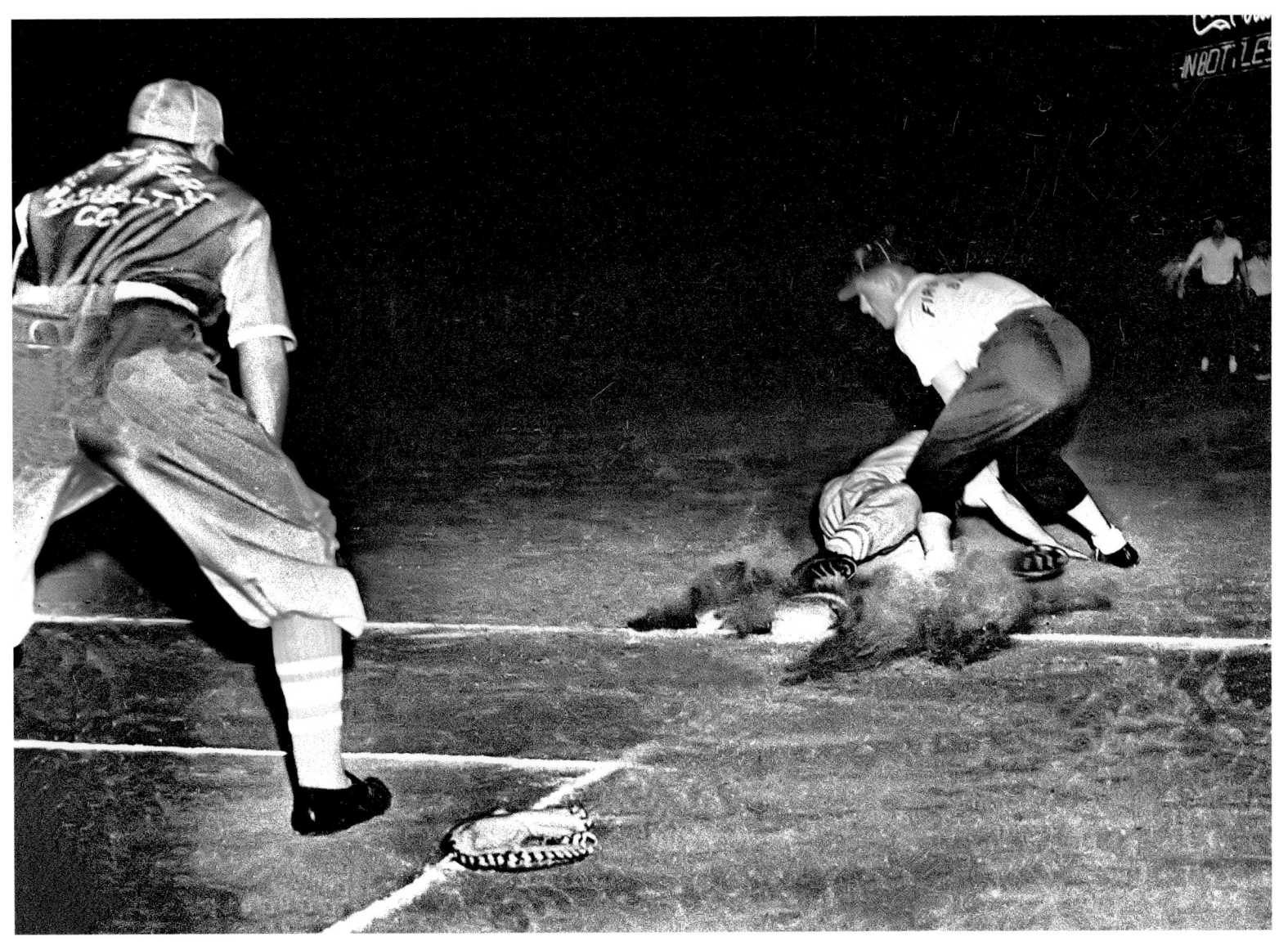

ABOVE: Player slides into home base. 1940s.

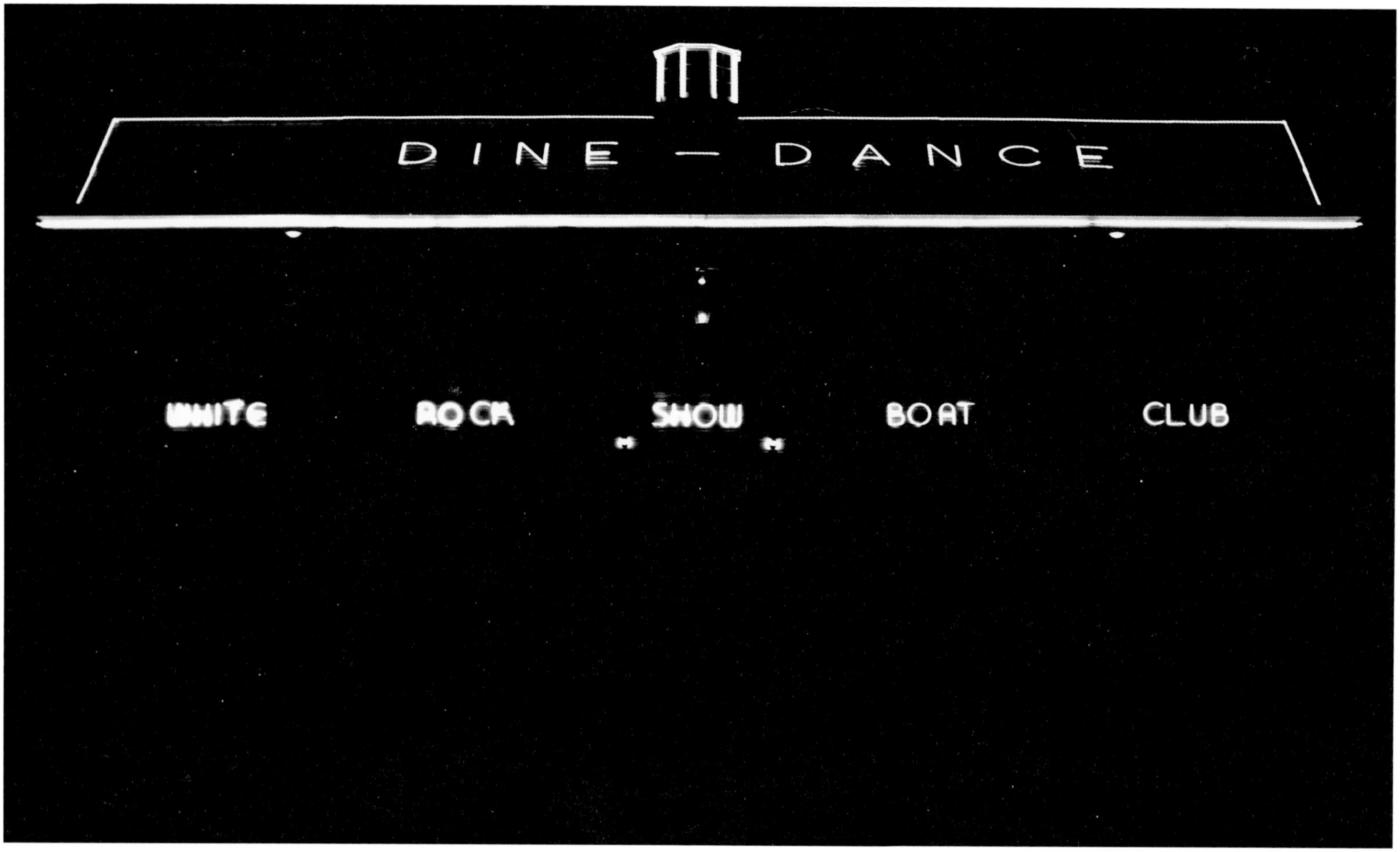

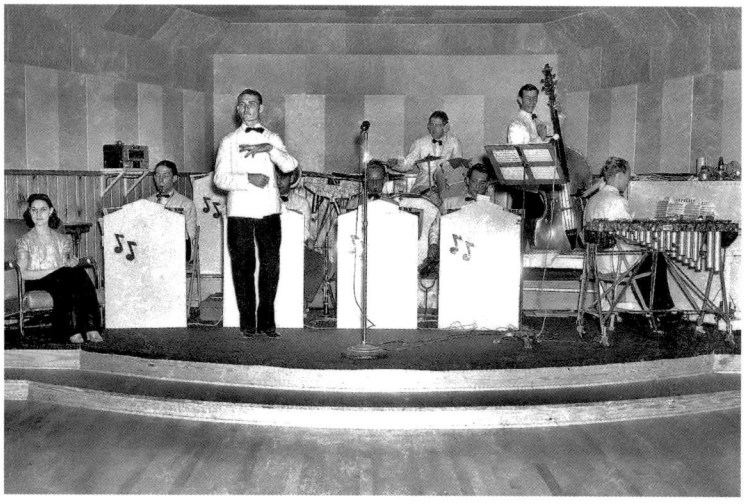

ABOVE: White Rock Showboat Club. 1940.

LEFT: White Rock Showboat Club orchestra. 1940.

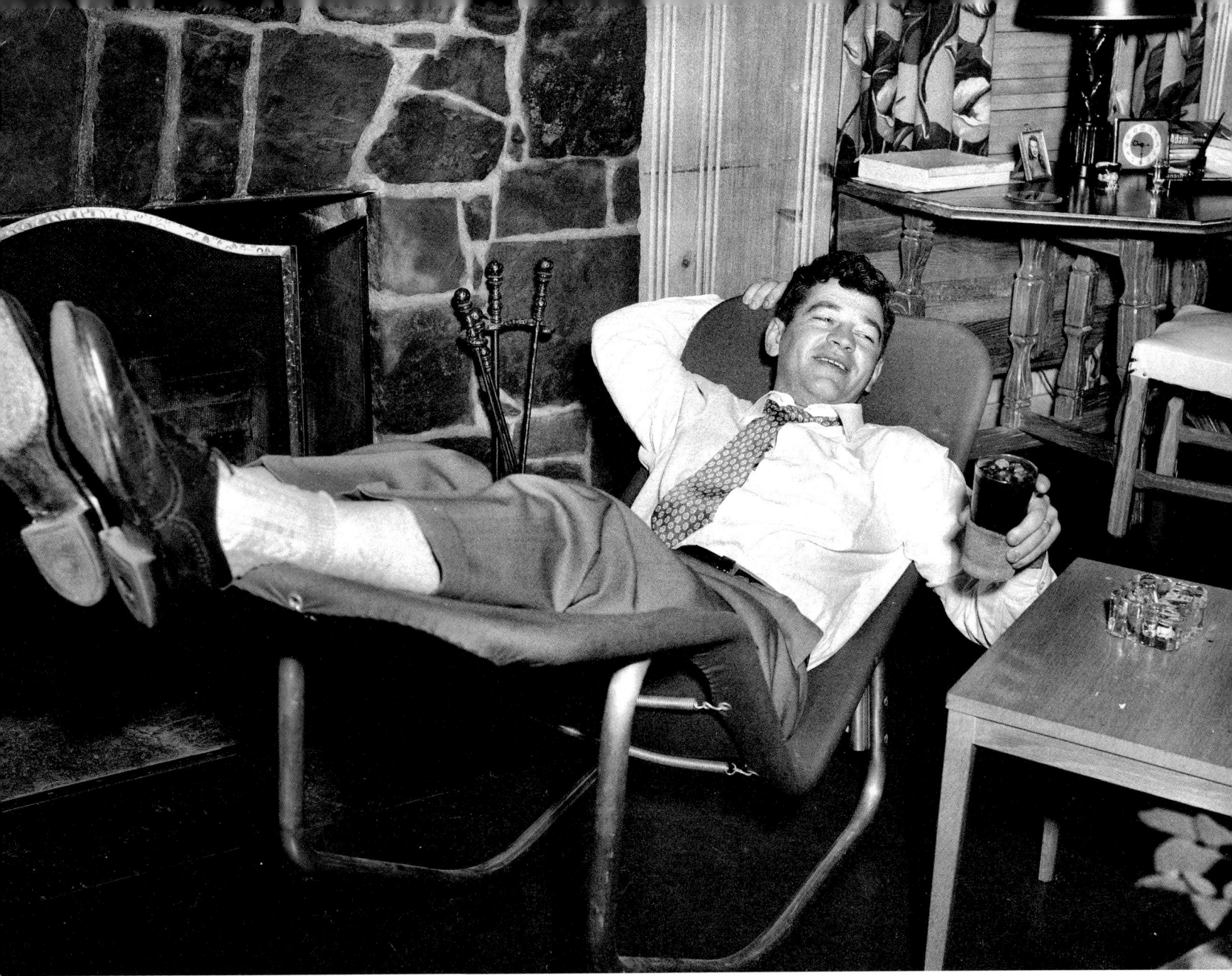

ABOVE: A group would gather at our house to listen to SMU's road games on the radio. This was a friend trying to relax after SMU's 27–29 loss to Notre Dame. With the win, the Fighting Irish completed their perfect 10–0 season and became the national champion. 1949.

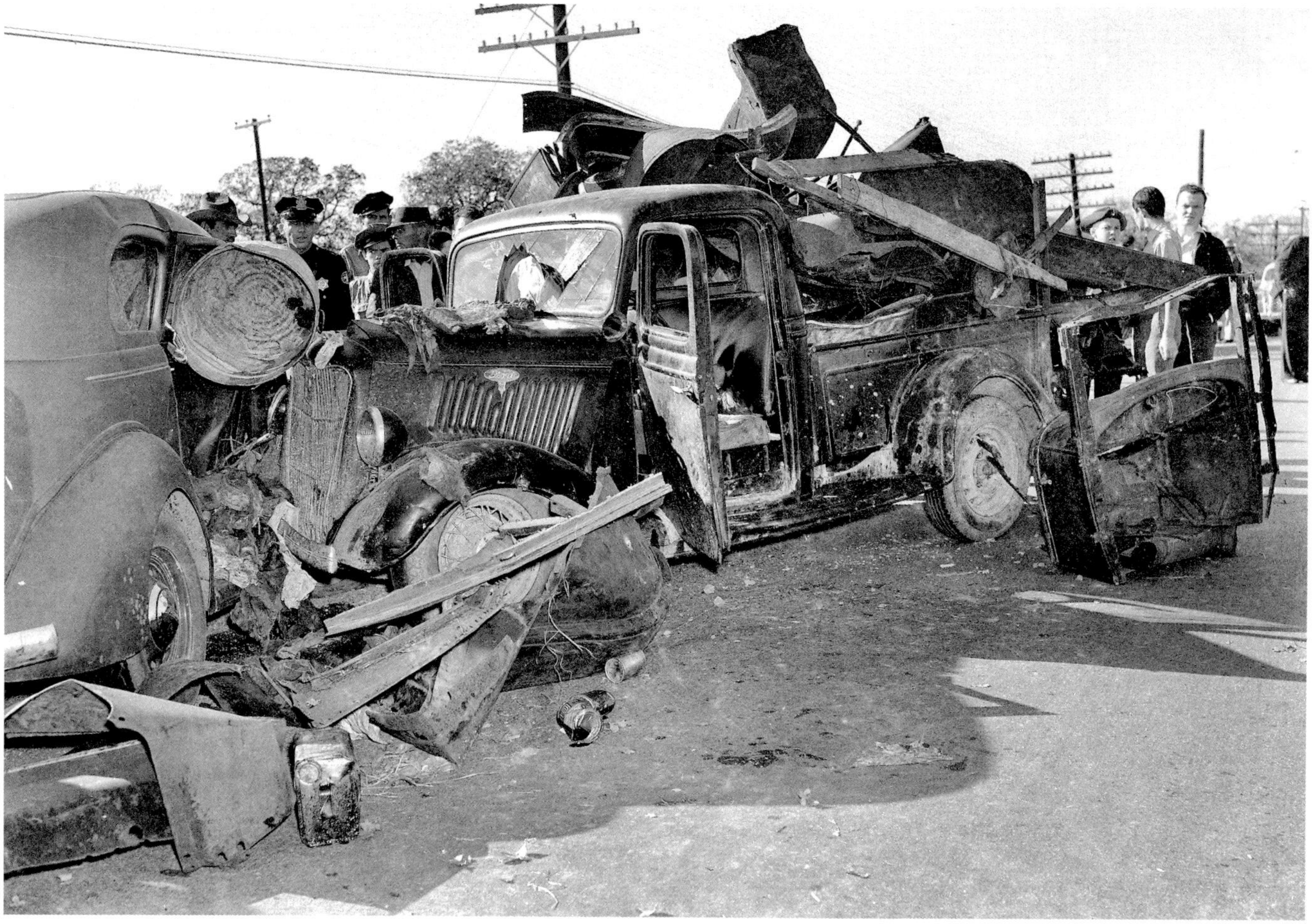

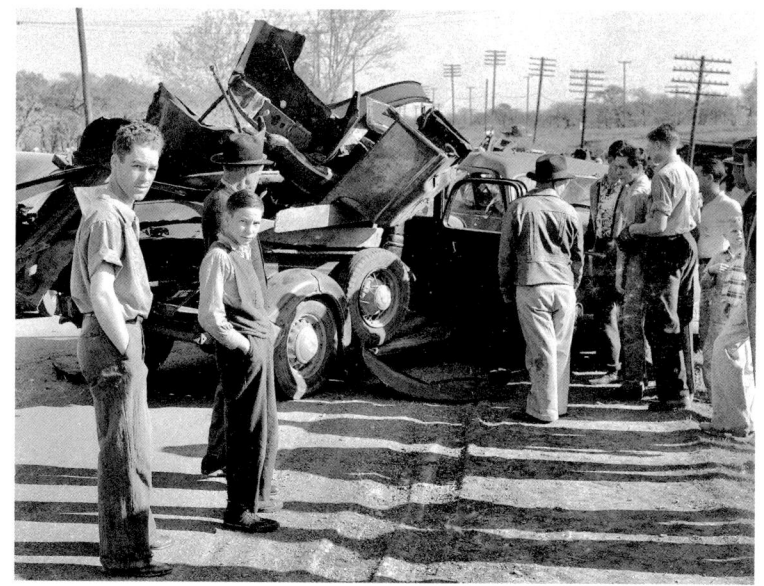

ABOVE: The front side of a bad crash between a truck and a car. 1939.

RIGHT: View from the back side of the above wreck. 1939.

OPPOSITE: Picnics with friends became a popular pastime after the war. 1948.

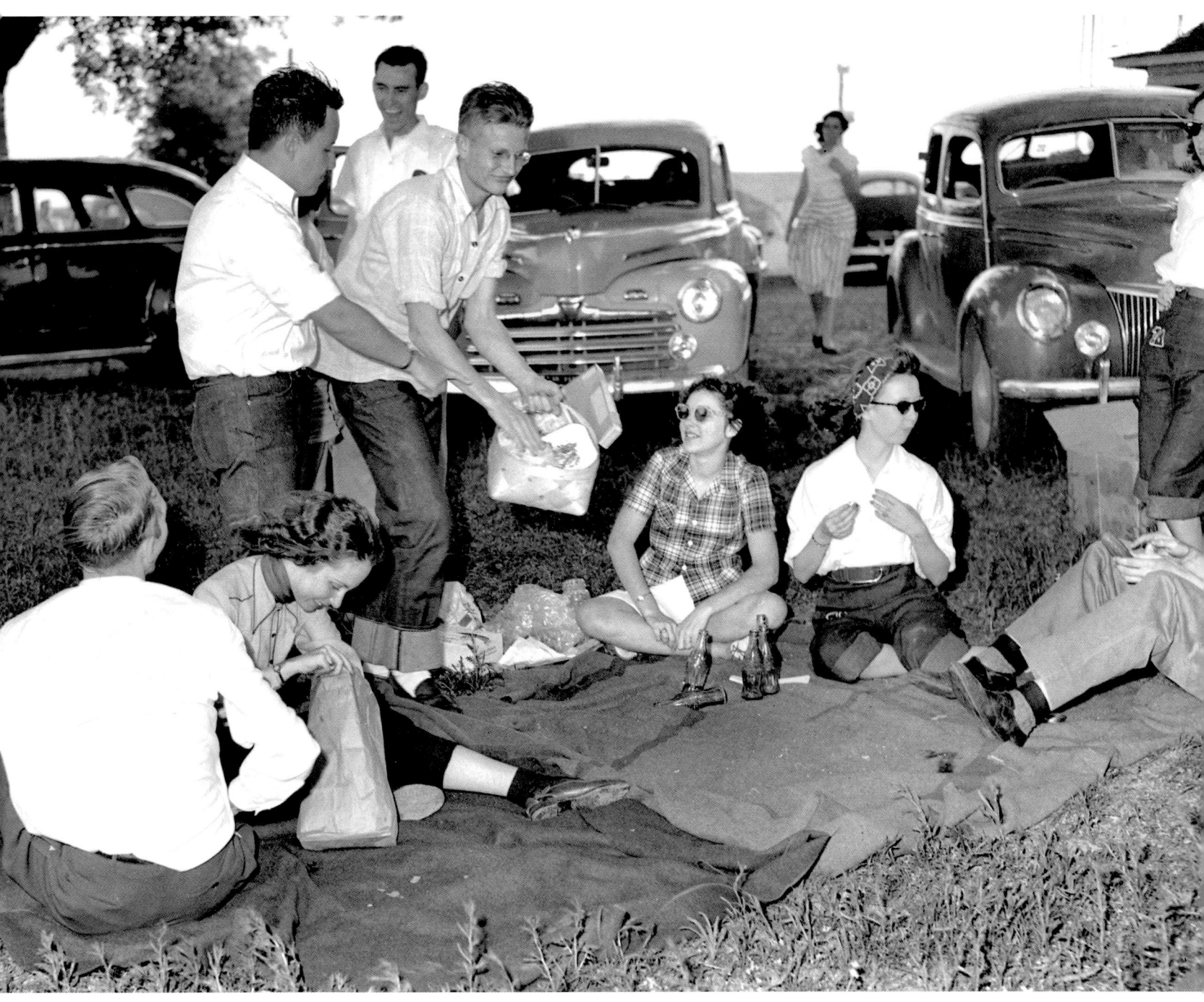

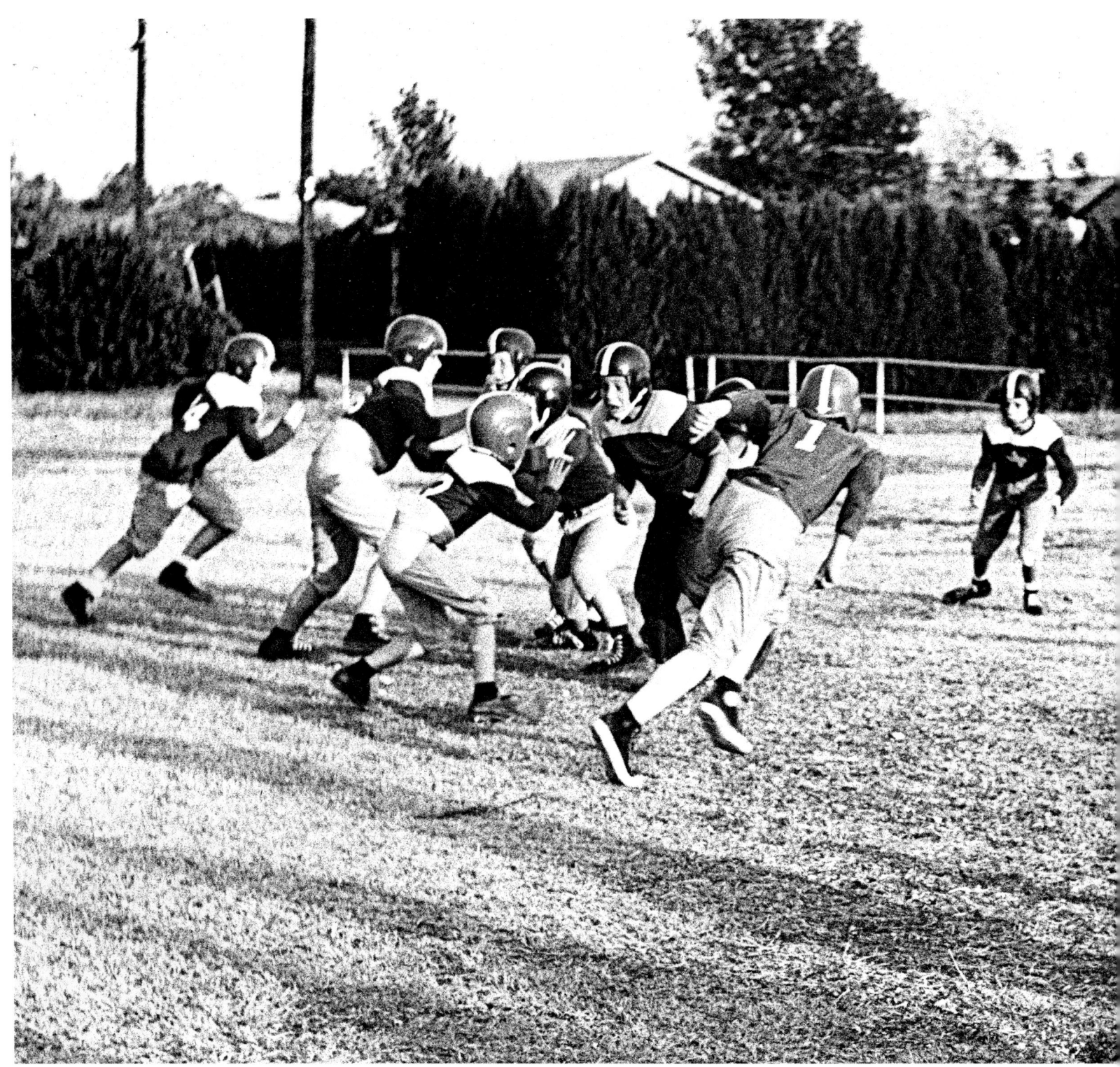

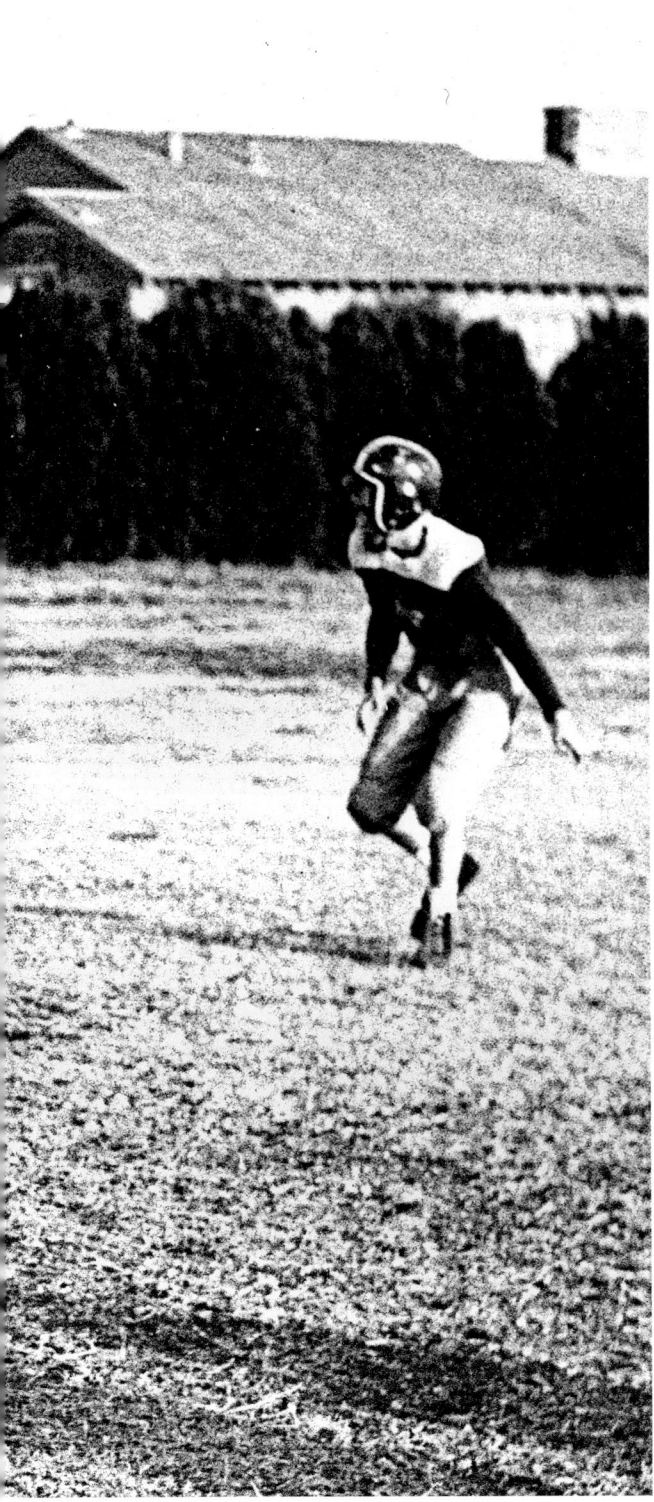

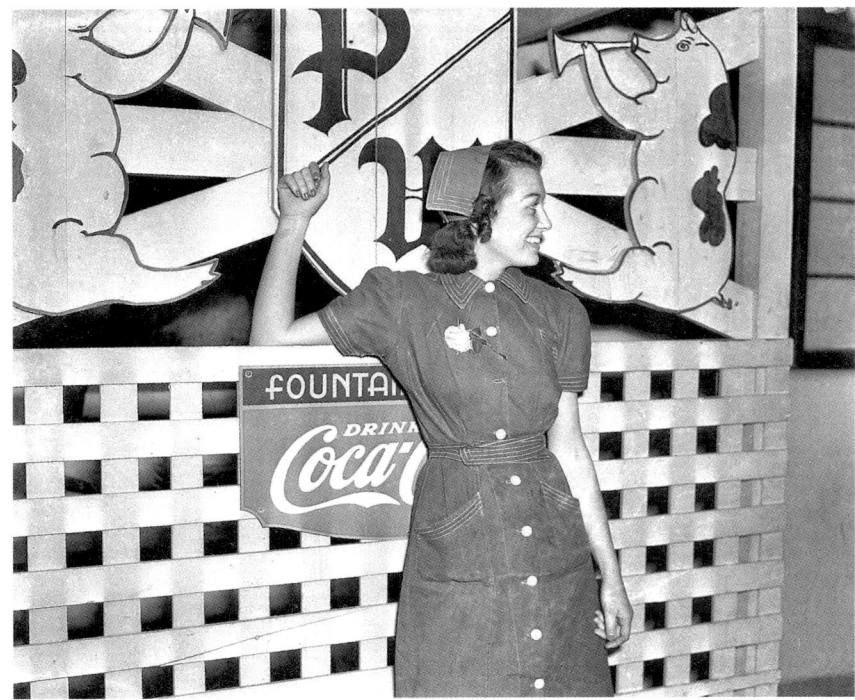

ABOVE: Waitress at the Pig 'n Whistle restaurant on North Zang Boulevard in Oak Cliff. 1949.

LEFT: Since Dad and my Uncle Giles brought big-time professional football to town that year with the original Dallas Texans, it was only fitting that, with my uncle as coach, we had a Park Cities YMCA little league football team, the Little Texans (in the darker jerseys). My cousin Ed (Giles's son) and I had a lot of fun playing on the team for two years, which, unfortunately, was longer than our family's NFL version lasted (with college football very hot and virtually no interest in the pro side of the game, we're still listed in the record book as the last team to go bankrupt in the NFL). 1952.

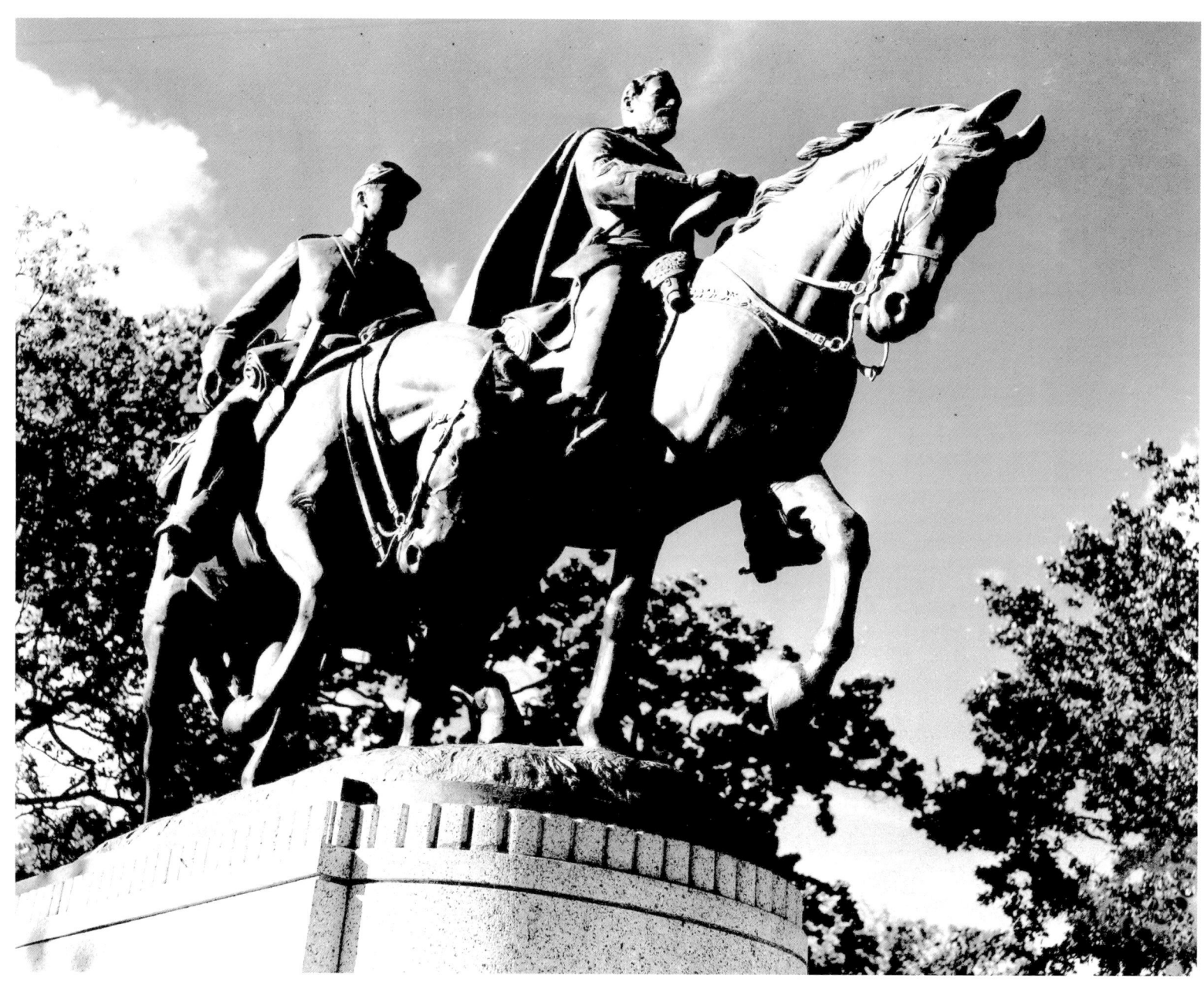

ABOVE: In 1936, a statue depicting Robert E. Lee and his aide was built in Dallas's Lee Park. It was removed in 2017 and now resides at a golf resort near Terlingua. 1939.

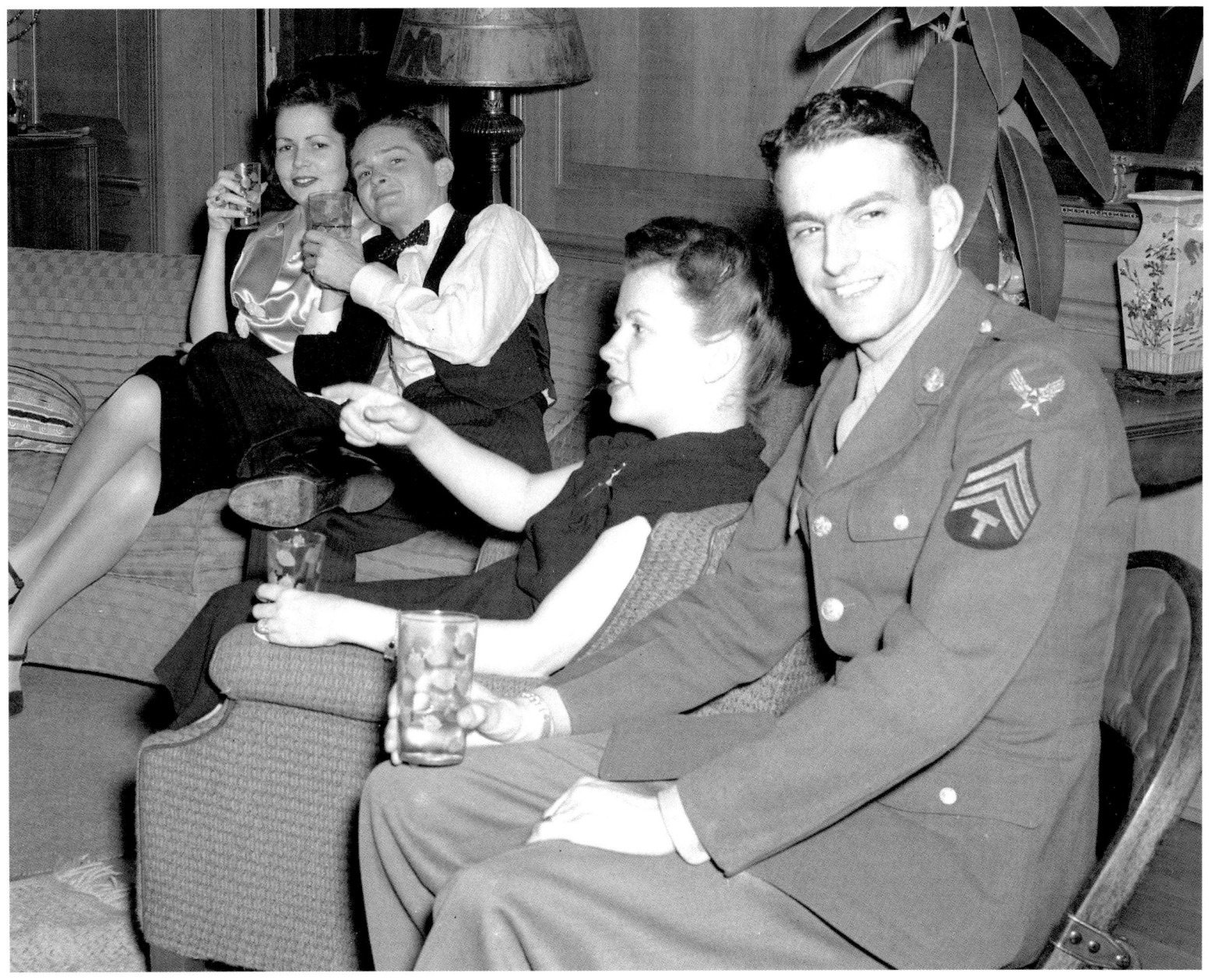

ABOVE: There were parties galore around Dallas as folks celebrated World War II coming to an end. 1945.

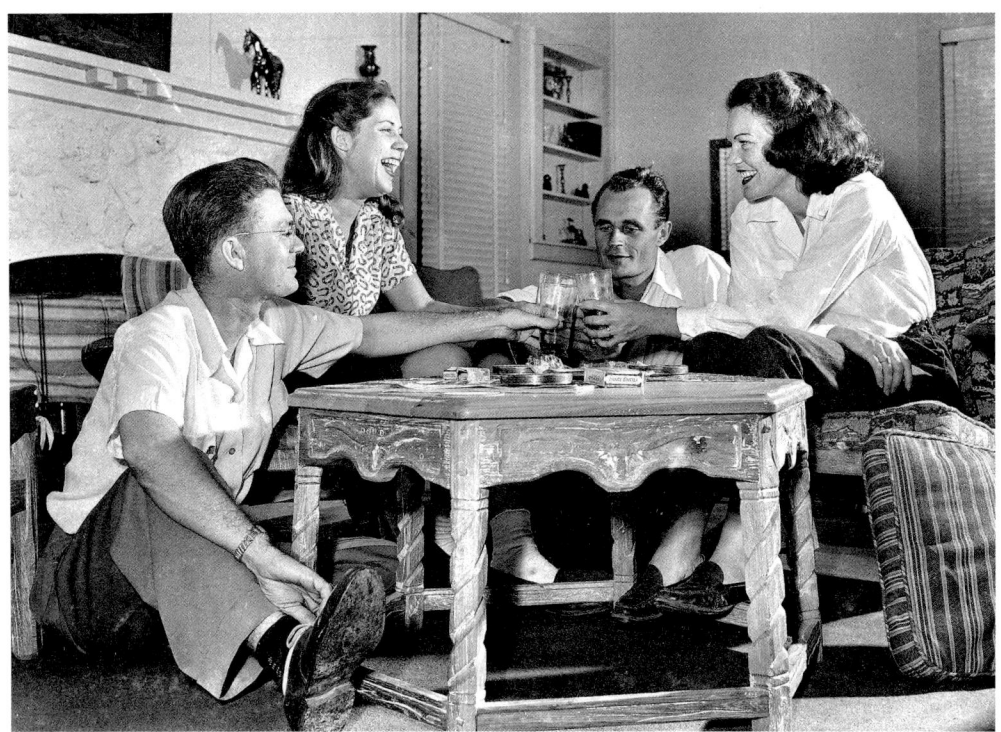

LEFT: Parties and get-togethers of friends became very popular after WWII. Incidentally, these folks are gathered around a cocktail table manufactured by the A. Brandt Ranch Oak Furniture Co. of Fort Worth. Pieces are very collectible today. 1948.

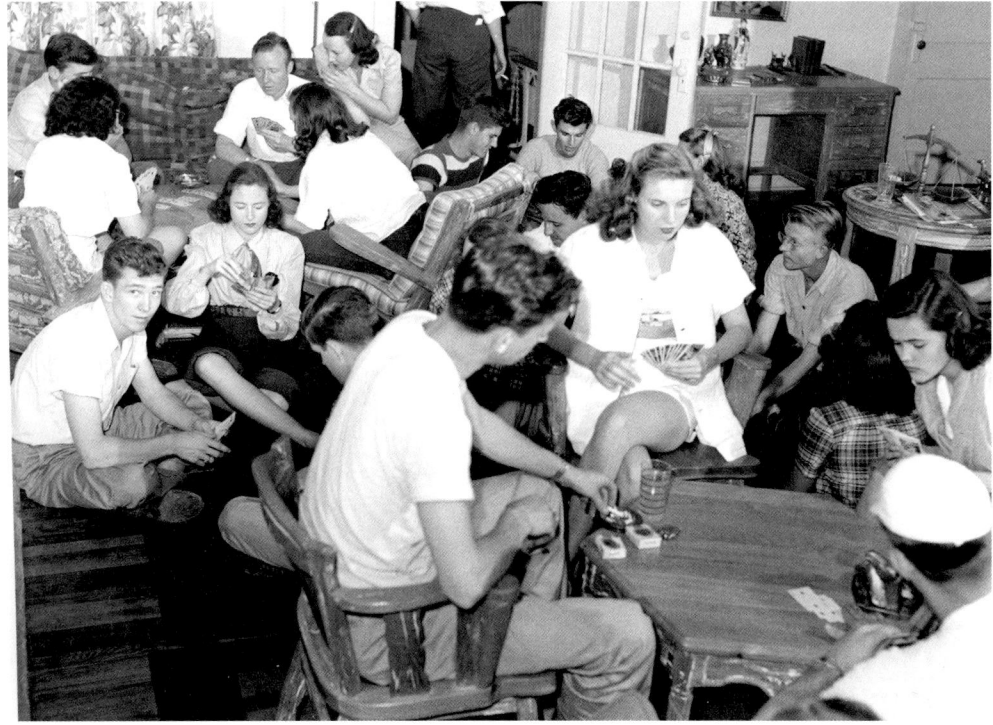

LEFT: Canasta and bridge were two card games that became very popular in the new post-war socializing. 1949.

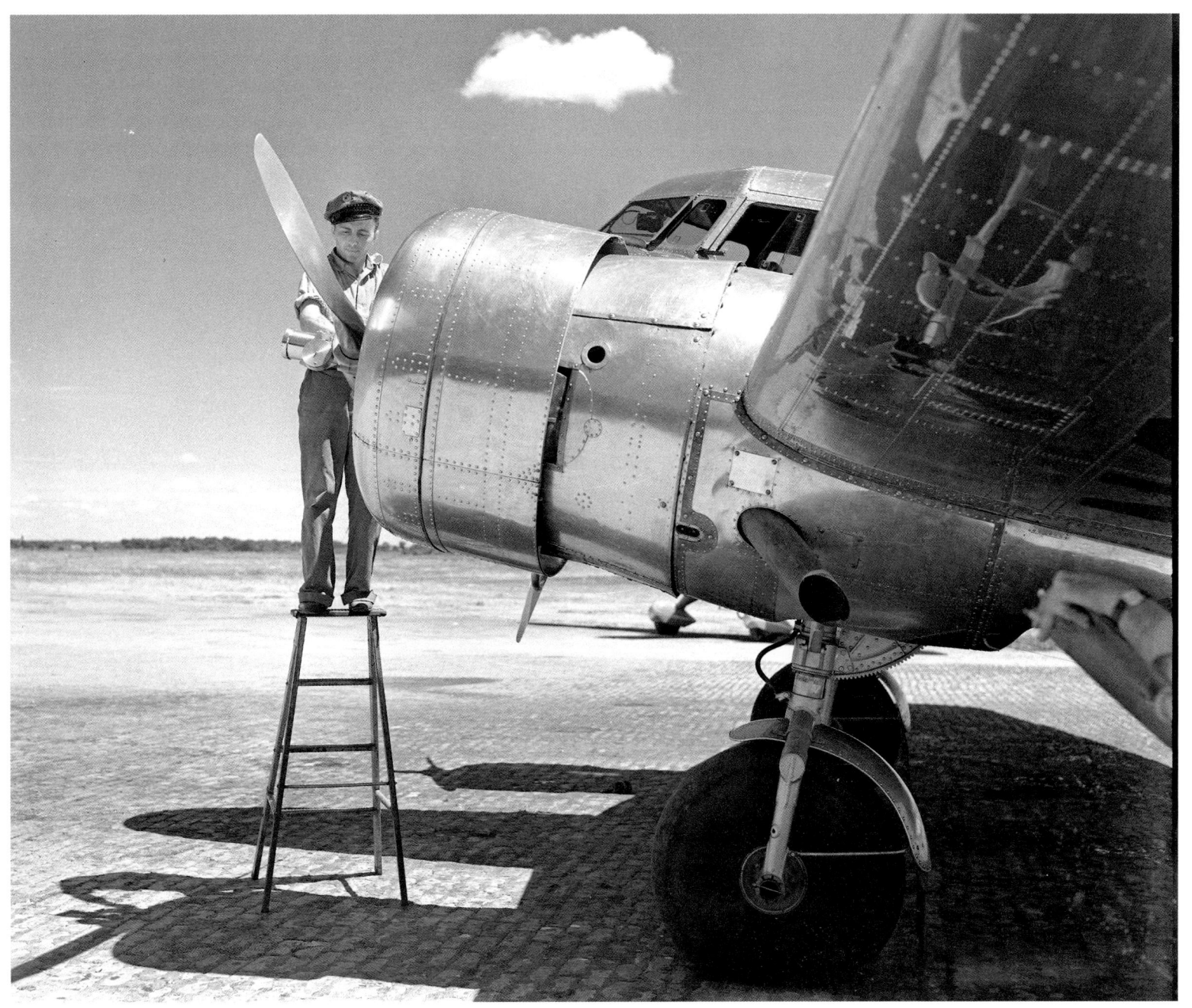

ABOVE: A little early morning maintenance at Dallas' Love Field. 1941.

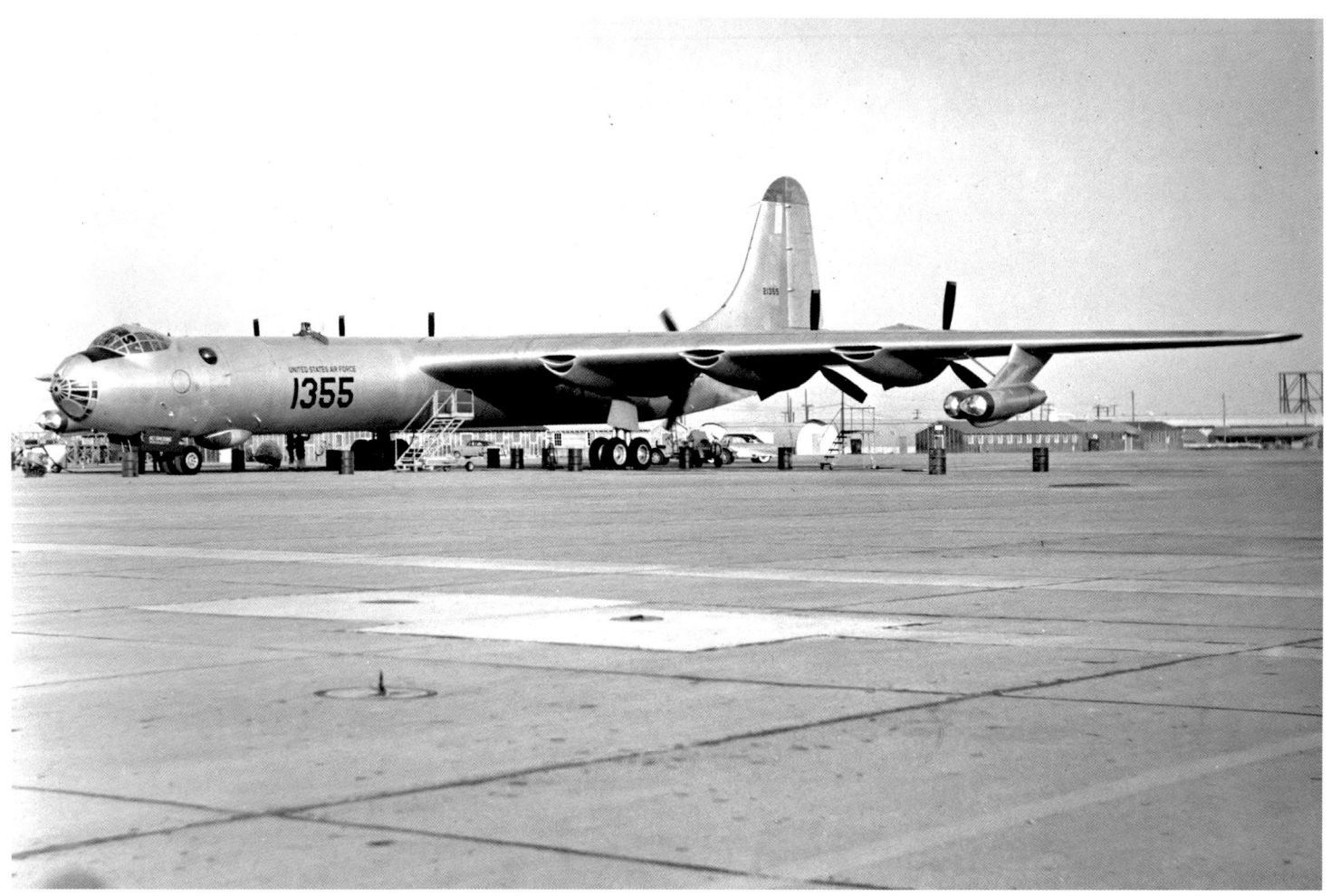

ABOVE: B-36 "Peacemaker" at Austin's Bergstrom AFB. Built by Convair in Fort Worth, these were massive, intimidating long-distance bombers, with a 230-foot wingspan, six 28-cylinder engines, top speeds of 435 mph, a 50,000-foot ceiling, and a range of up to 12,000 miles carrying a massive payload. Only four remain intact today, including the last one built named the "City of Fort Worth." Dad took this as he and I were pulling into Bergstrom along with a contingent of Dallas sportscar owners and drivers the day before a big SCCA race event. 1954.

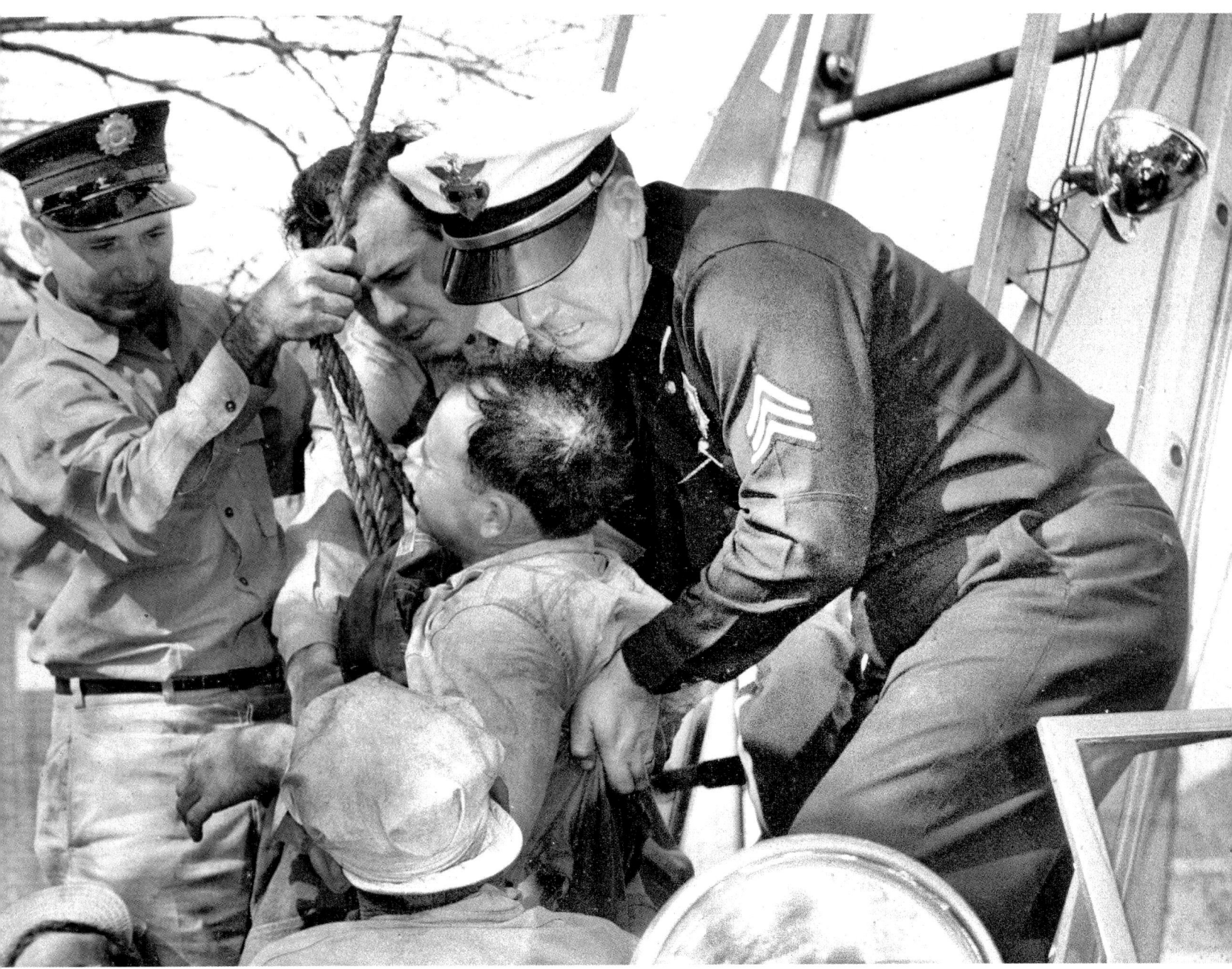

ABOVE: Rescue from a water tower. 1948.

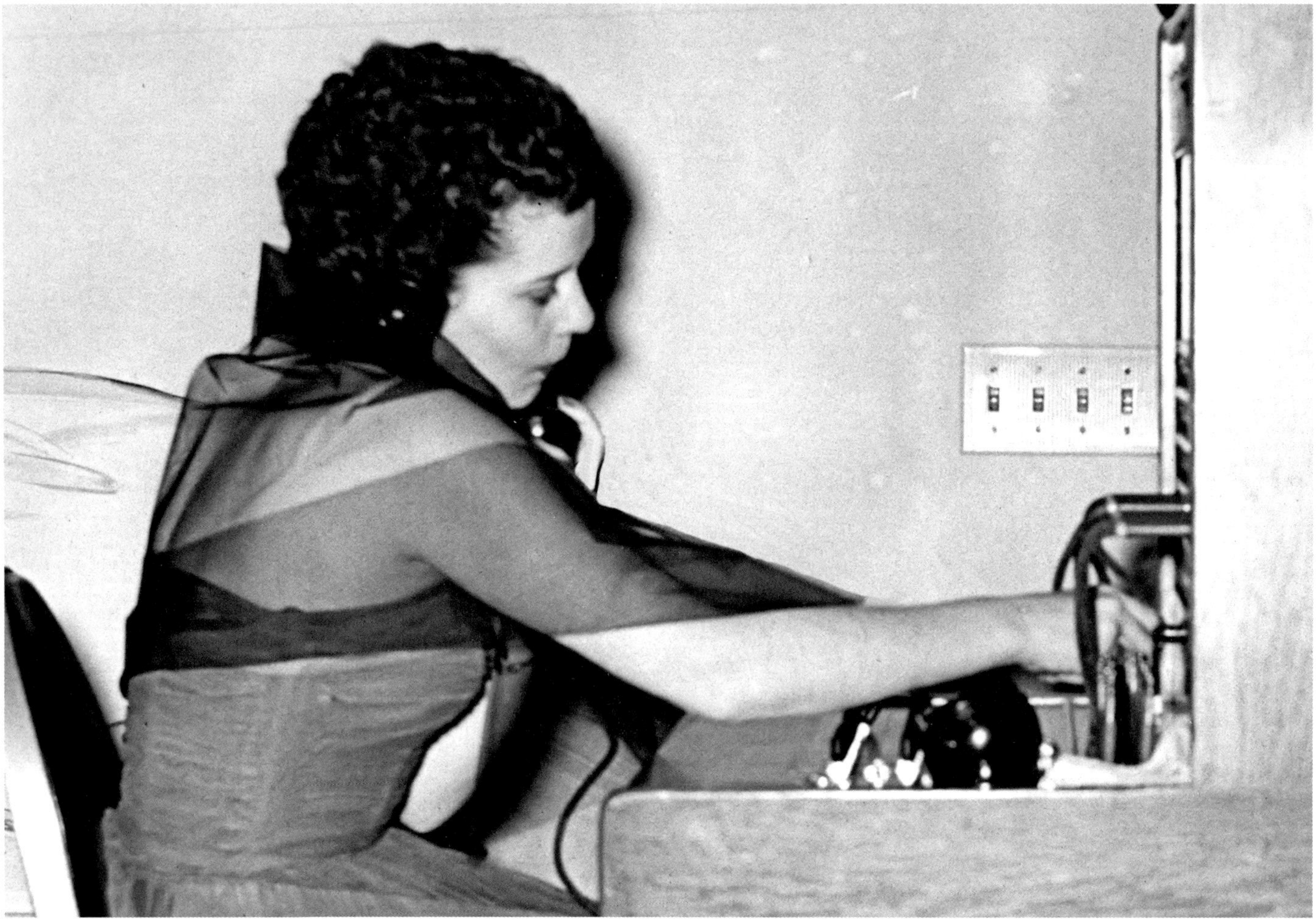

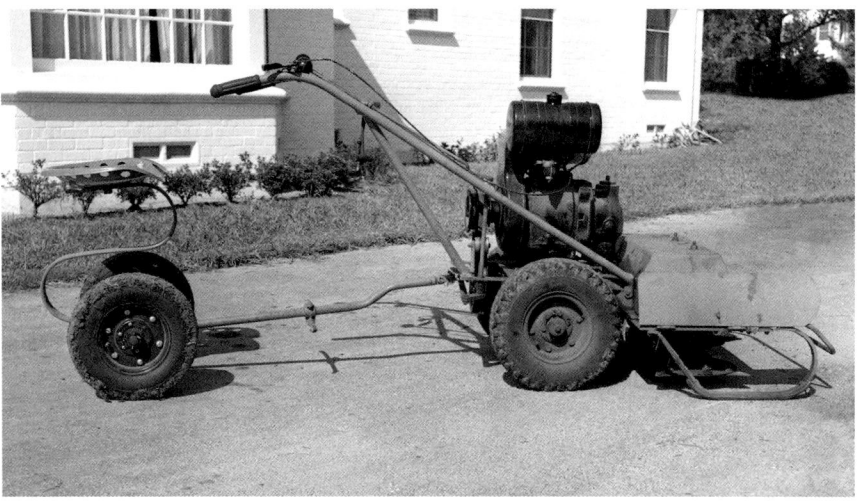

ABOVE: Dallas company switchboard operator. 1950s.

LEFT: Gravely riding mower— state of the art. 1951.

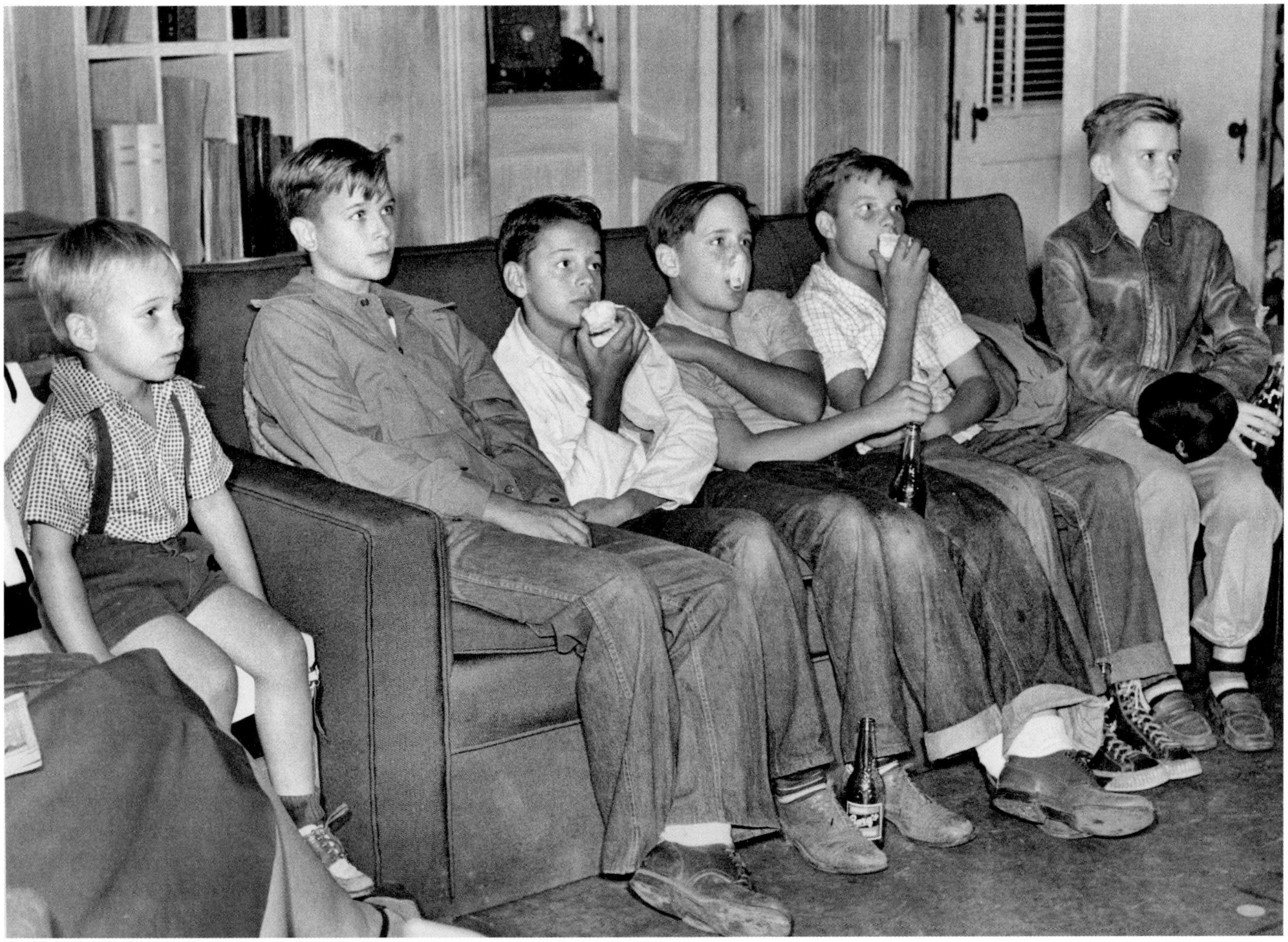

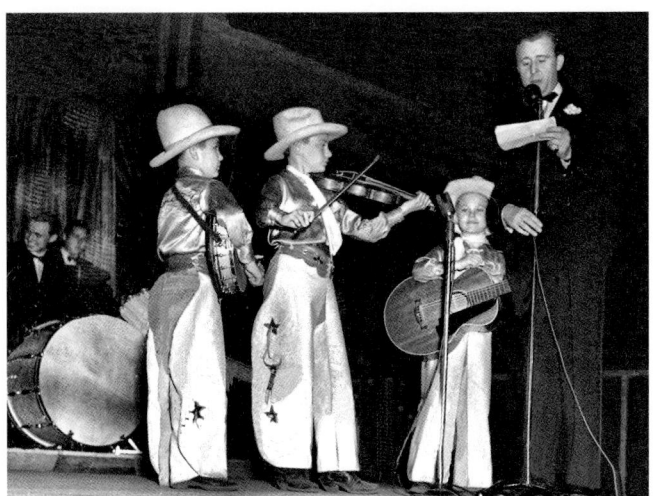

ABOVE: Neighborhood kids watching movies at a home in University Park. 1948.

LEFT: Early 1940's talent contest with three li'l buckaroos. 1942.

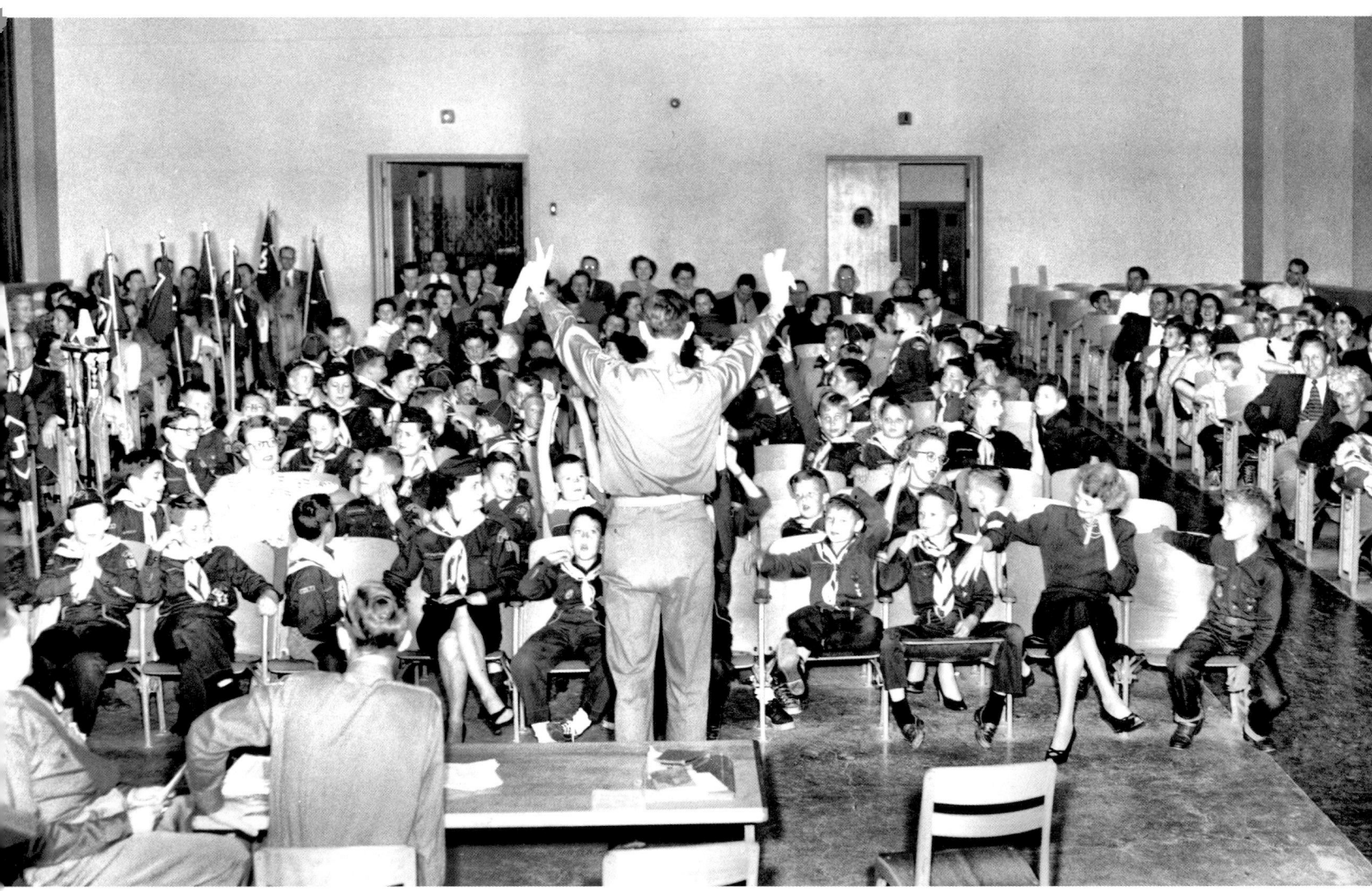

ABOVE: Cub Scout assembly at H. W. Longfellow in Dallas. 1952.

PAGES 54-55: Meeting of several Cub Scout dens at H. W. Longfellow Elementary School. Fourth row up is my brother Alex (in plaid shirt on end). Next to him is my mother, who was also our pack's den mother. I'm the Cub Scout to the left of her facing the camera. 1952.

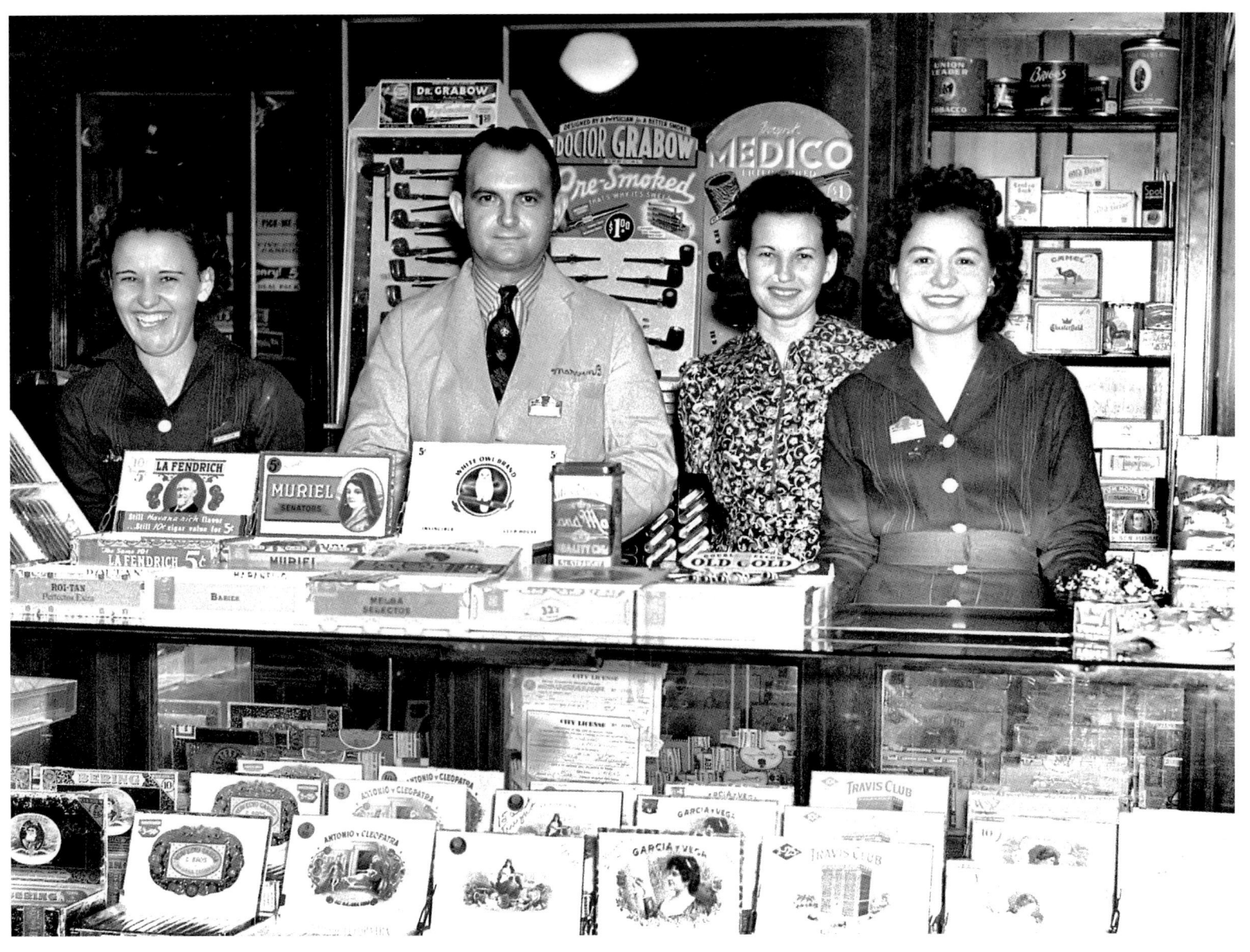

ABOVE: Employees of Marvin's Drug Store. Early 1940s.

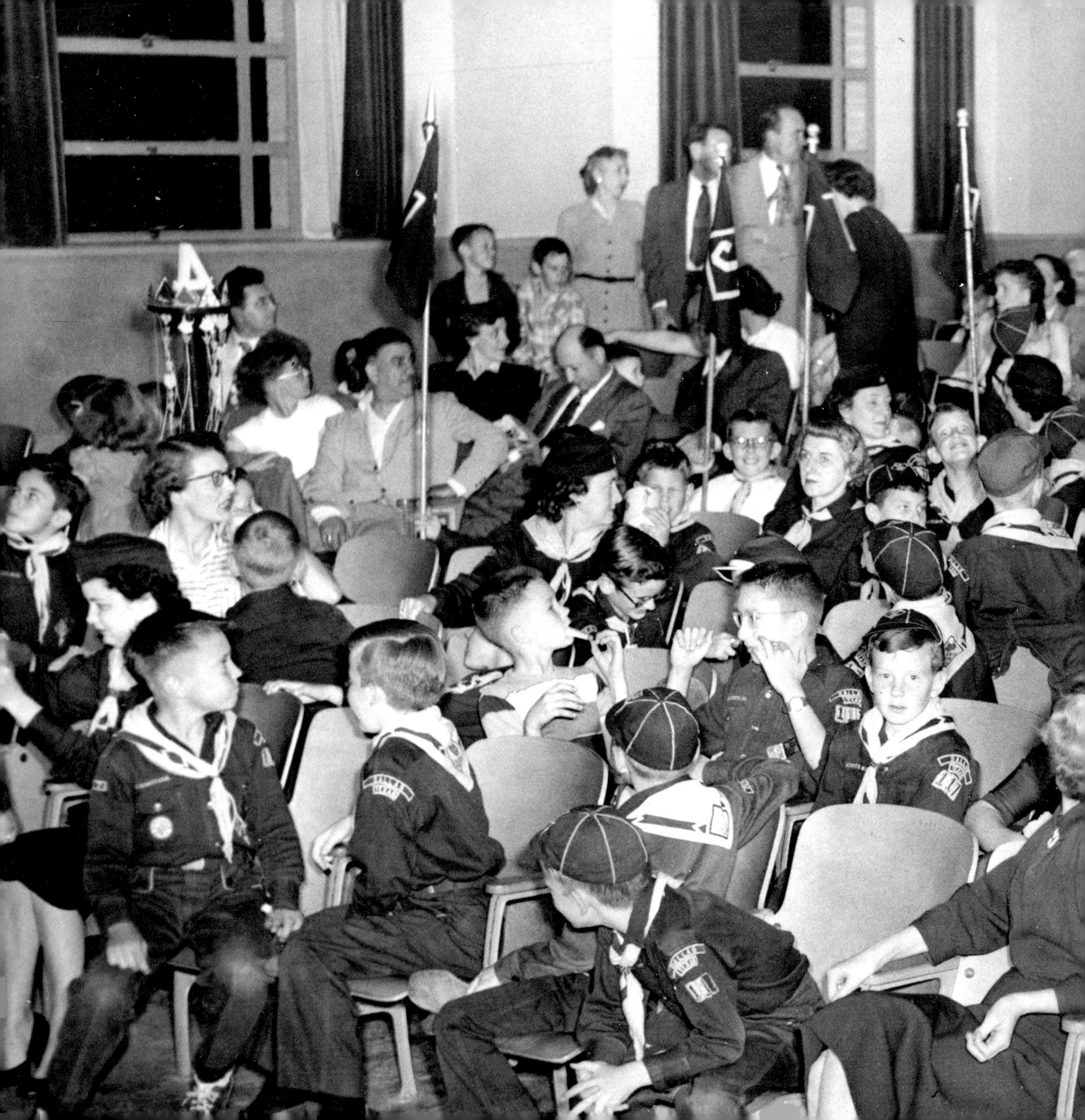

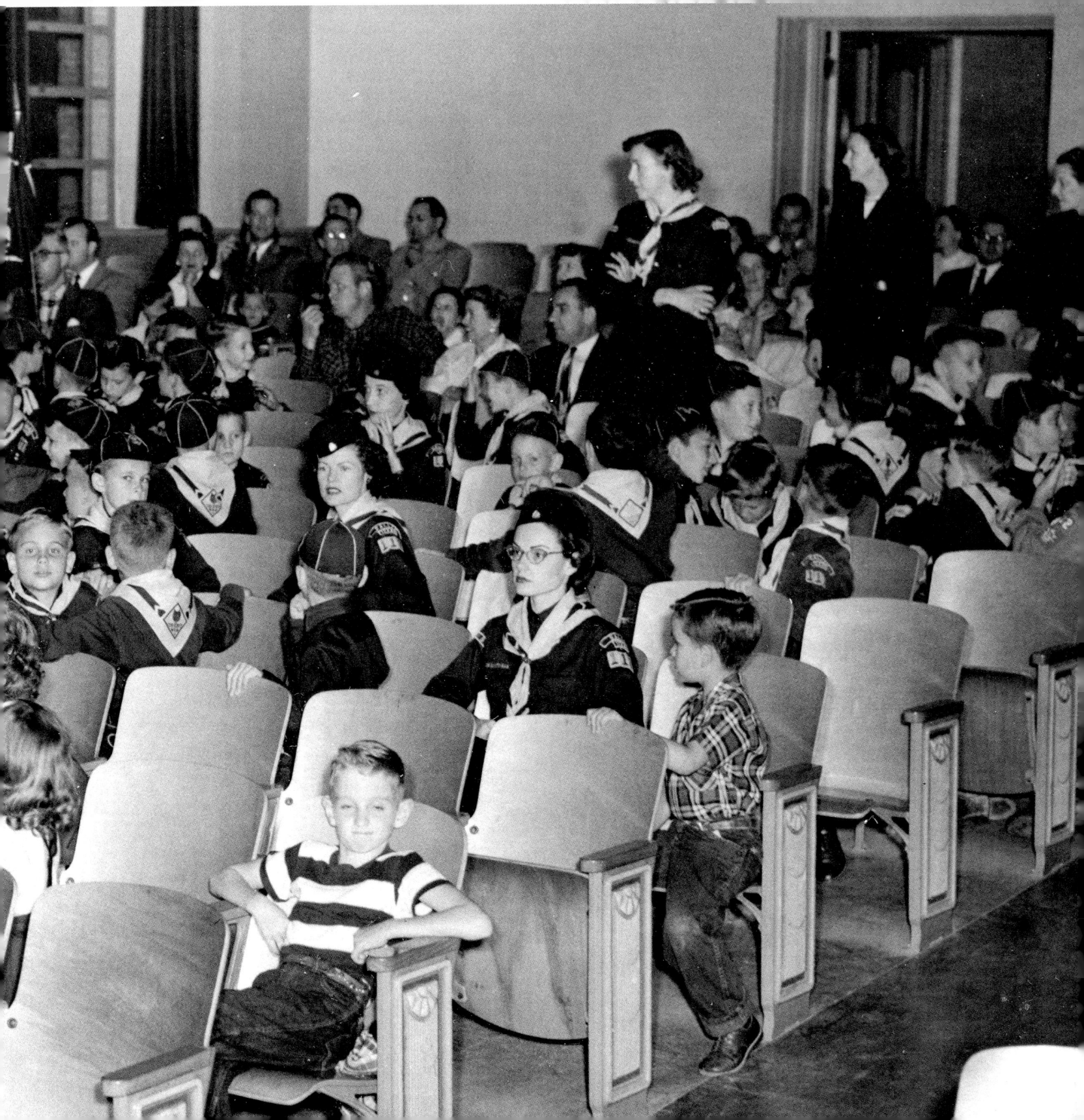

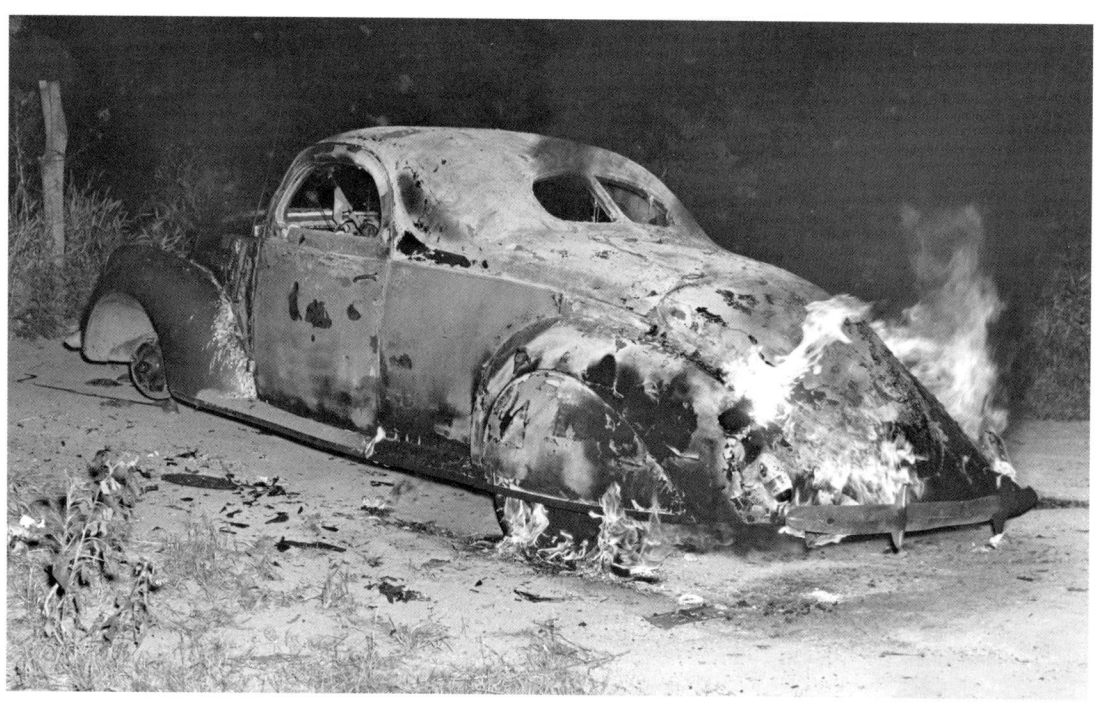

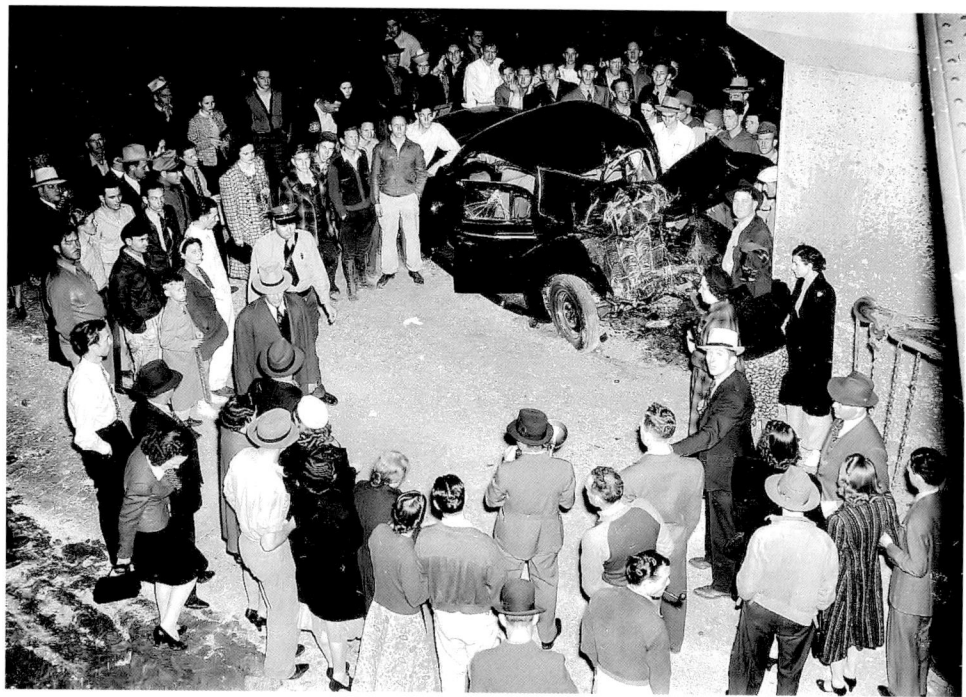

ABOVE: The flames were still burning when he shot this 1939 Lincoln Zephyr coupe. Early 1940s.

LEFT: Crowd gathered at the underpass on Buckner Boulevard after Jack Kirk crashed into it at high speed. Ruled a suicide. 1940.

OPPOSITE: Pouring a footing for a new house in Greenway Parks. 1951.

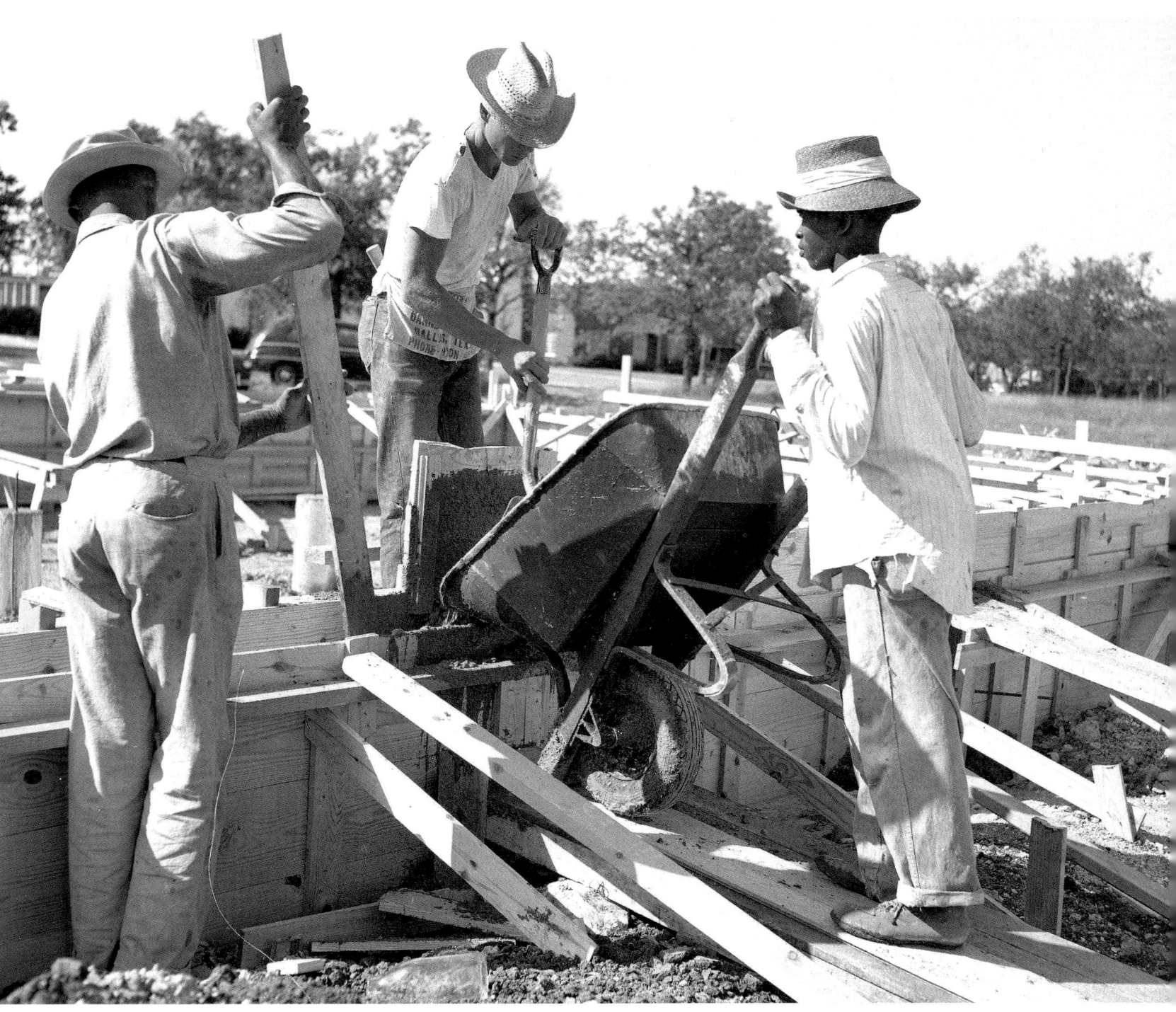

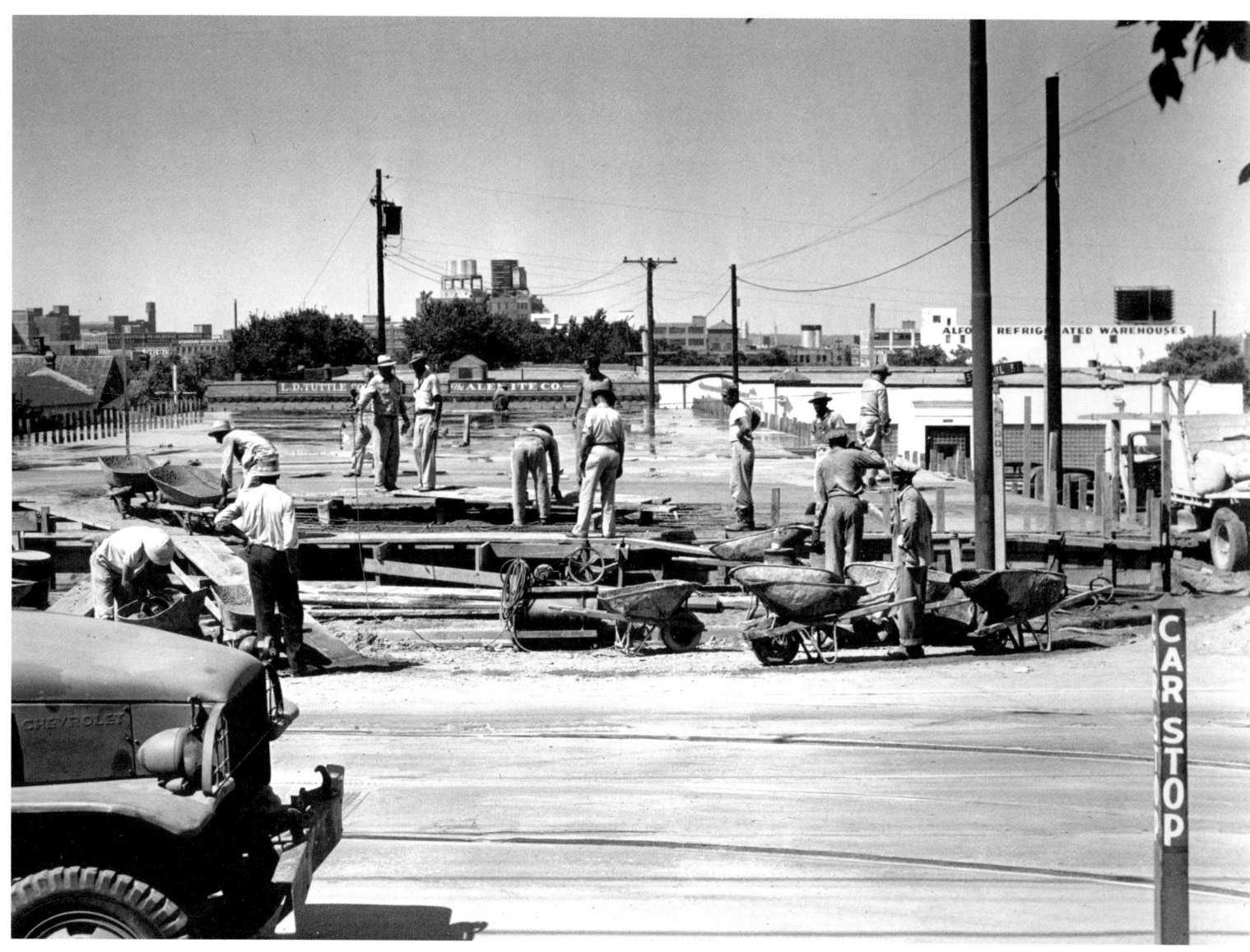

ABOVE: Building in Dallas, both residential and commercial, was at a furious pace in the late 1940s.

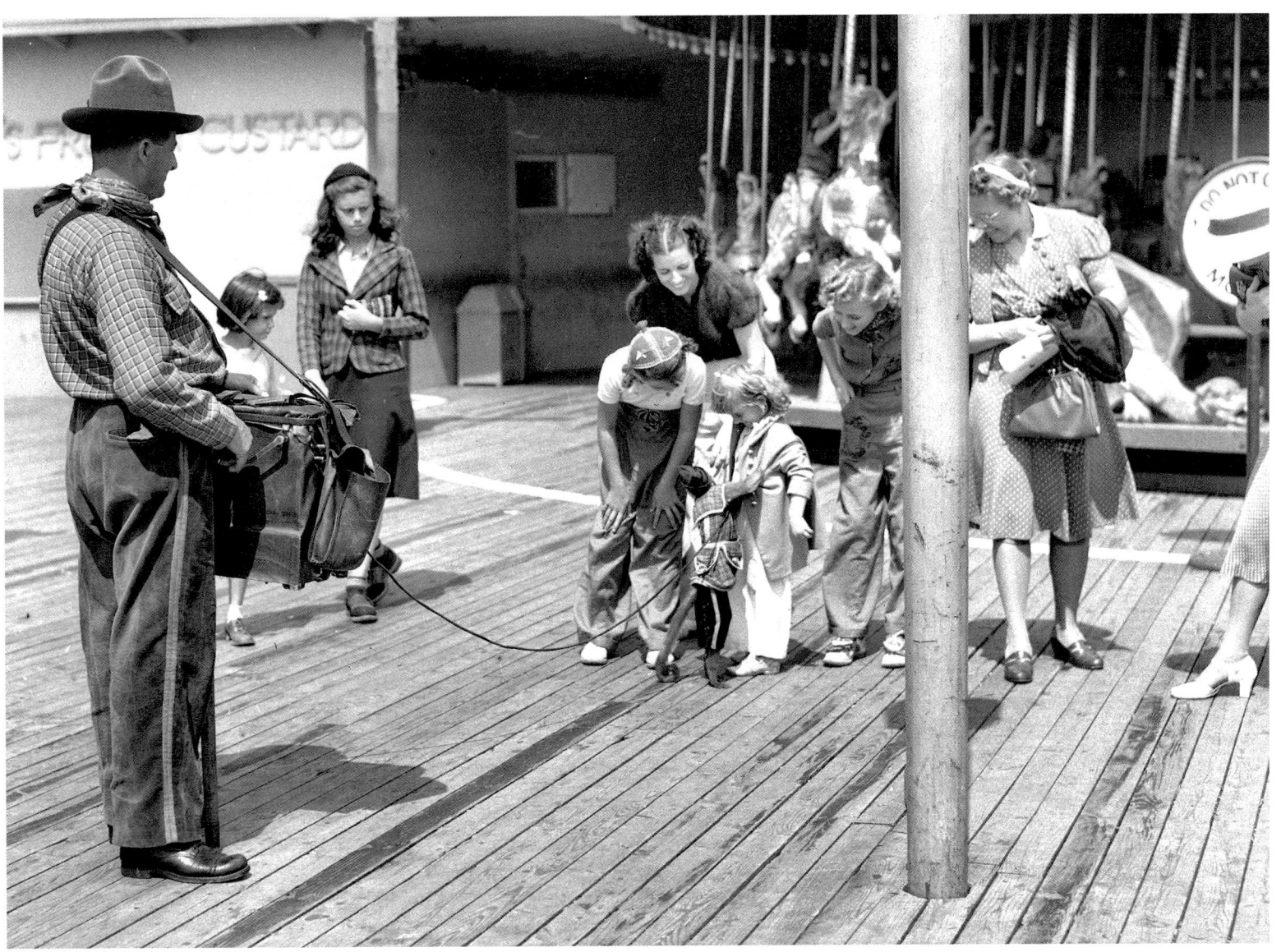

ABOVE: Organ grinder and his monkey entertaining kids for tips. I remember seeing him—and his monkey—performing at some of the shopping centers as late as the mid-fifties. 1945.

SMU

———

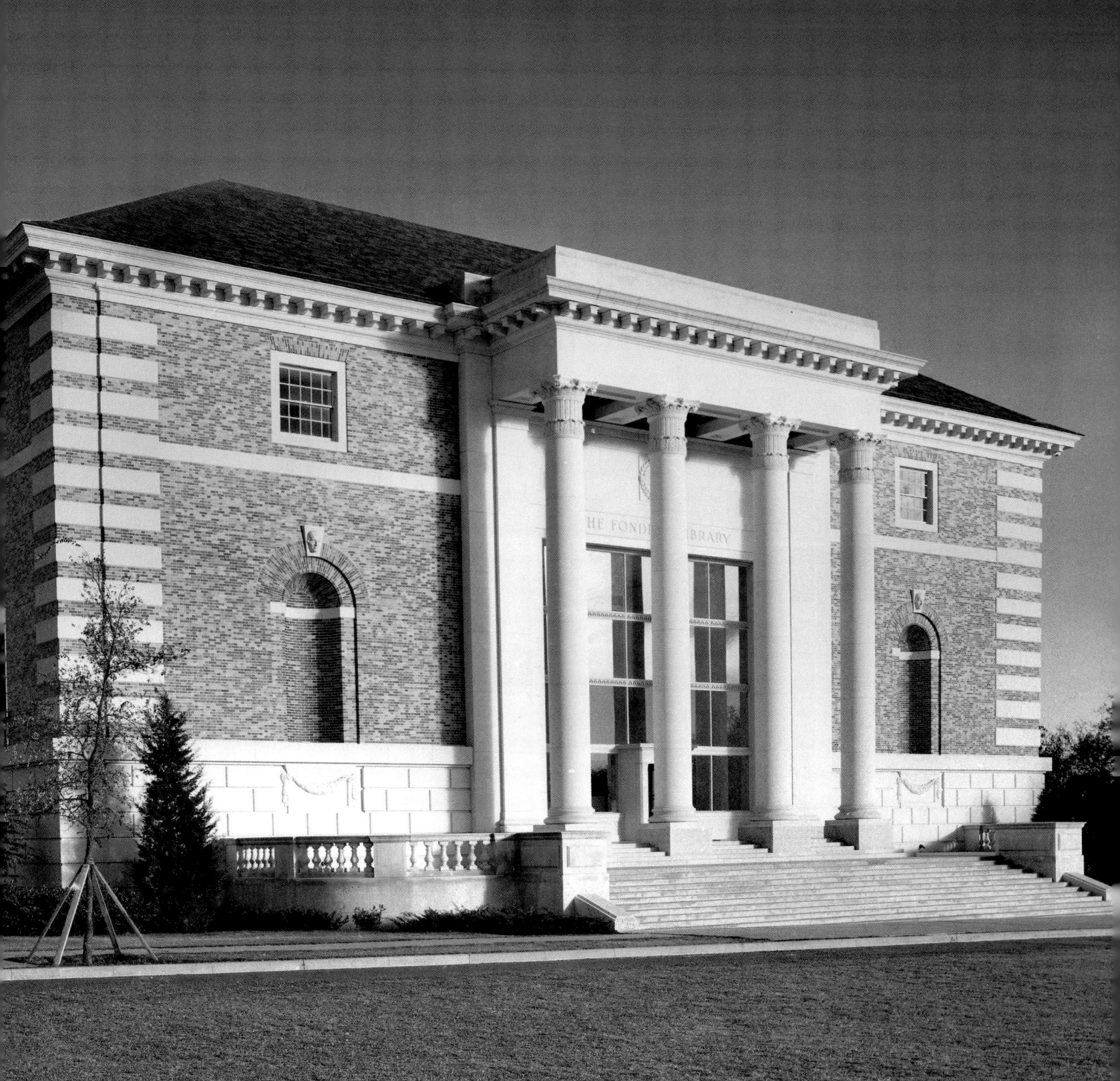

While attending SMU and before he married my mother, my father was living at his parents' home at 5112 Swiss Avenue, where he set up a darkroom and learned to develop film and print his own photographs. To provide money to help support the expenses associated with his hobby, he would go to the fraternities and sororities at the university and take group photos, which he would then sell to the students.

My mother and father loved SMU, and they made quite a few lifelong friends there—from classmates and his Delta Chi fraternity brothers and her Delta Gamma sorority sisters to several of the professors from his business classes and hers from the music department. Like many of the era, they were big football fans and became good friends with several of the players, including Doak Walker, who would go on to win the Heisman Trophy in 1948.

Doak and Norma (his first wife) would stop by occasionally when visiting her parents, who lived nearby. On one occasion, while tossing a football around with my brother, Alex, Doak showed me the correct way to hold the ball when throwing a spiral pass. Another time, he took us for rides in his brand-new 1953 Corvette, one of the first in Dallas. Such a nice guy and a terrific athlete. He was certainly a role model for us youngsters in the late forties and early fifties.

Dad shot these images around the SMU campus between 1939 and 1947.

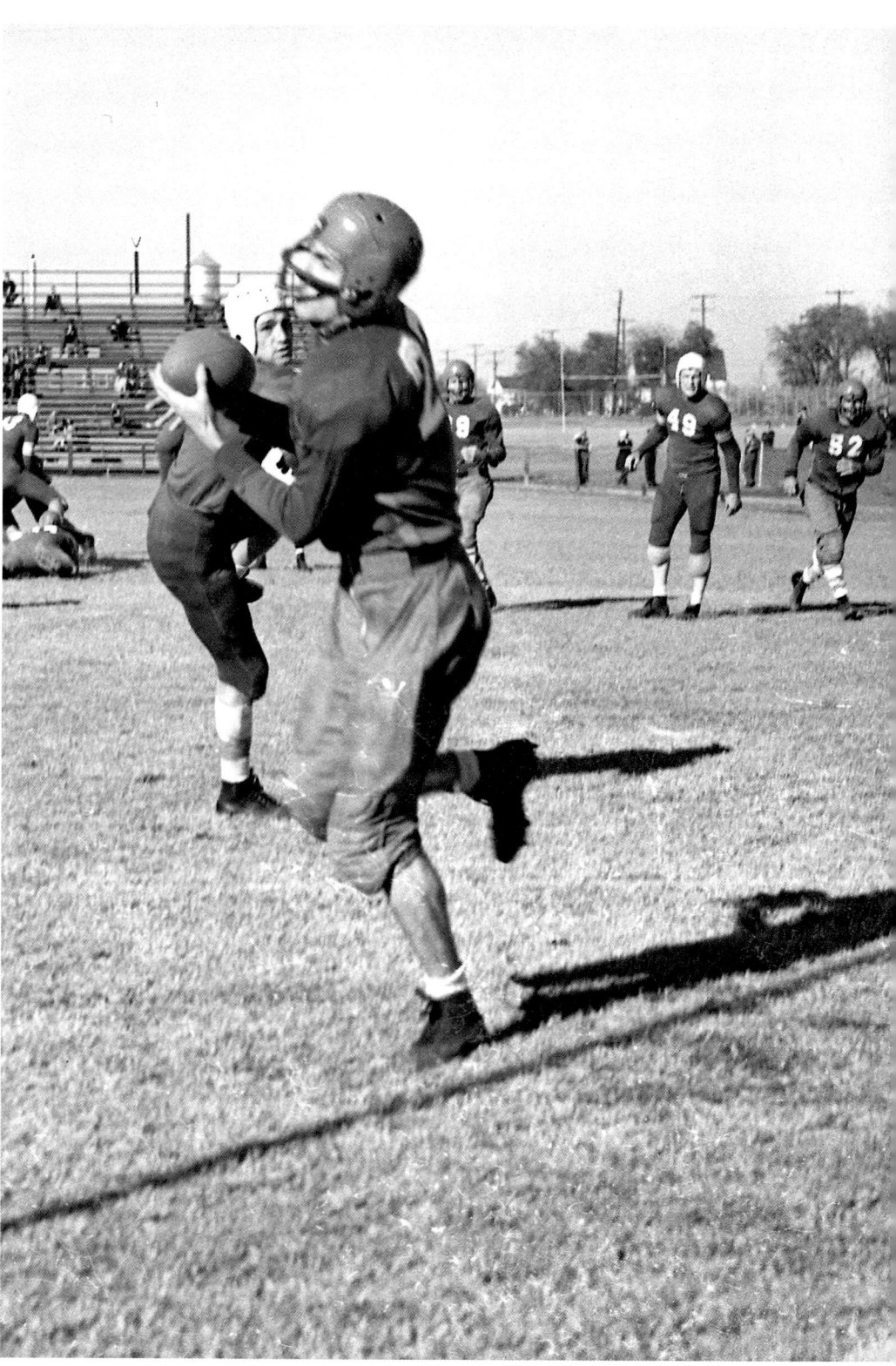

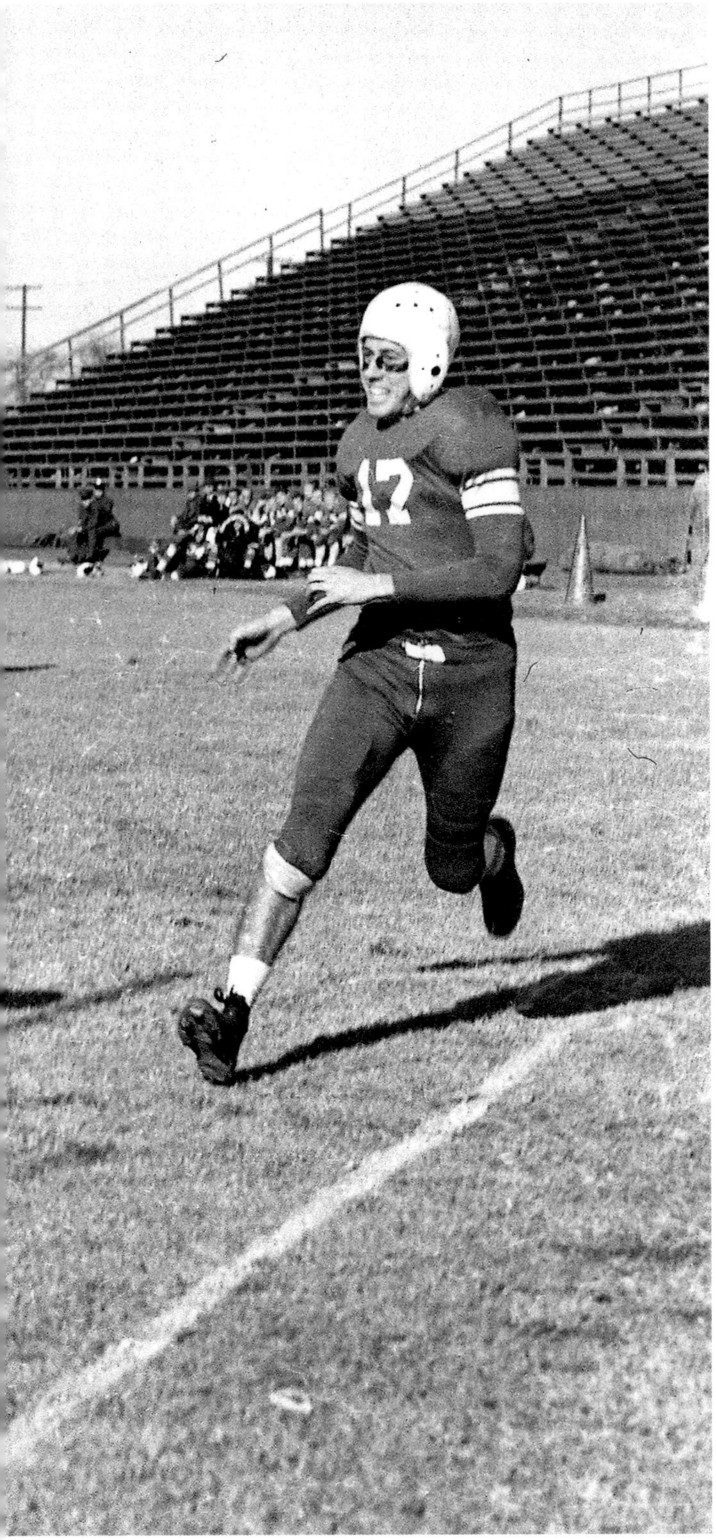

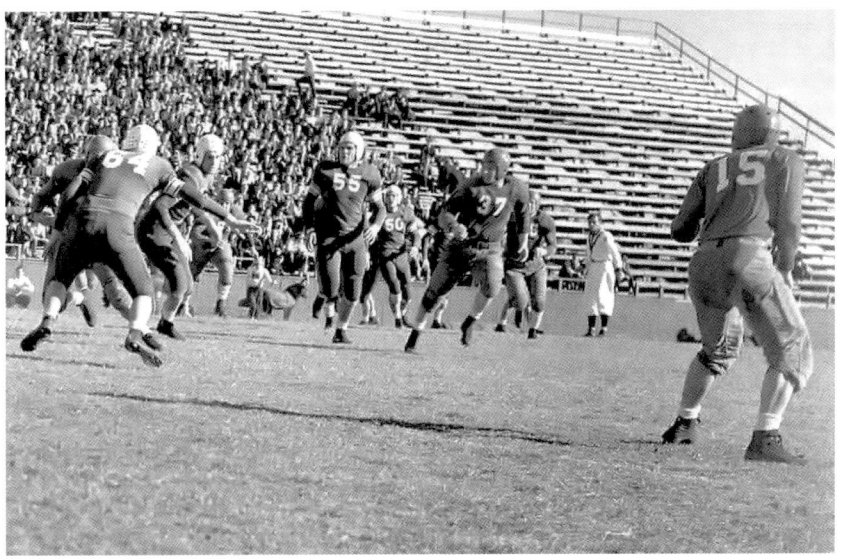

ABOVE: A scrimmage at SMU's Ownby Stadium. One of the best to ever play the game was Doak Walker (#37). "The Doaker" left SMU a three-time All-American and as the 1948 Heisman Trophy winner. He then went on to play with the Detroit Lions. In 1950, he was the Rookie of the Year, the league's scoring leader, and a Pro Bowl participant. In the six years he played, he won two NFL scoring titles and was selected to play in five Pro Bowls. He was Mr. Do Everything—rushing, passing, receiving, place-kicking, punt and kickoff returns, and punting. In 1986, Doak was inducted into the Pro Football Hall of Fame. 1947.

LEFT: Scrimmage at Ownby Stadium. 1947.

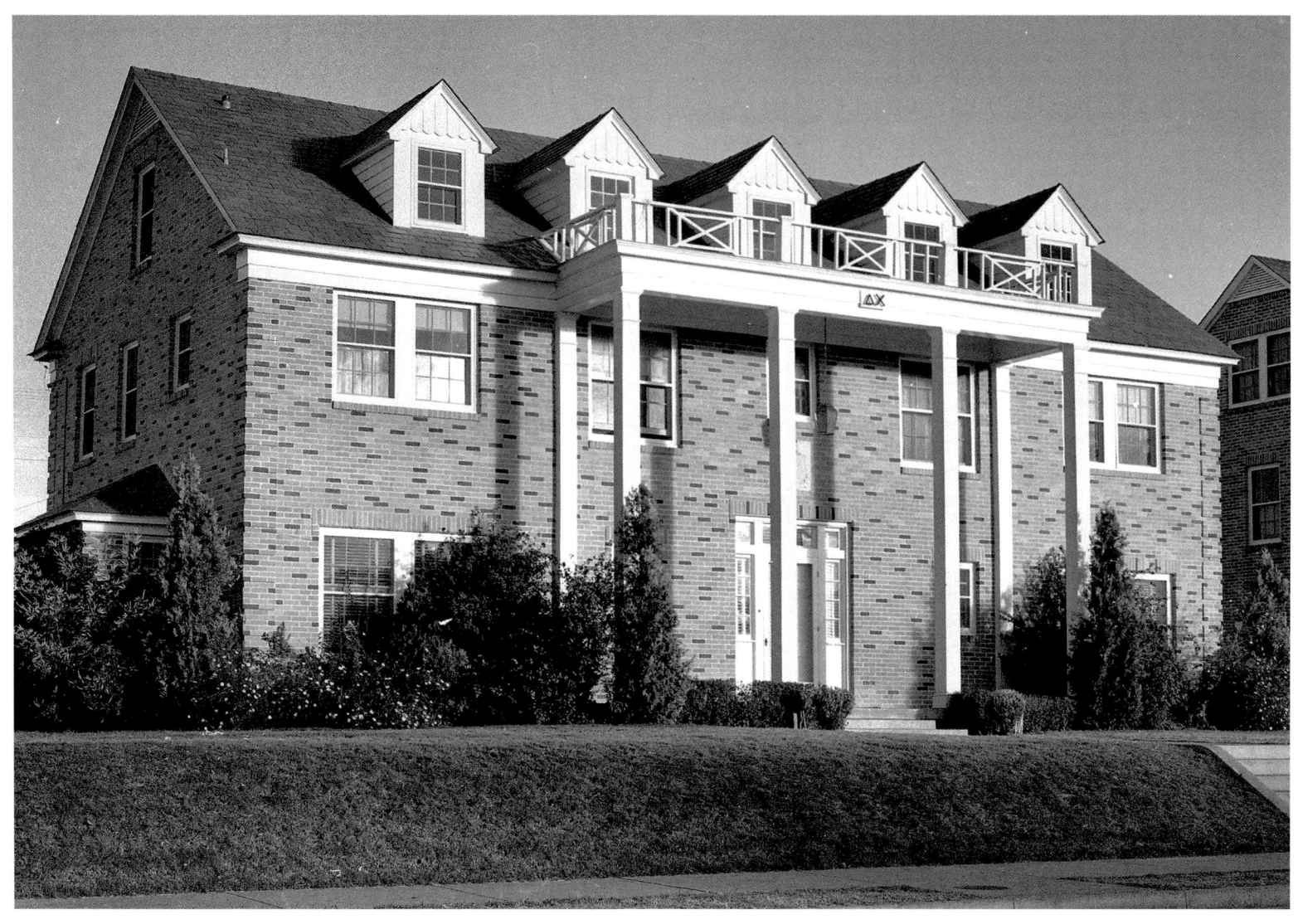

ABOVE: Delta Chi Fraternity. 1940.

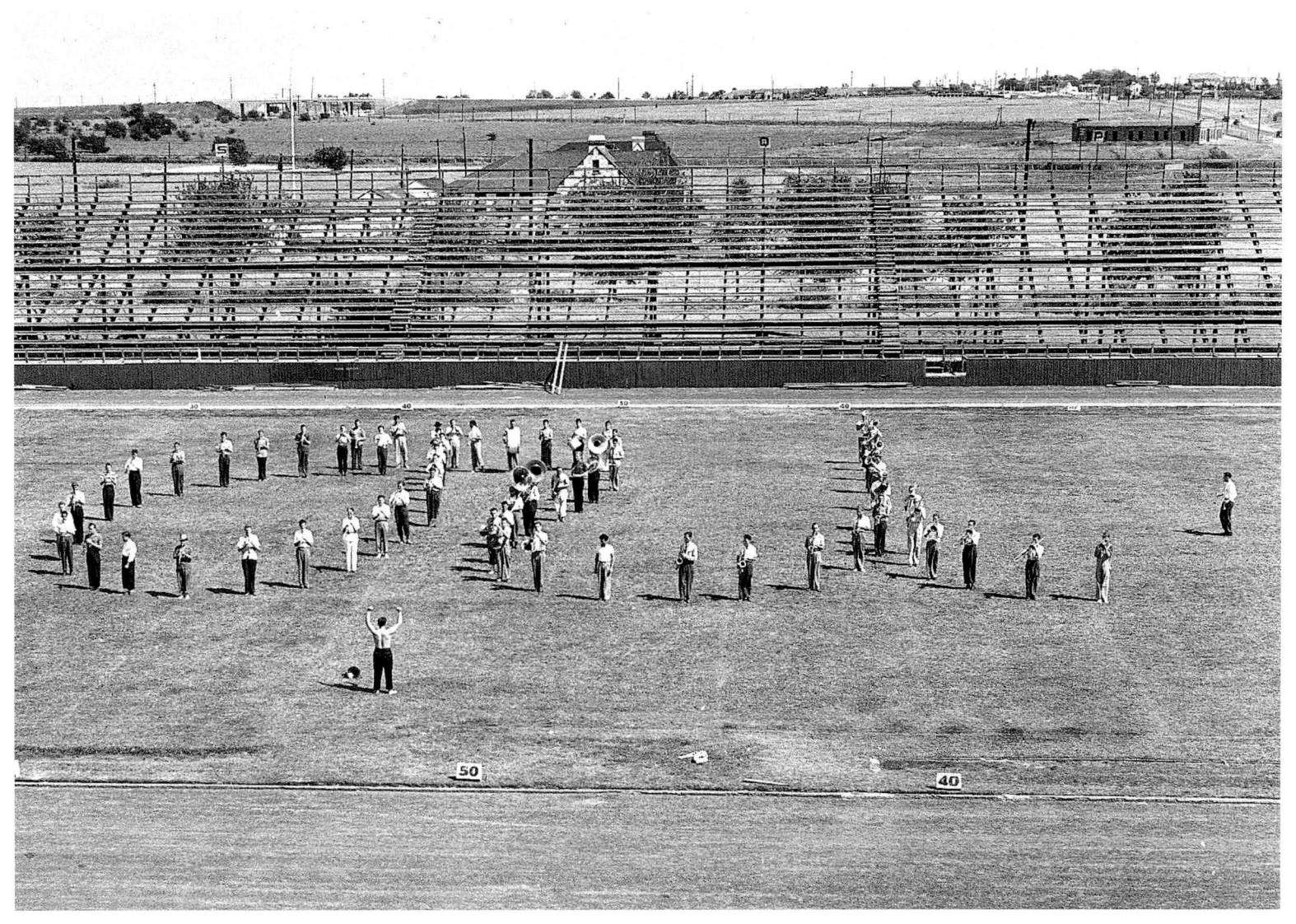

ABOVE: Band drill at Ownby Stadium. In 1998, Ownby Stadium was demolished to build Gerald J. Ford Stadium on the site. 1939.

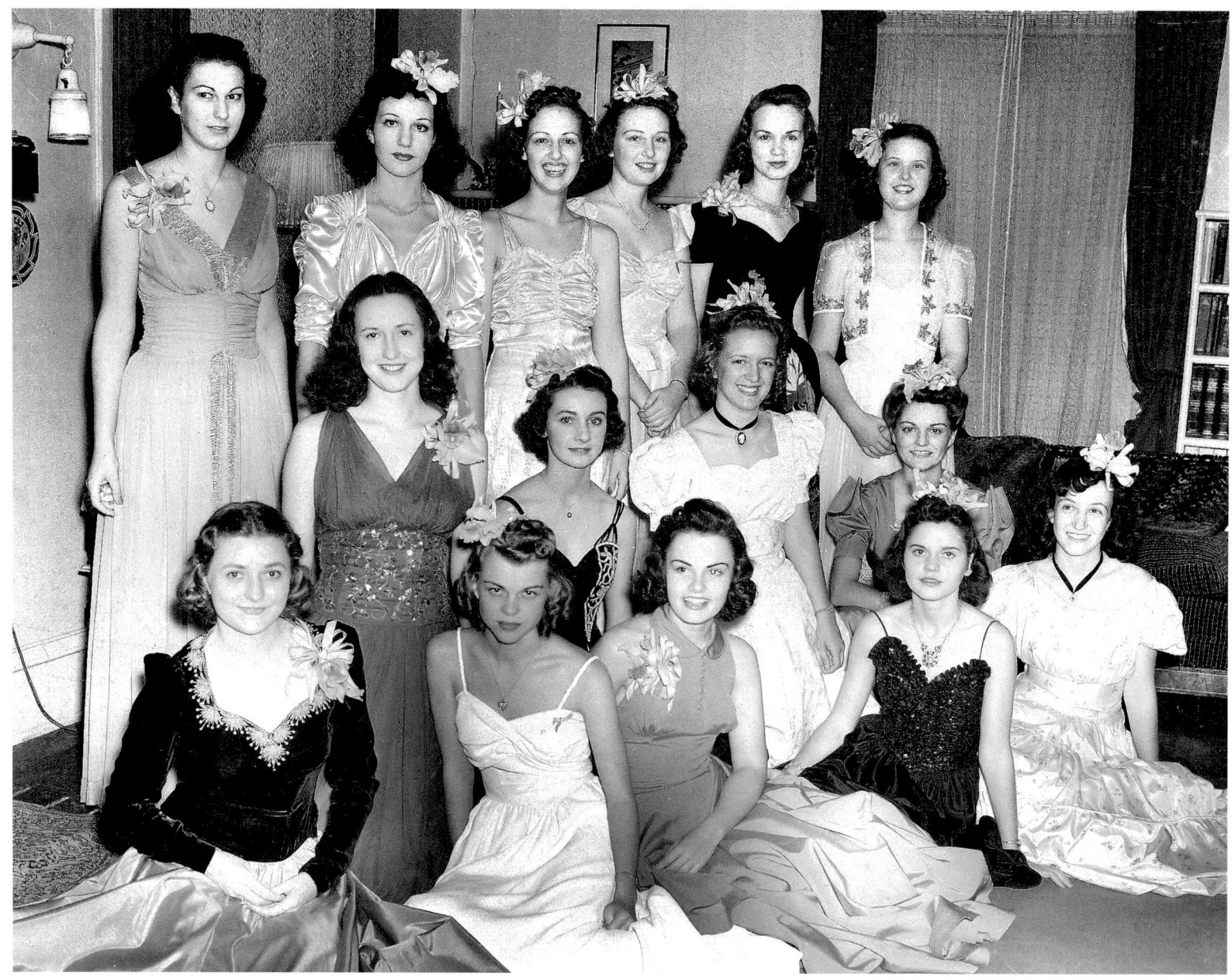

ABOVE: Delta Gamma Sorority pledge class. While taking this photo, Dad started talking to the attractive young woman in the middle of the front row (sitting). She was a nineteen-year-old freshman from Nowata, Oklahoma, who had just finished preparatory school at Ward-Belmont in Nashville. That meeting resulted in a date, and in July 1942, they were married. In June 1943, they had the first of three sons ... me! 1940.

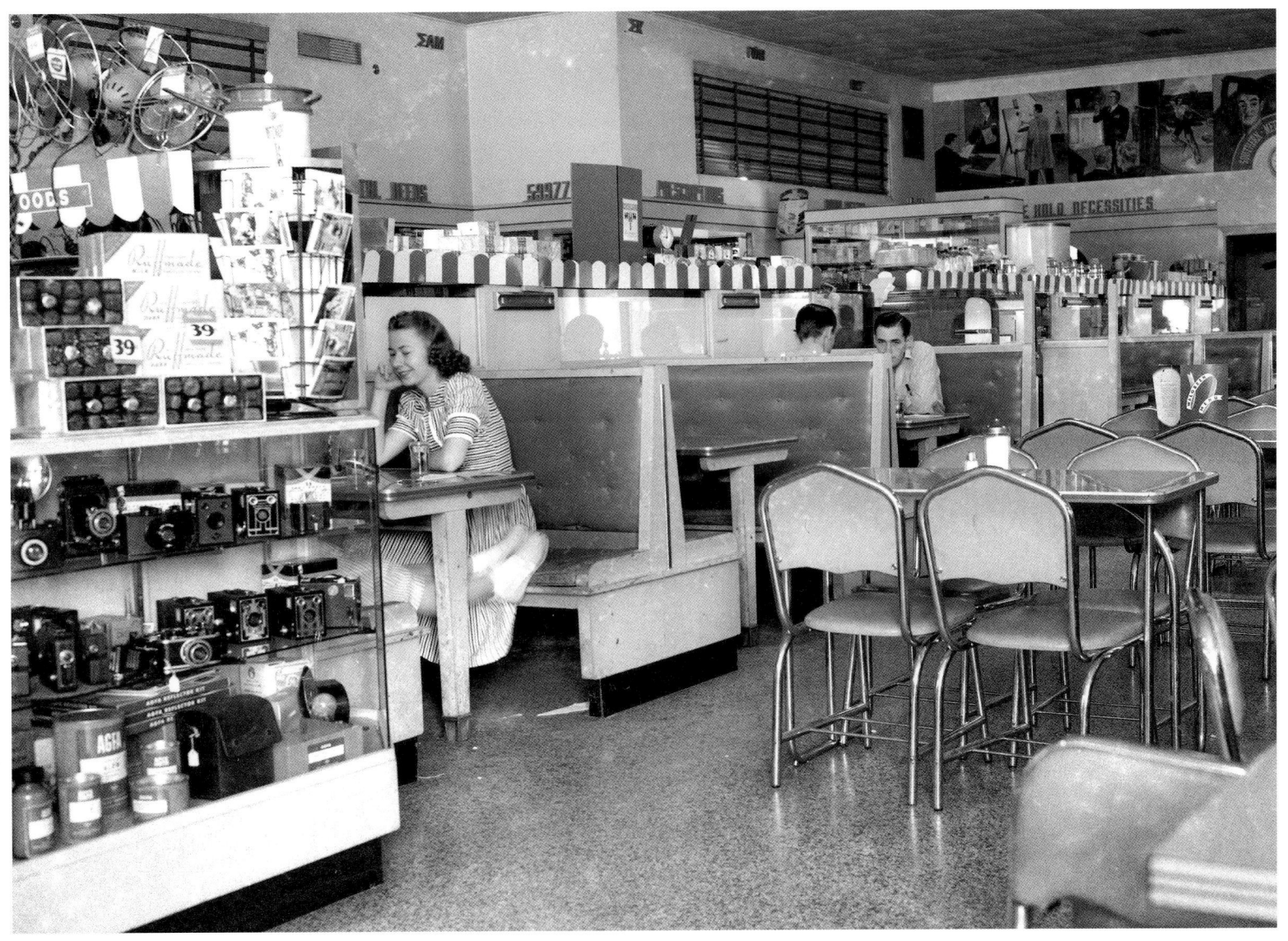

ABOVE: A popular place where SMU students could grab a Coke and a burger after class, or maybe a fan, camera, toiletries, their prescription, or a box of chocolates. 1941.

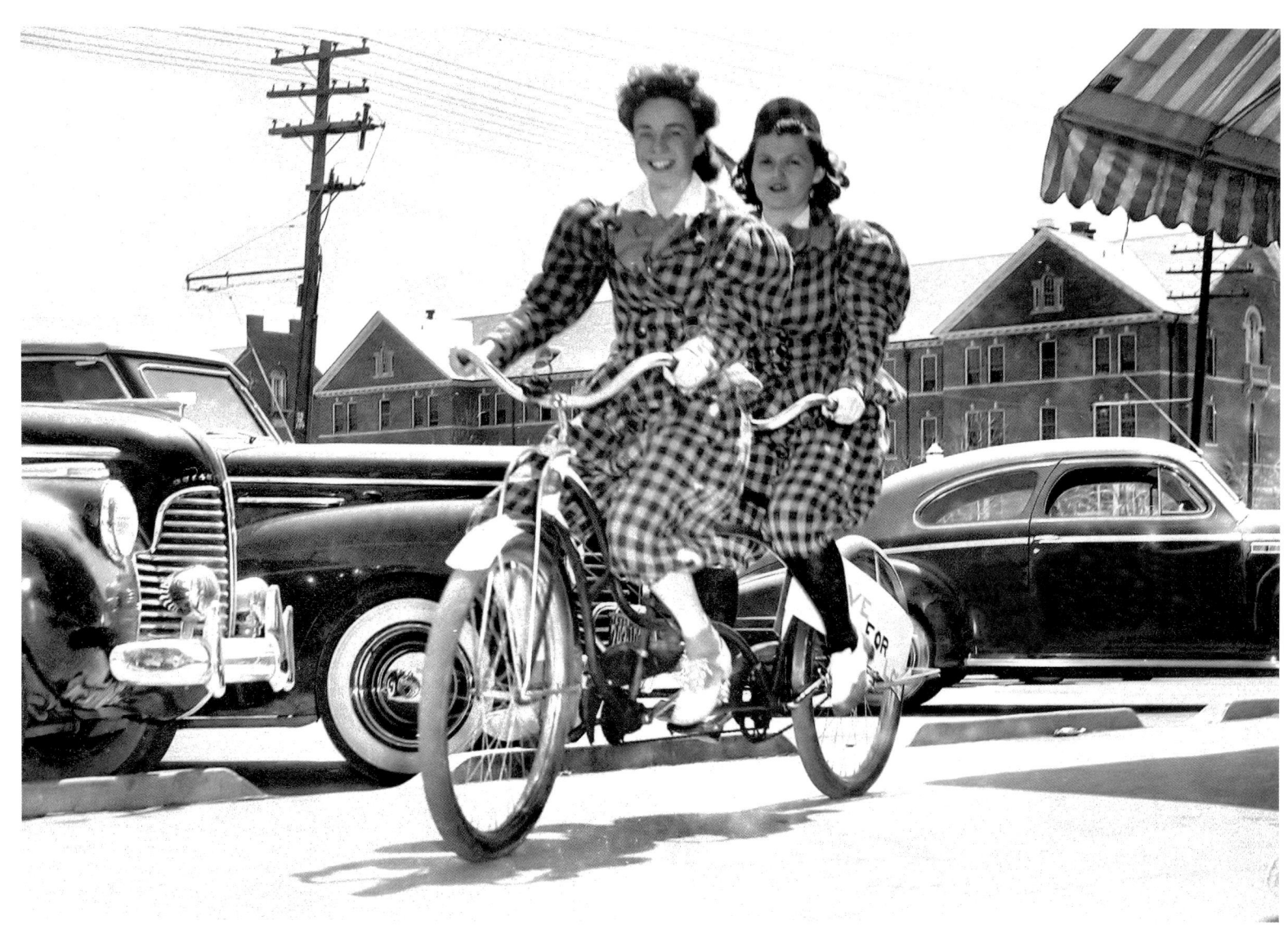

ABOVE: SMU students havin' fun! 1941.

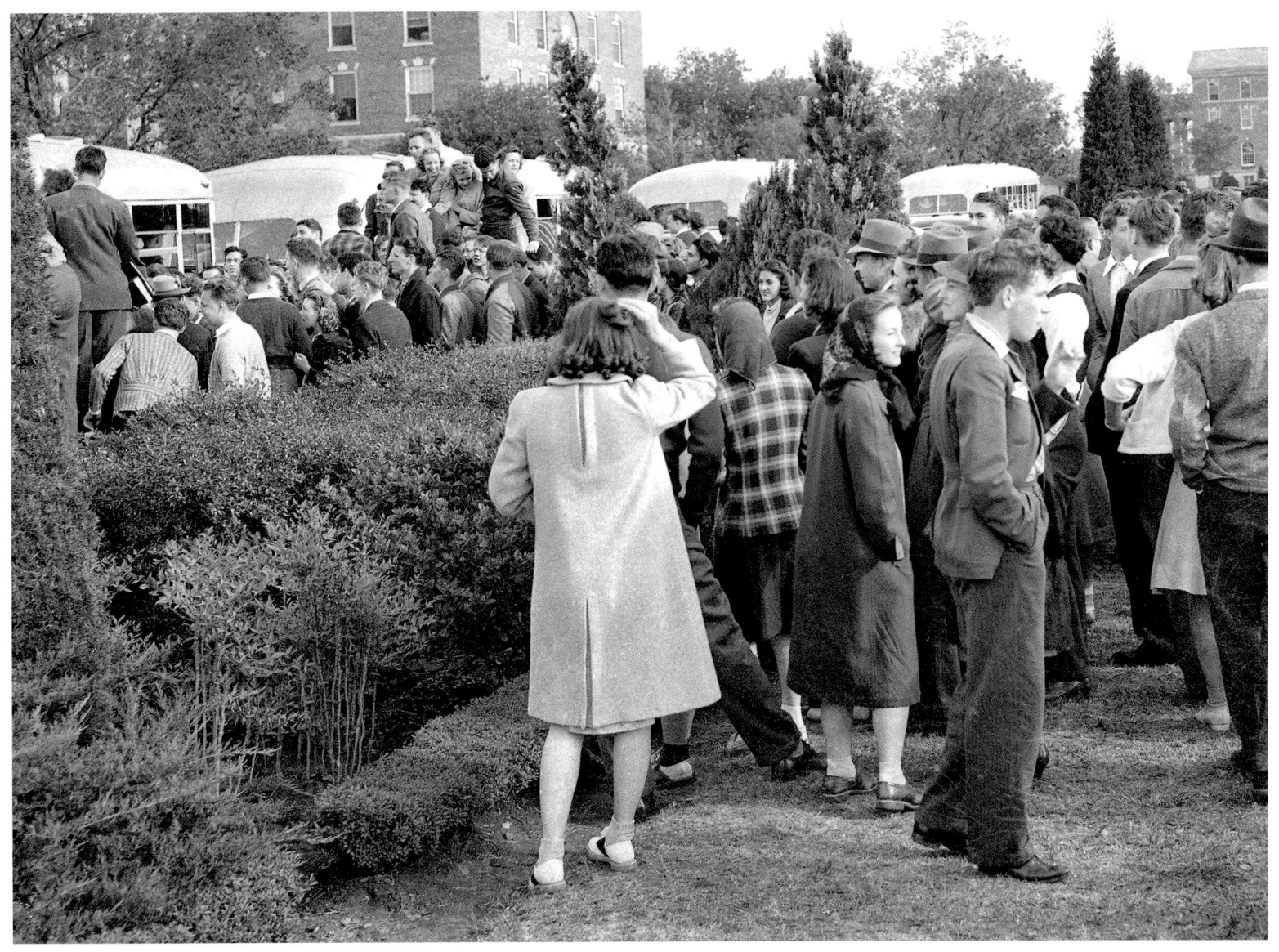

ABOVE: Pigskin Saturday! SMU students loading the buses up that will take them to the Cotton Bowl to watch the Mustangs do battle with one of their Southwest Conference foes. 1939.

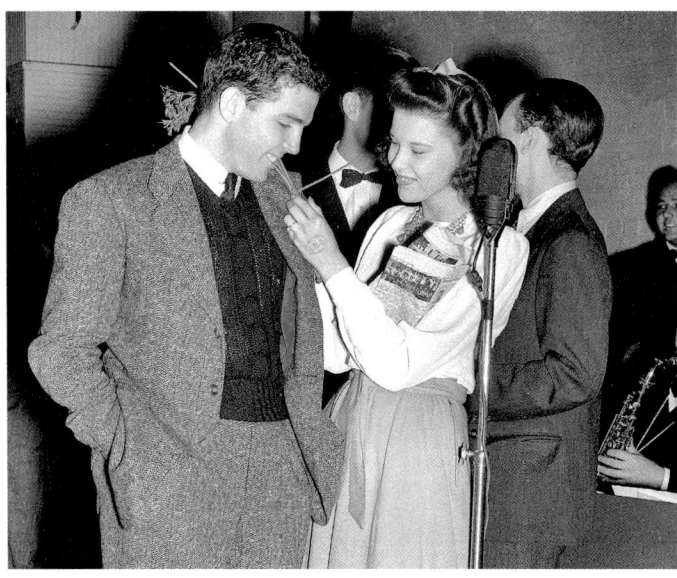

ABOVE: First dance. 1940.

RIGHT: SMU dance. 1940.

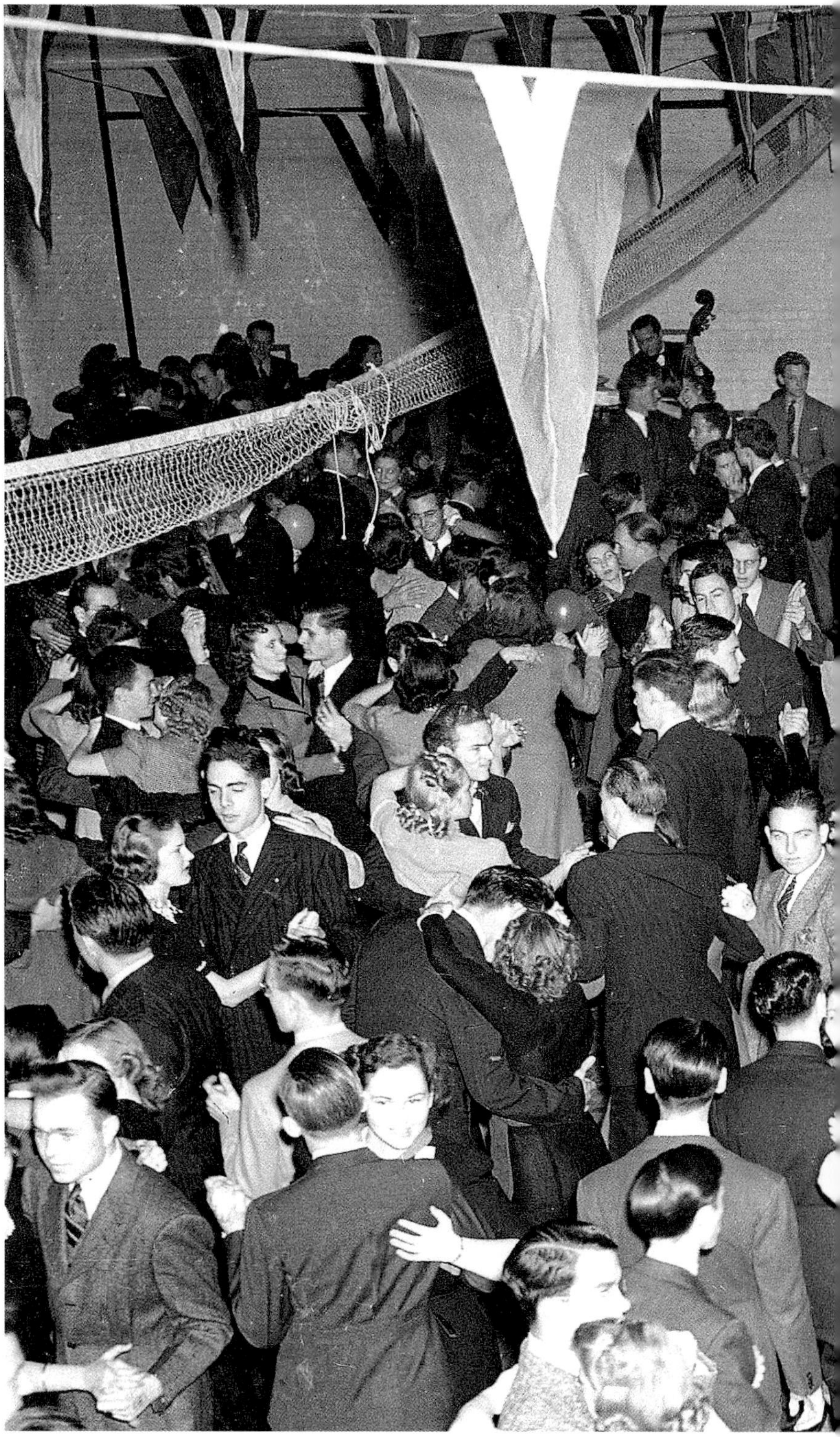

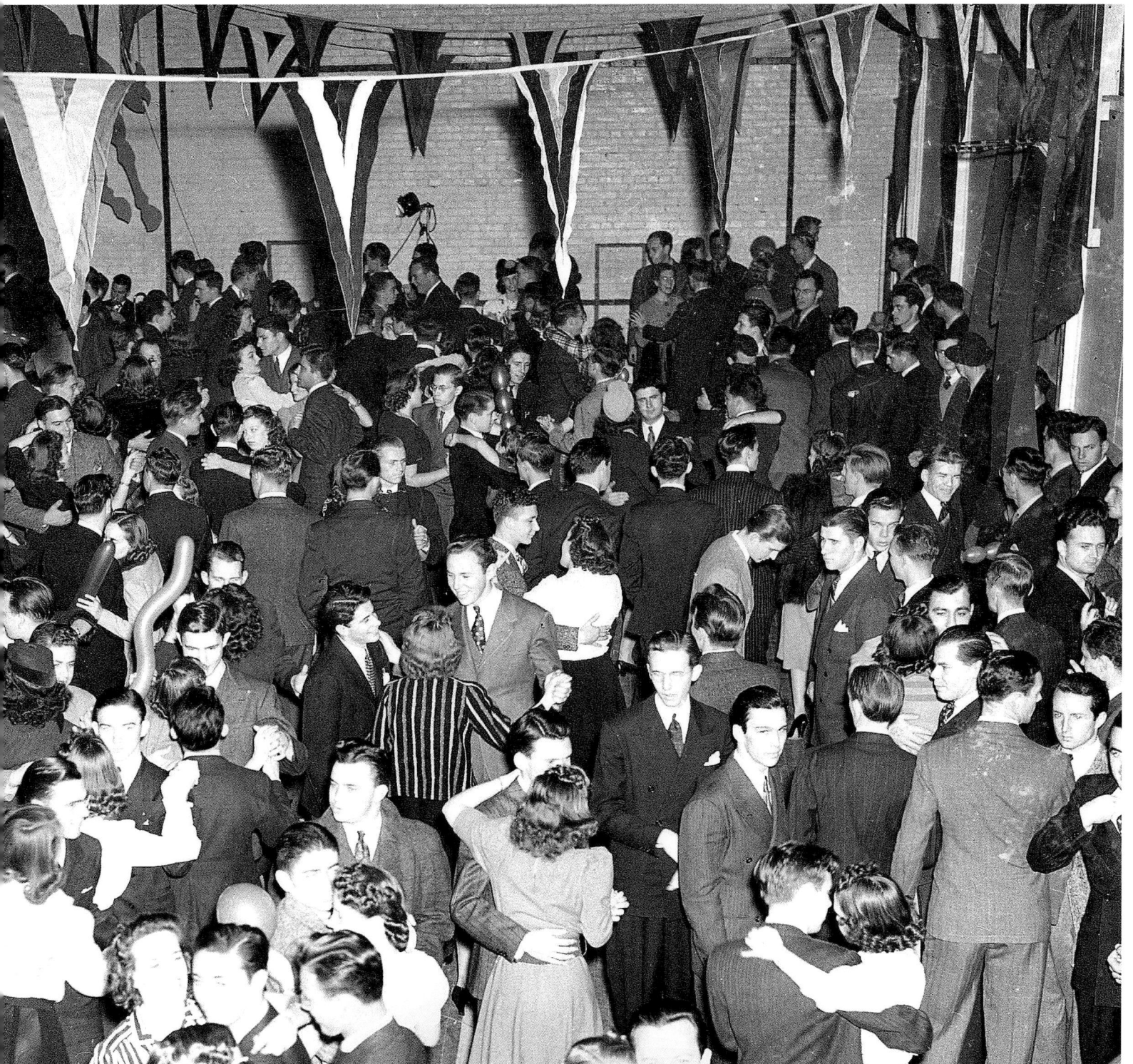

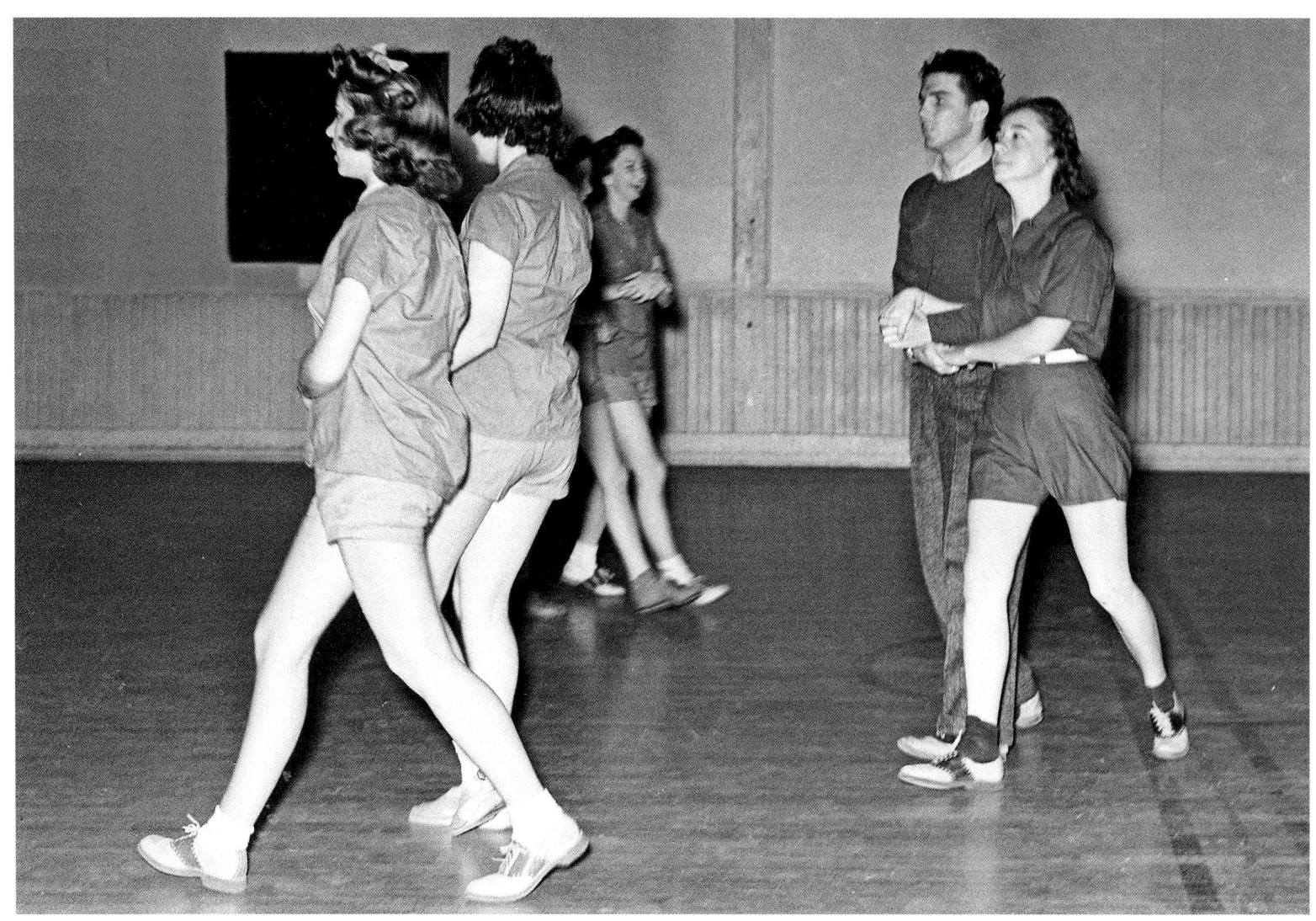

ABOVE: Wayne Woodruff in dance class. Woodruff was a Knight in the Cycen Fjodr, a men's honor society at SMU. Membership for the Knights is based upon outstanding academic achievement, general leadership qualities, and service to the university beyond the call of duty. 1941.

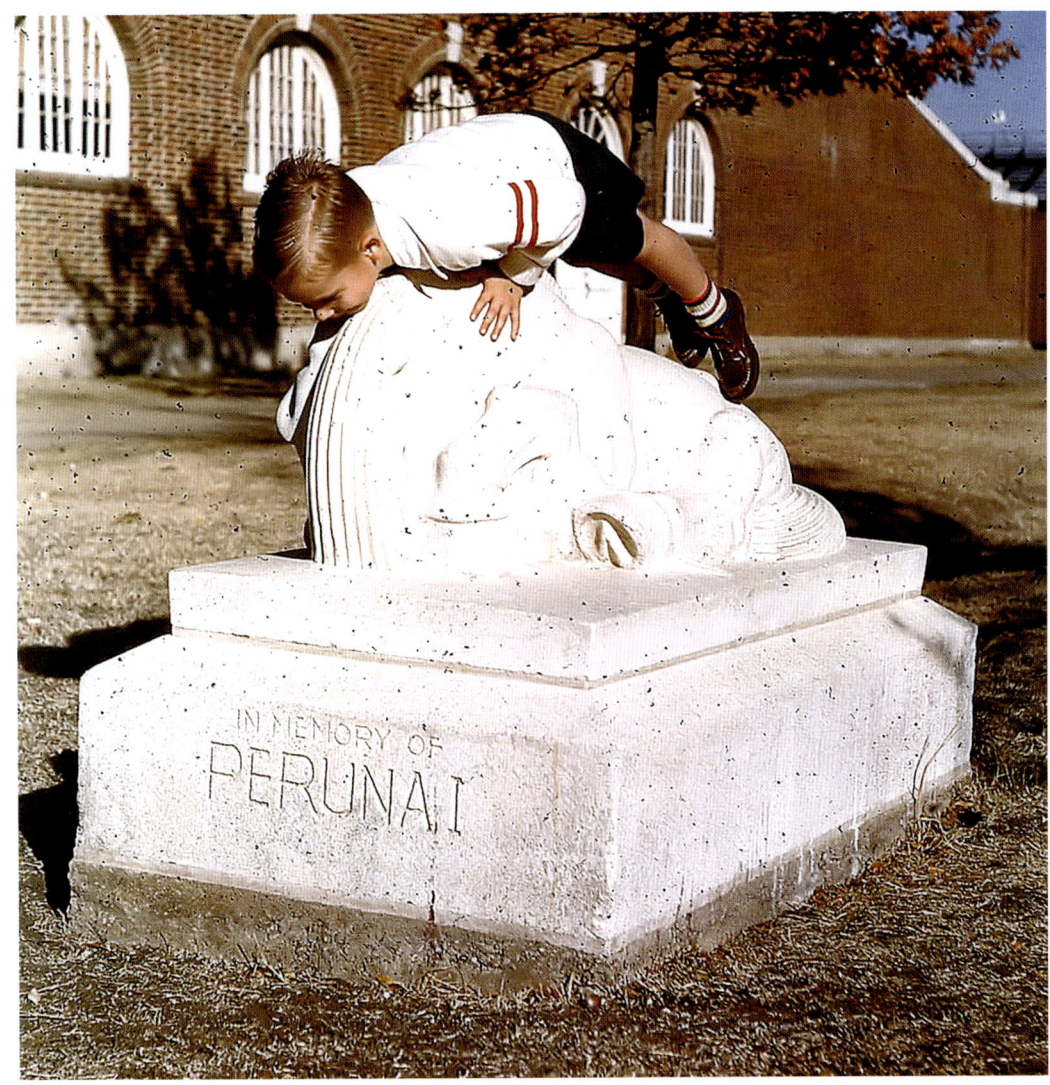

ABOVE: I am that young football fan at Mustang mascot Peruna's burial site on the SMU campus. 1950.

Manufacturing

———

OPPOSITE: Cotton mill worker
in McKinney. 1939.

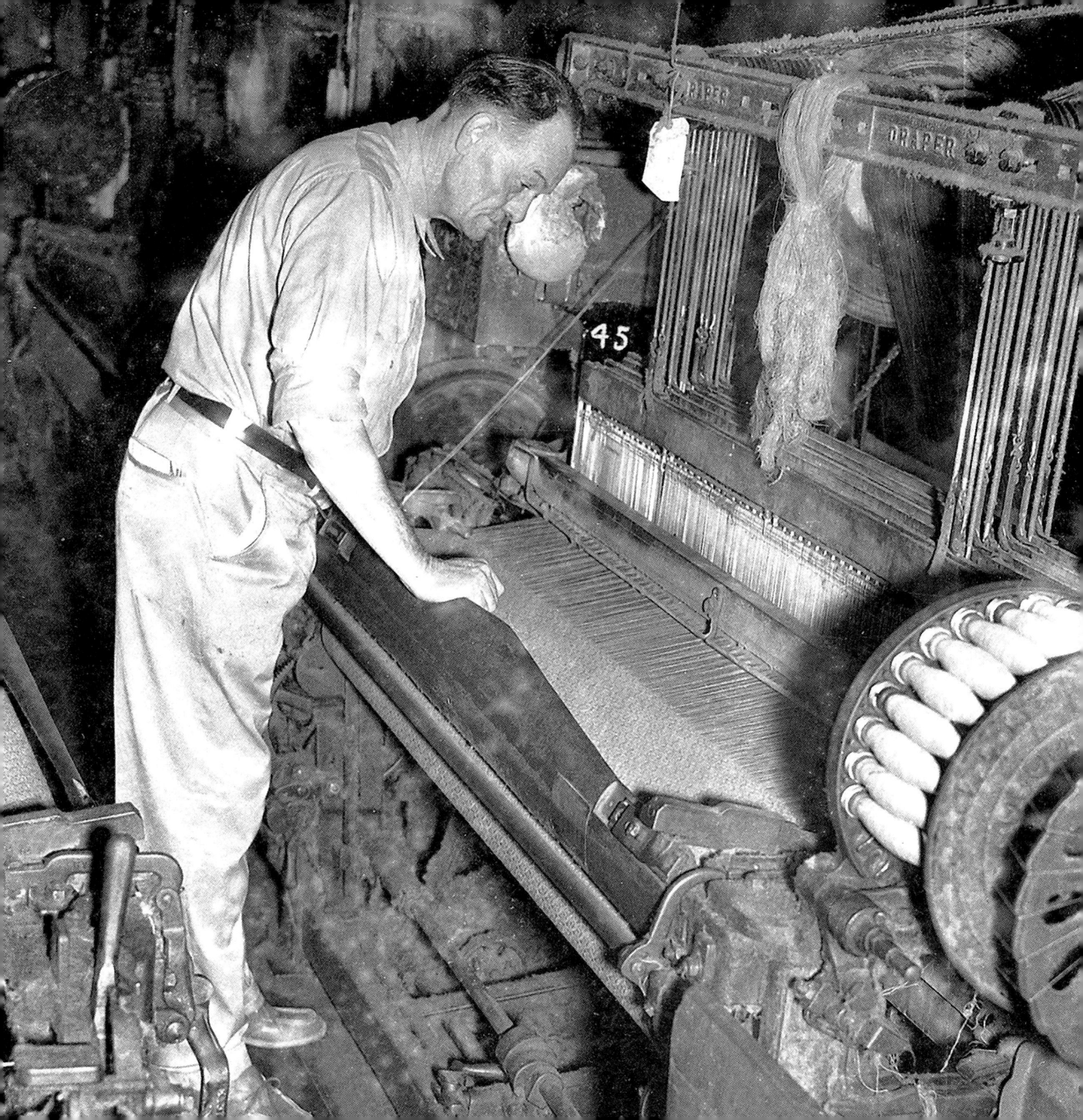

As the country pulled out of the Great Depression, the groundwork began being laid that would eventually result in Dallas becoming one of the major centers of business in the US. A confluence of factors, detailed below, created a certain "synergism" that certainly had much to do with the emergence of this formerly sleepy and small "big" city into the sprawling and very much wide-awake metropolis of today.

Texas was blessed with vast natural resources such as cotton and oil which, with its huge cattle and farming industries, were the foundation upon which the state would grow. Farsighted businessmen in Dallas were determined to make their city a leader in this growth. One of these was the future four-time Mayor of Dallas, R. L. Thornton, whom our family and his friends called "Uncle Bob." Along with three others, Thornton founded the Mercantile National Bank, which by the 1940s had become the leading banking operation in the Southwest.

With the end of World War II, there was now a sizable workforce available with experience in building tanks, airplanes, ships, cars, and trucks coming in to find jobs in manufacturing waiting for them at the new factories being built or at those that were springing back to life after shuttering their doors during the wartime years.

To move its manufactured or produced goods to other states, Dallas's highways and railroad lines branched out in every direction, and shipping by air was also happening with the growth of commercial aviation from Love Field.

————

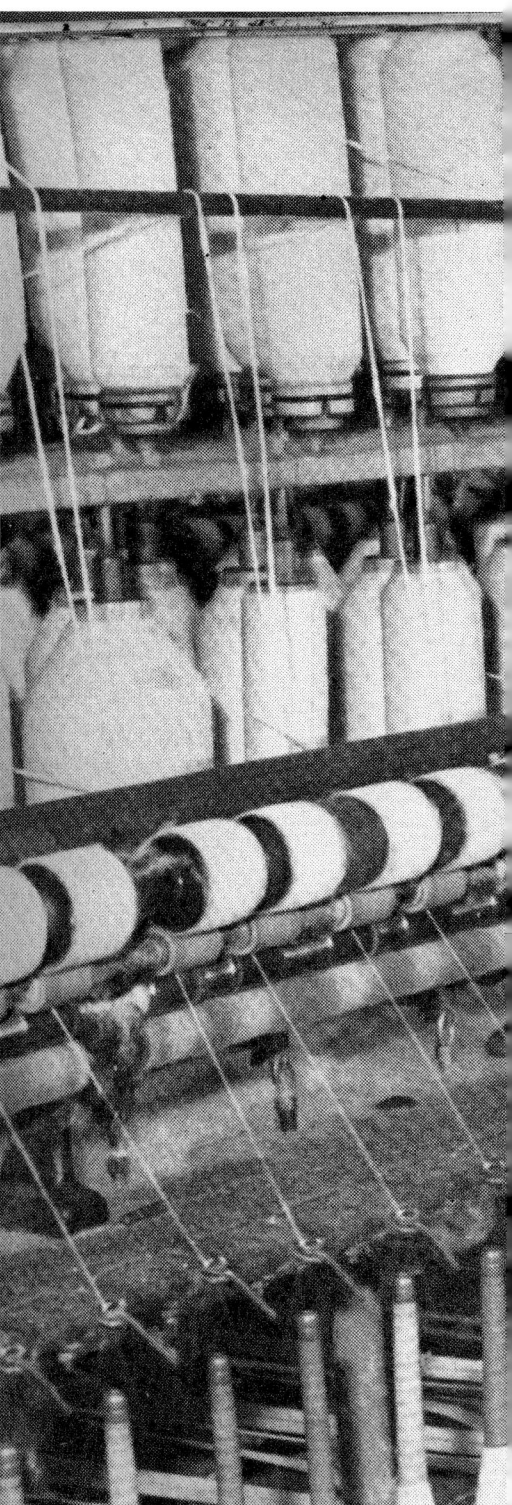

RIGHT: Spinning room worker in McKinney. 1939.

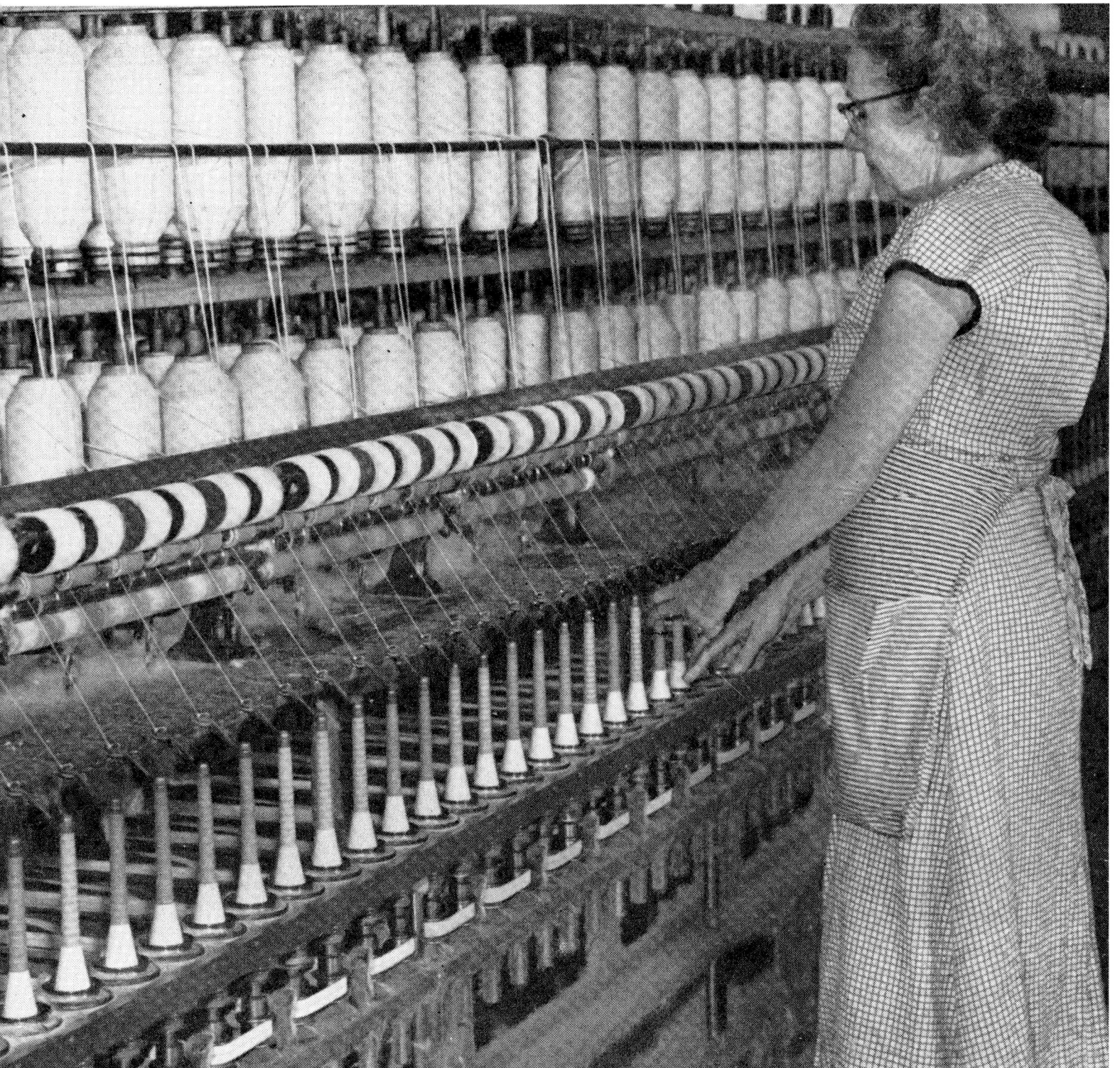

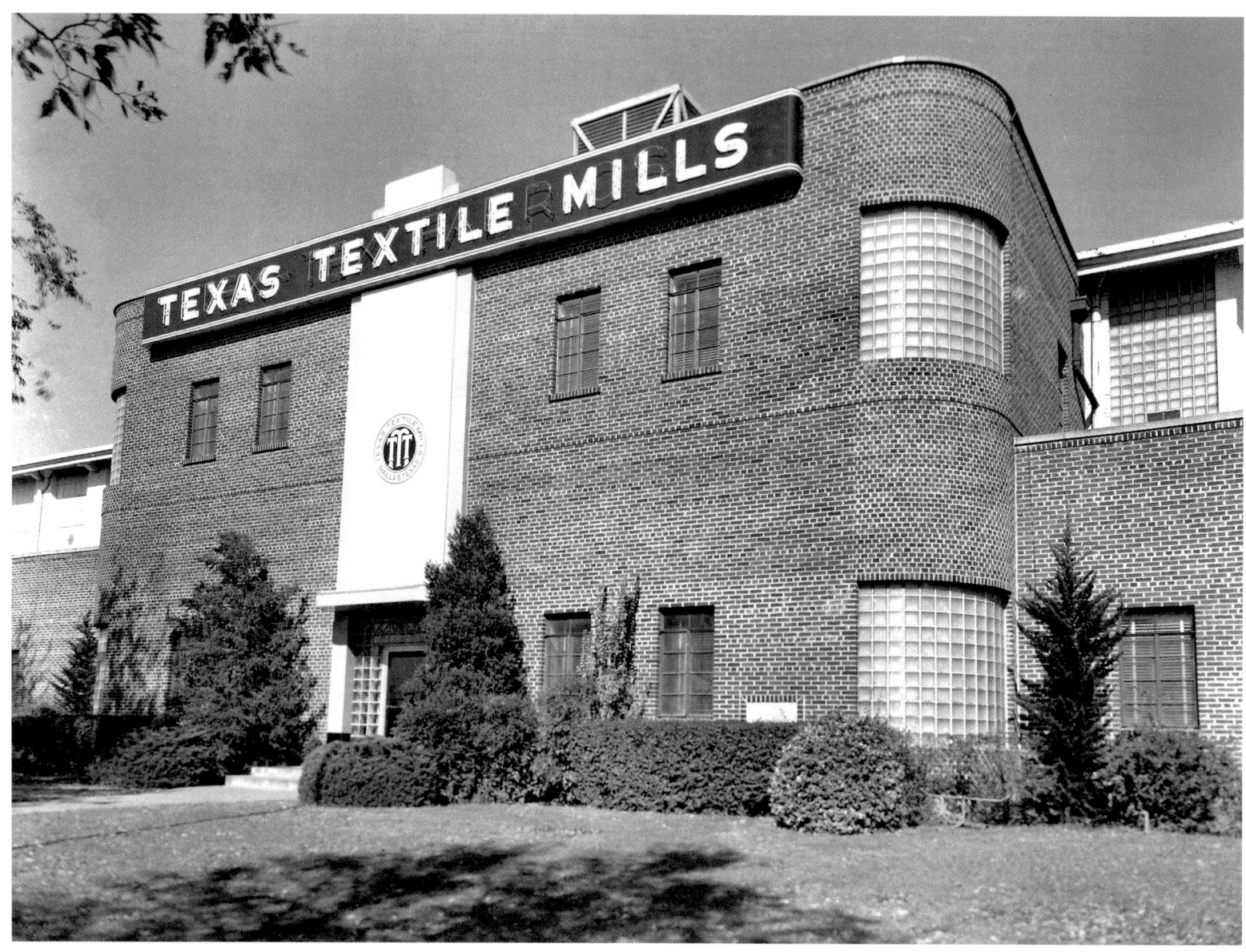

ABOVE: Texas Textile Mills headquarters and main milling operation near Love Field. 1949.

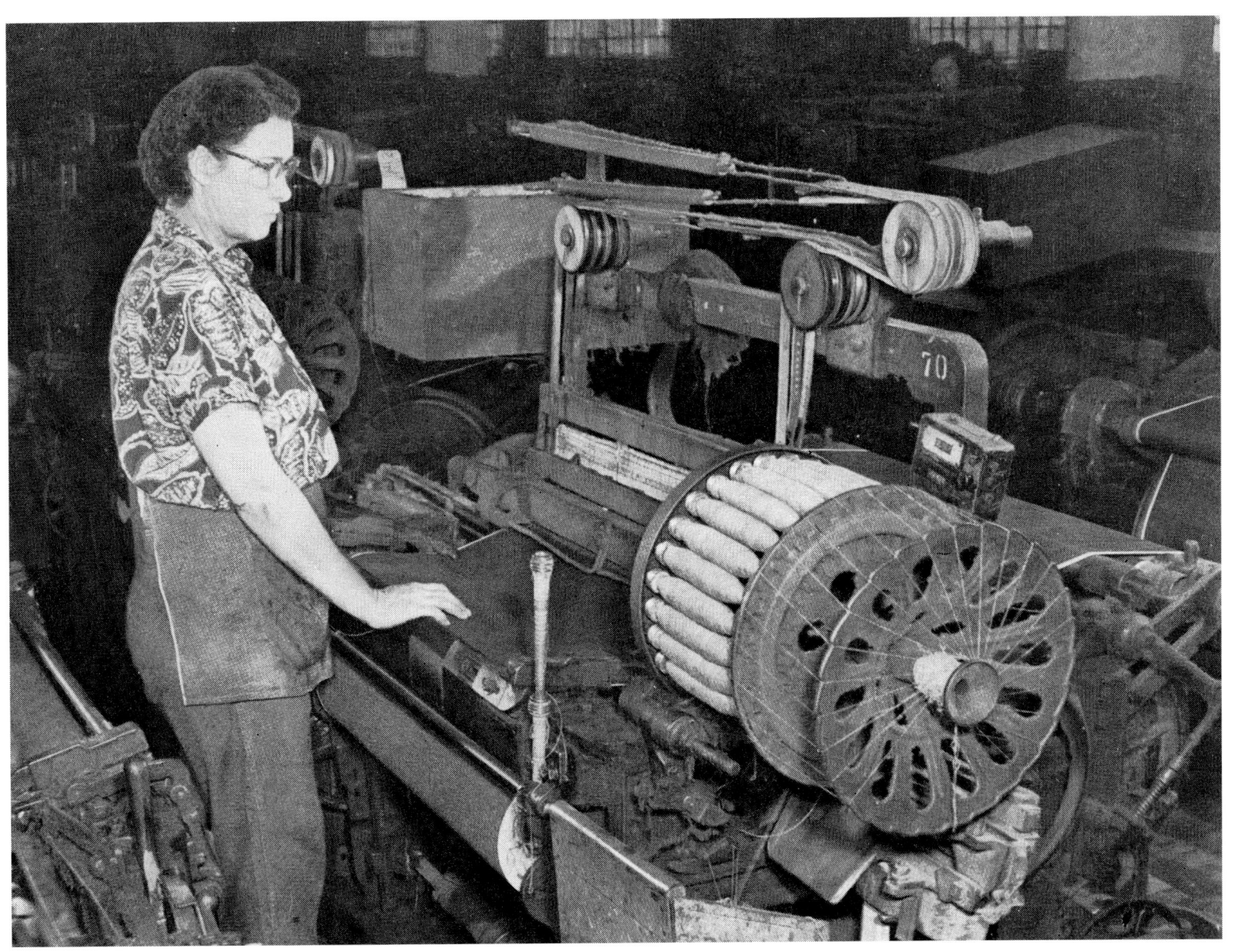

ABOVE: Worker in McKinney Mill. 1939

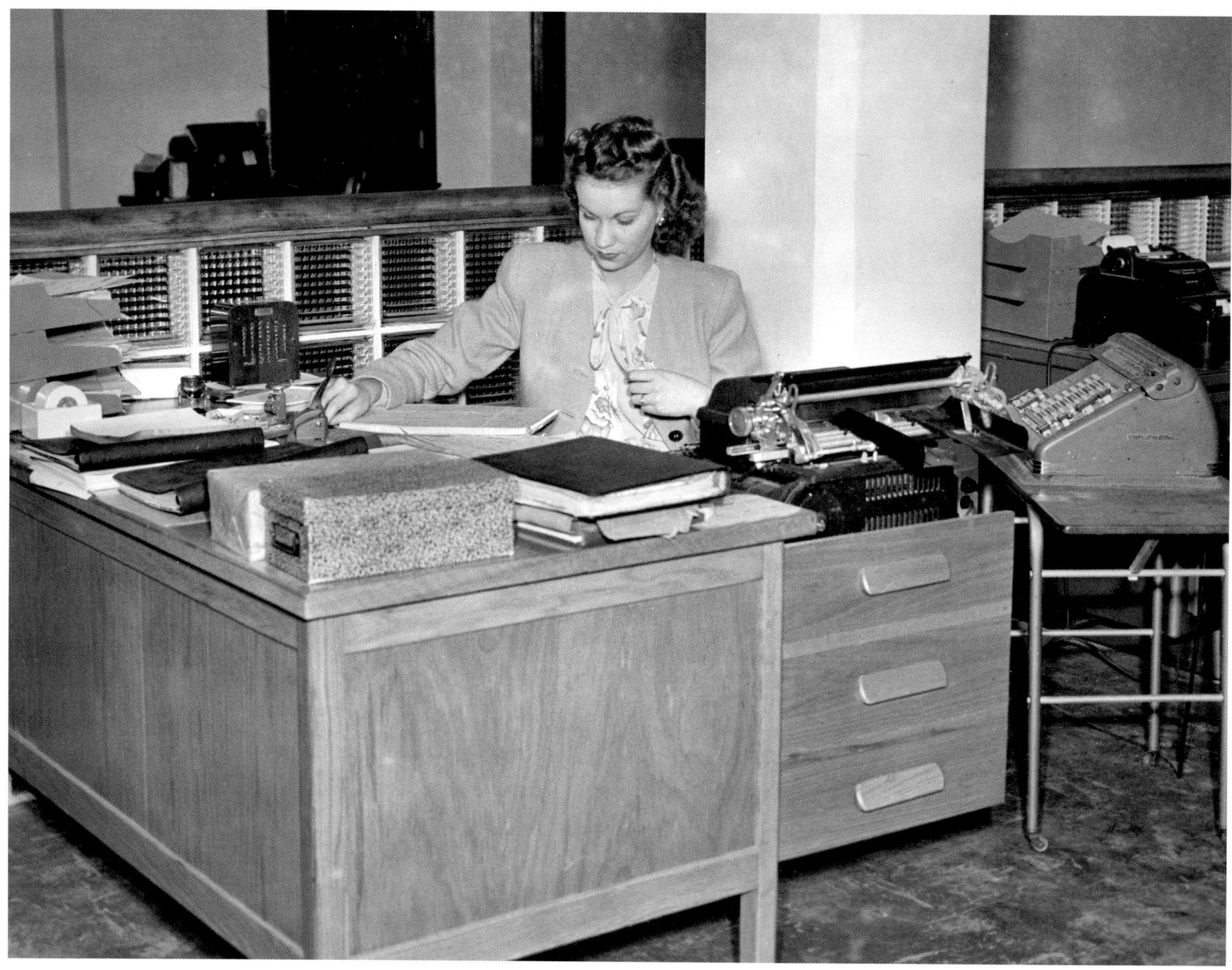

ABOVE: Secretary and her state-of-the-art office equipment. Her properly organized desk with the large typewriter and manual adding machine, small desktop file box, and all the other papers and folders would be replaced with just a computer monitor, keyboard, and mouse on today's office desk! 1948.

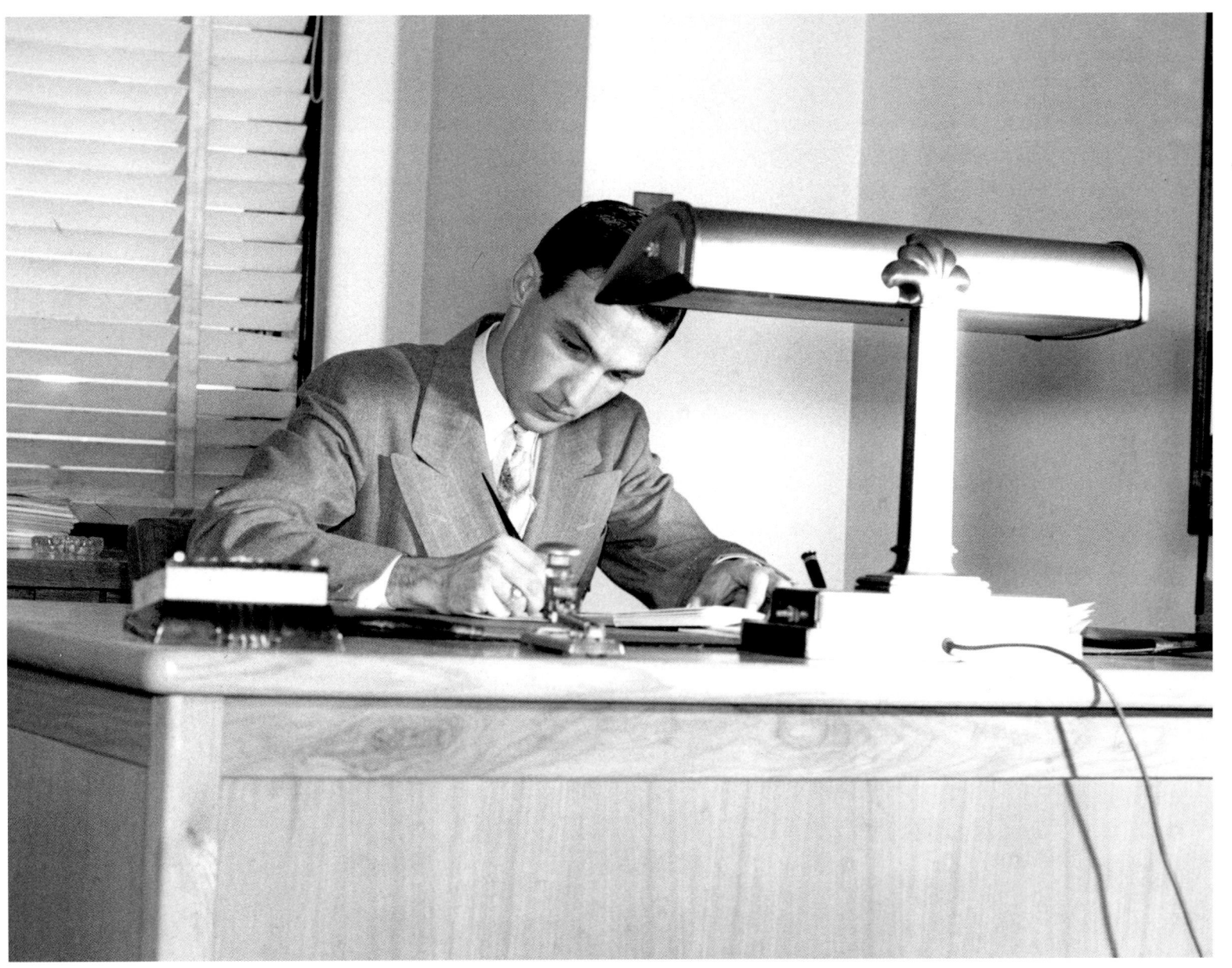

ABOVE: An office worker. 1948.

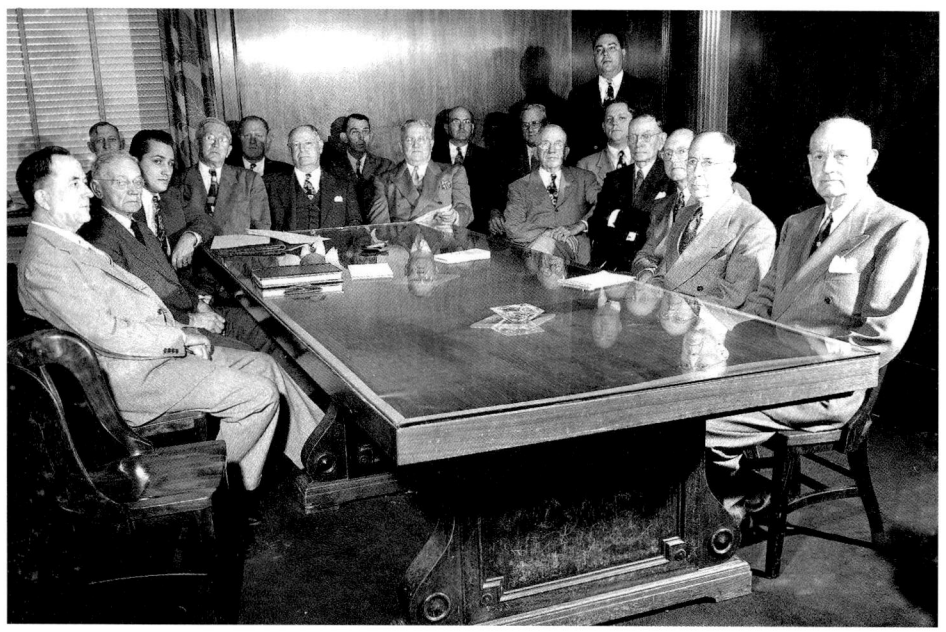

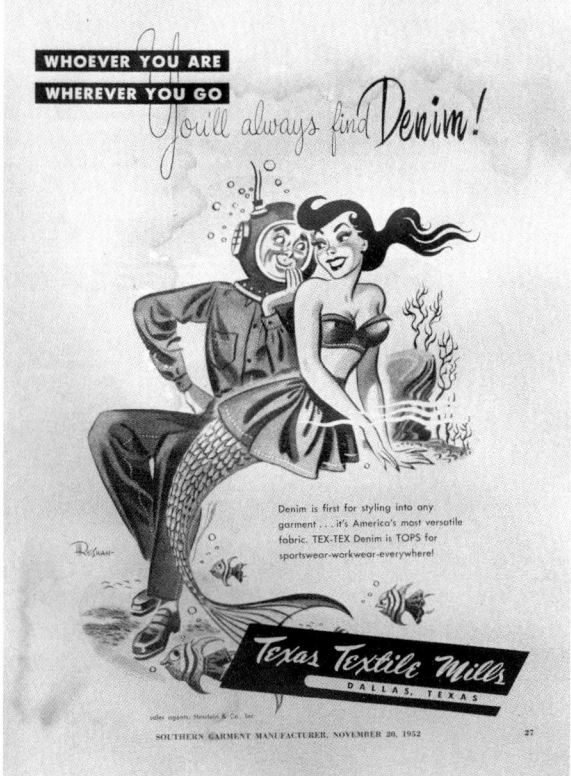

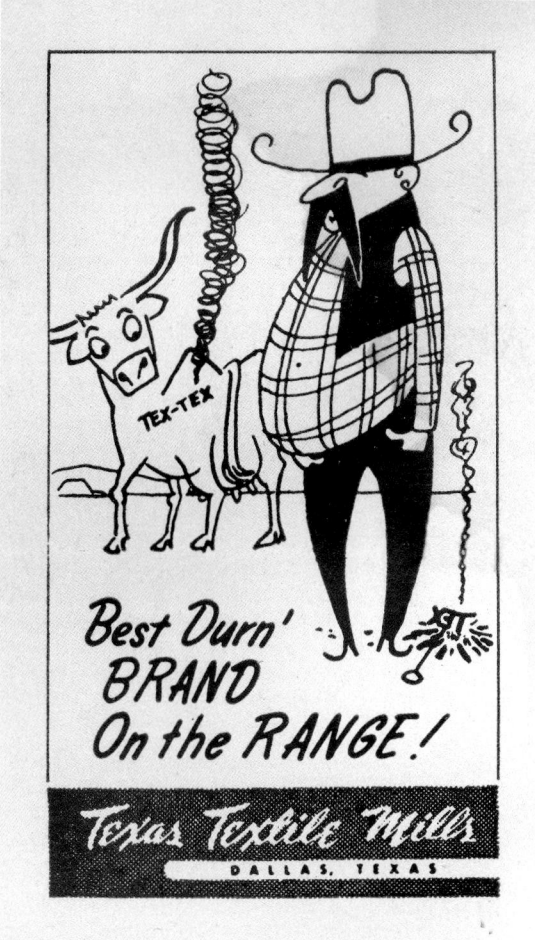

ABOVE: Texas Textile Mills board meeting. Founder and Chairman C. R. Miller is in the light suit at far corner of table. 1949.

LEFT: Texas Textile Mills advertisement. 1952.

ABOVE: The Tex-Tex Cowboy was part of the company's branding (no pun intended). 1952.

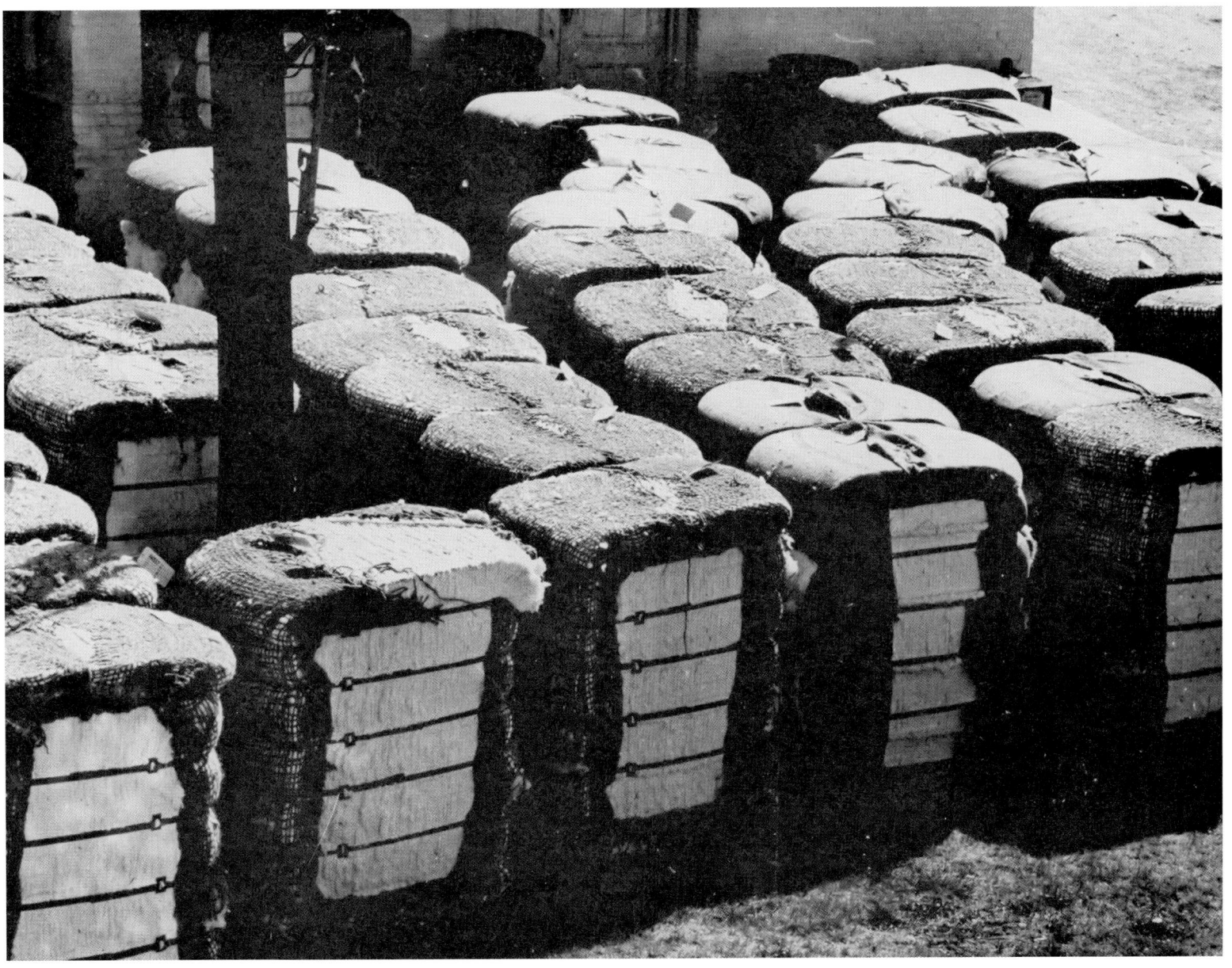

ABOVE: Before foreign imports and the advent of synthetic fabrics, Texas's number one cash crop was cotton. It still remains at the top, and according to the Texas Almanac, in 2020, the annual Texas cotton harvest produced around 37.5 percent of the total cotton in the United States. 1950.

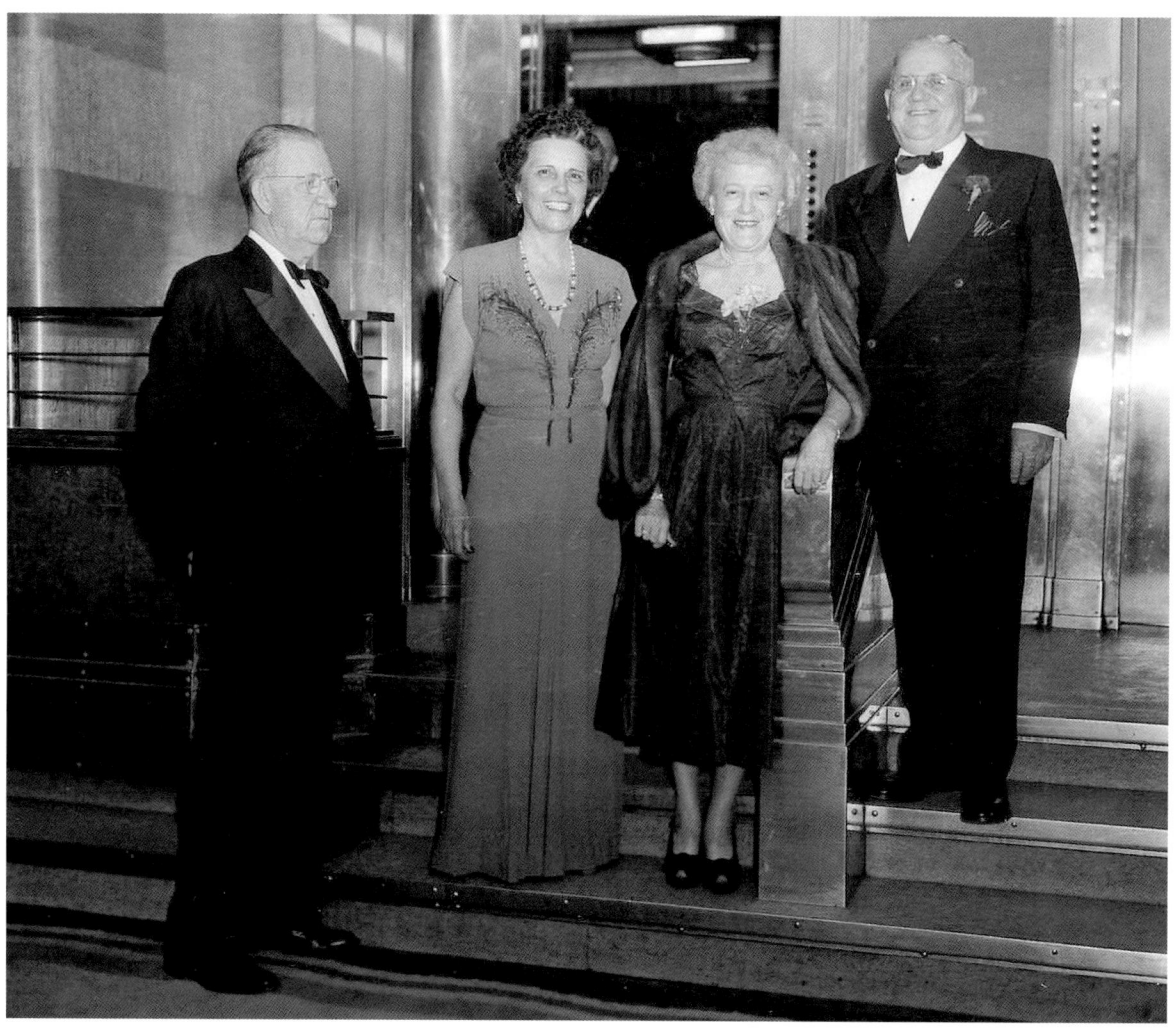

ABOVE: Two titans of industry in Dallas and their wives: R. L. Thornton, founder of the Mercantile National Bank and future four-time mayor, Esther Miller (my grandmother), Mary Thornton, and Clarence Miller, my grandfather and founder and president of Dallas-based Texas Textile Mills. They were aboard the RMS *Queen Mary*, sailing to England. 1948.

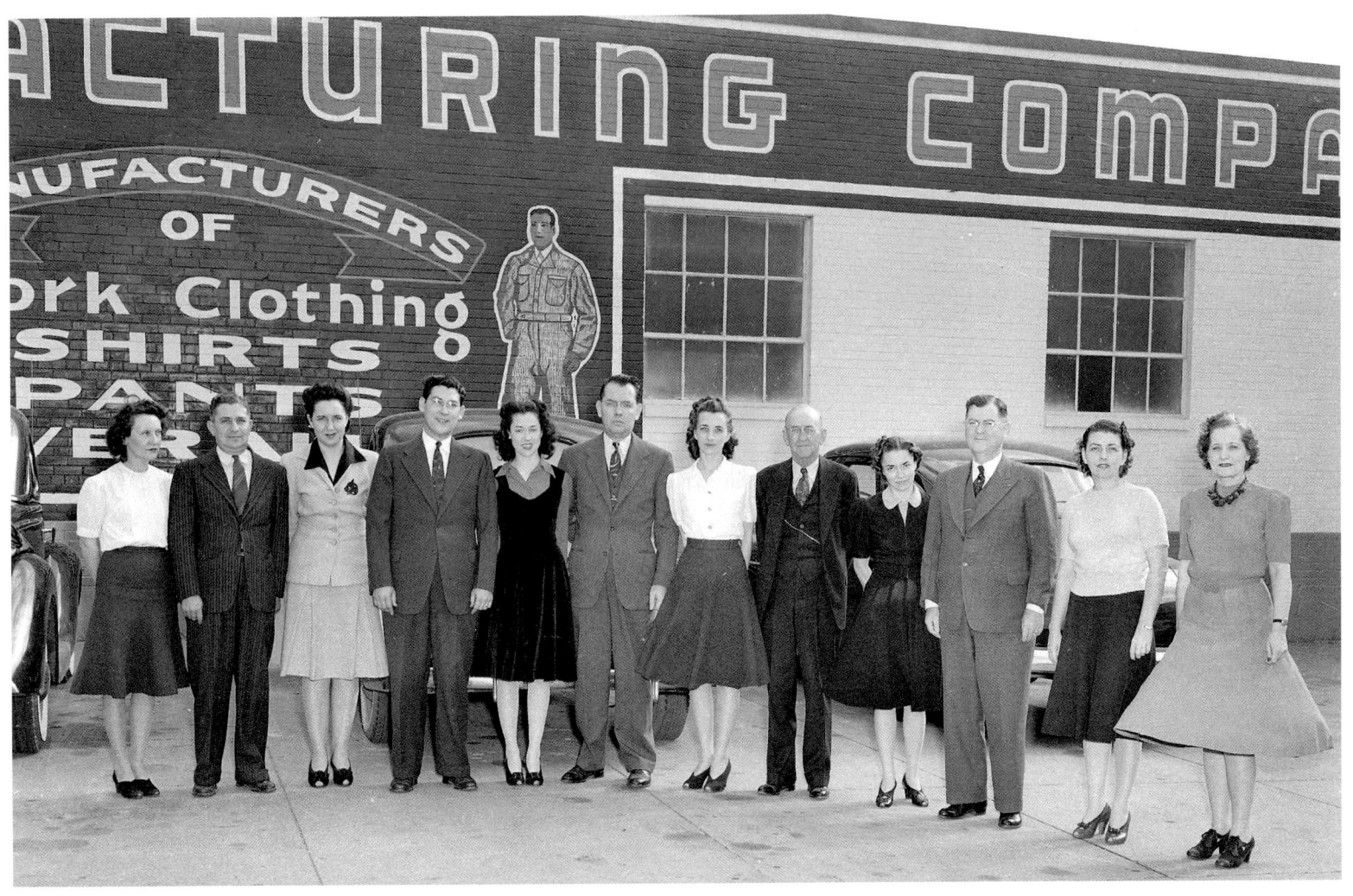

ABOVE: Executives and front office workers at Conro Manufacturing Co., located at 615 North Good Street (located on the west side of the street in the general area of the old Good Latimer Tunnel). This was the manufacturing facility of our family's Texas Textile Mills. We made denim work jackets, shirts, and pants. During WWII we also made most of the duffel bags carried by members of our armed forces. When the decision was made to put Texas Textile Mills and its subsidiary "to bed," Dickies purchased most of Conro's machinery. That is my wonderful great-aunt Lee Miller Blake on the far right. 1940s.

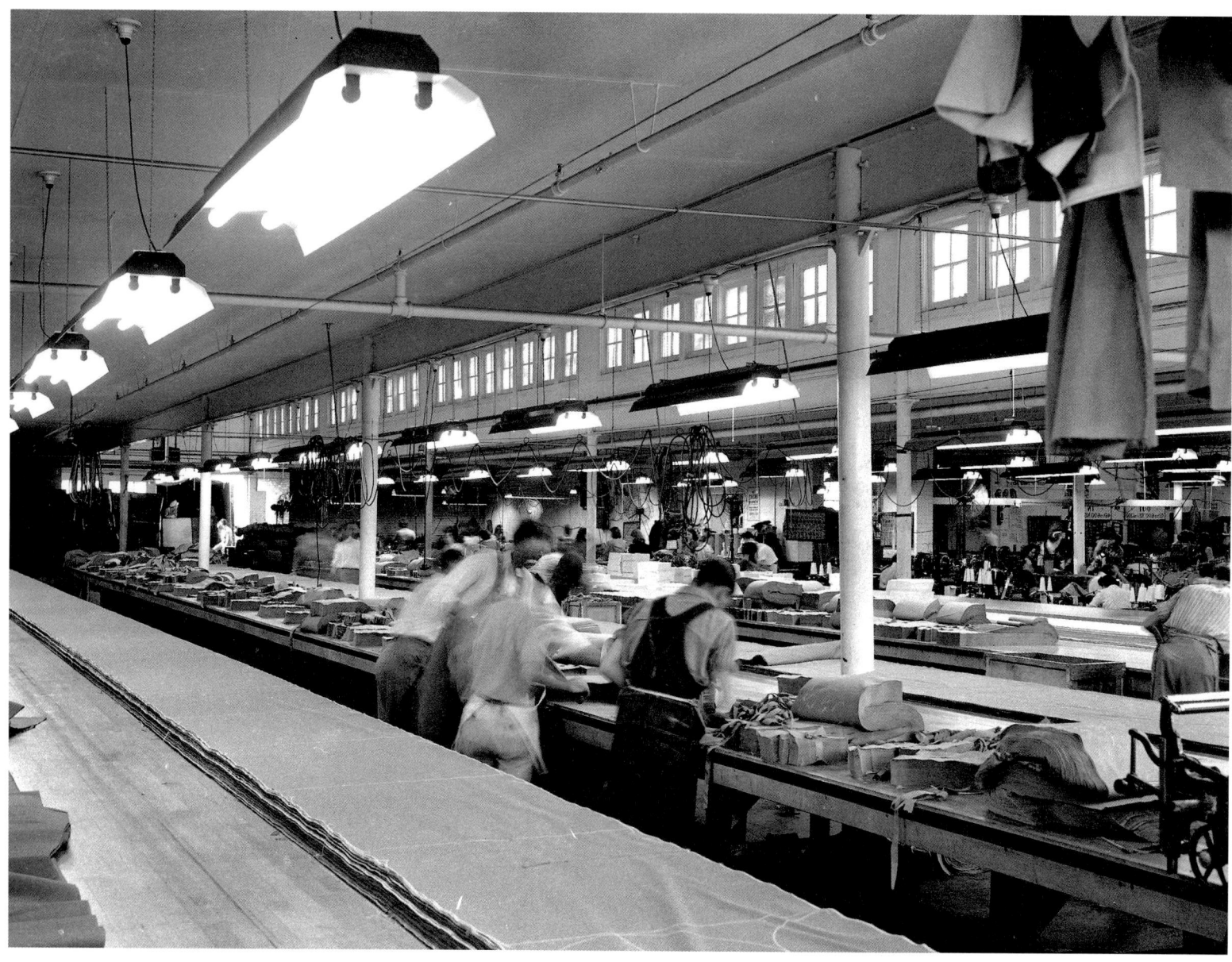

ABOVE: Part of the cutting room at Conro. Next, the pattern-cut fabric would go to the sewing room. 1940s.

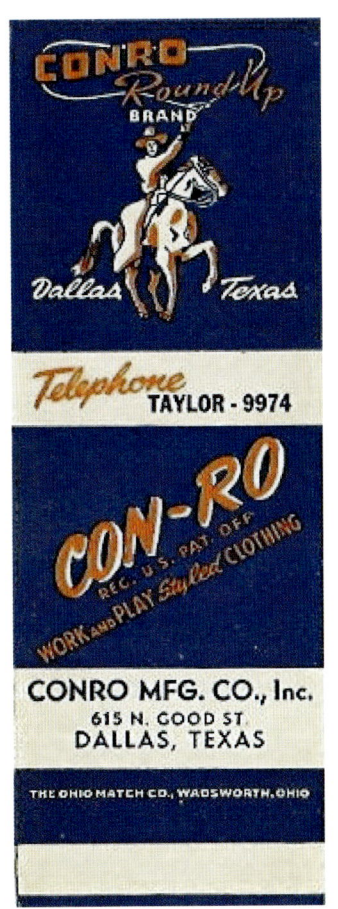

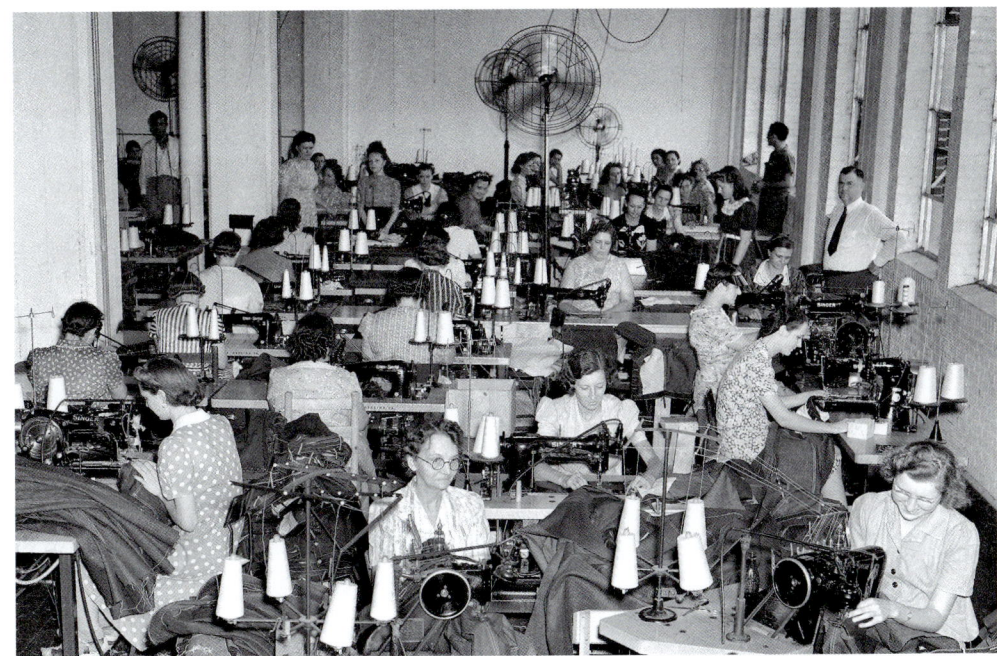

ABOVE: Sewers busy joining the left and right sides of work pants and jeans. 1940s.

ABOVE: Matchbook cover from Conro. 1940s.

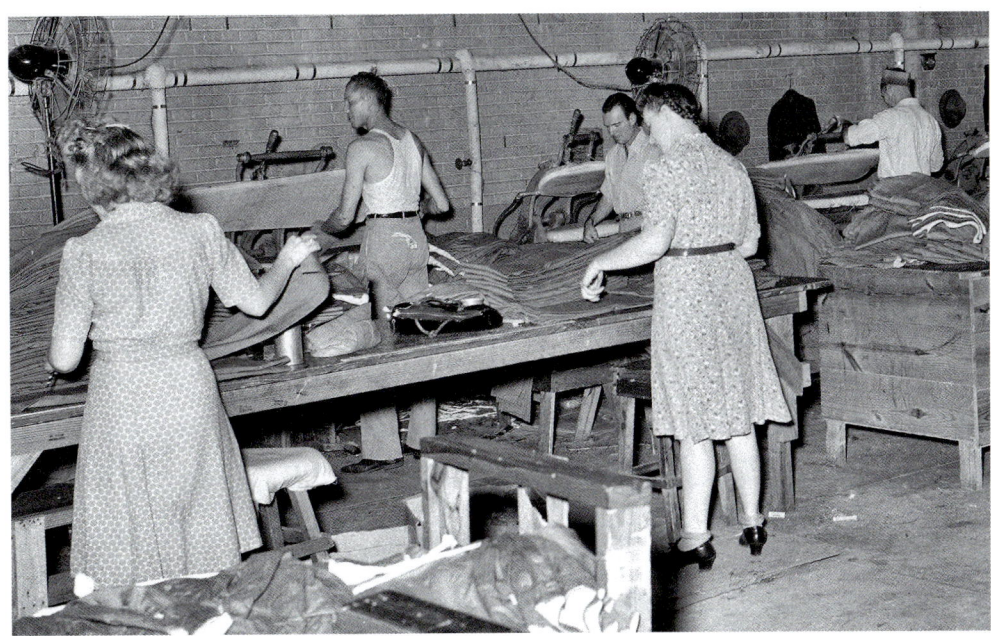

RIGHT: Sewn pants were then gathered and pressed by industrial-type ironing machines (back, against the wall). 1940s.

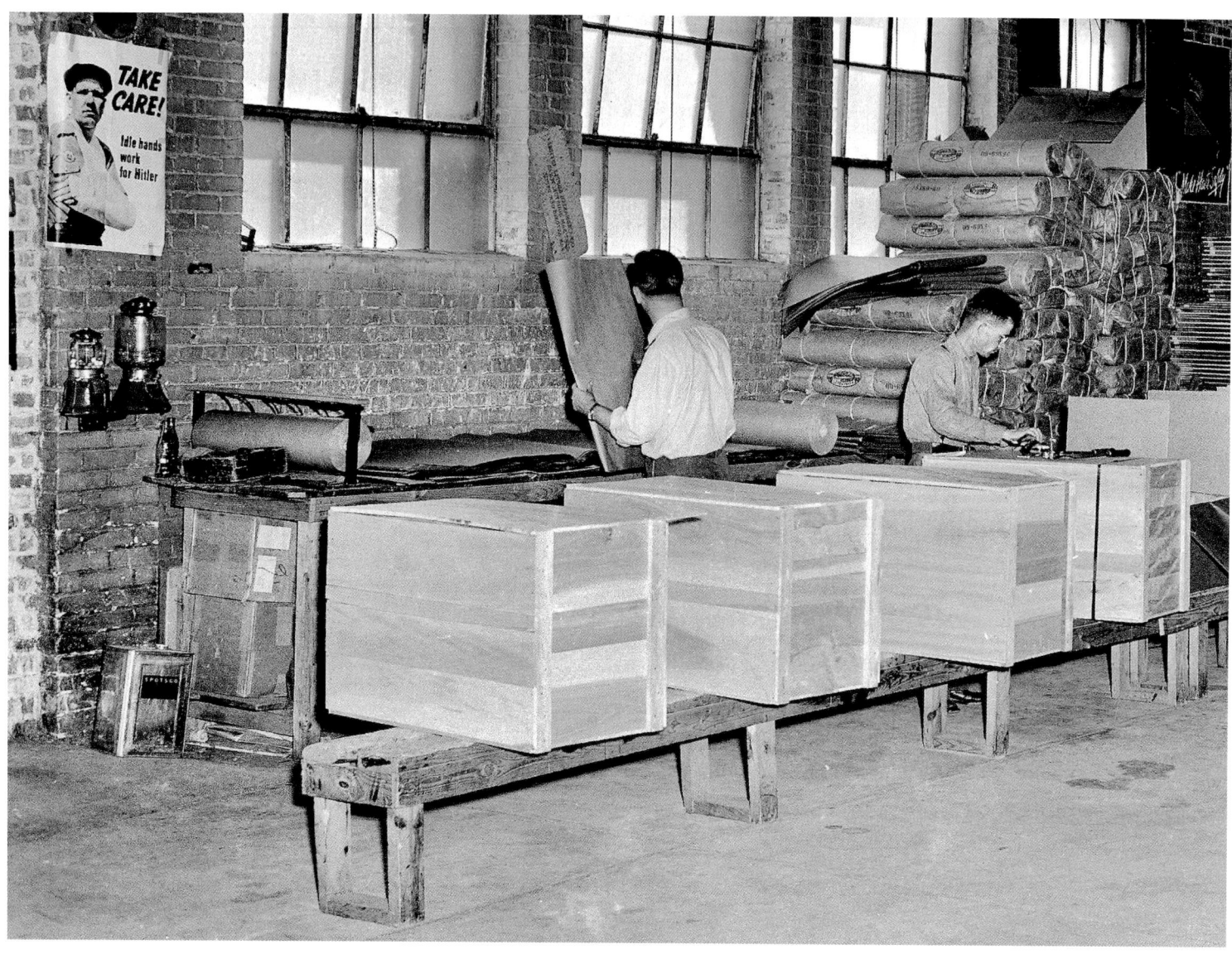

ABOVE: After pressing, pants were then sorted, packaged, and labeled, ready for shipping to various stores and suppliers around the country. 1940s.

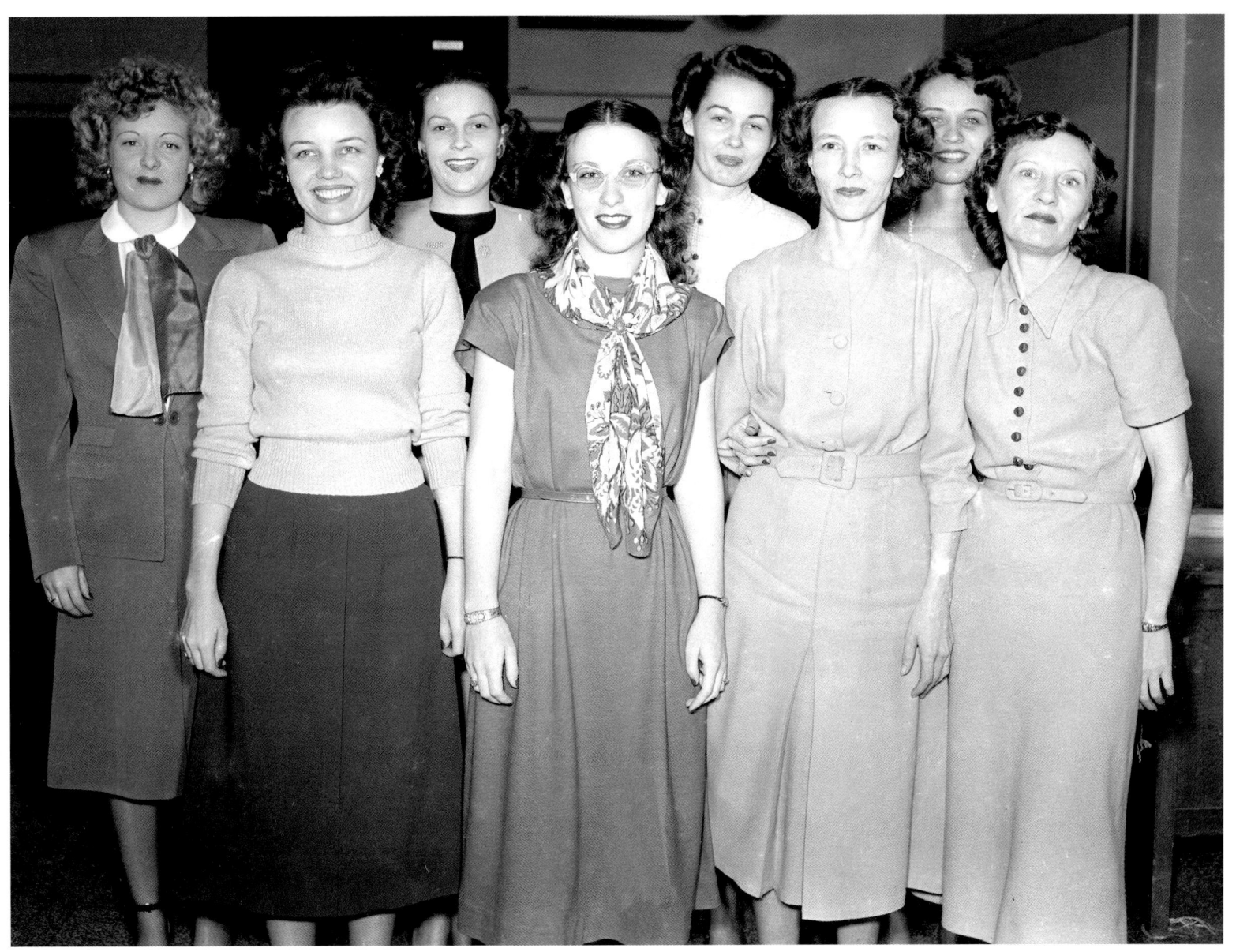

ABOVE: Office workers at Conro. 1940s.

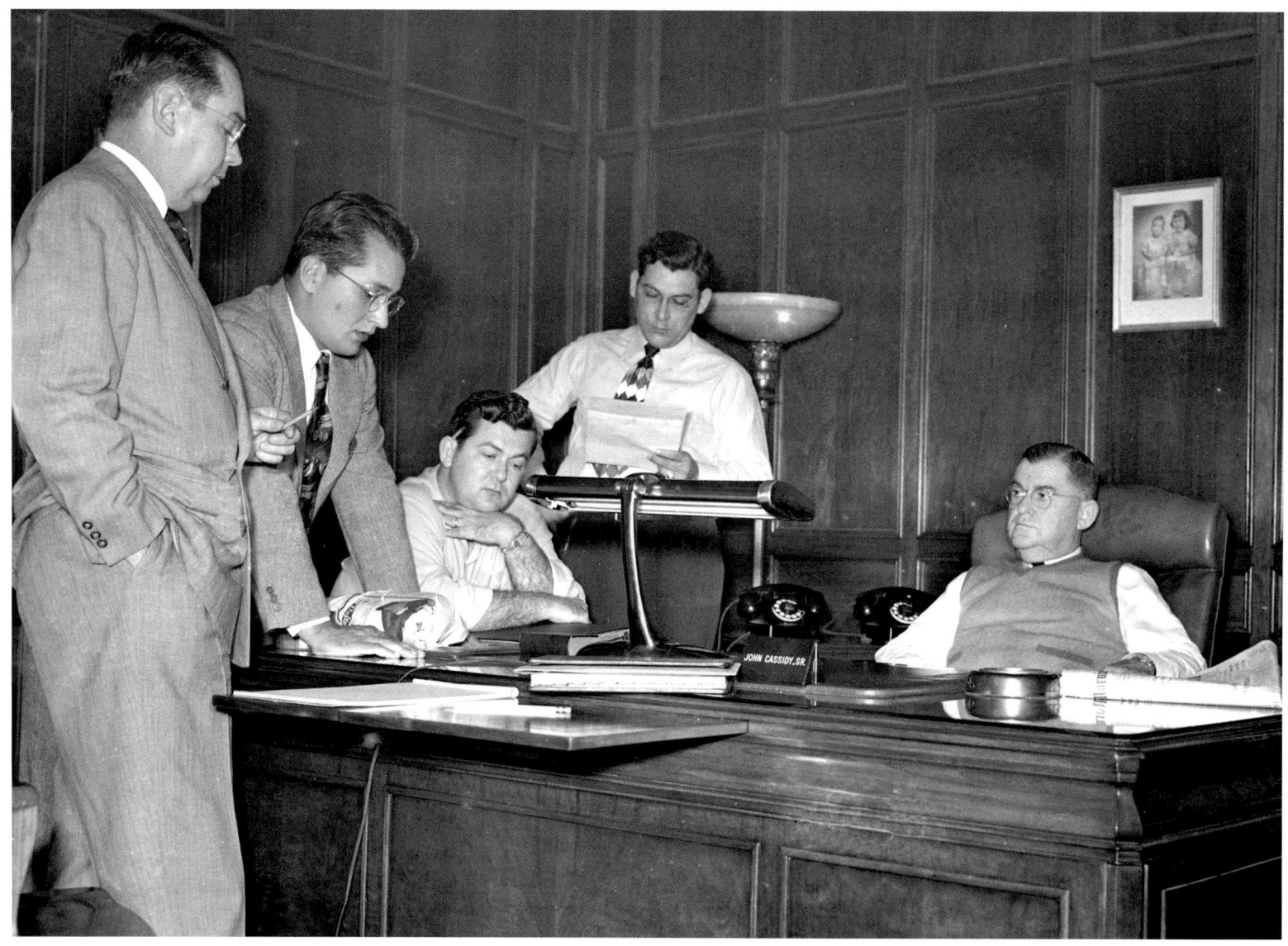

ABOVE: Executive leadership at Conro Manufacturing Co. My uncle Giles is second from the left. My dad, Connell R. Miller Sr., was also part of the leadership team at Conro and Texas Textile Mills as an owner and executive vice president but was seldom pictured as he was usually the one taking the photos. 1940s.

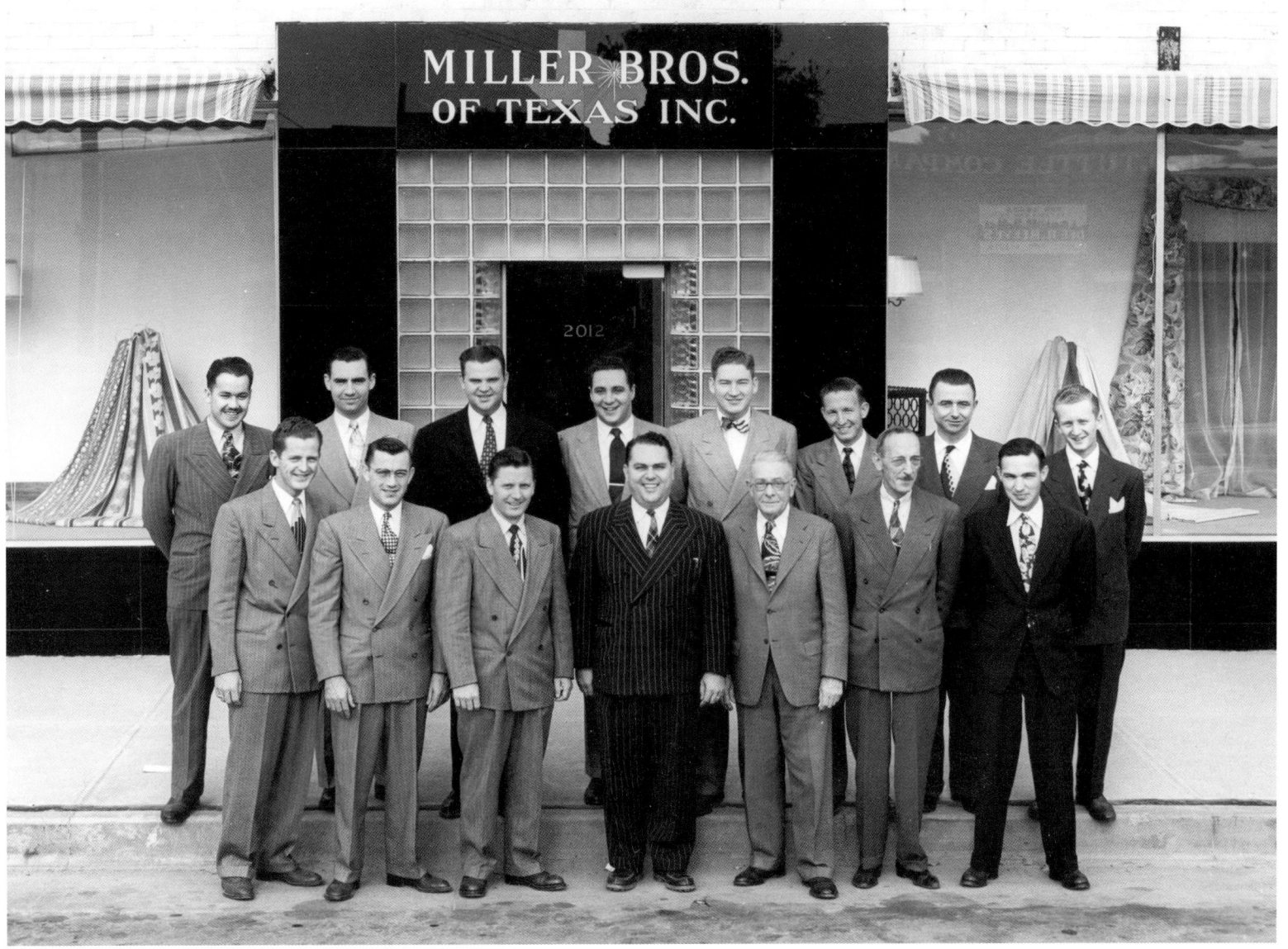

ABOVE: The opening of Miller Bros. of Texas in their just-completed building on Akard Street in Dallas. Connell R. Miller Sr., my father, is in the dark suit in the middle of the front row. The company was the sales arm of Texas Textile Mills, the largest cotton milling operation west of the Mississippi. We also had a sales rep based on the west coast and one in an office in the Empire State Building in NYC. 1947.

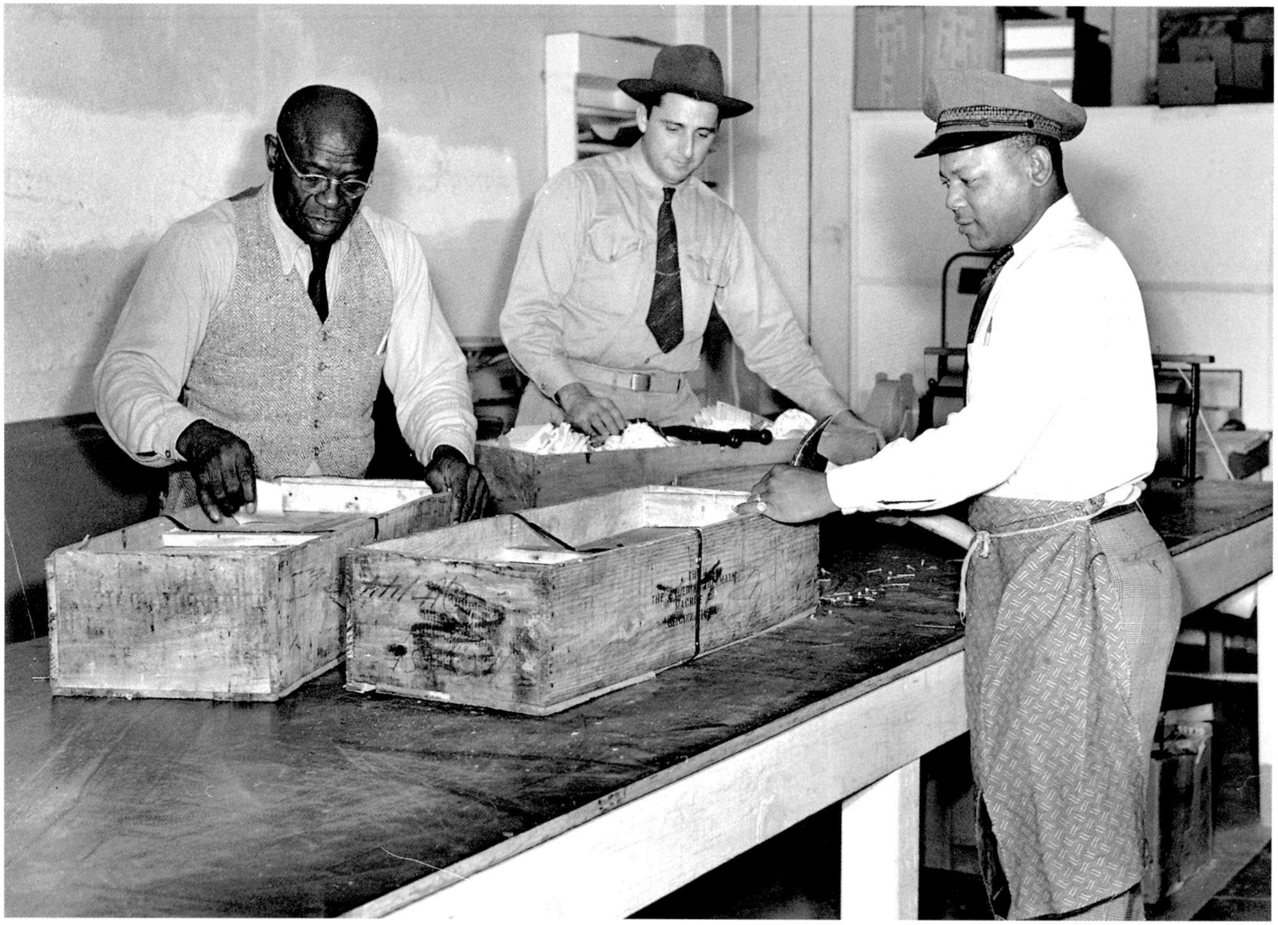

ABOVE: Samples are prepared for shipment to fabric buyers across the country by D. C. Goins, unidentified, and Cecil "Romeo" Phillips. 1947.

RIGHT: D. C. Goins was also our hospitality manager, and visiting buyers raved about the lunch fare that he served. 1947.

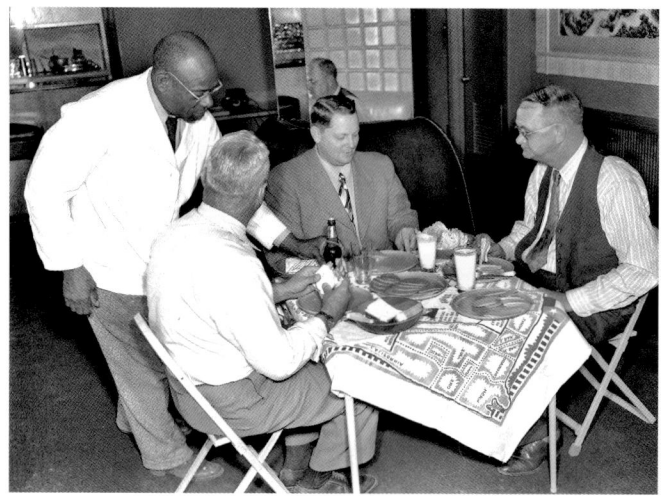

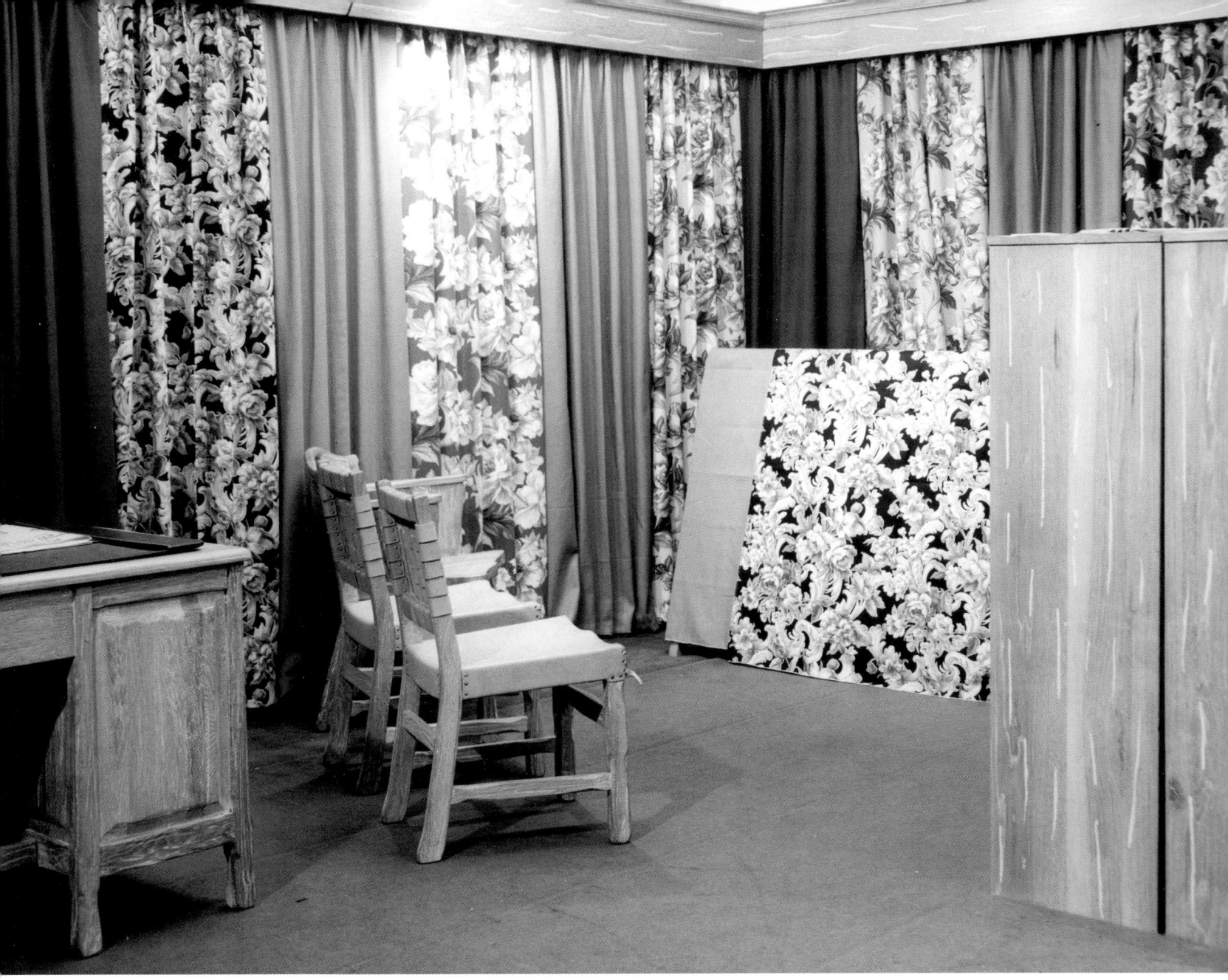

ABOVE: One of the showrooms at Miller Bros. The Ranch oak furniture was manufactured by Fort Worth's A. Brandt. 1947.

1948 McKinney, Texas, Tornado

—

OPPOSITE: A lot of spinning machines
were damaged beyond repair. 1948.

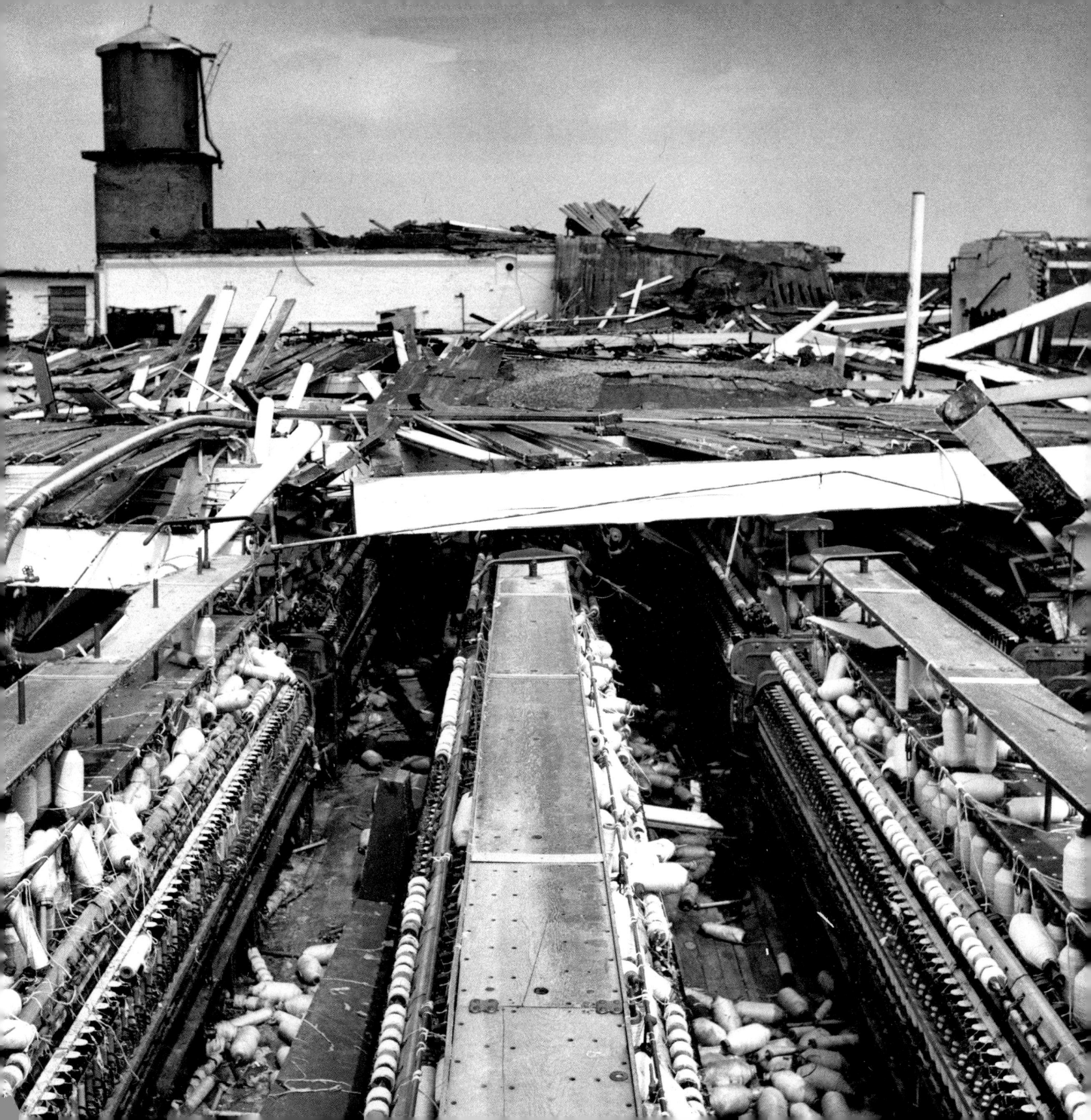

In the afternoon on May 3, 1948, an F3 tornado roared through McKinney and destroyed several hundred homes and businesses, leaving three dead and many injured. One of the hardest hit buildings was the town's largest employer, our family's textile mill on Elm Street, just east of State Highway 5. We were fortunate there were no deaths among our office and plant personnel. The tornado hit between shifts with few people in the building at the time. Dad raced from our headquarters in Dallas to McKinney immediately and, after meeting with the employees, took several photos of the carnage.

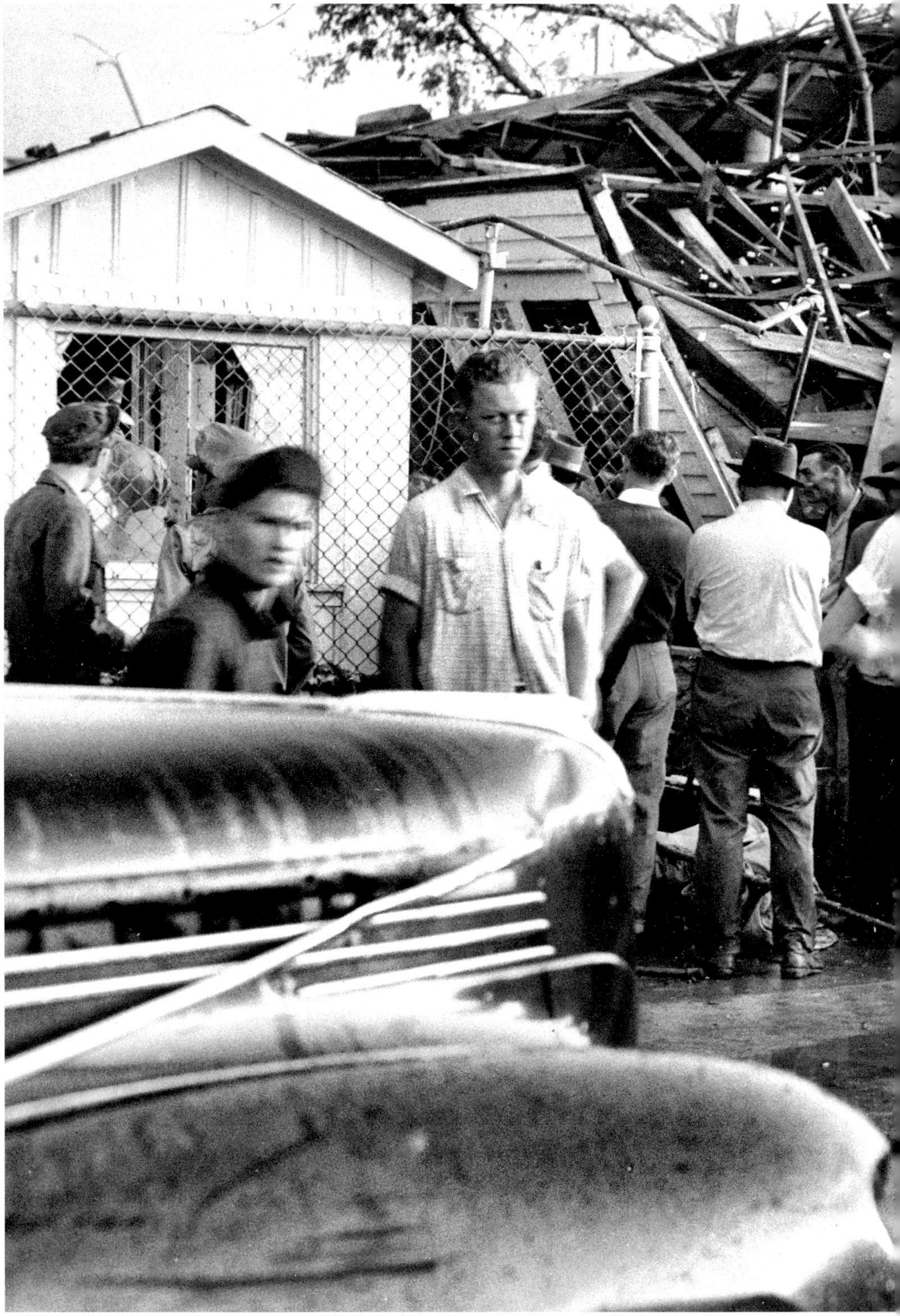

RIGHT: Crowds of people gather to assess the damage brought about by the tornado. 1948.

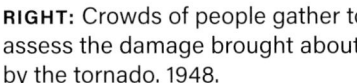

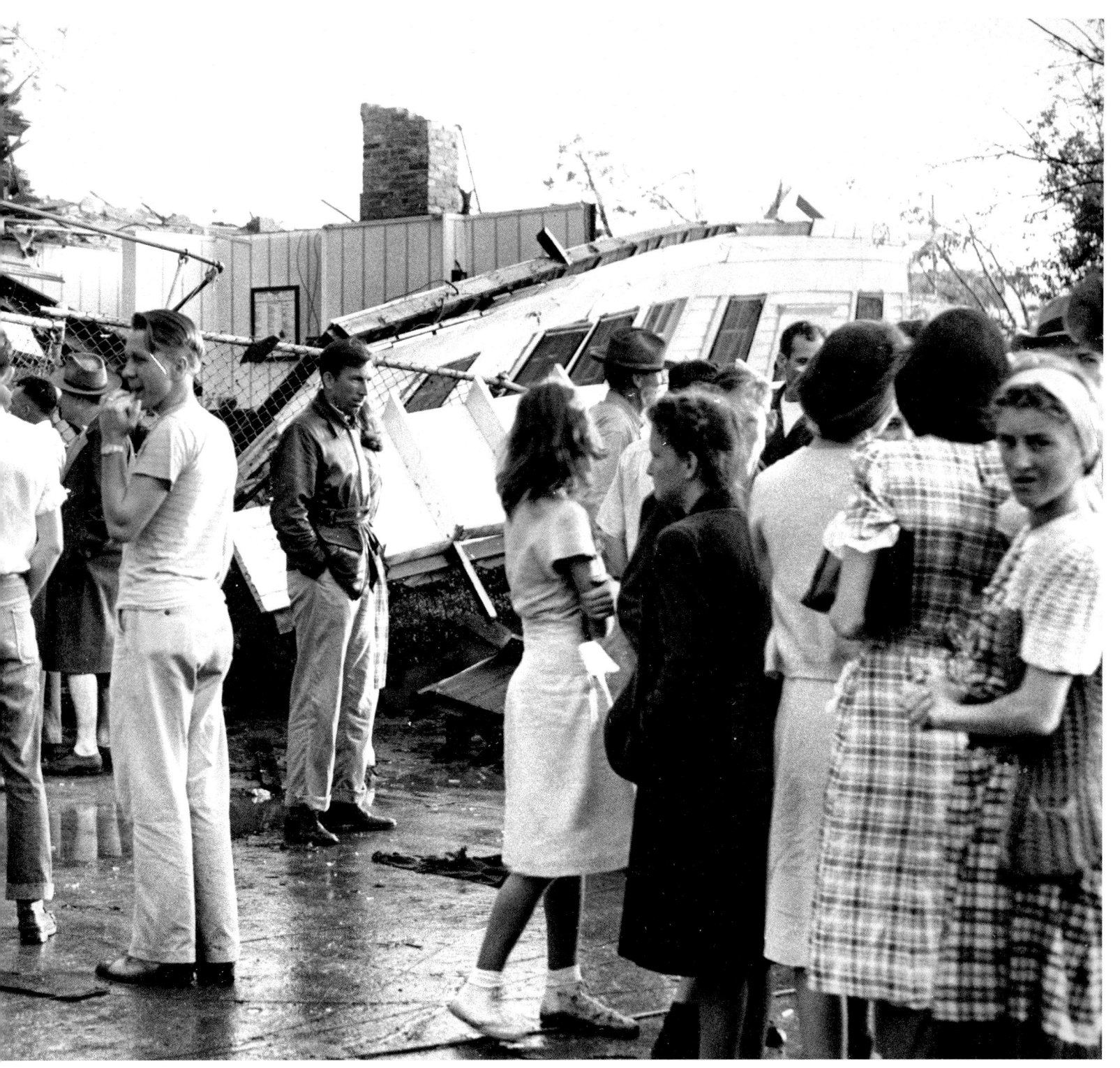

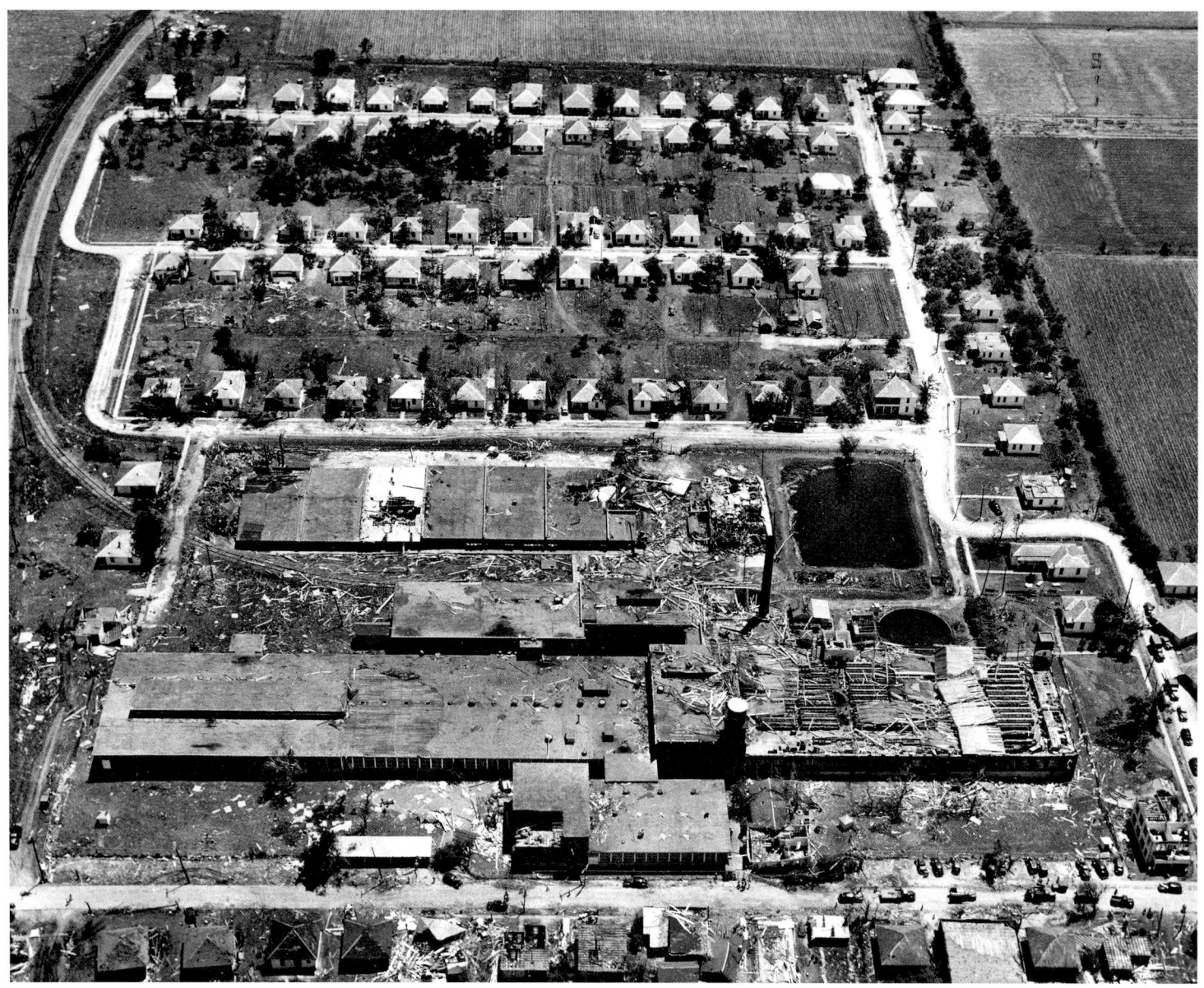

ABOVE: This is an aerial shot by an unknown photographer from the next day. Most of the homes (at the top) Texas Textile Mills had built for their workers. Fortunately, many of them did not sustain severe damage and were repaired quickly. The mill itself took a little longer, and our mills in Waco and Gonzales were pressed to up their output until McKinney was back online. 1948.

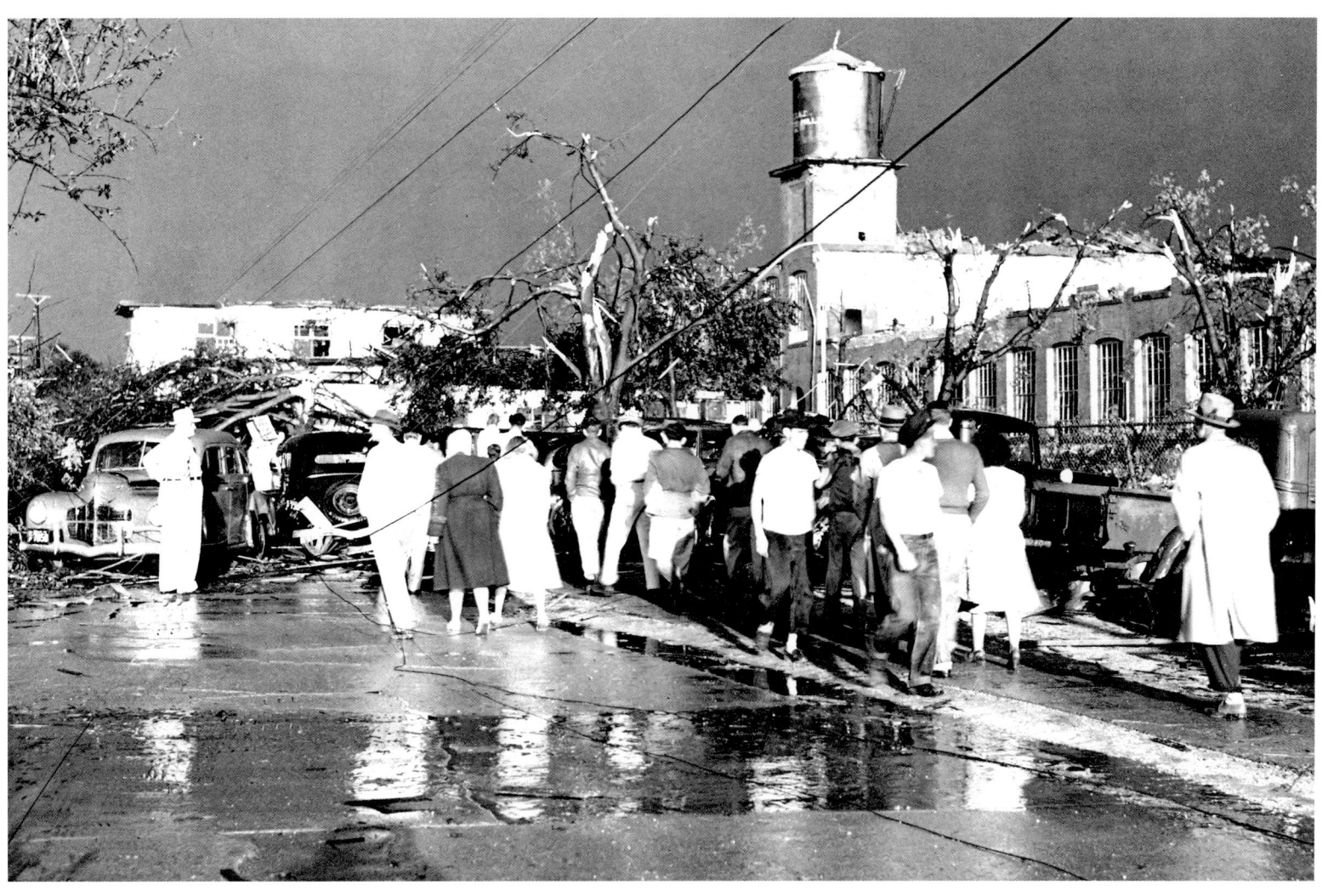

ABOVE: In the waning sunlight, everyone walked around with looks of disbelief at the damage. 1948.

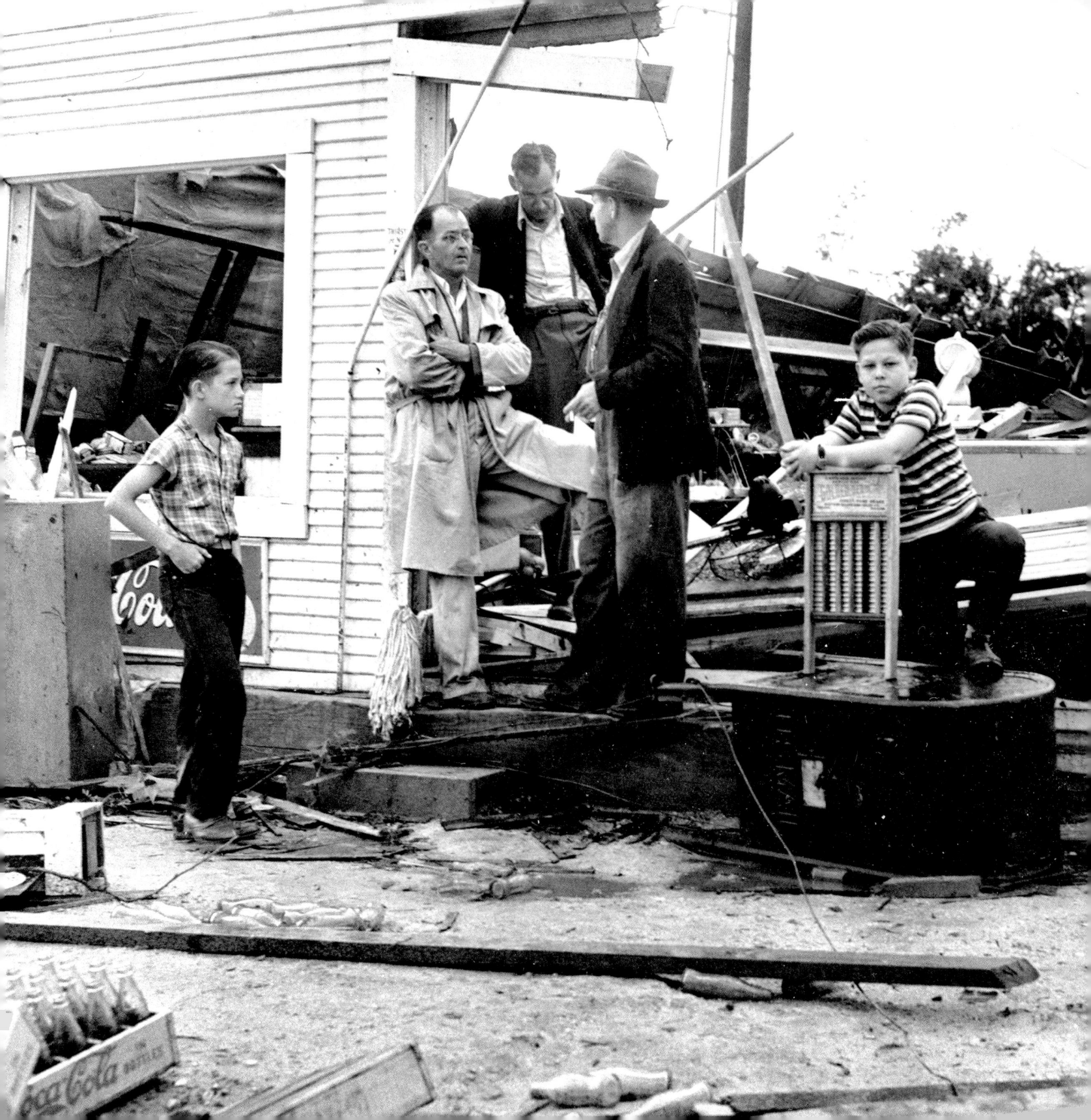

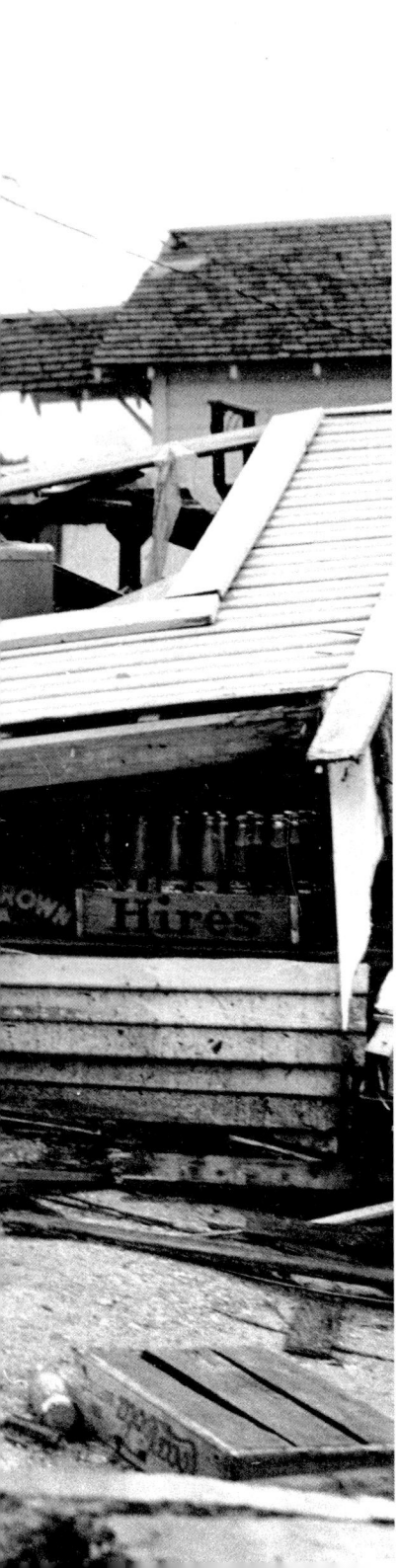

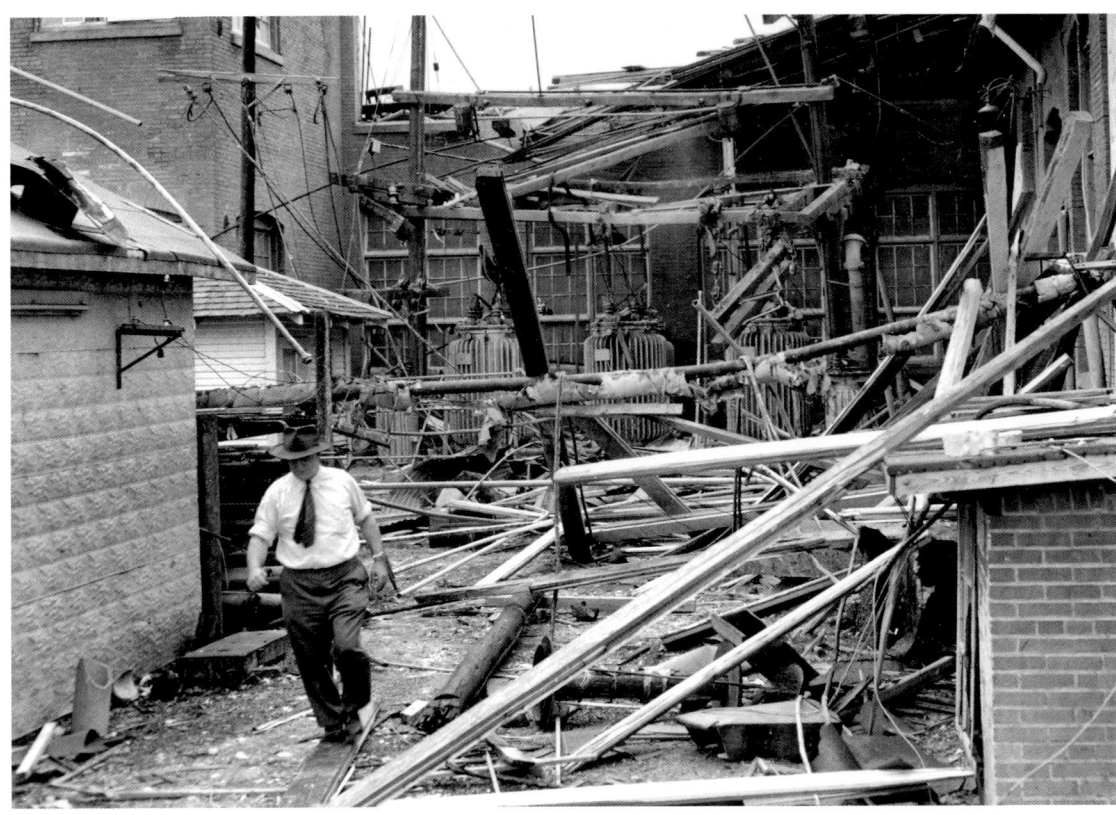

ABOVE: My grandfather, Clarence Miller, president and CEO of Texas Textile Mills, assessing the damage as he walked through the ruins in McKinney, the largest of our mills in Texas. 1948.

LEFT: Workers were naturally worried about the mill's future. It was rebuilt and operating again as quickly as possible. 1948.

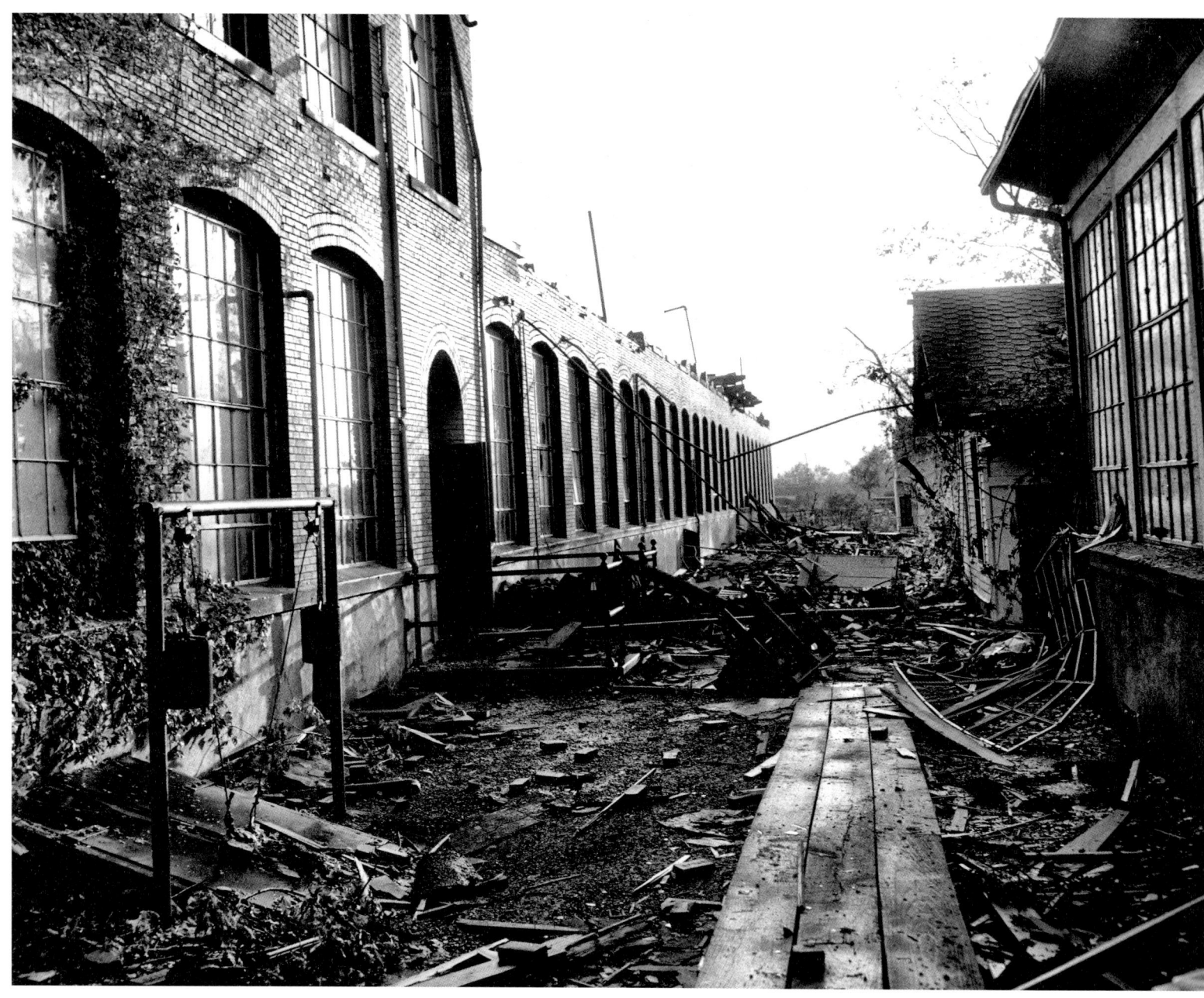

ABOVE: Decisions had to be made on what could be rebuilt
and what would have to be razed and built anew. 1948.

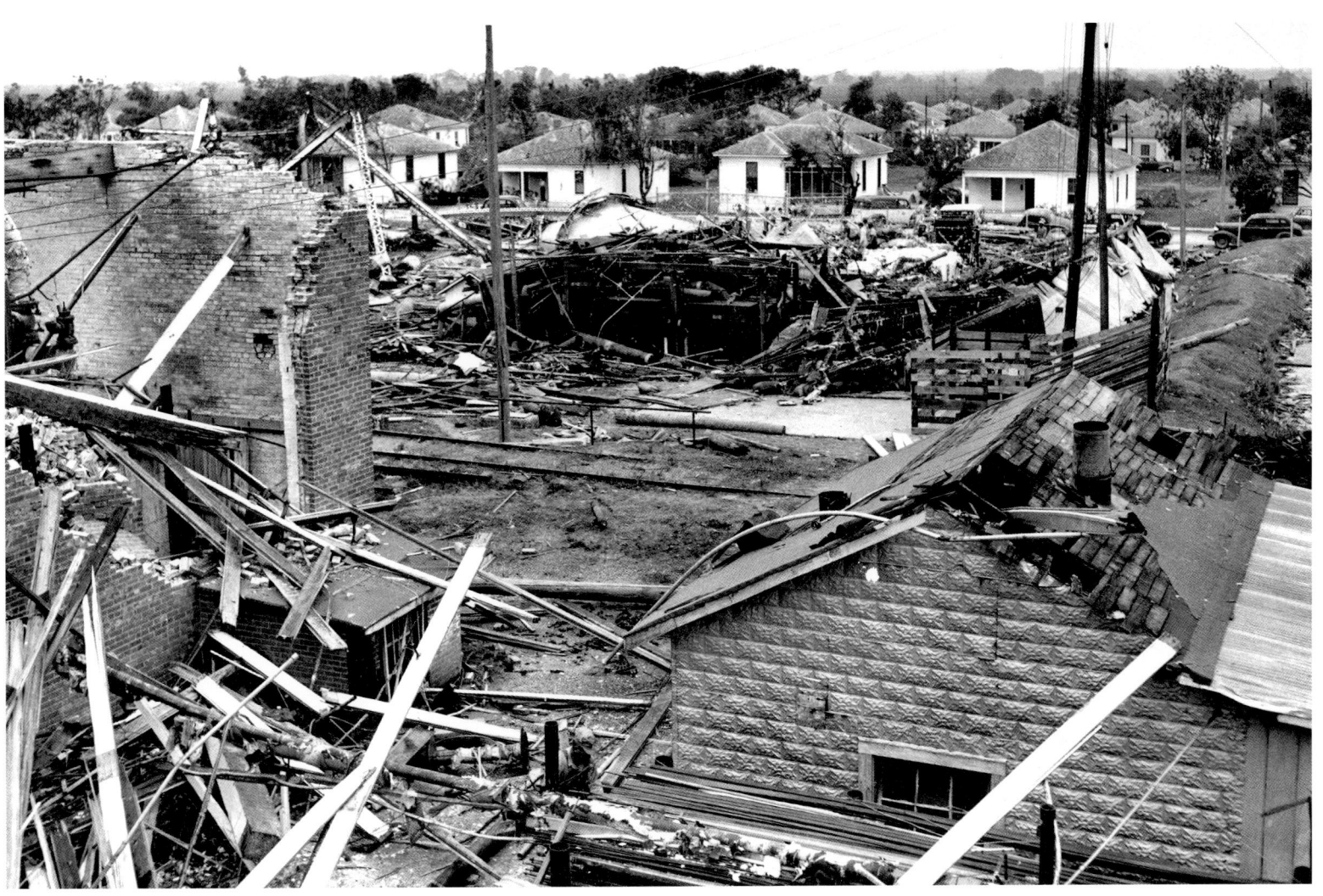

ABOVE: Several homes destroyed
by the tornado. 1948.

Goins Foundation

———

OPPOSITE: The Goins Club basketball team. 1948.

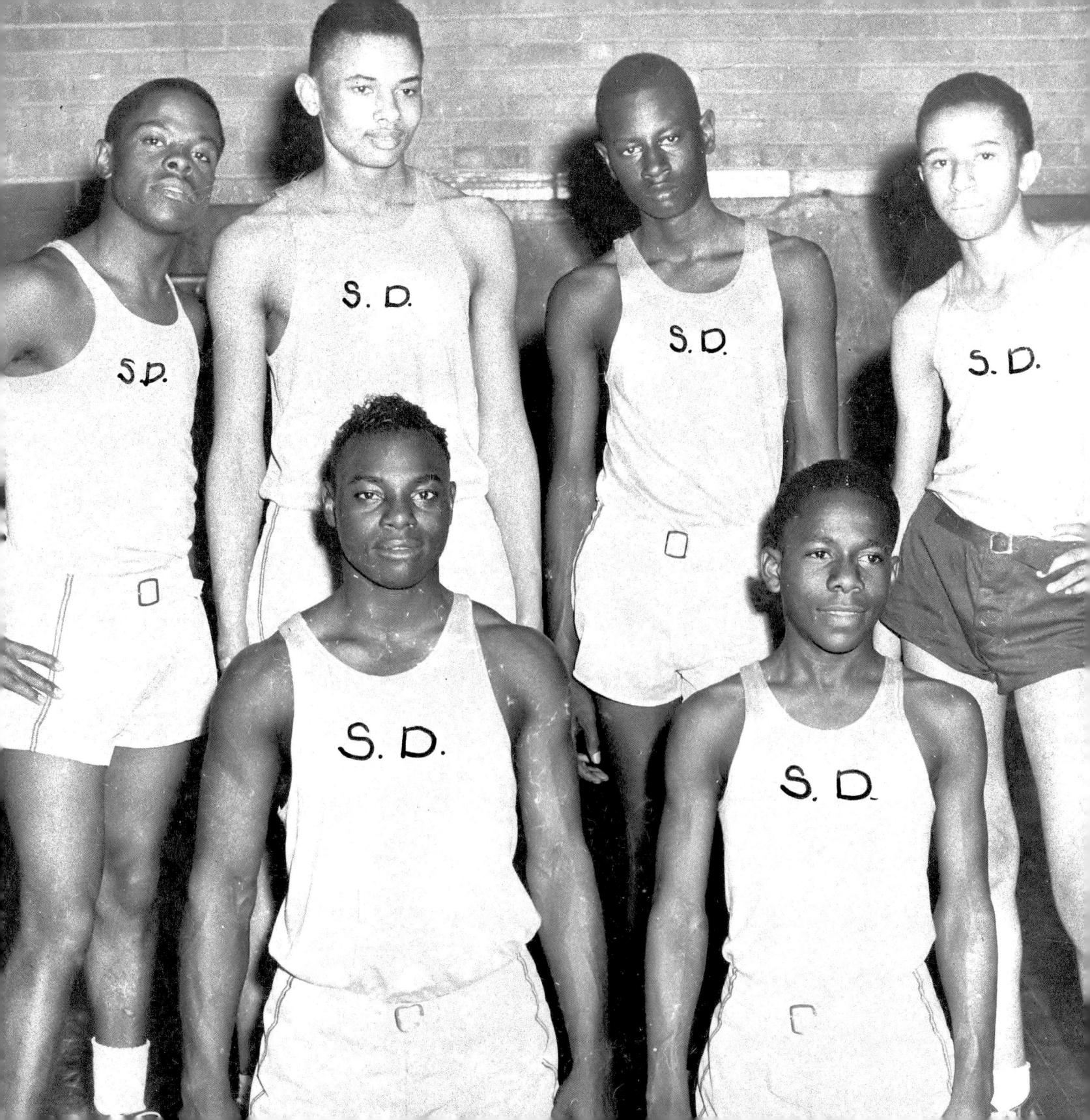

Earl Goins, after leaving the army after World War I, became a much-beloved employee of our family from the 1920s until his passing in 1963. In the 1940s, my dad, uncle, and grandfather worked with Earl to set up the Goins Foundation in 1948. They obtained a building in South Dallas that they furnished with a ping-pong table, pool table, record player, radio, refrigerator, etc. It was a place where kids could go to meet after school or on the weekend and have fun. On Sundays, there was usually a small church service. Sports were included as well with a foundation-sponsored football and basketball team. Earl told me one time in the early sixties, "I only had one of my kids that ever went bad." He and Rosina—or Rosie, as we called her—his wife, were well known and respected by city leaders. There were undoubtedly over a thousand people at Earl's funeral, and I'm estimating close to one-half were white.

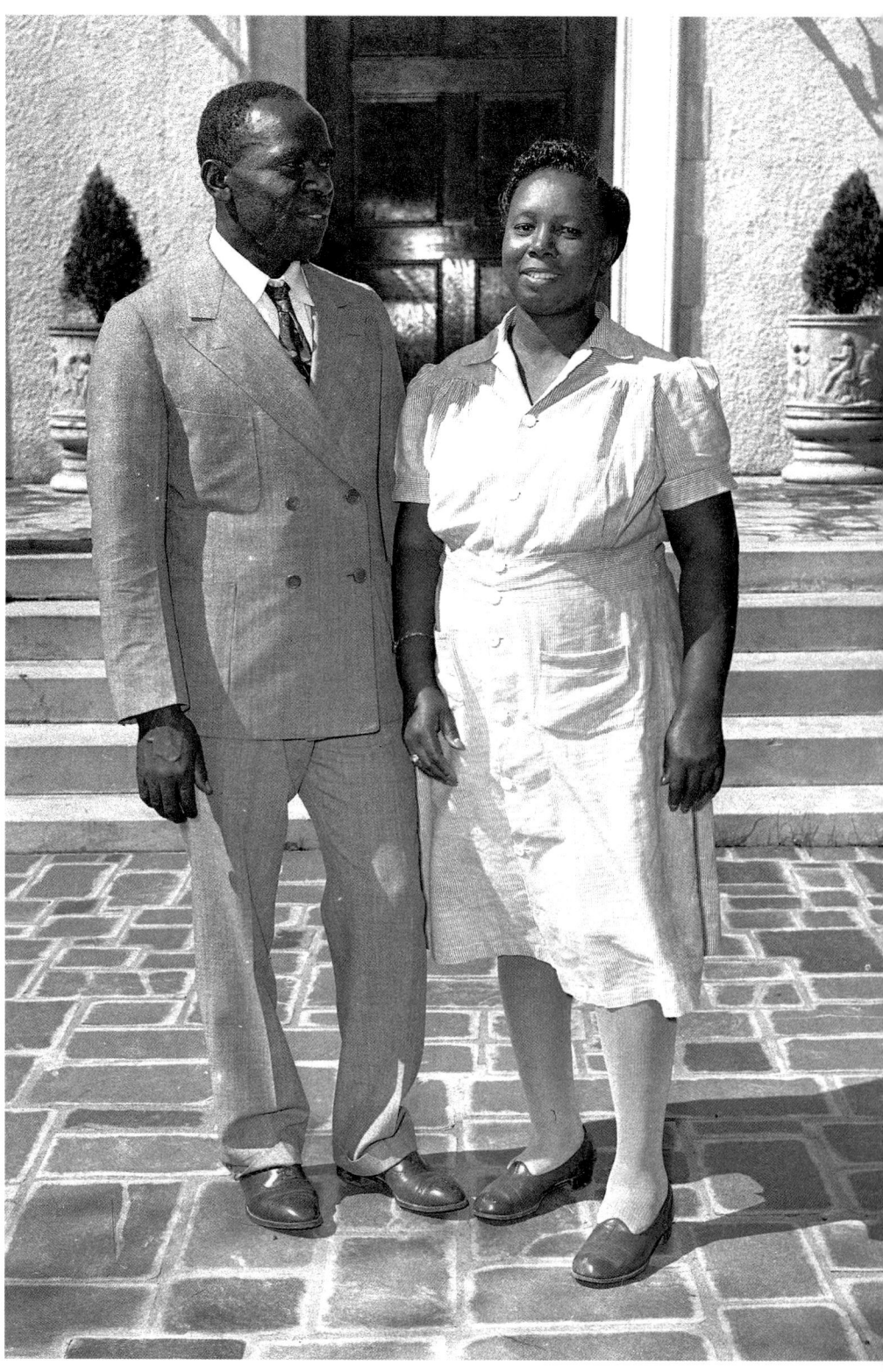

RIGHT: Earl and Rosie Goins. 1944.

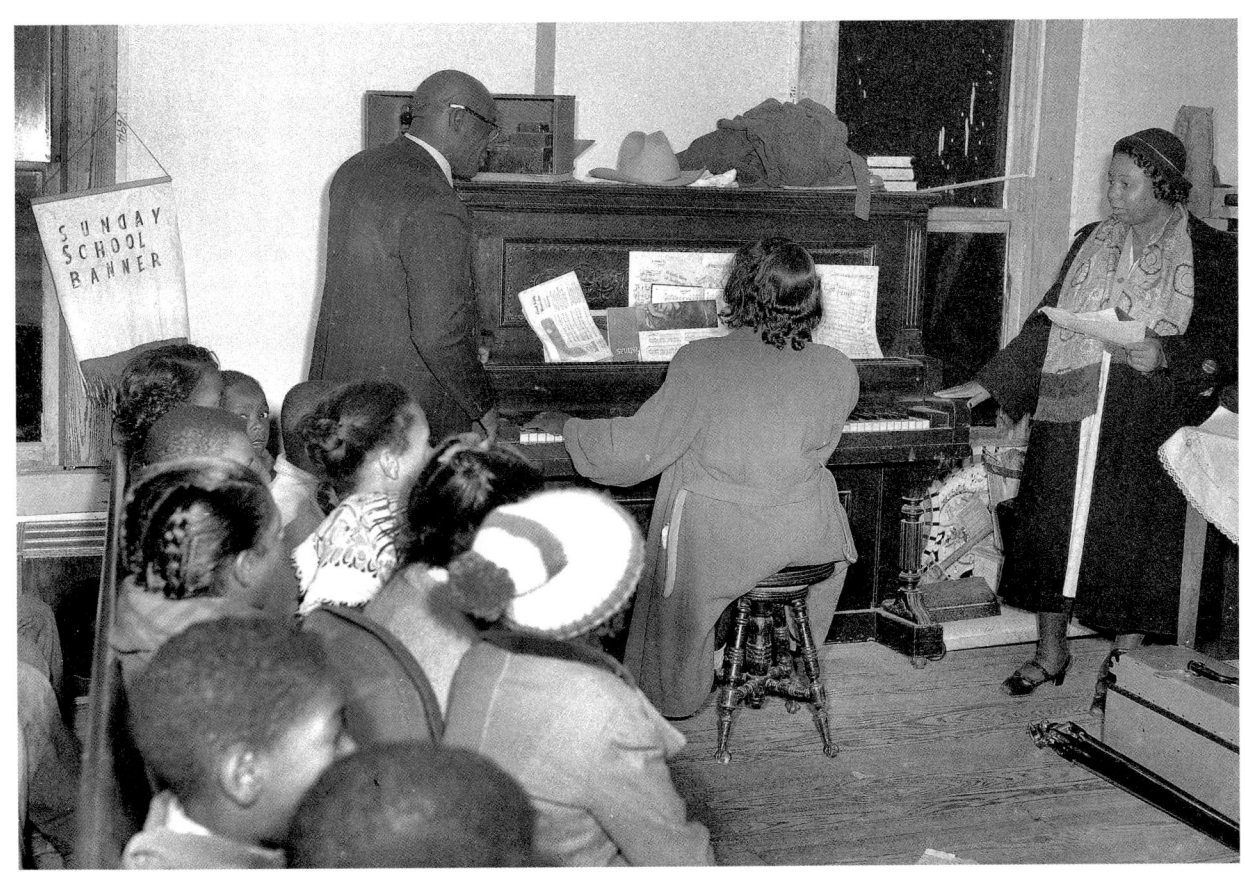

ABOVE: Church service at the foundation's clubhouse. 1949.

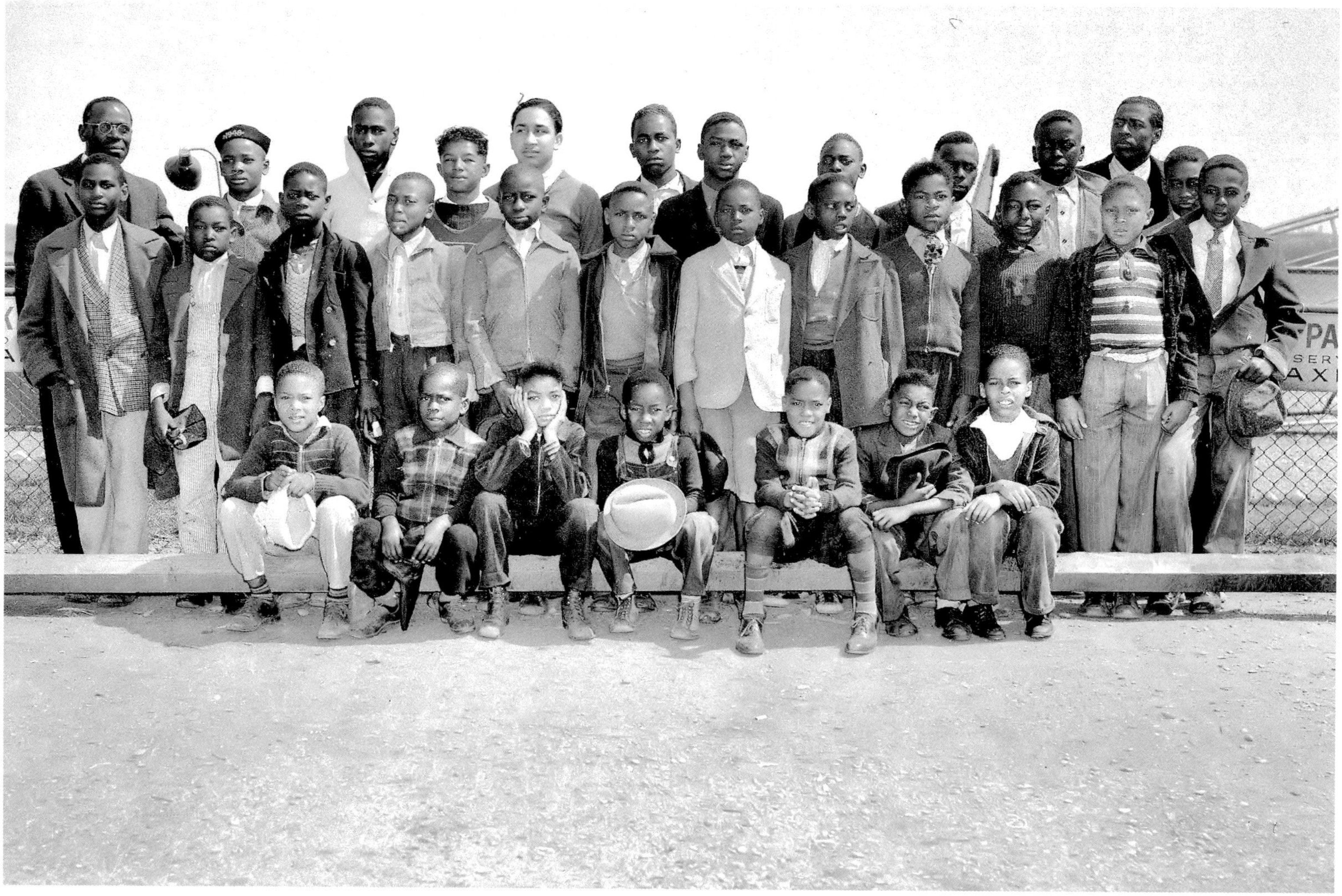

ABOVE: Earl Goins and some of "his kids."
Earl is on the back row, far left. 1950.

RIGHT: Goins Foundation football team. Earl is back
on the right, and Cecil Phillips is on the left. 1953.

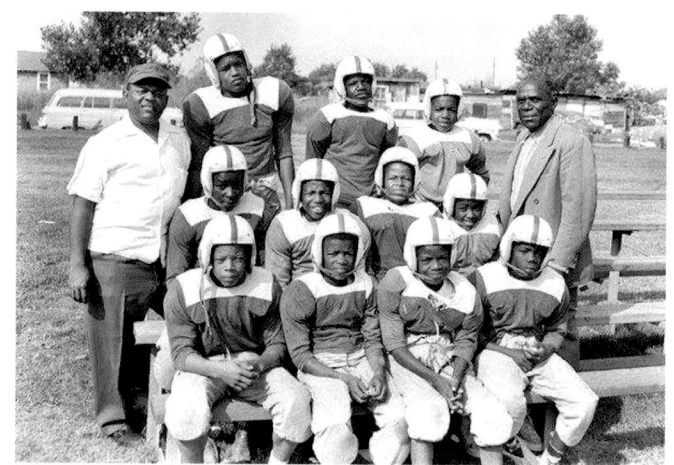

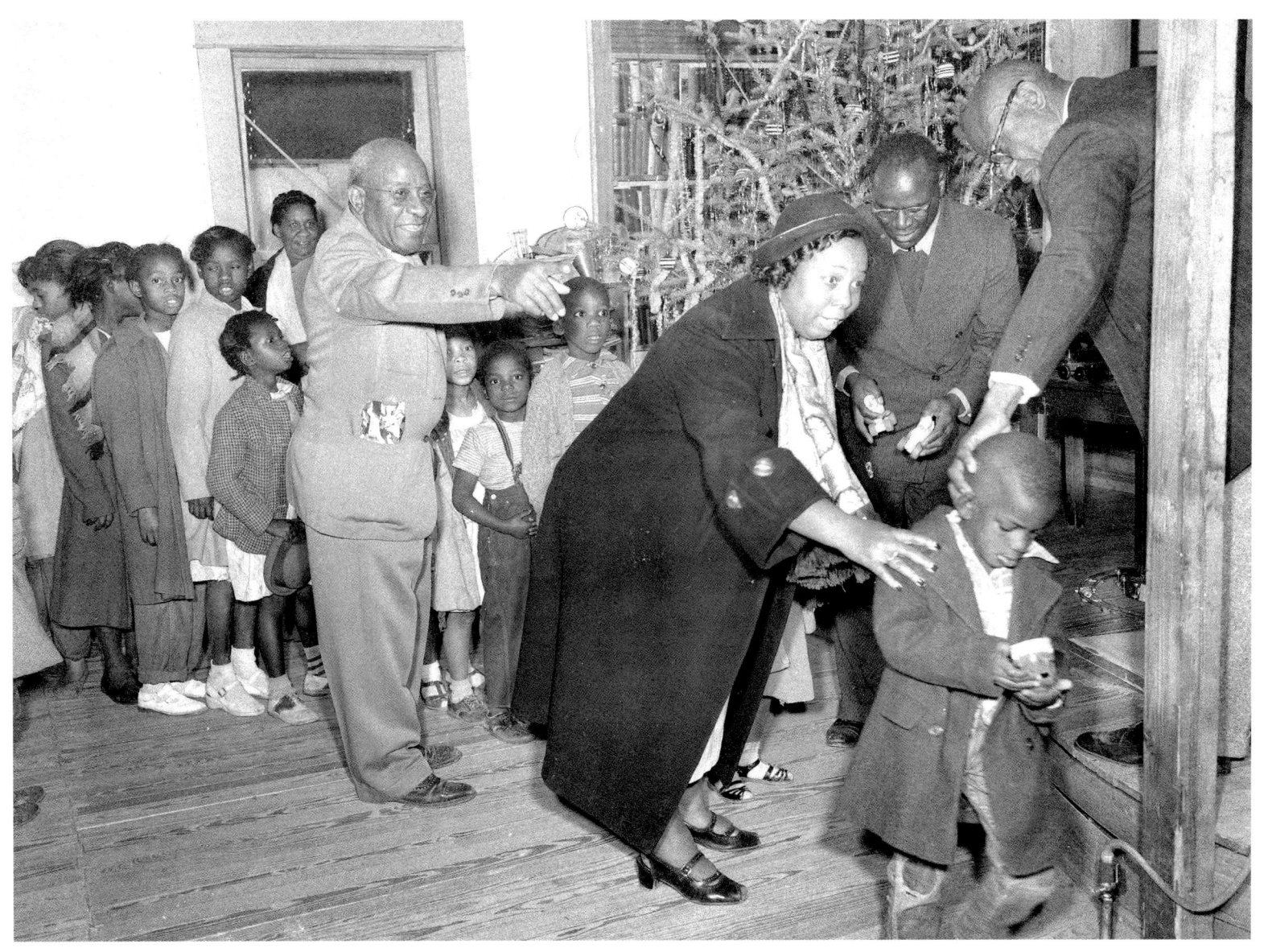

ABOVE: Christmas at the Goins Foundation. That's Earl in a dark suit holding a gift in each hand. 1949.

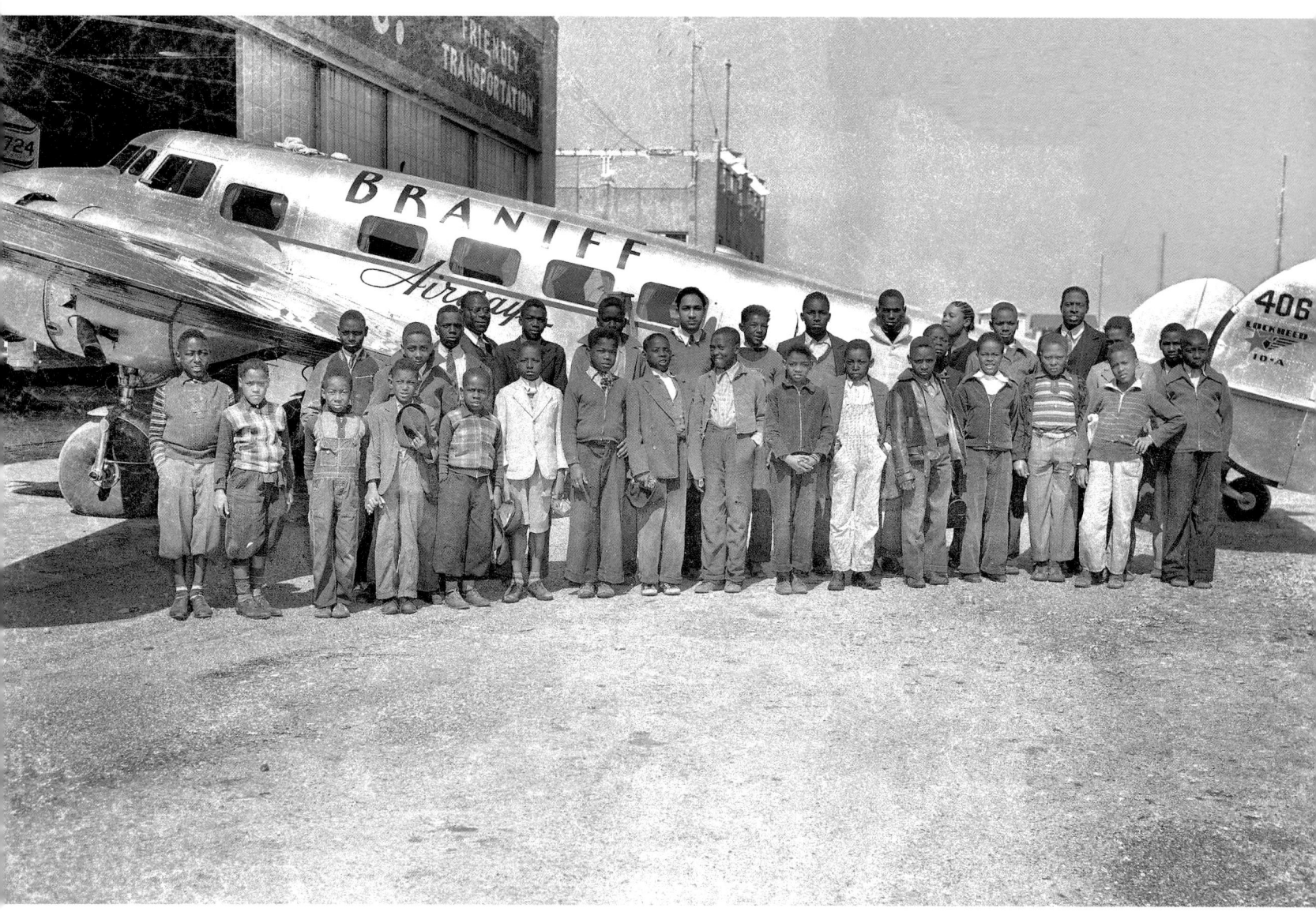

ABOVE: Earl taking his kids on flights around the Metroplex courtesy of Tom Braniff and his Braniff Airways. 1949.

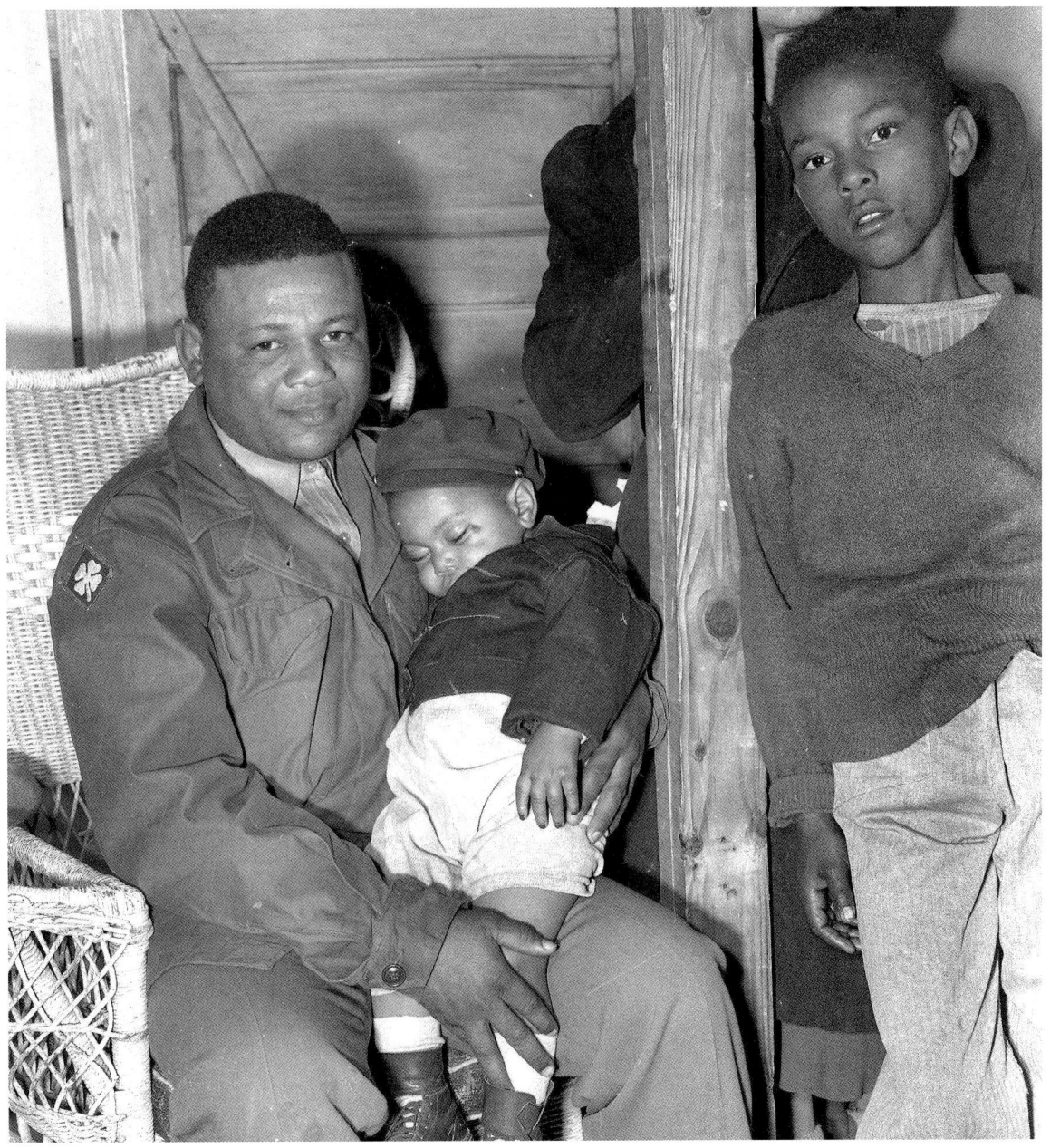

ABOVE: Everyone called him Romeo, but his real name was Cecil Phillips, and he worked for Conro, the clothing manufacturing arm of Texas Textile Mills. Here he is holding a little boy at the foundation clubhouse. Romeo took over the reins running the Goins Foundation after Earl passed away in August 1963. 1950.

Leisure on the Water

———

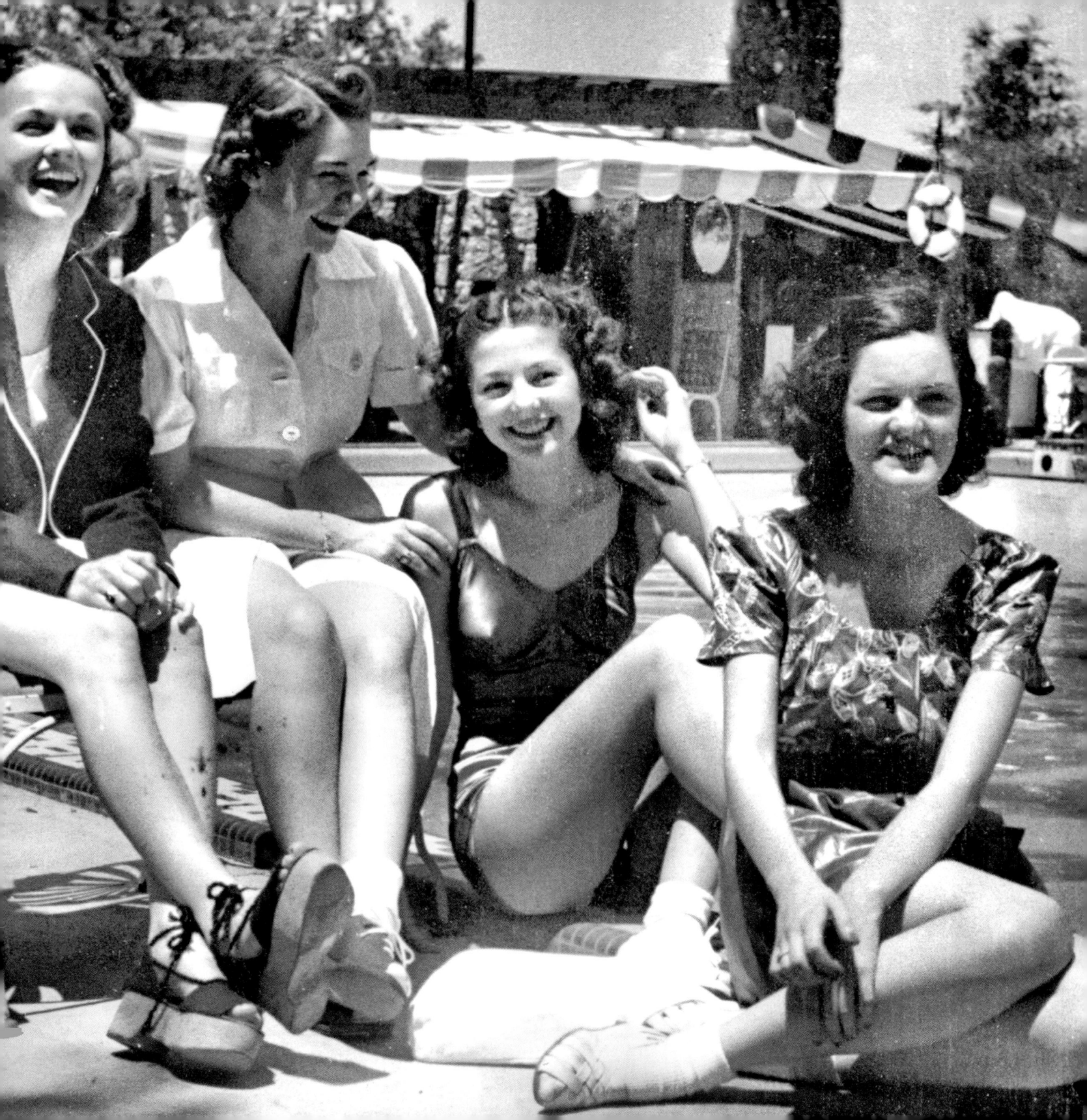

Dallas residents look forward to being outside every year, especially near water, as Texas often experiences warm spring temperatures, blazing hot summers, and mild fall weather. The postwar years saw the construction of dams, creating new lakes and adding new docks and camping areas to already existing ones. Powered sailboats line up at the lakes' ramps, and pools fill up quickly at country clubs, neighborhood parks, and individual residences as the temperatures begin to rise each year!

RIGHT: Young man casting a line. 1939.

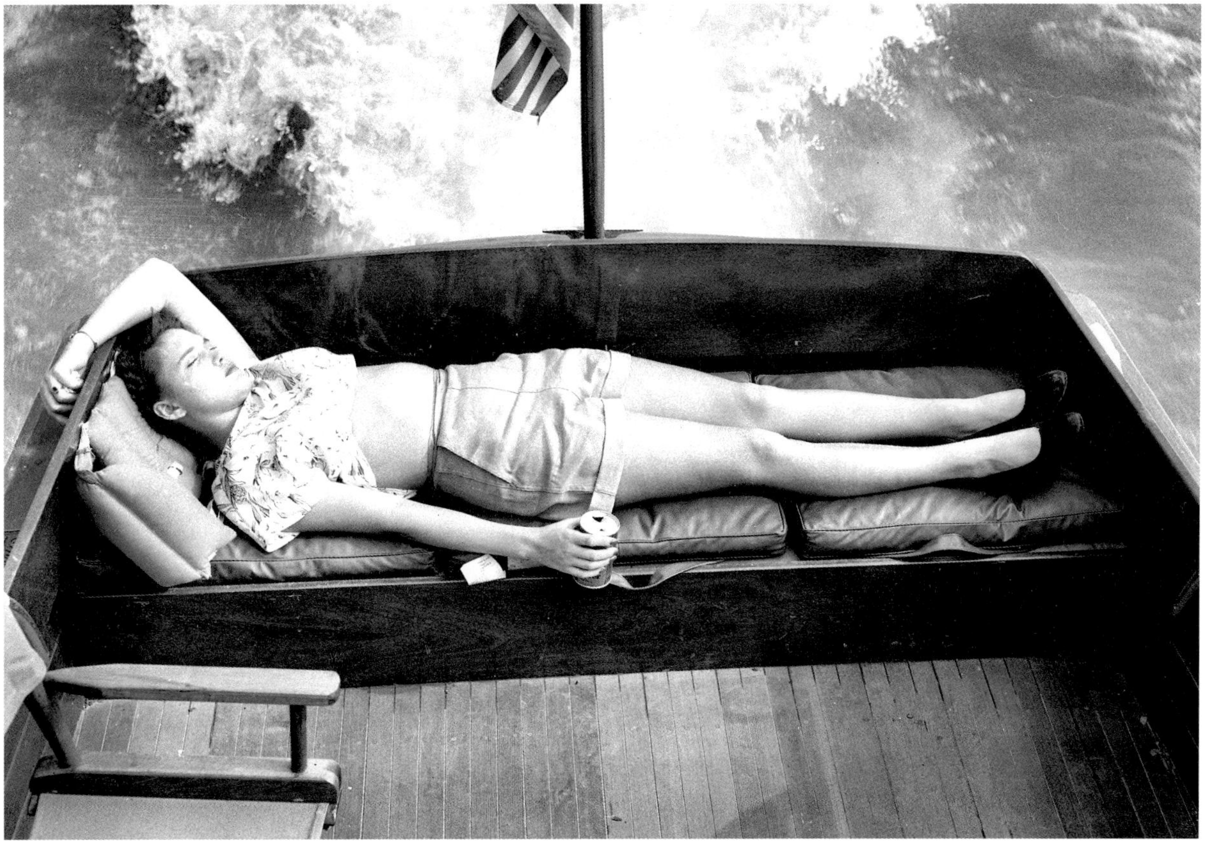

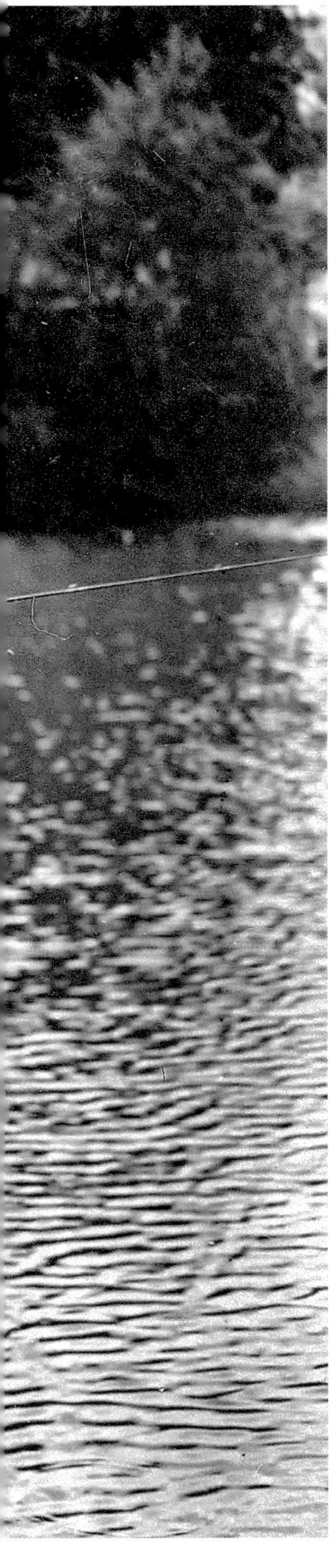

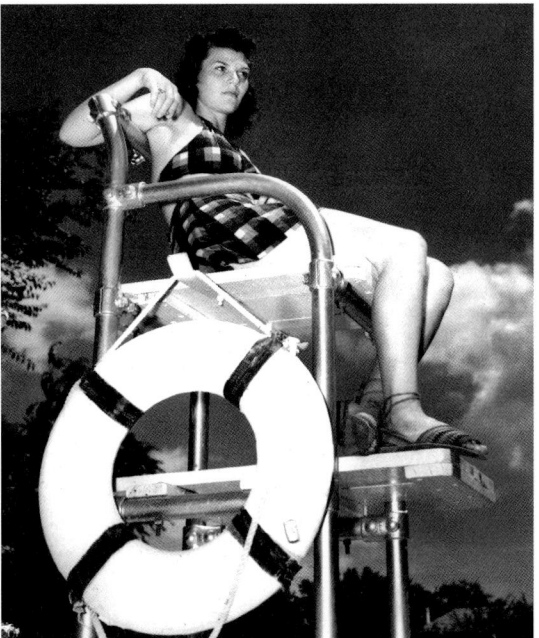

ABOVE: Cruising Lake Dallas on a sunny summer day. 1949.

LEFT: Lifeguard. 1940.

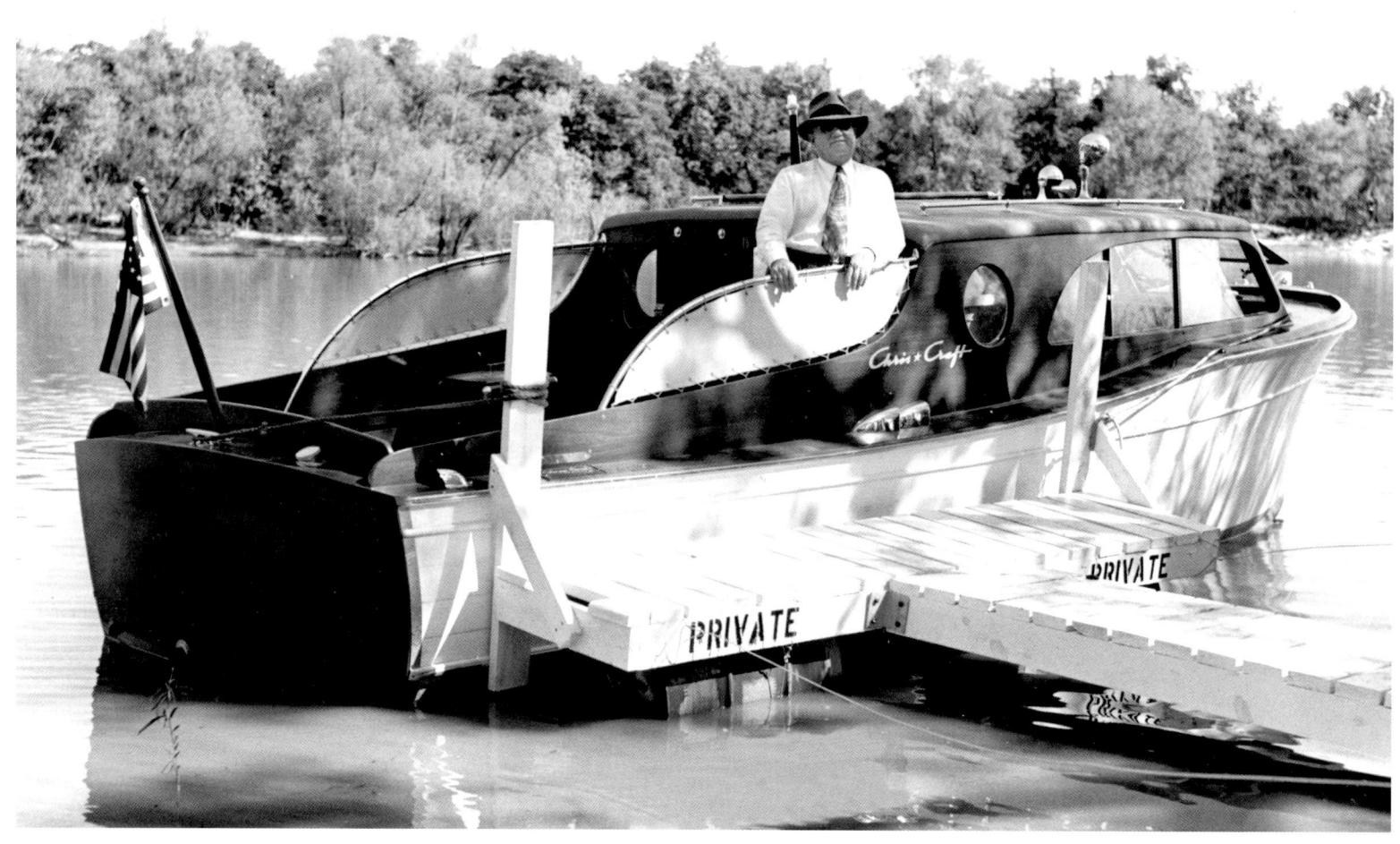

ABOVE: Twenty-six-foot Chris-Craft boat named *Seacrest*, sold new by Hundley Marine on Lake Dallas. 1947.

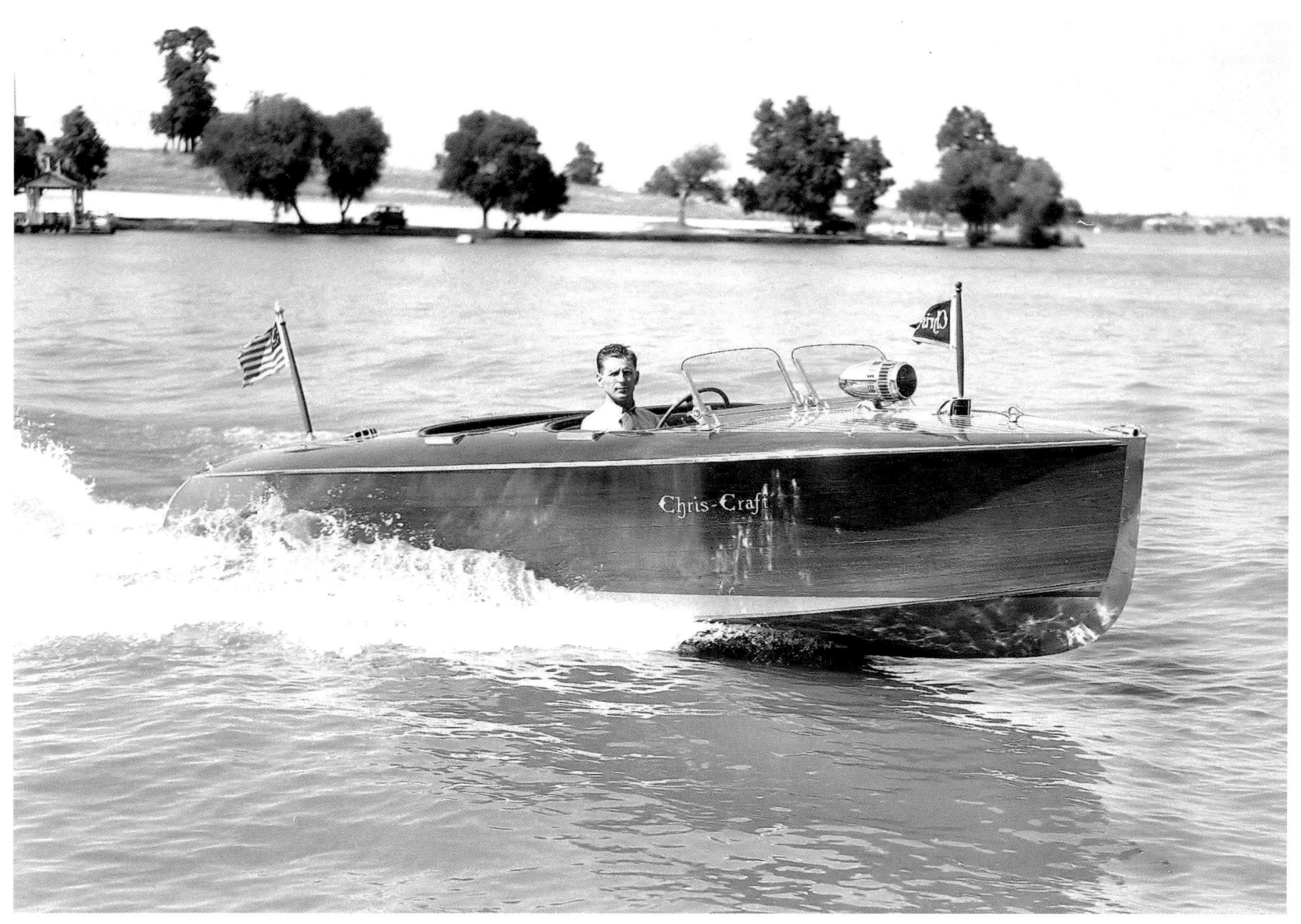

ABOVE: Red Harris's Chris-Craft in Lake Dallas. Late 1940s.

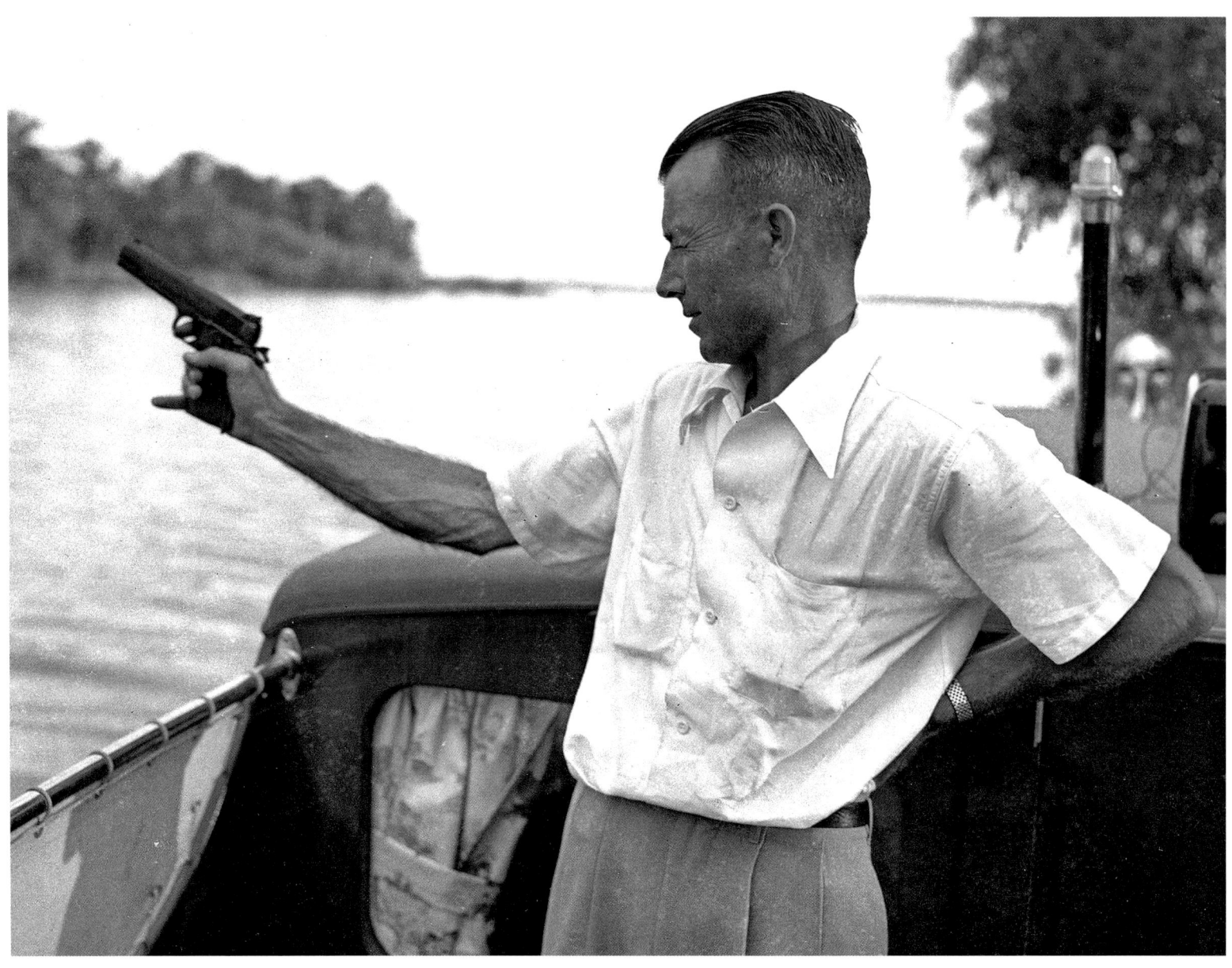

ABOVE: Family friend Guion McCaleb doing some target practice at the bank. This was in an inlet of Lake Dallas where our family's ranch had a long shoreline with no inhabitants in that area. 1950.

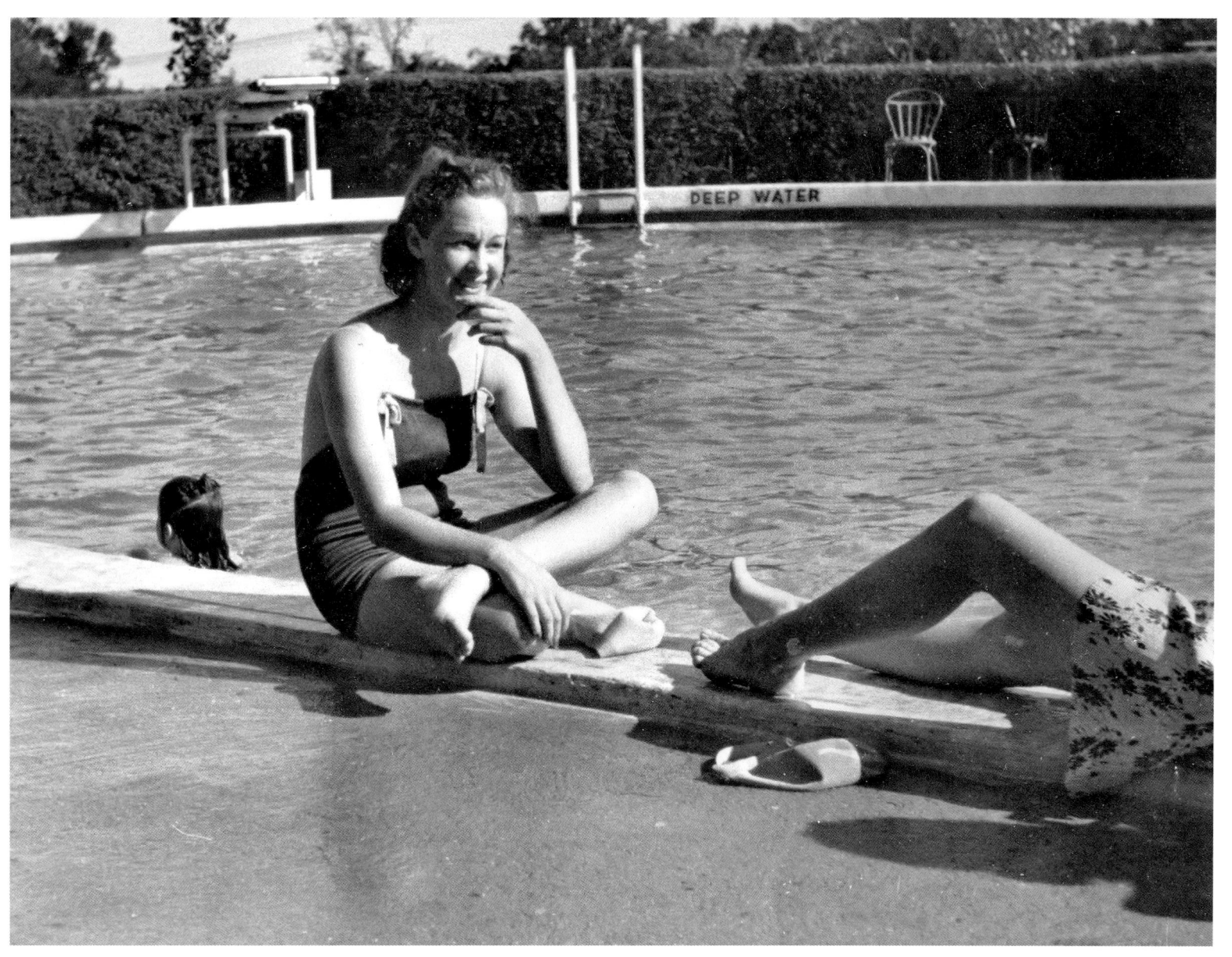

ABOVE: Young woman enjoying swimming pool in Dallas. 1940.

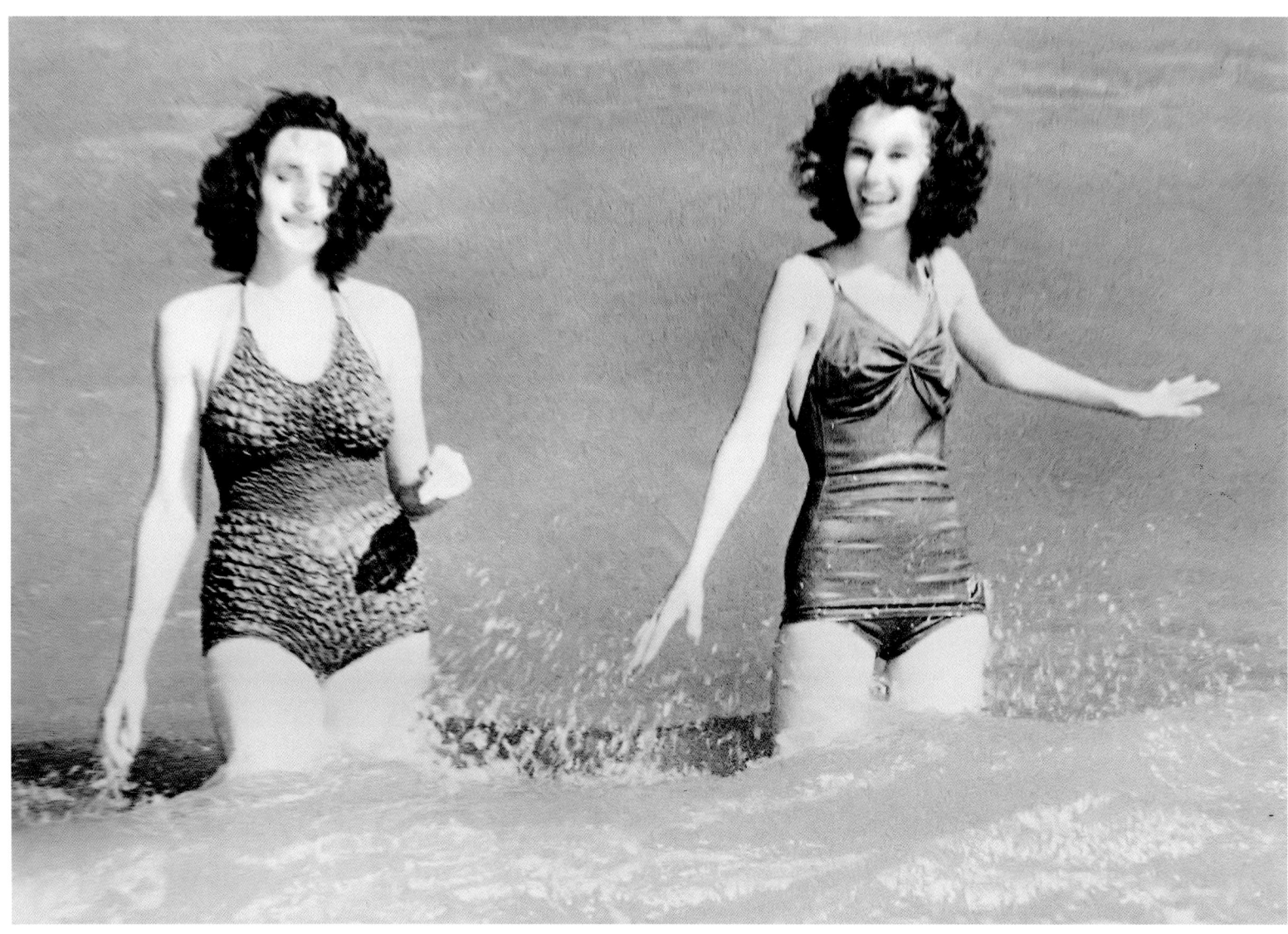

ABOVE: Having fun at
White Rock Lake. 1939.

OPPOSITE: White Rock Lake,
Dallas. Early 1940s.

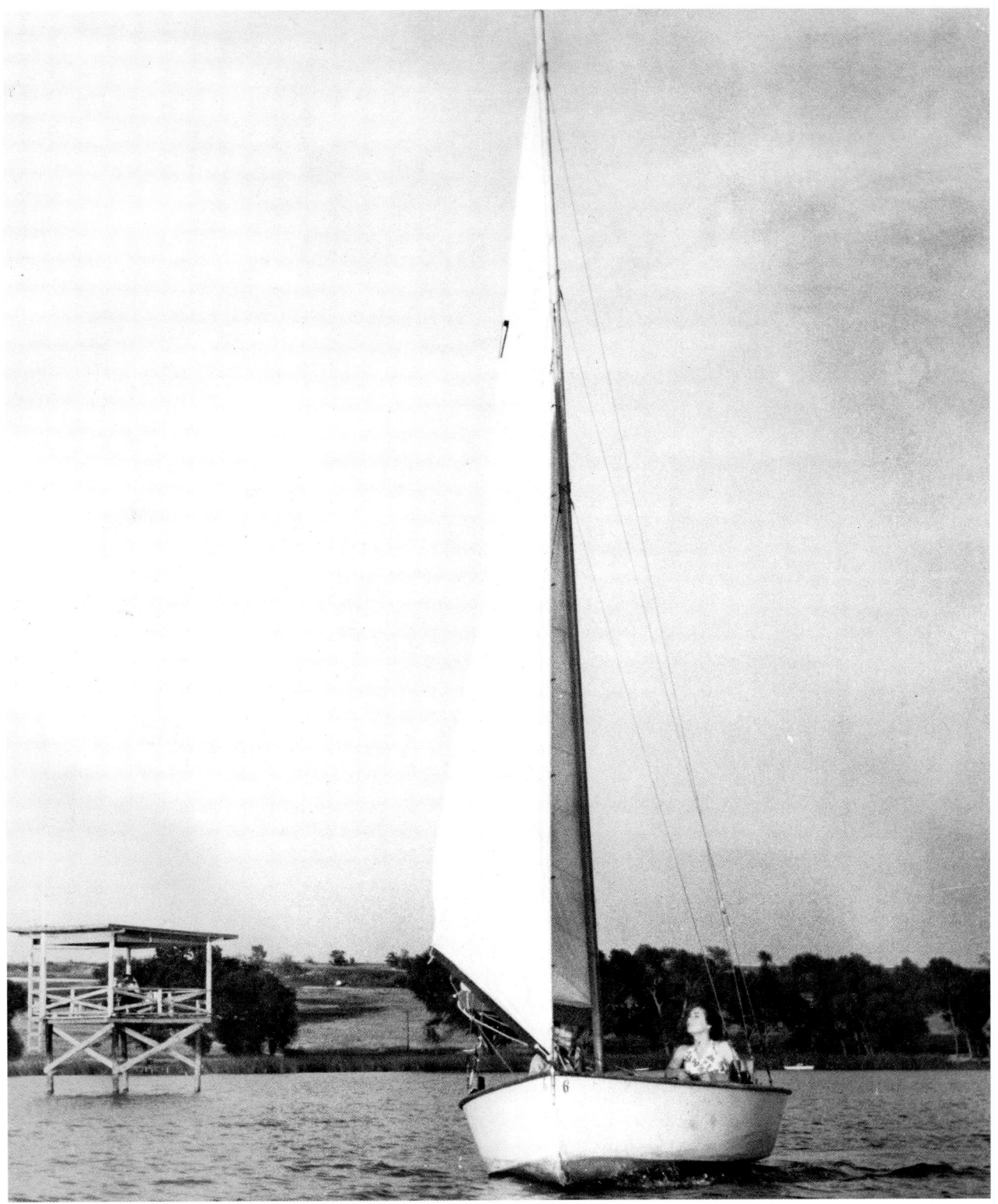

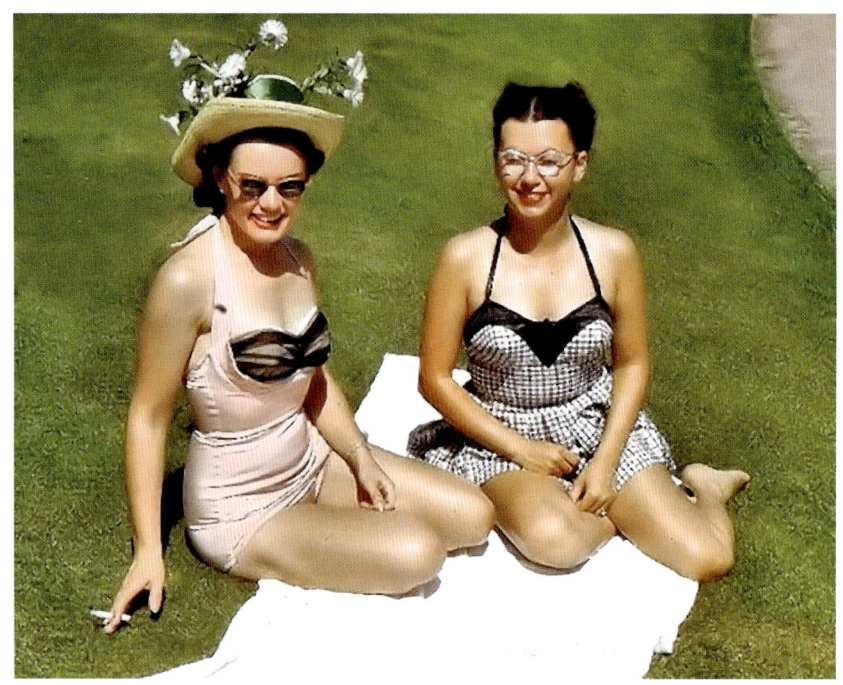

ABOVE: My mother, Martha, and my aunt, Betty Jane, at the beach. Two years later they would become the first women to be on the board of an NFL team when my dad and uncle bought the New York Yanks and brought them to town as the Dallas Texans. College football was at its peak, and in 1952 no one wanted to see grown men play the game, so we are still listed as the last NFL team to go bankrupt. 1950.

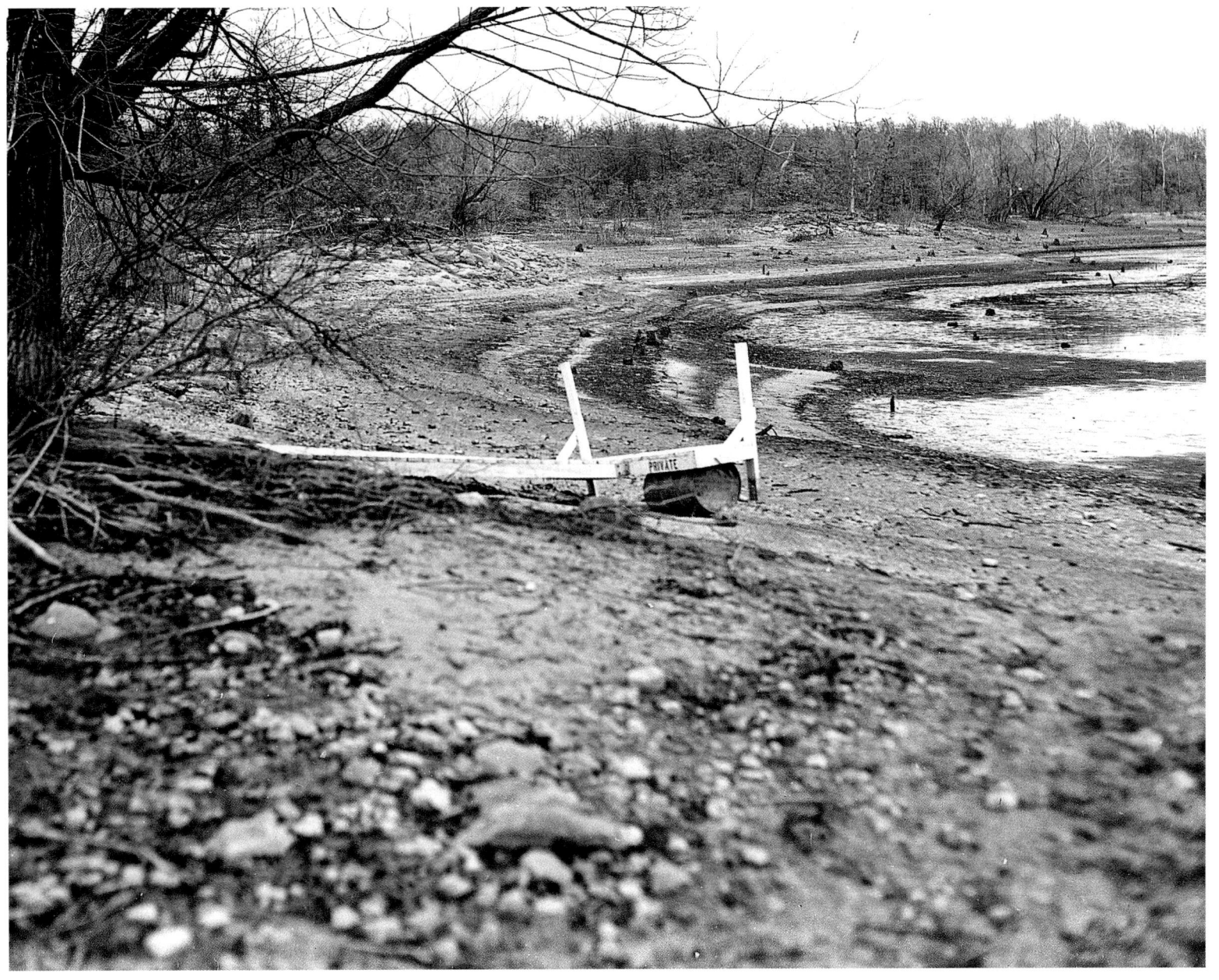

ABOVE: A several-years-long Texas drought began in 1948, bringing down lake levels everywhere. This is the small dock that belonged to our family's Crescent Oaks Ranch that had a quarter mile of Lake Dallas shoreline. Late 1940s.

Mid-Century
Interior Design

———

OPPOSITE: The home hi-fi rig, complete with plenty of shelf space for all those records. Hard to imagine that every song on every one of those albums could now be put on an external hard drive small enough to rattle around in your shirt pocket. 1950.

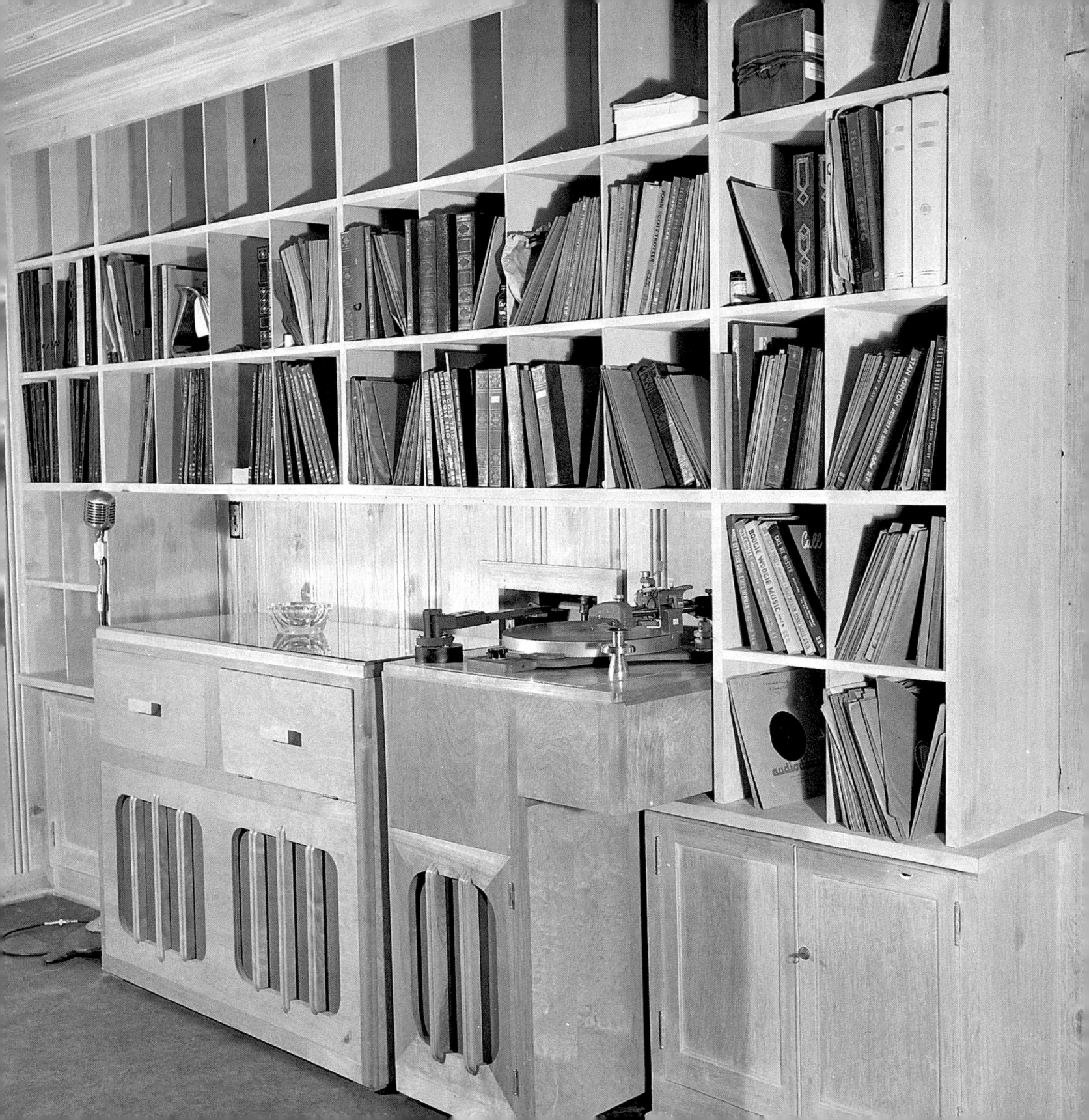

The term "mid-century design" now resonates strongly with everyone from interior designers to furniture builders to home restorers to "flippers." Providing historical context, designer Liza Kuhn explains, "In a post-World War II environment, designers and architects were eager to develop new ideas that married the mass production and technology invented during the first half of the twentieth century with a more optimistic outlook for the future." Since that style is considered existing from the post-art deco mid-1930s all the way to the space age's mid-1960s, it is not so easy to think that mid-century styling can be put in a box for display or illustrated in one or two pages of a magazine. Here we have some examples my father photographed during that period of both residential rooms and business offices.

———

RIGHT: A good example of mid-century casual furniture in this living area of my family's weekend retreat, a small cabin near Lewisville, Texas. Grady Cates, another Dallasite with a weekend retreat close to us, owned an old 1918 American LaFrance firetruck and would take all the kids in the area riding around nearby roads. 1954.

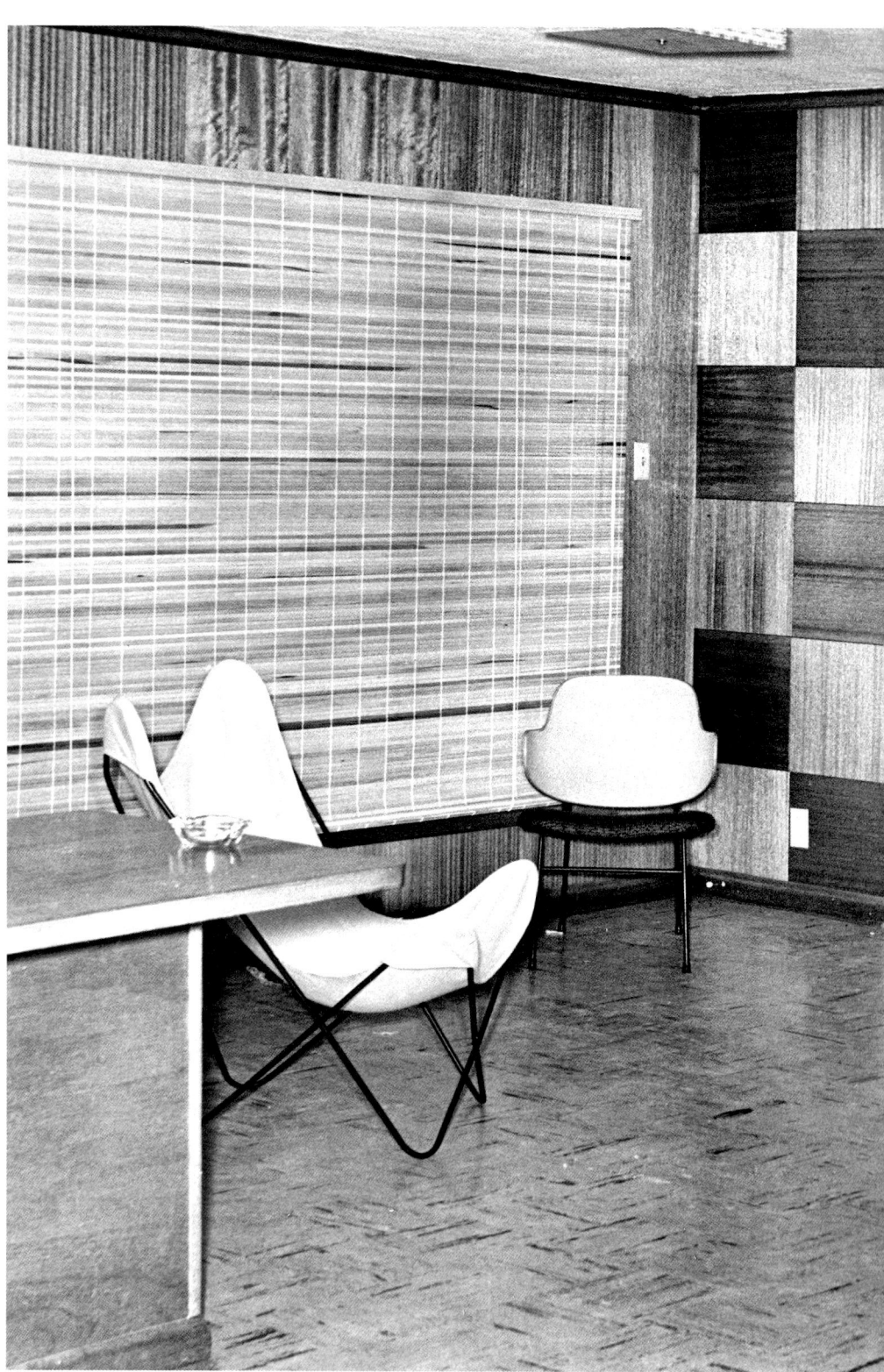

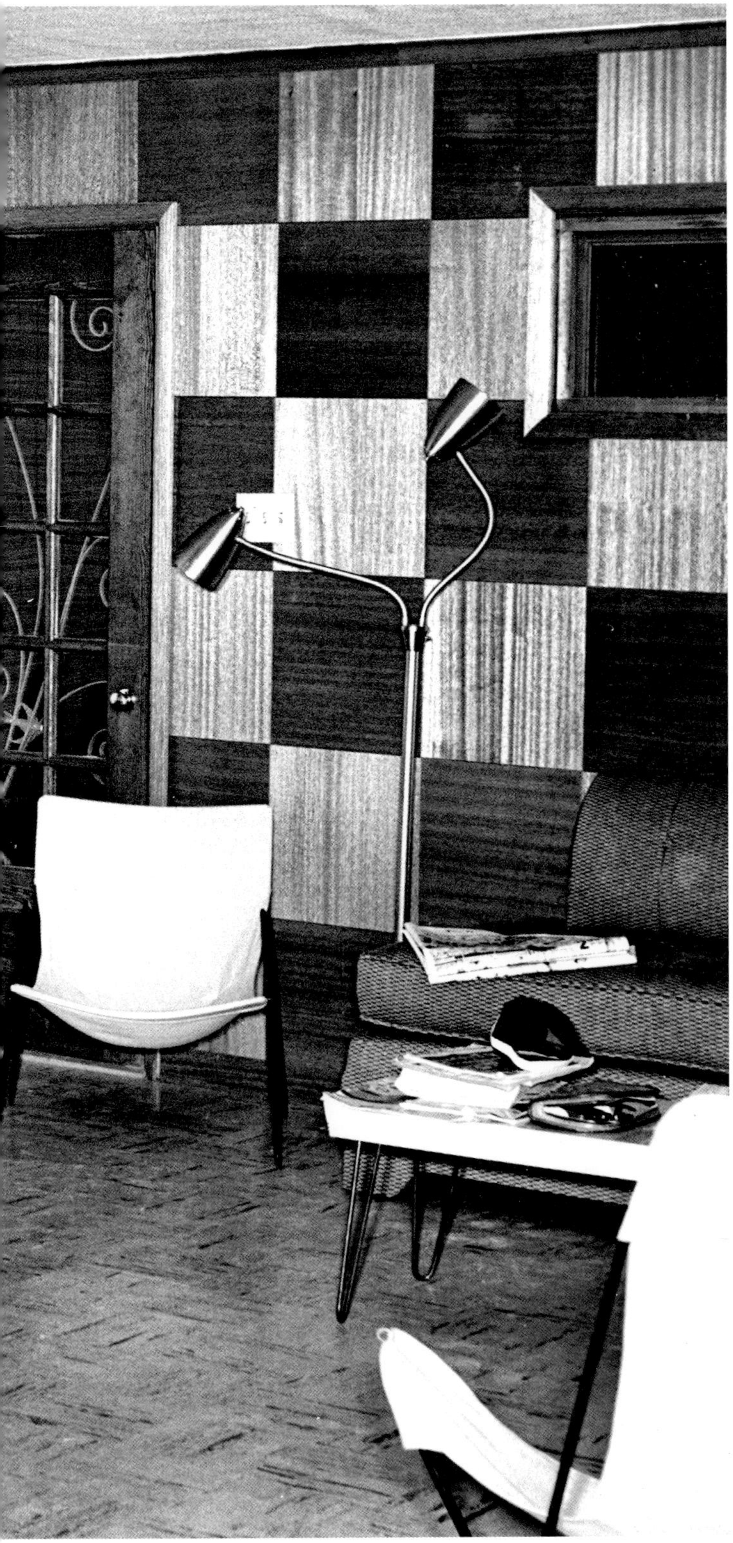

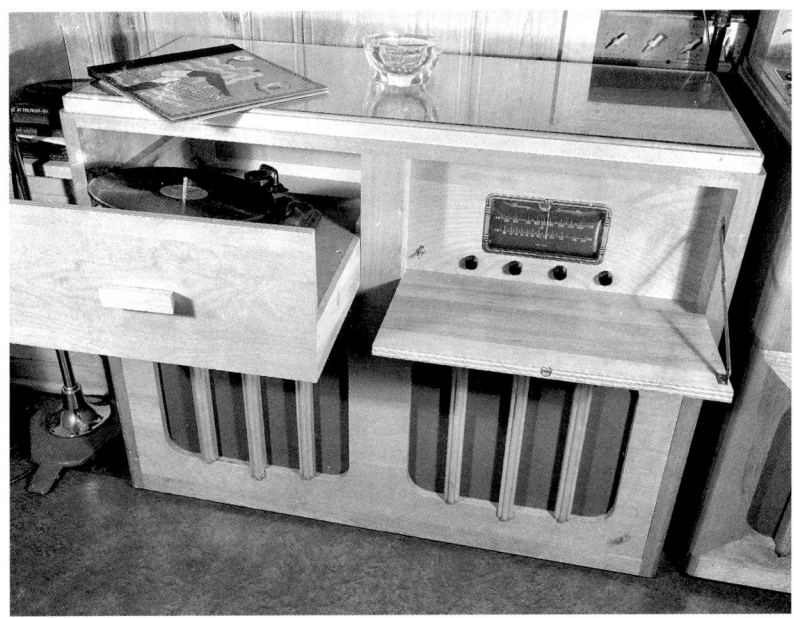

ABOVE: High-end 1947 home record player and radio set up. It was monaural (one channel) hi-fi that preceded the left and right stereo channels of today. The two speakers below only served to "fatten" the sound of the single musical track. 1950.

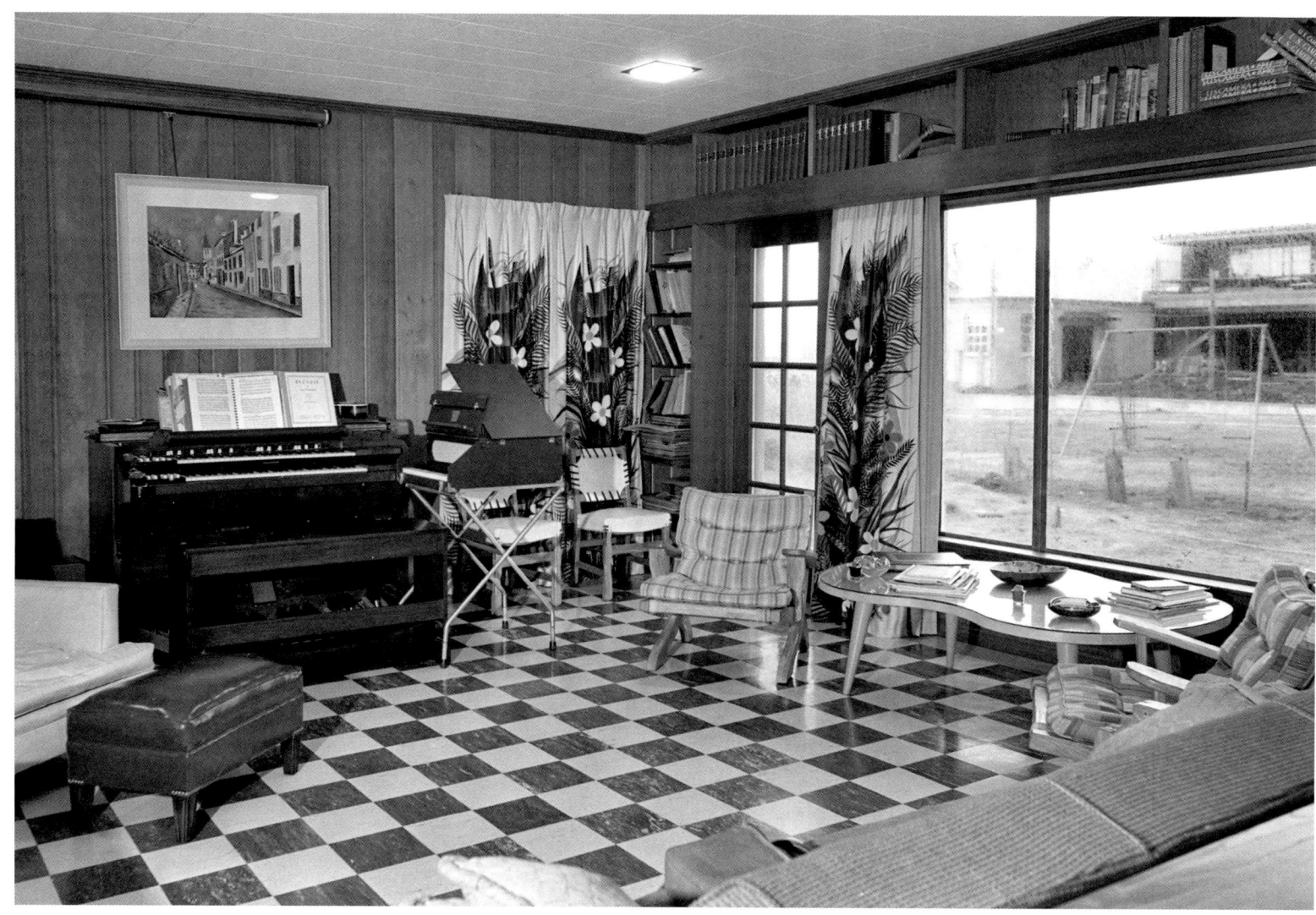

ABOVE: This was the game room of our home at 5373 Wenonah Drive in the Greenway Parks subdivision of Dallas. It was completed in 1952, and we lived there until 1959. Unfortunately, it no longer exists as it was sold in 2023, and the new owner immediately demolished it to build a new house. 1953.

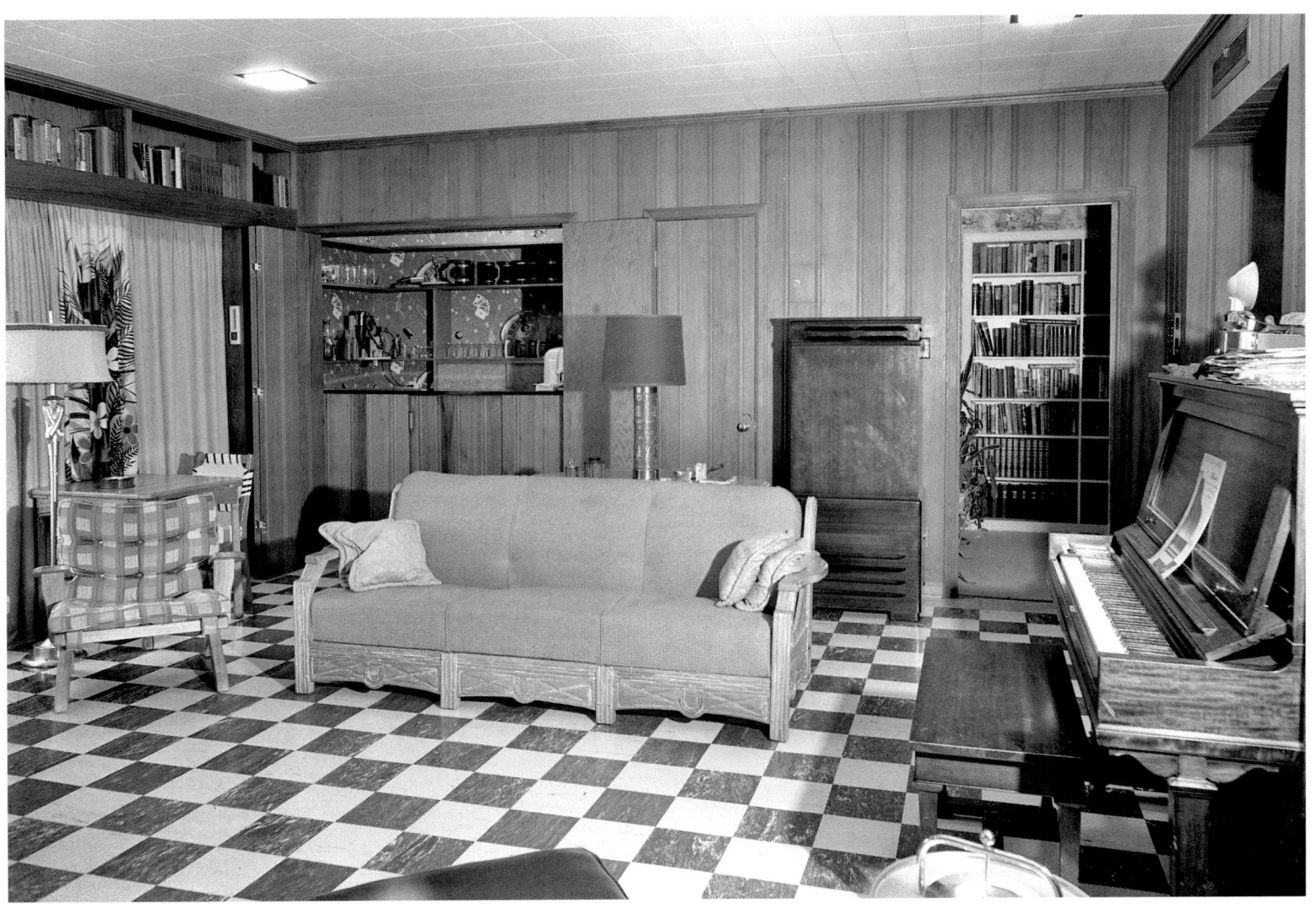

ABOVE: The other side of the game room. The bar area in the back was big enough for two and featured a refrigerator and sink. 1953.

Law Enforcement

———

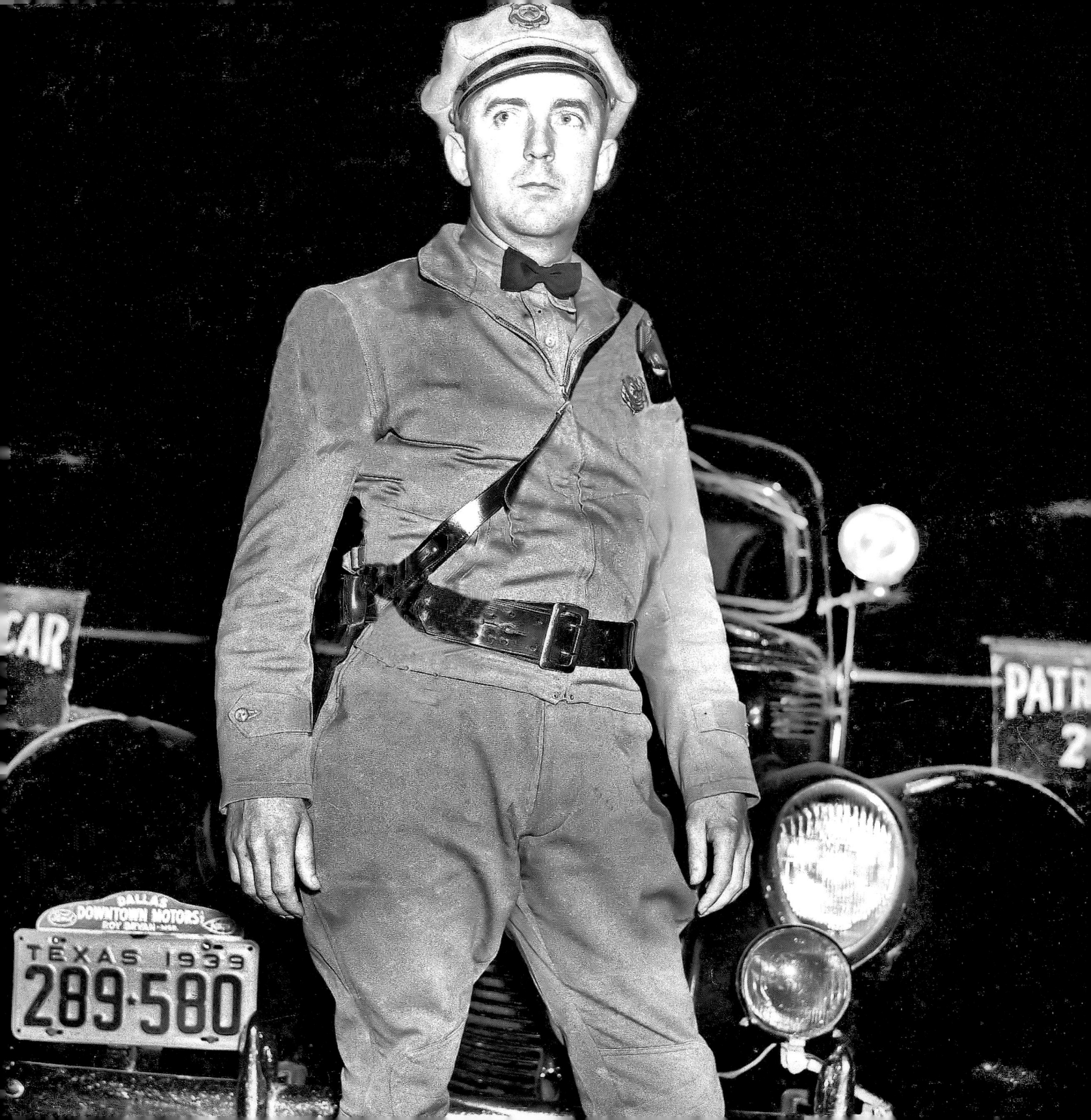

Over the years, through his "street" photography and being called upon on occasion to shoot law enforcement affairs and occasional police and sheriff's department assistance at Bonehead Club events, Dad developed many friends in both departments. After working on a few projects with the Tarrant County Sheriff's Office in 1947, he was even made a Deputy Sheriff (and with no "Honorary" marked on his certificate!). Unfortunately, I have no knowledge of his side career as a Tarrant County crime fighter.

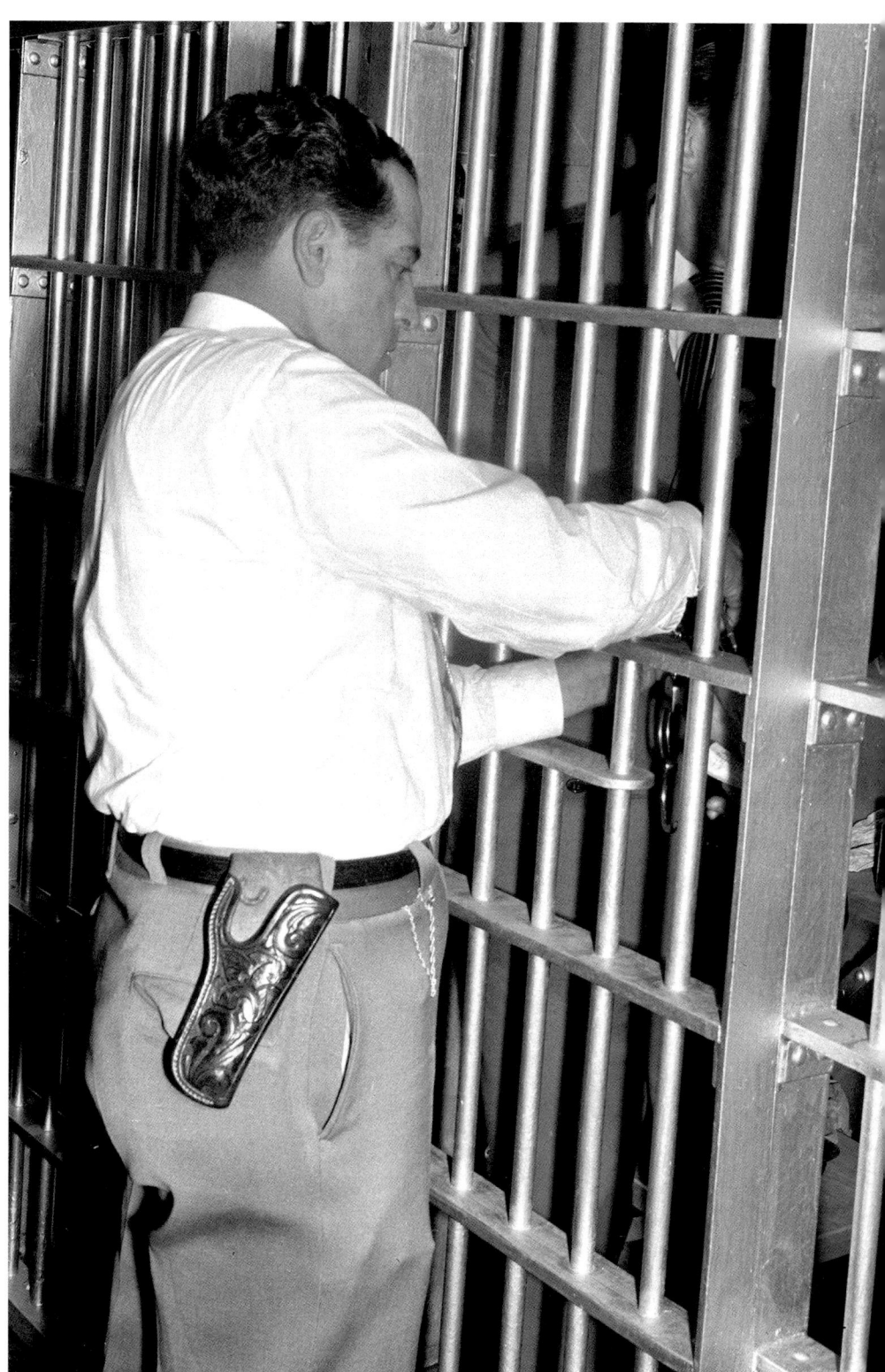

RIGHT: Members of the Dallas Police Department demonstrating lock up procedures on a colleague. 1947.

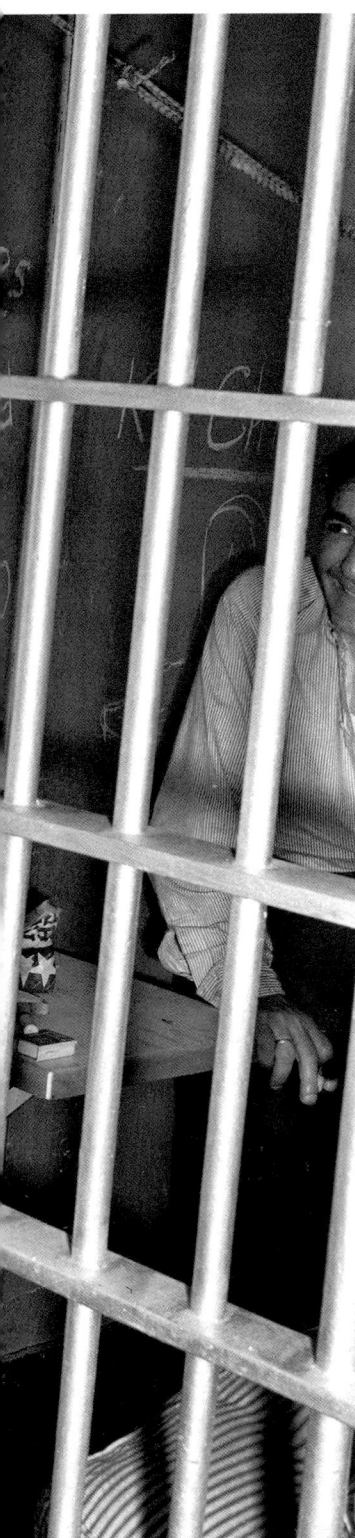

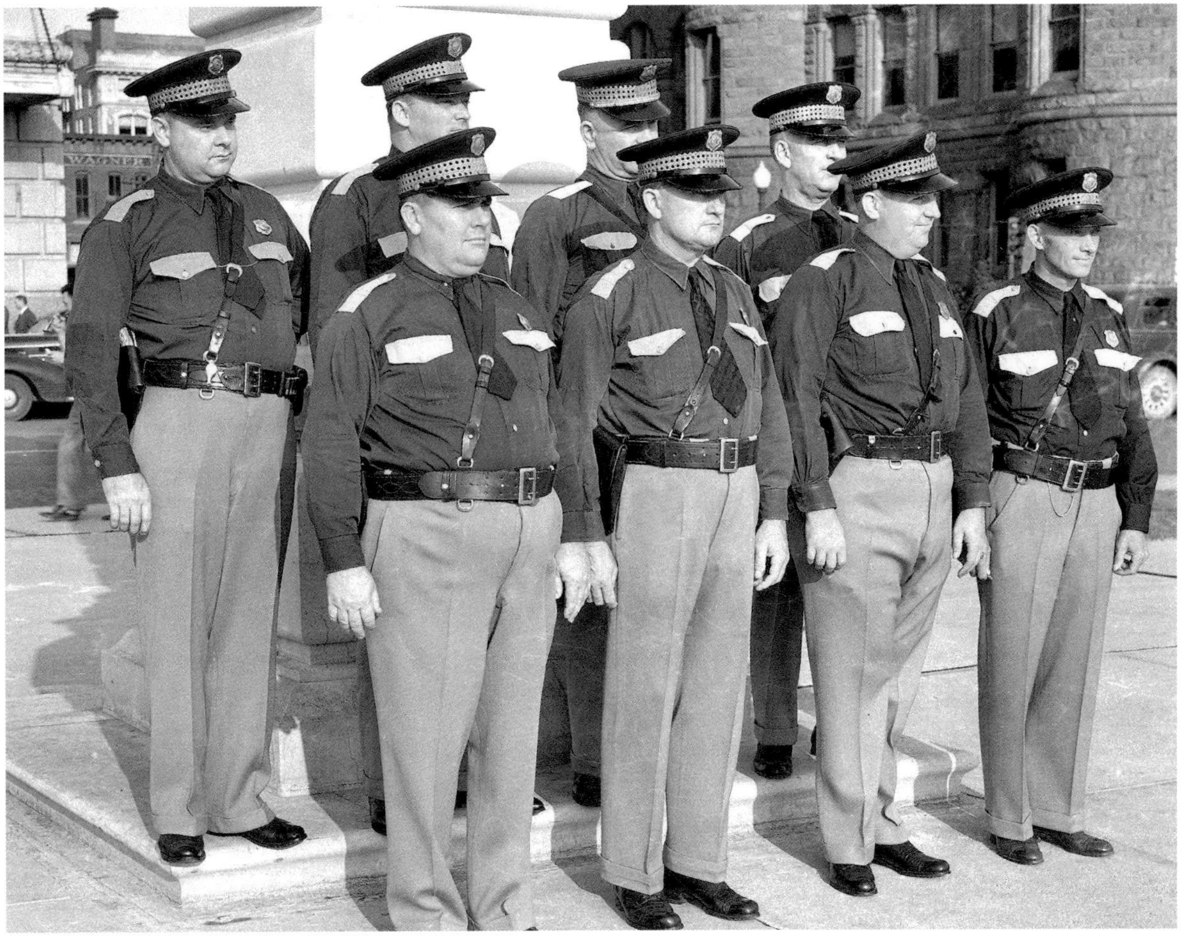

ABOVE: Members of Dallas Police Department. Early 1940s.

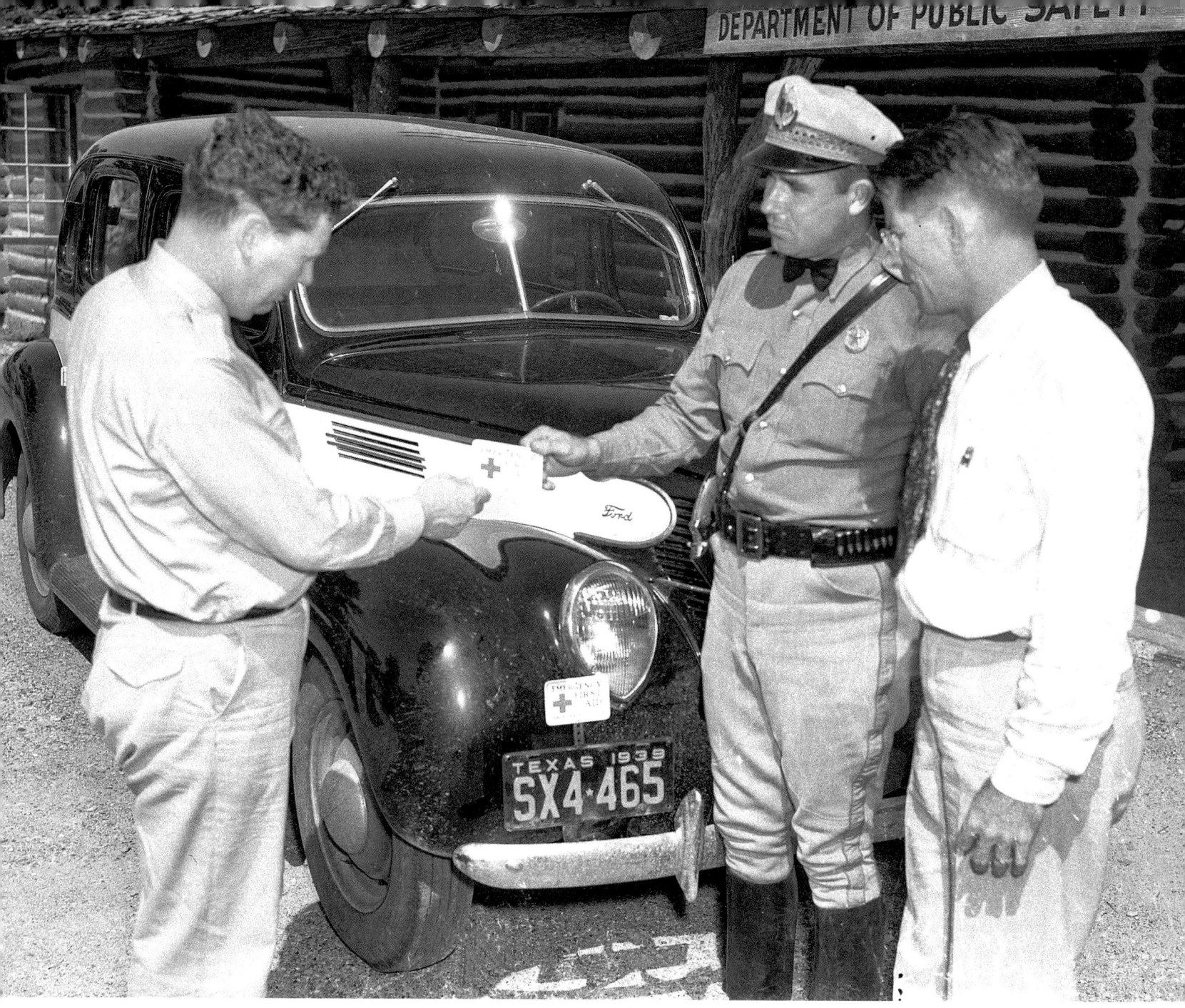

ABOVE: Capt. Draper of the Dallas station of the Texas Department of Public Safety issuing a permit, possibly a hospital parking pass. 1939.

RIGHT: For those that are prone to run, this was a deterrent used by the Dallas Police Department. Photo taken at downtown Dallas police station. 1941.

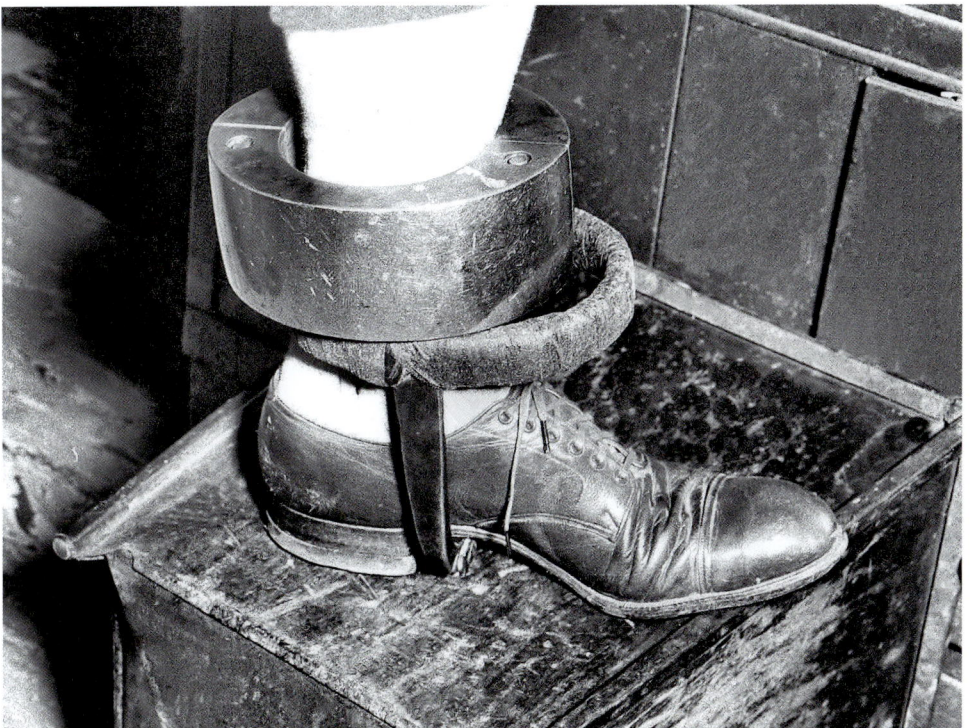

	T-Man No. **867**
License No._____	Date_____
Traveling N, S, E, W, Inbound, Outbound, Time_____ A. M._____ P. M._____
On_____ At_____

☐ Speeding
☐ Ran Red Light   ☐ Flashing Red Light
☐ Ran Stop Sign
☐ Disregarded Pedestrians
☐ Turned from Wrong Lane
☐ Driving Wrong Side of Street
☐ Driving Wrong Way on One-Way Street
☐ Illegal left turn

☐ Illegal Parking (specify kind)
☐ Cutting in Ahead of Another Vehicle
☐ Passing Stopped Streetcar or Bus
☐ Reckless Weaving
☐ No Arm Signal   ☐ Wrong Signal
☐ Defective Headlights
☐ Defective Tail-Light
☐ Double Parked

Remarks:
_____
_____

Owner_____

Address_____

ABOVE: In 1953, Dallas created the Citizens Traffic Commission, and Dad was on it. The T-Man cards contained blanks where information regarding someone's driving infraction was to be noted. After the city received it, the offender would receive a letter stating his or her infraction and the city's hope that it would not happen again. 1953.

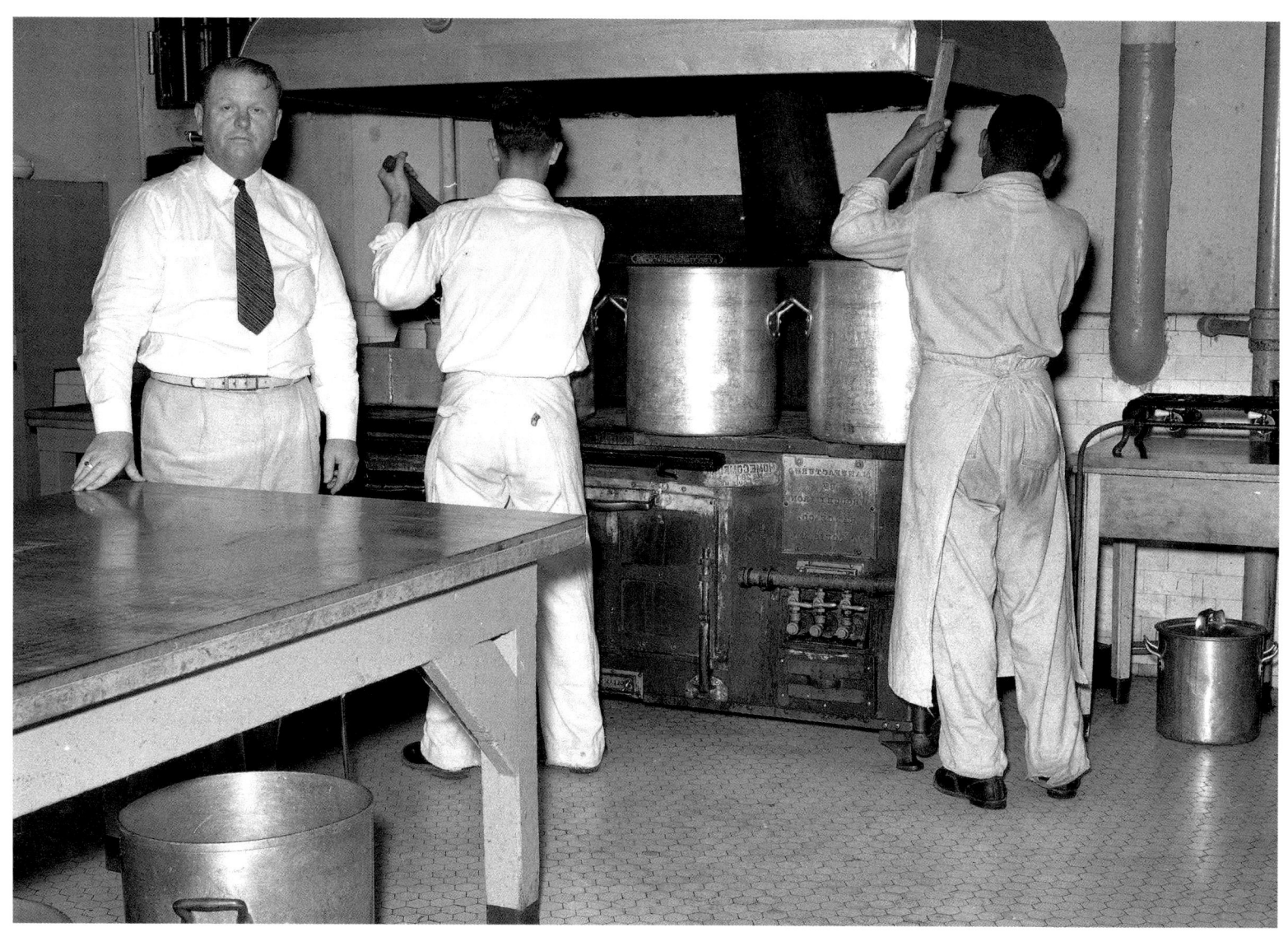

ABOVE: Dallas City Jail kitchen. 1947.

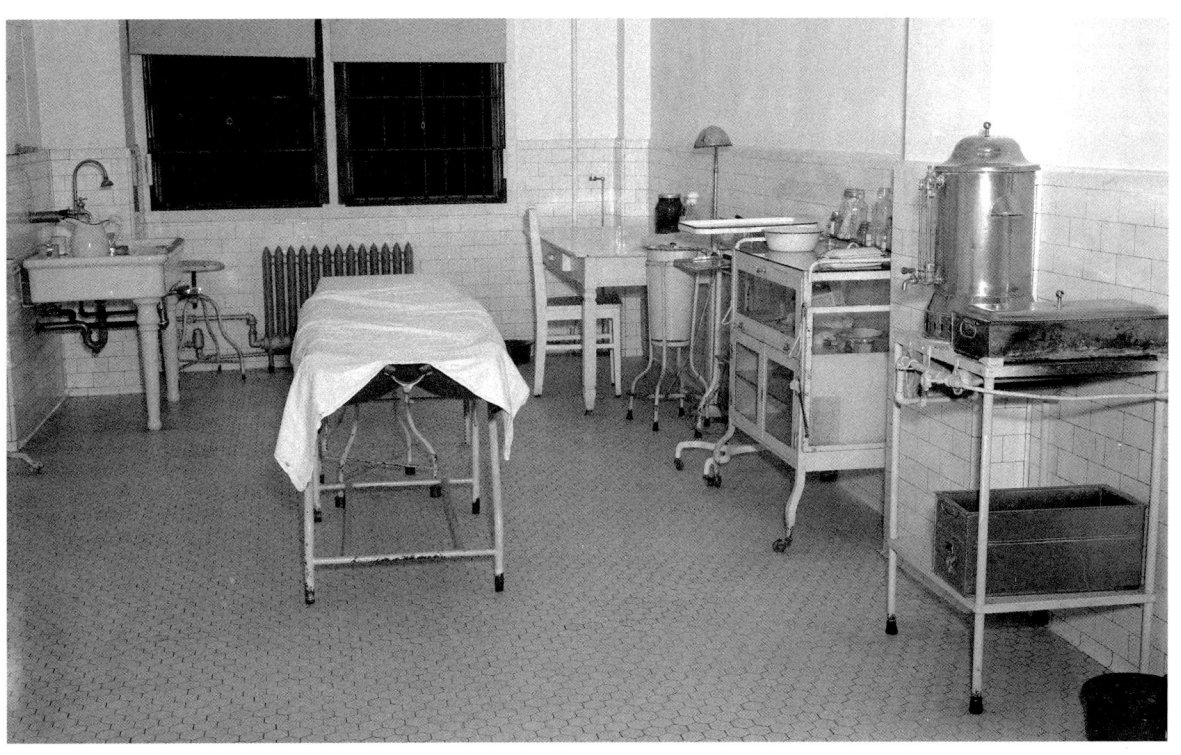

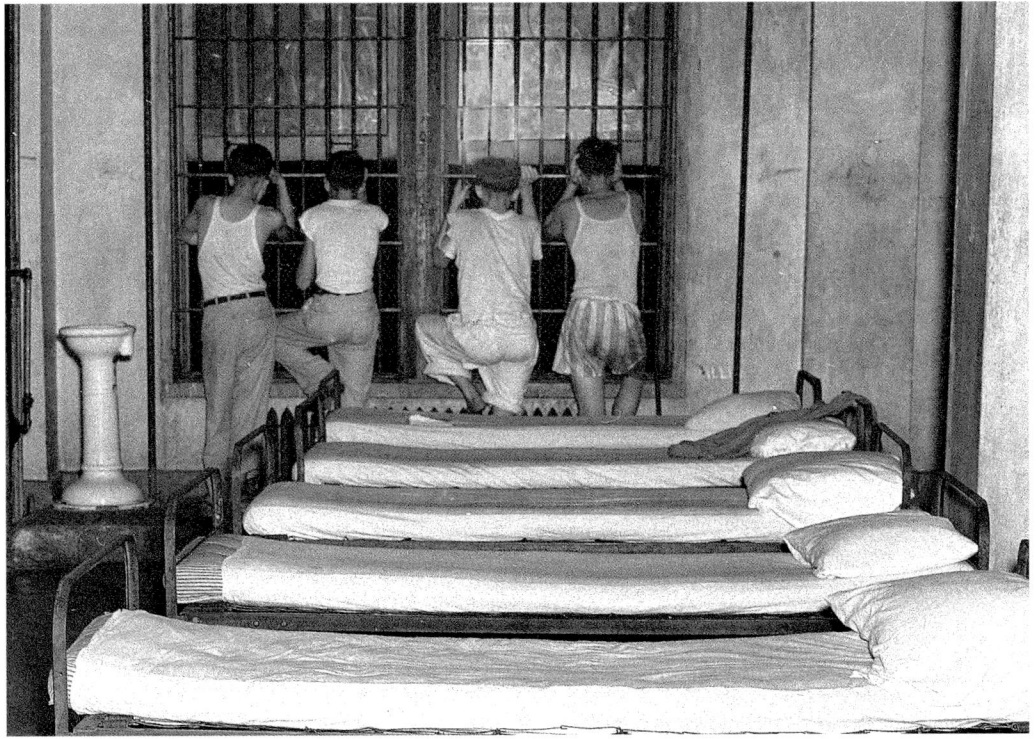

ABOVE: Autopsy room in the Dallas City Jail. 1947.

LEFT: Four young males peering through barred windows in Dallas City Jail and their sleeping accommodations. 1947.

Bonehead Club

———

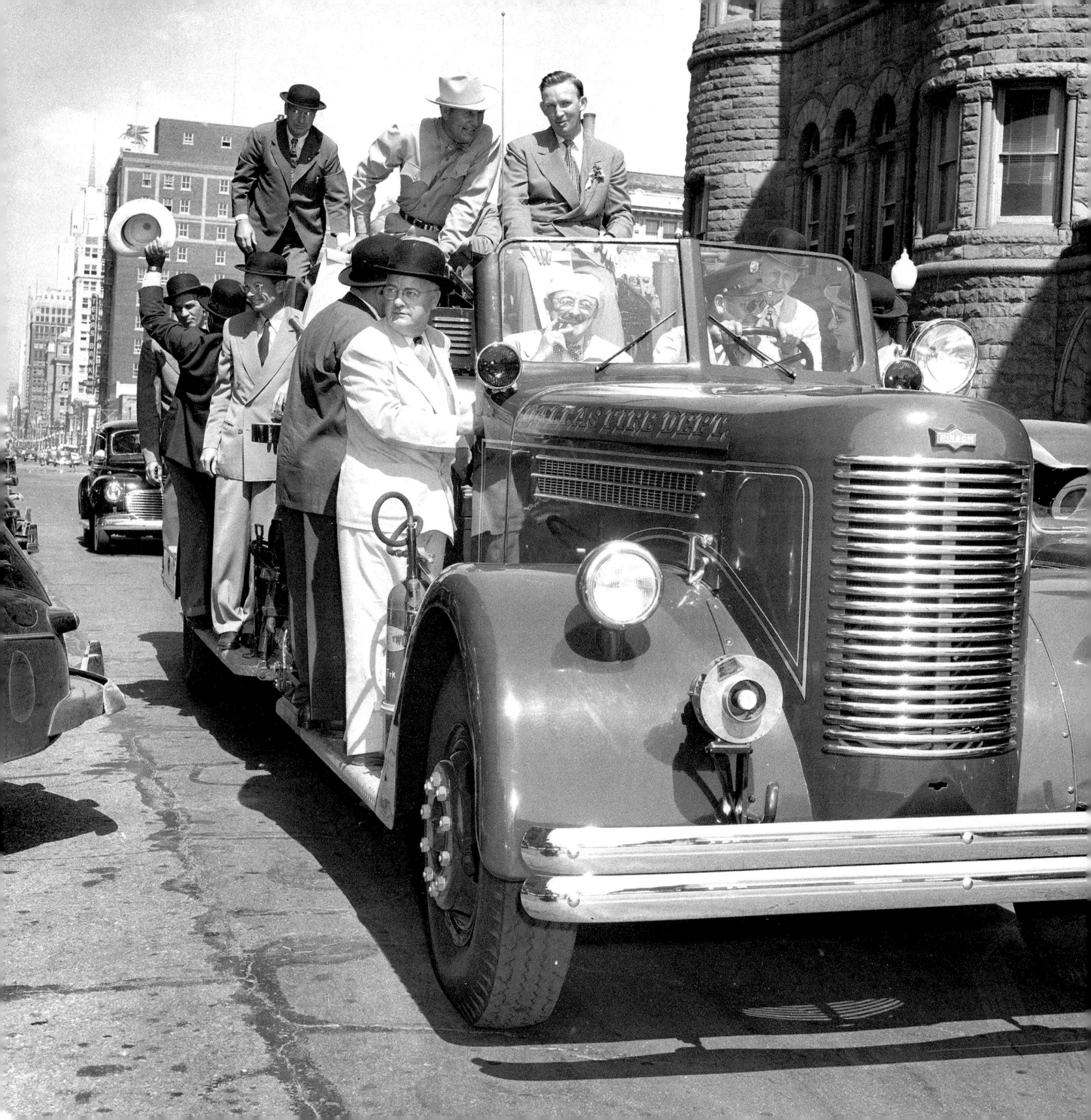

During World War I, a number of Dallas businessmen, lawyers, doctors, and other professionals would gather at a local hotel's dining room to share any news from the front lines their sons were sending back. To overcome the usual somberness of what they were receiving, they decided humor was their saving grace as the war reportage grew worse. They started wearing women's hats to the meetings and, as it developed into a real club, began electing officers, with the president being called the "Big Chief" and all the other members being given the title of "Vice President."

As their meetings undoubtedly became more boisterous, club lore tells us that when a complaint was lodged with the manager of the restaurant, his response was: "Sorry, there's nothing I can do about those boneheads." And suddenly they had a name!

The Bonehead Club continues to this day, and the city of Dallas has always enjoyed their antics. Perhaps the best known and longest lasting one over the years is the annual ride on a firetruck to the State Fair grounds to "officially" close the fair the day before it officially opens! My dad was a Bonehead member—the "Big Chief" in 1948—and in 1953, I got to ride on the firetruck with him to do the annual "closing" for that year.

Among the more well-known projects the Bonehead Club has sponsored was the wedding of Josephine and Napoleon, the Dallas Zoo's camels. The club's participation in a Dallas beautification project was to plant a large oak tree in the center of the intersection of Akard and Commerce streets. Another time they sent a small bottle of water taken from the Trinity River to a soldier in Korea to help him think of home. Their Christmas parties are usually held in April. After Herbert and Nelson "Bunker" Hunt lost almost a billion dollars in their attempt to corner the silver market in the late seventies, they were given the Bonehead of the Year Award at a large banquet. The brothers smiled, graciously accepting the award while wearing outrageously flowered ladies hats!

The Boneheads constantly remind everyone not to take things too seriously. The club's longstanding motto is: "To learn more and more about less and less until, eventually, we shall know everything about nothing."

————

RIGHT: "Big Chief" Connell Miller standing in front of a relic of the Bonehead U Driving School. 1949.

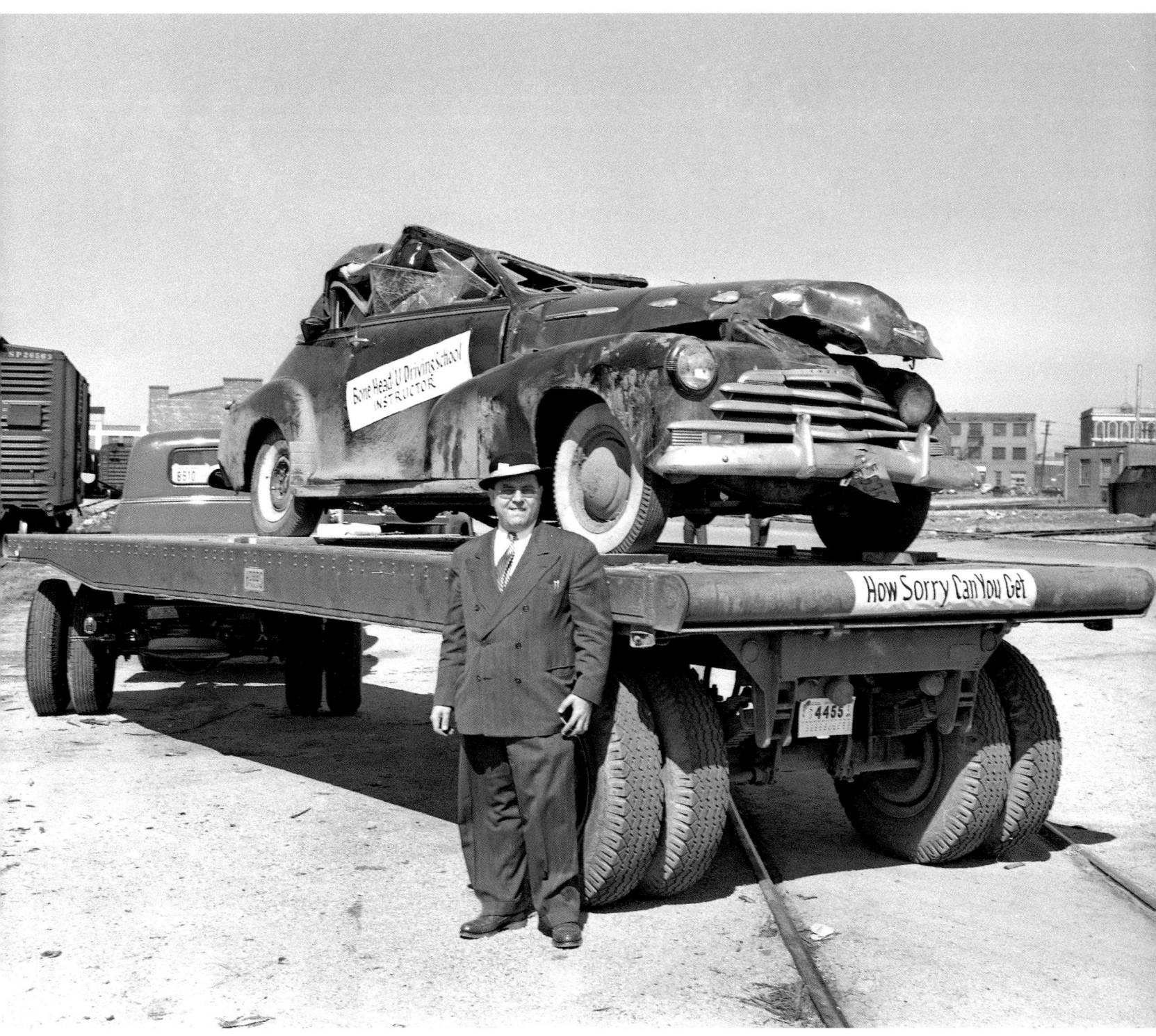

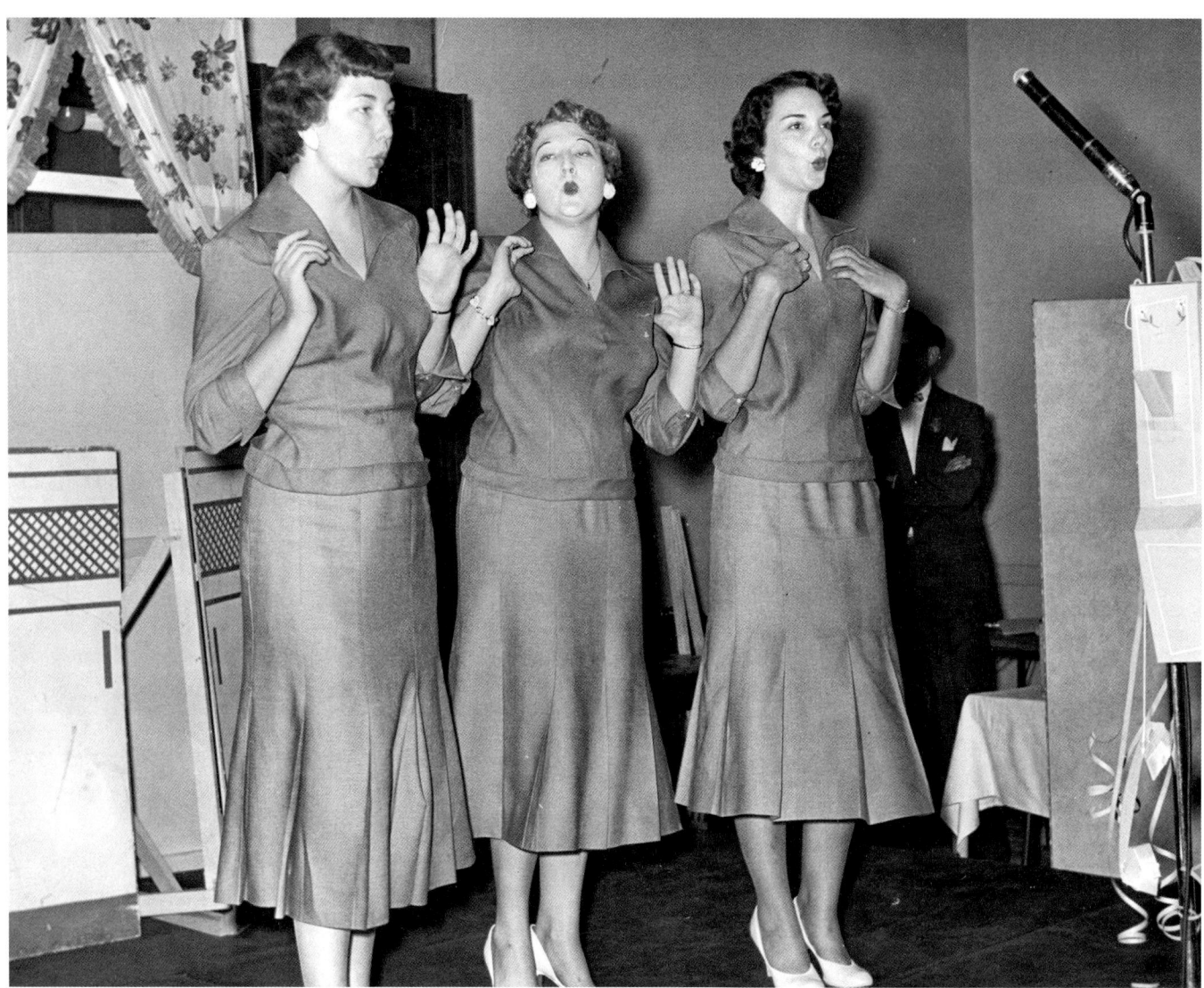

ABOVE: A little entertainment during the
Christmas Party . . . held in April, of course. 1954.

OPPOSITE: "Cigarette Girl" circulating at the
Christmas Party. 1954.

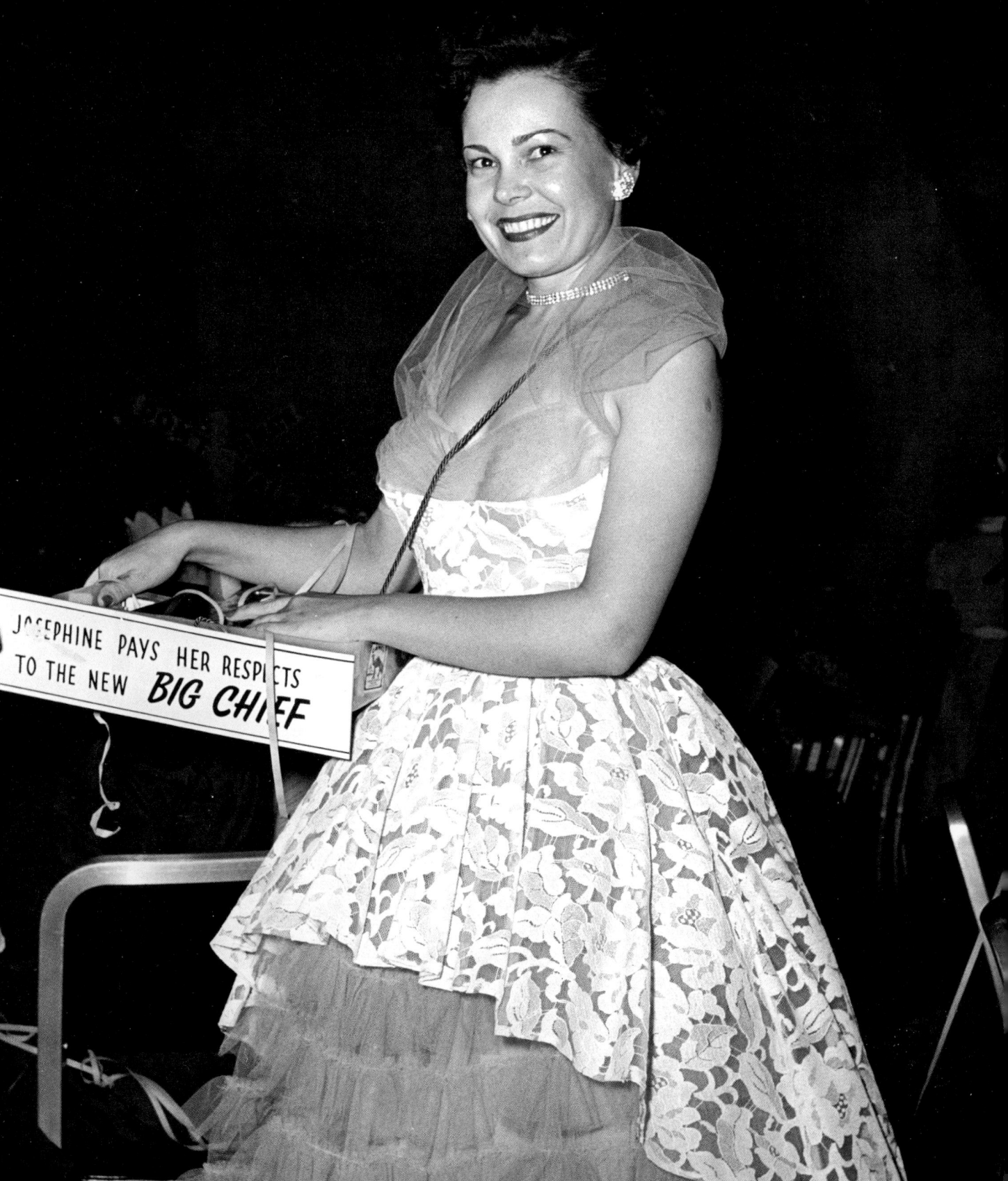

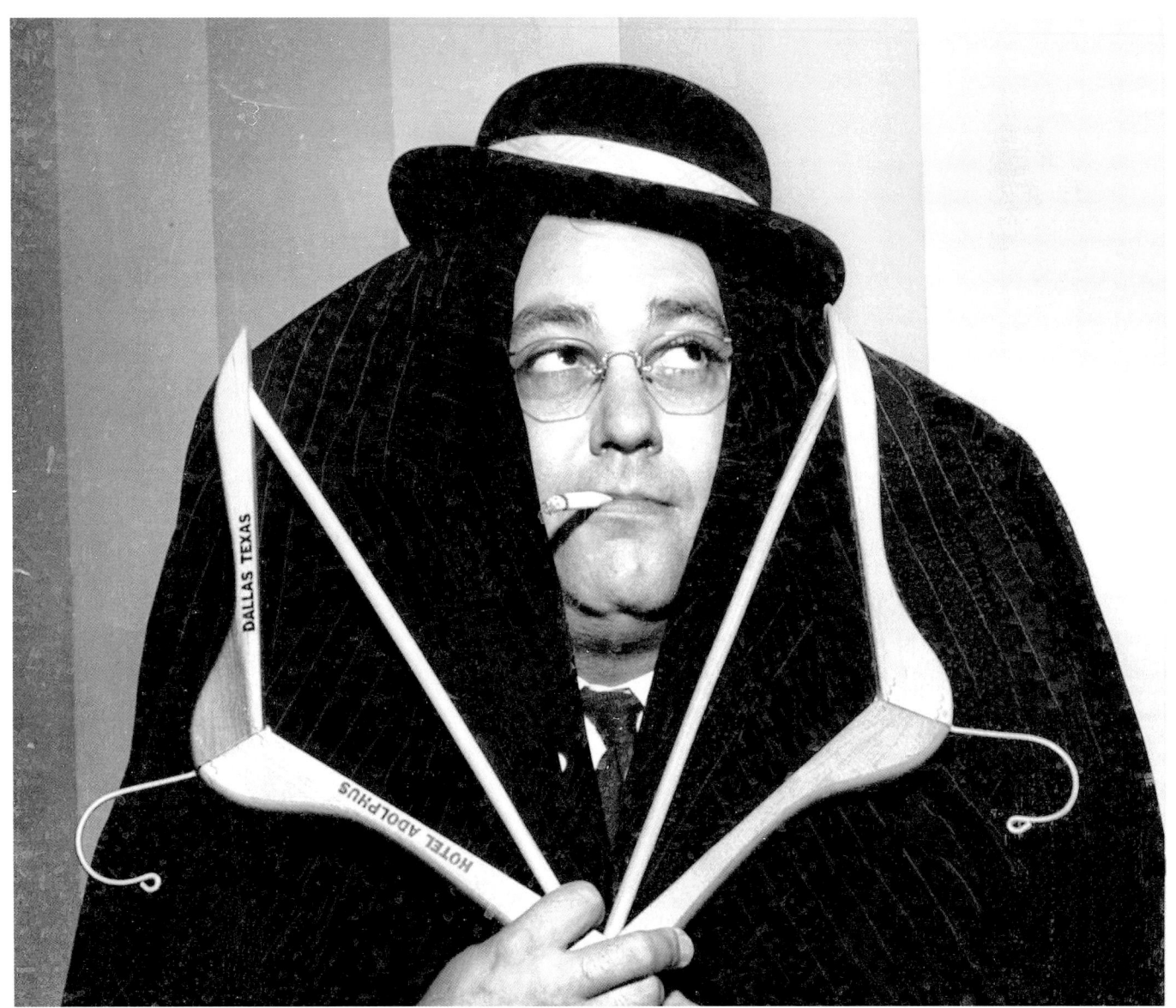

ABOVE: My dad, who was also a Bonehead member, posing for a formal club photo. 1951.

OPPOSITE: Sometimes the best ideas come to you while you're playing music! Early 1950s.

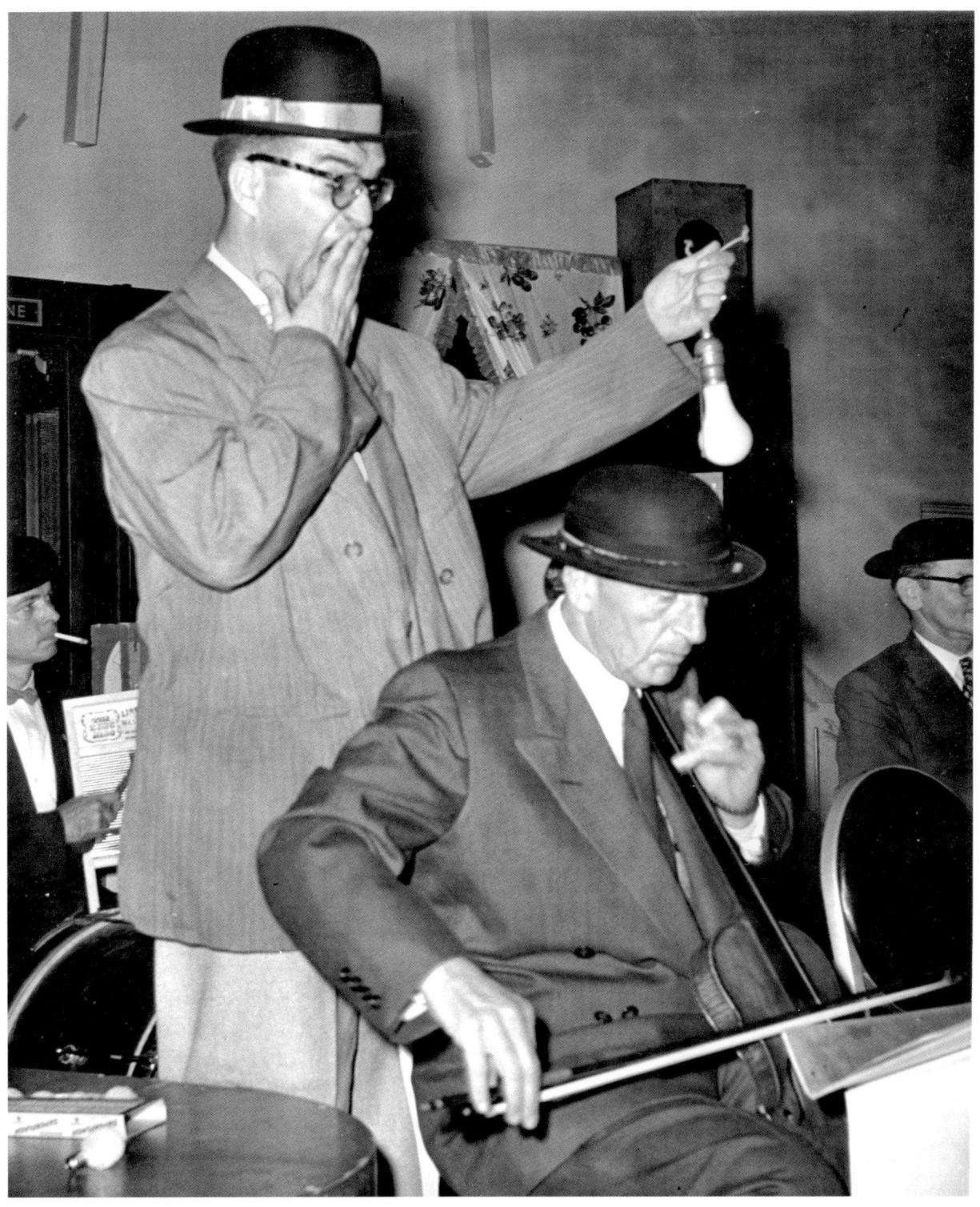

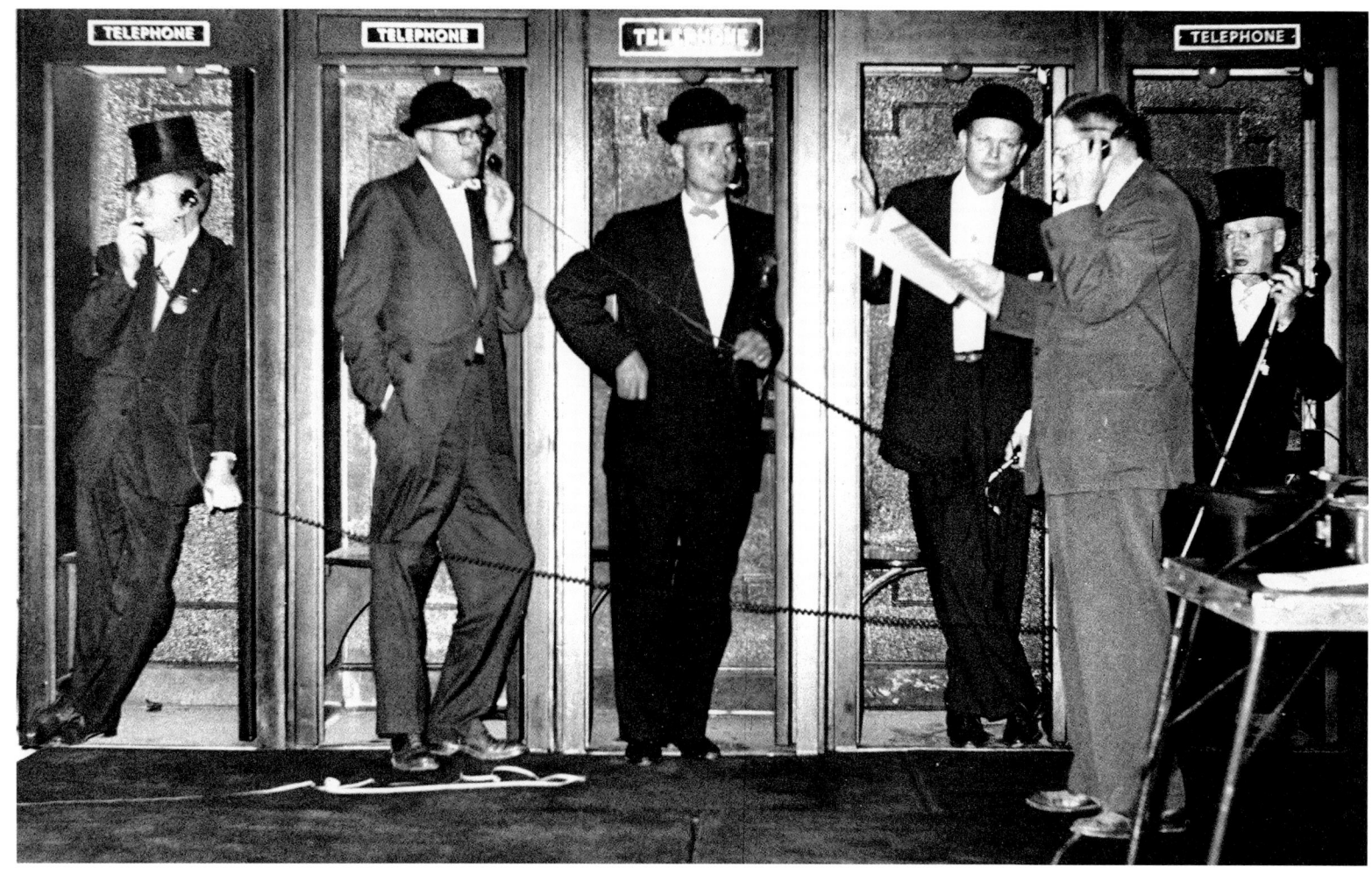

ABOVE: Four Bonehead Club members posing in telephone booths. Almost tempted to call this the Bonehead Club's "Call Center." 1951.

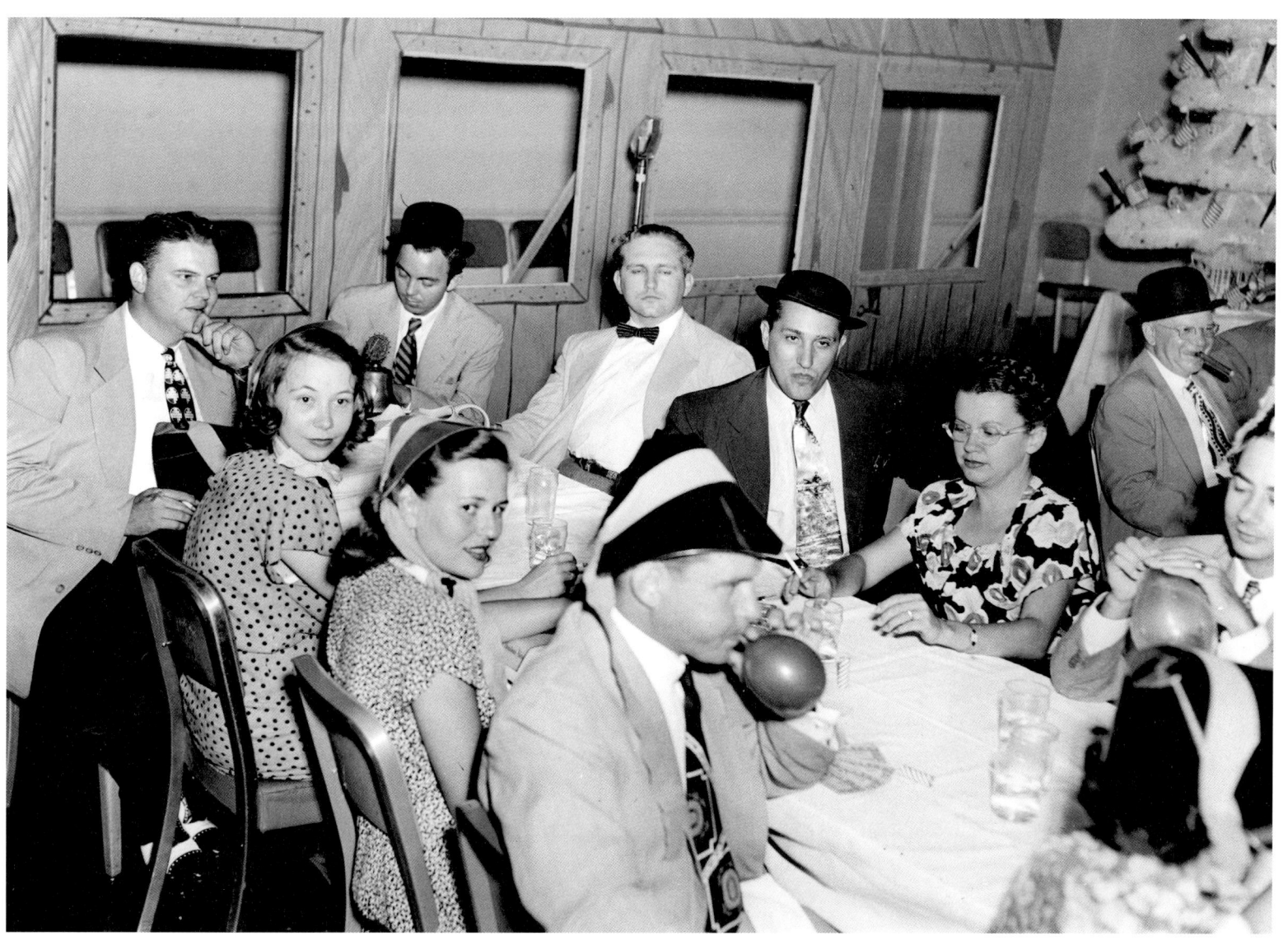

ABOVE: Bonehead Club dinner. With his hand on his chin, Miller Bros. executive Scott DeLee is seated on the far left, with his wife Nancy next to him. Gordon McLendon, dubbed the "Old Scotchman" and radio empresario of KLIF, appears across from him, staring down with a bowler hat. My Uncle Giles, wearing a dark suit and a bowler hat, is sitting next to my Aunt Betty. 1950s.

Automobiles

———

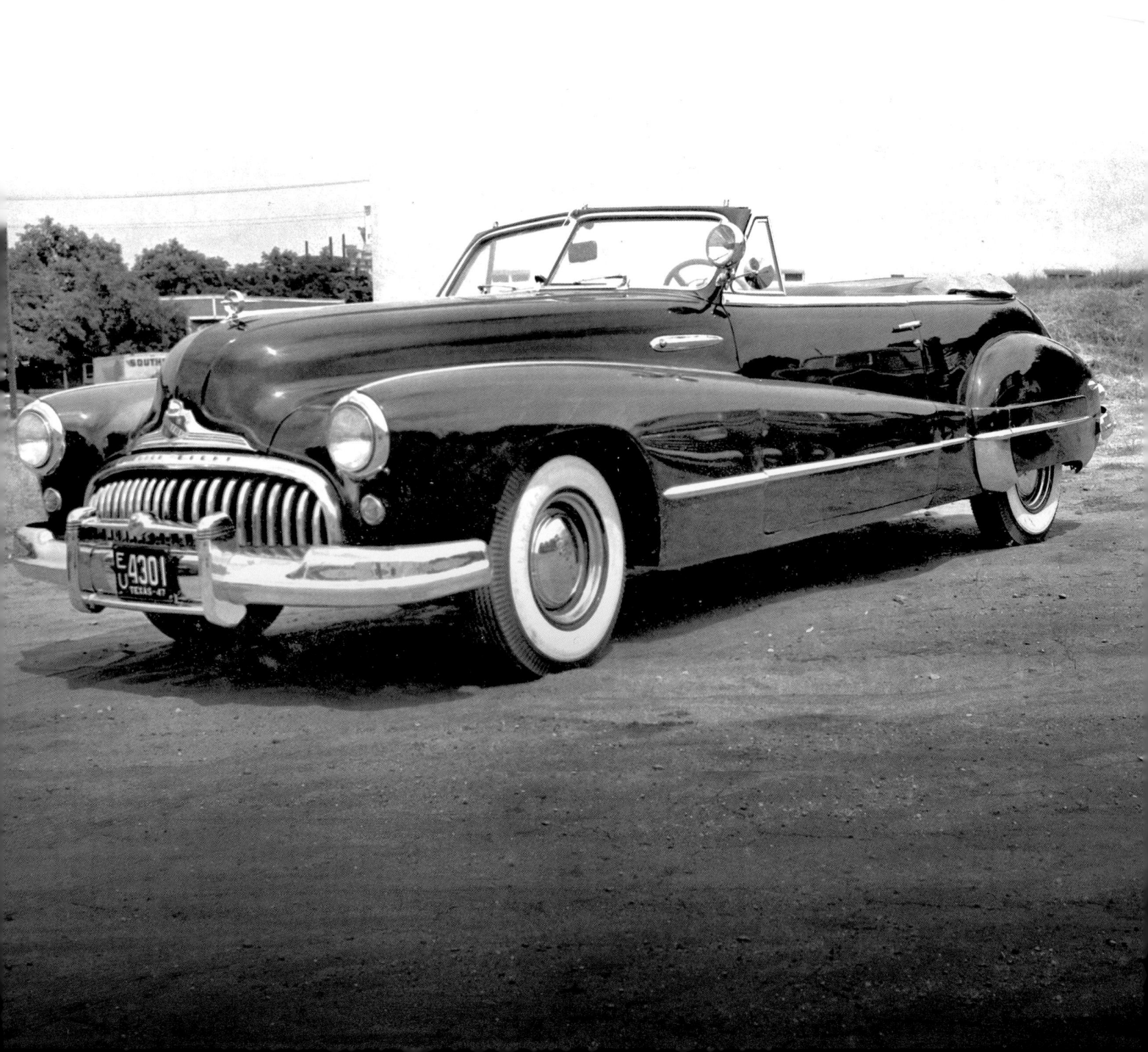

Dad was a true automotive gearhead here in a city that absolutely loves anything on wheels driven by a motor! Whether it was shiny new autos on a showroom floor, an old flivver parked in a field, or a sleek race car speeding down one of the many tracks in the Dallas area, he was often there, Speed Graphic in hand, to photograph it. This section begins with the images of a few of the cars our family owned over the years, plus two early Packard's, one of which, a 1940 model, belonged to Dad's friend.

With his interest in motorsports, you will also see a few of his racing photos taken at Dallas-area tracks. If one wonders when automobile racing first began here, it likely resulted from the moment one car owner said to another: "I'll bet my car is faster than yours!" The story of a local Dallasite issuing such a boast to his friend seems to persist more often than the others, so I will go with it.

However, we can pinpoint the owner of the first car in Dallas—Col. E. H. R. Green, a local railroad owner and son of financier Hetty Green, who was known as the "Witch of Wall Street." Hetty was also called the most miserly woman in America. Despite her wealth, she would not pay for medical treatment for her son's broken leg, which resulted in its amputation. She was also said to keep small scraps of soap in a box to use.

Green's opponent, who probably countered with: "I believe my horseless carriage can easily outrun yours," is said to have been one Samuel H. Boren,

according to his son, Horace Boren. The elder Boren was a Dallas oilman whose wife, Ella, was the daughter of United States Senator Horace Chilton. Unfortunately, the details and result of that first car race have been lost to time and there is now no one still around who may have witnessed it.

After those beginnings, racing took a foothold and several horse racing tracks being used for the automobiles were supplemented by new ones built strictly for car racing events. Here are photographs my father shot at several different race tracks, starting in the late 1930s. Most are of the midgets, a class that was at the peak of popularity with both racers and spectators all the way up to the '60s. The three tracks drawing the largest crowds and who were among those that stood the test of time, keeping their gates open the longest, were: (1) the track by the Cotton Bowl on the State Fairgrounds, (2) Arlington Downs in Arlington, and (3) the Devil's Bowl, located behind the Buckner Boulevard Drive-In Theatre in Dallas. The Devil's Bowl, where the World of Outlaws sprint car organization later was founded, is still open and hosting weekly race events in its newer Mesquite location.

Dad was also the chief photographer for the Texas Region of the Sports Car Club of America. In March 1954, he and I went to Austin to shoot the huge "Lone Star National Sports Car Race" at Bergstrom Air Force Base, the next to last race we covered before his death in November. The event's grand

marshal was actor and Lieutenant. Colonel (and future Brigadier General) Jimmy Stewart, and the special guest was the last living veteran of the Civil War, 111-year-old Walter Williams. This was during the years when Air Force General Curtis E. LeMay, a racing devotee who owned an English-made Allard with a Cadillac engine, approved of using military airbases for sports car racing events. His reasoning was that the facilities would boost troop morale, make money from concessions they sold, and generate interest in that branch of the service with young spectators of military age. LeMay's Allard later was bought and drag raced by Dallas photographer L. C. Kirby, who lived in the old Higginbotham home on Swiss Avenue. Kirby eventually sold the Allard to build the smaller and lighter Cadillac-powered, Italian Bandini that most racegoers remember.

———

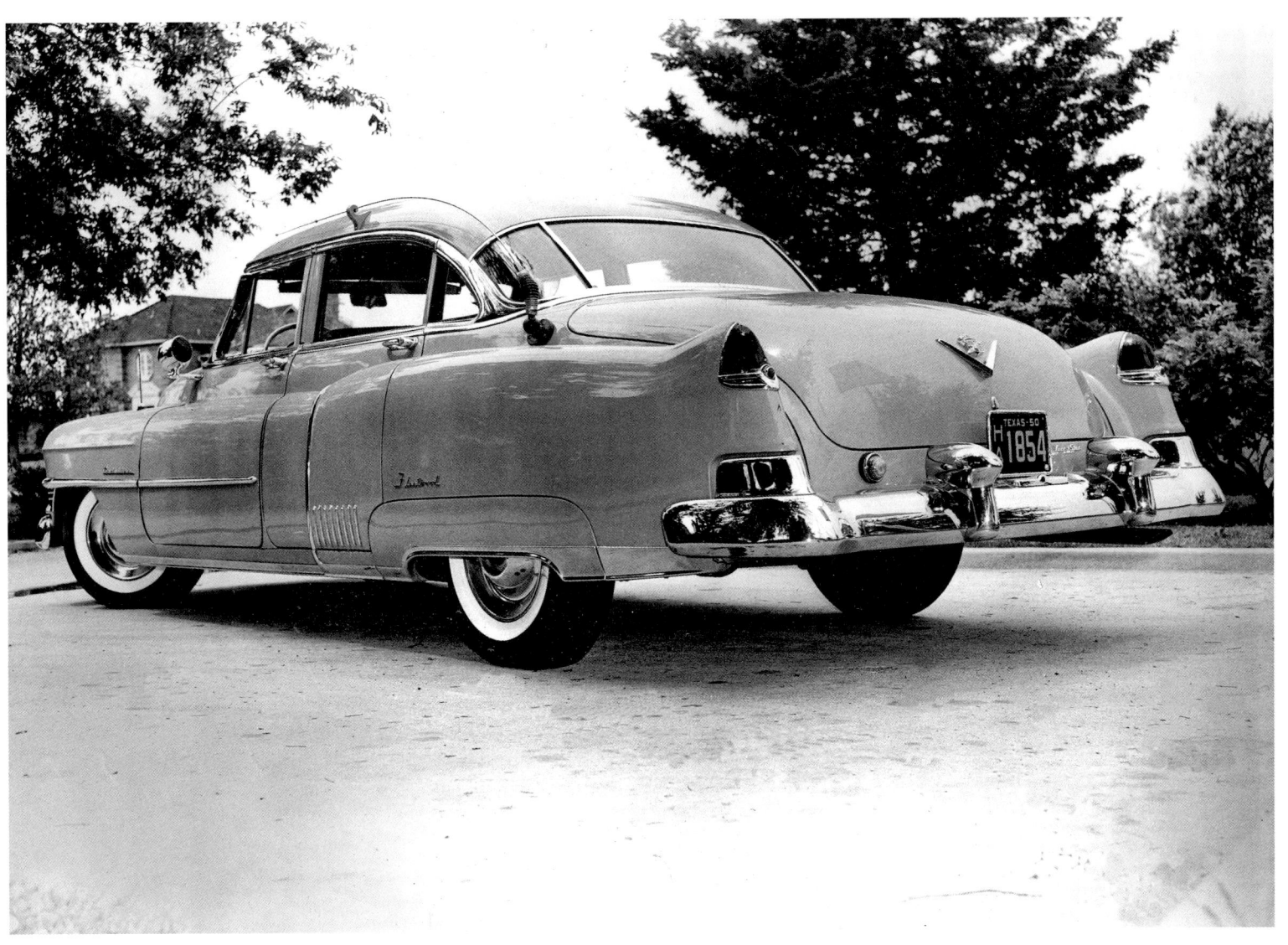

ABOVE: Dad's 1950 Cadillac Fleetwood that had a telephone and police radio. We used this car for so many of his photo shoots in the 1950s. 1950.

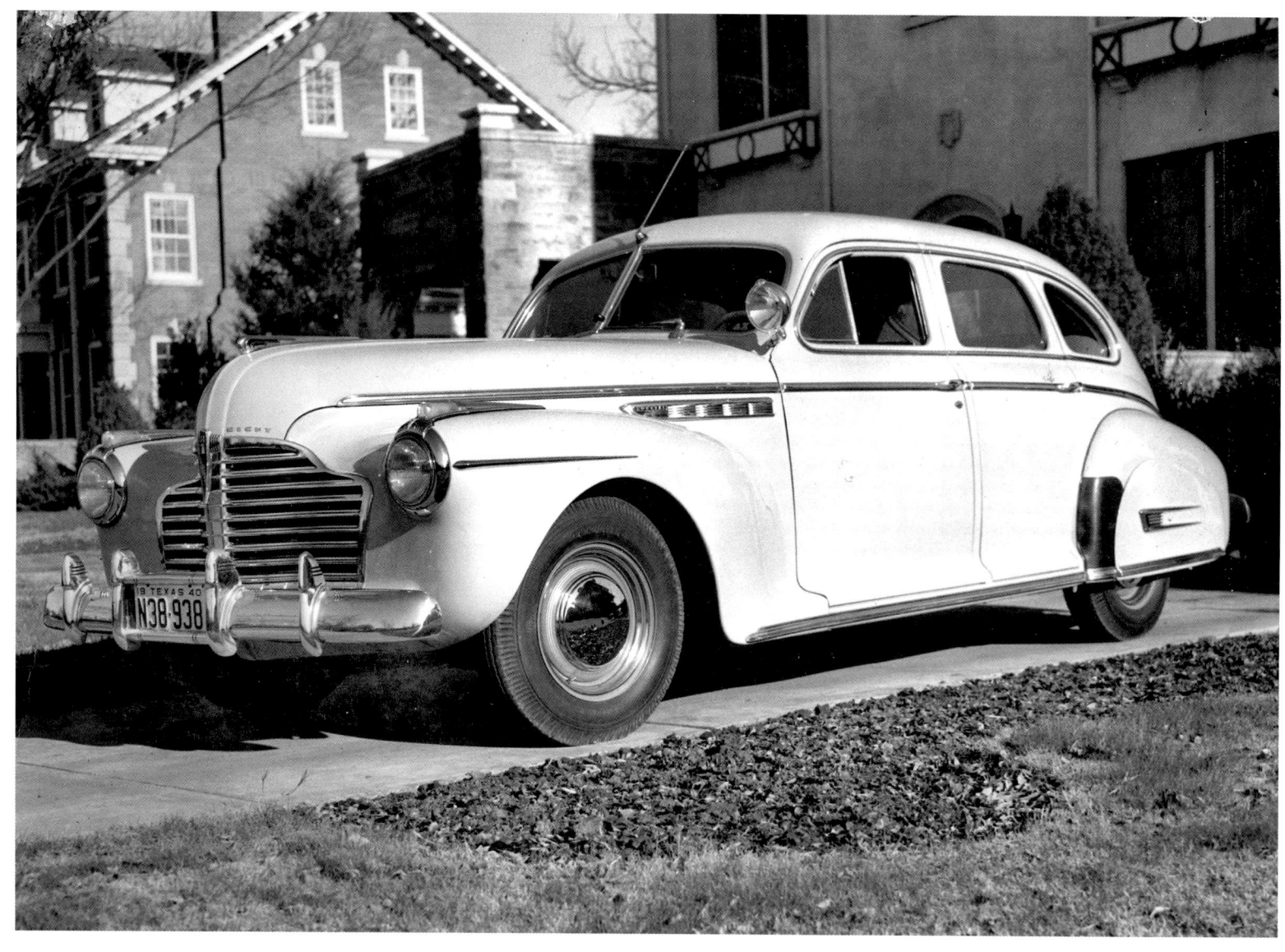

ABOVE: 1940 Buick. 1940.

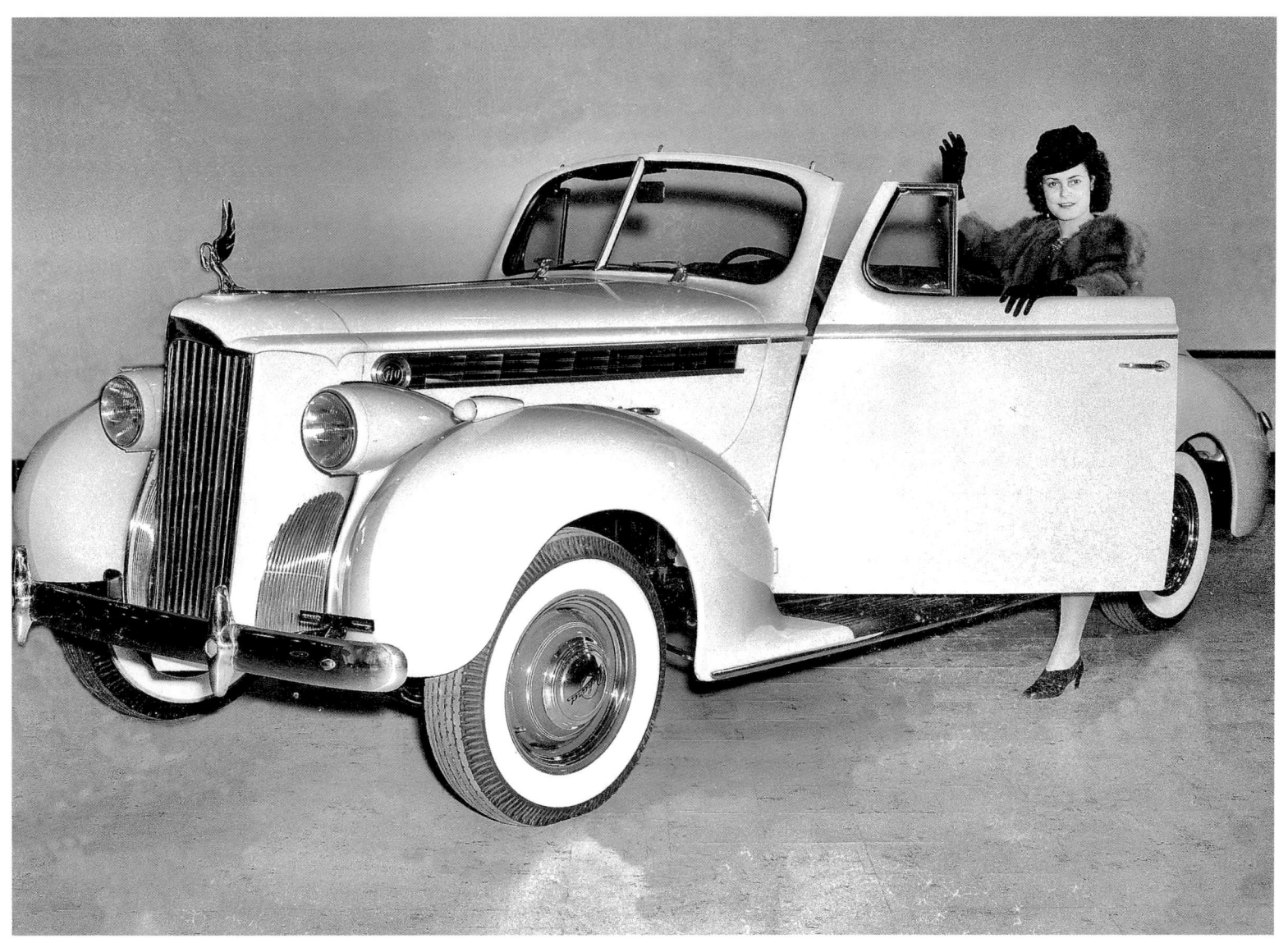

ABOVE: Dallas socialite Hazel Ashley
and her new 1940 Packard Roadster. 1941.

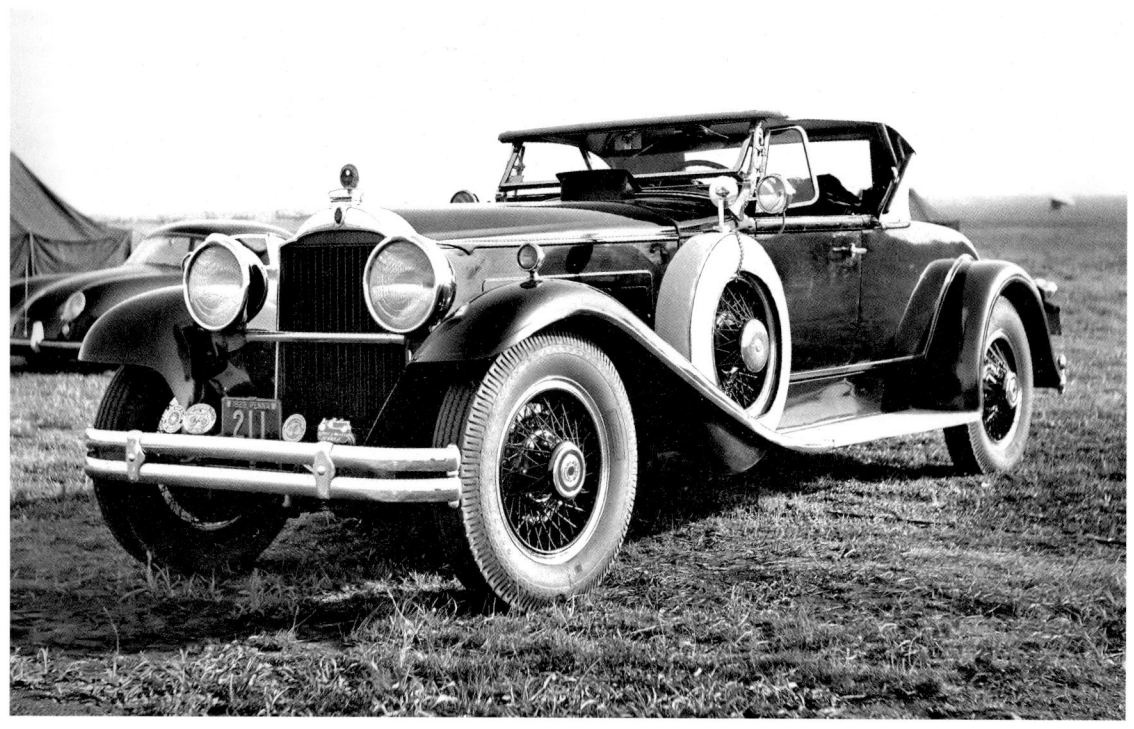

ABOVE: This was not our 1929 Packard Roadster, just one that we saw parked at an event. Gorgeous car and Dad, of course, had to shoot it. 1954.

RIGHT: After deciding his 1952 MG-TD just wasn't fast enough, here's Dad's next new car—a 1953 Jaguar XK-120M coupe (the "M" was some factory modification that upped the horsepower a bit from stock). The XK-120 Jags were among the most beautiful cars ever built. One time Dad and I, coming back from a time-trials event in Fort Worth, got on a newly paved but not yet open to the public stretch of highway and, with the very accurate Jaeger-LeCoultre speedometer facing me (it was mounted right of the Jaeger tachometer), I saw the needle hover just above the 130-mph mark for a short period before slowing and exiting our own personal racetrack. 1953.

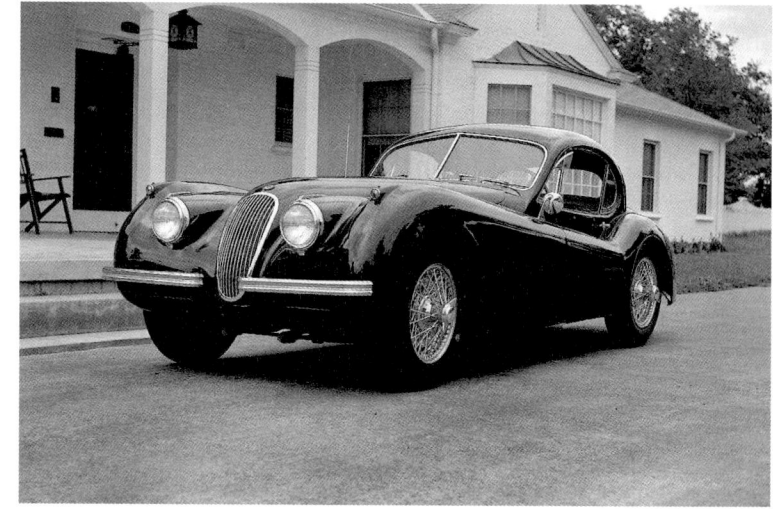

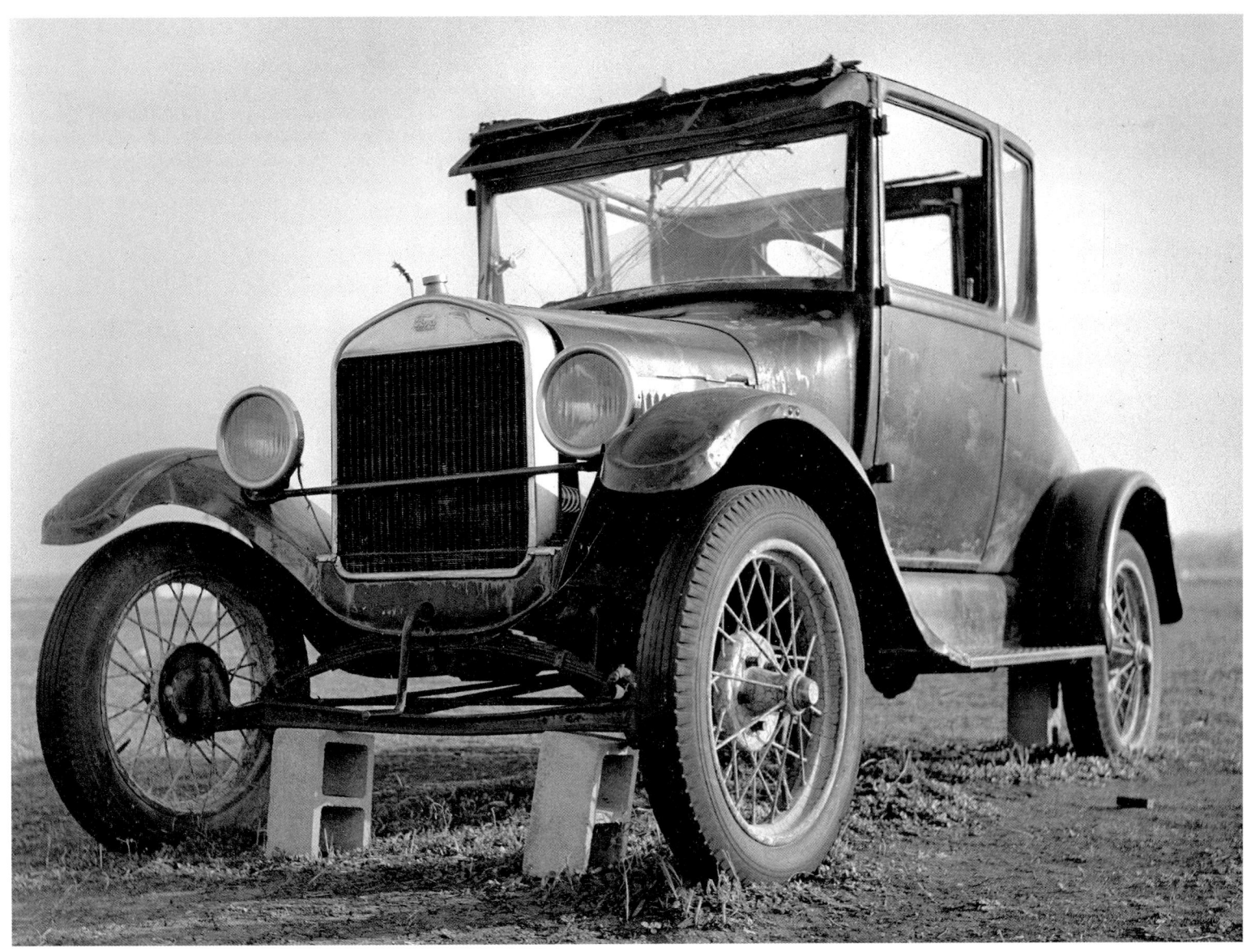

ABOVE: This is a 1927 Model T coupe that Dad and his good friend Scott DeLee were restoring. After Dad's death, Scott took ownership of it and finished the car. It looked like the day it rolled off the assembly line at Henry Ford's Highland Park plant in Michigan. 1953.

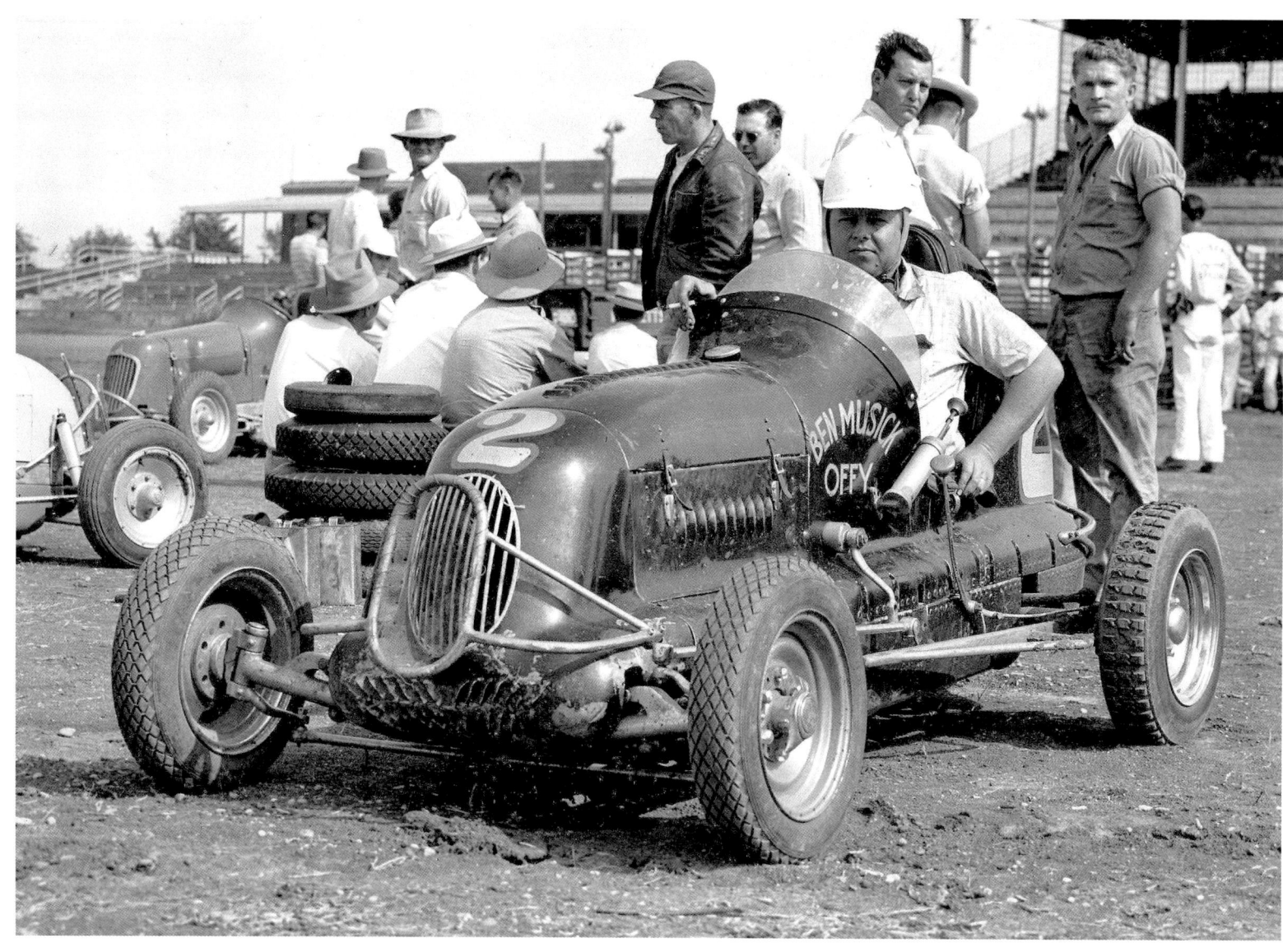

ABOVE: I believe this is the track
at the Fairgrounds in Dallas. 1940s.

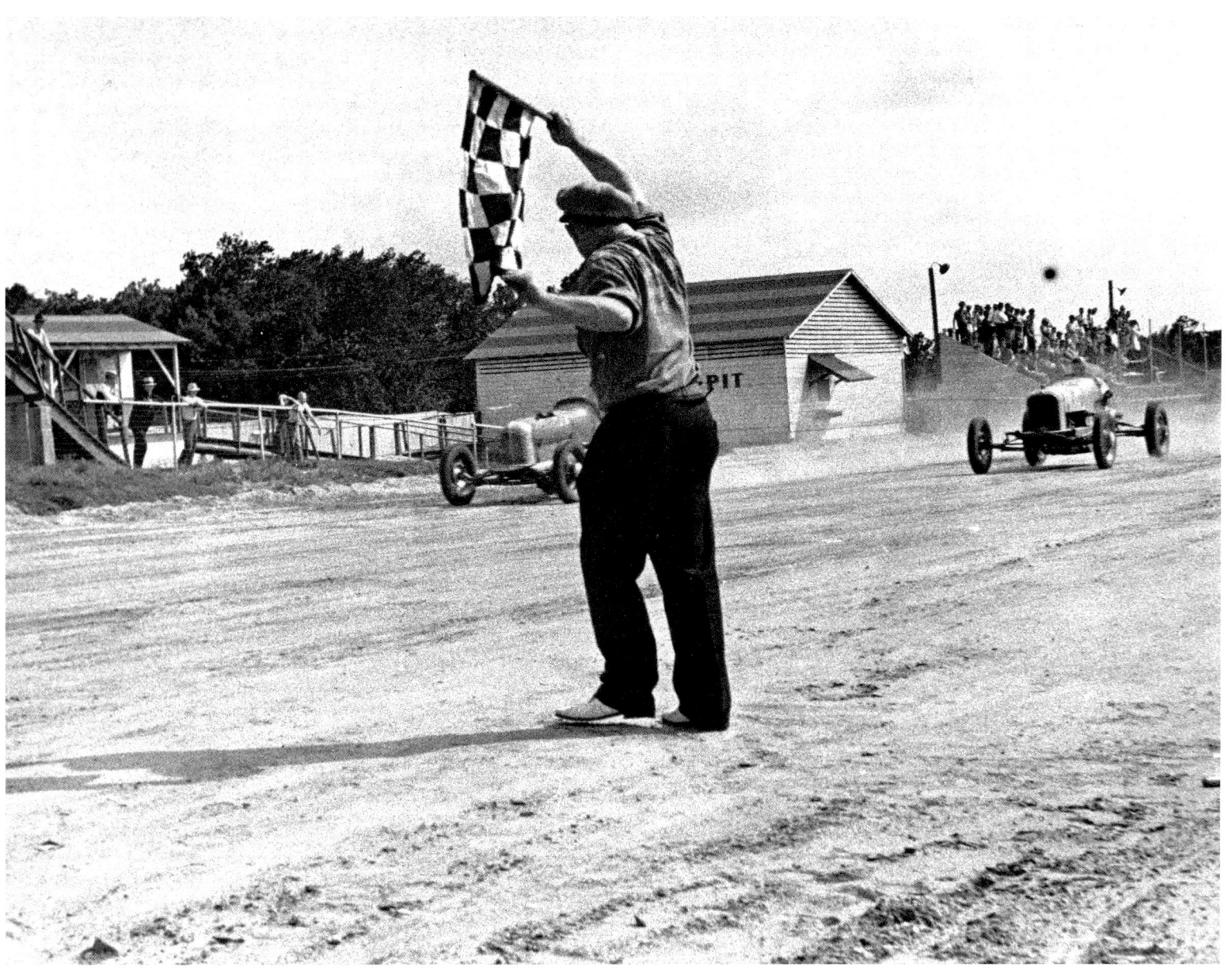

ABOVE: Les Butler poised and ready to drop the checkered flag on the winner. Butler was the promoter at several Dallas-area racetracks, including the one at the State Fair. He was usually the flagman at the events as well. 1939.

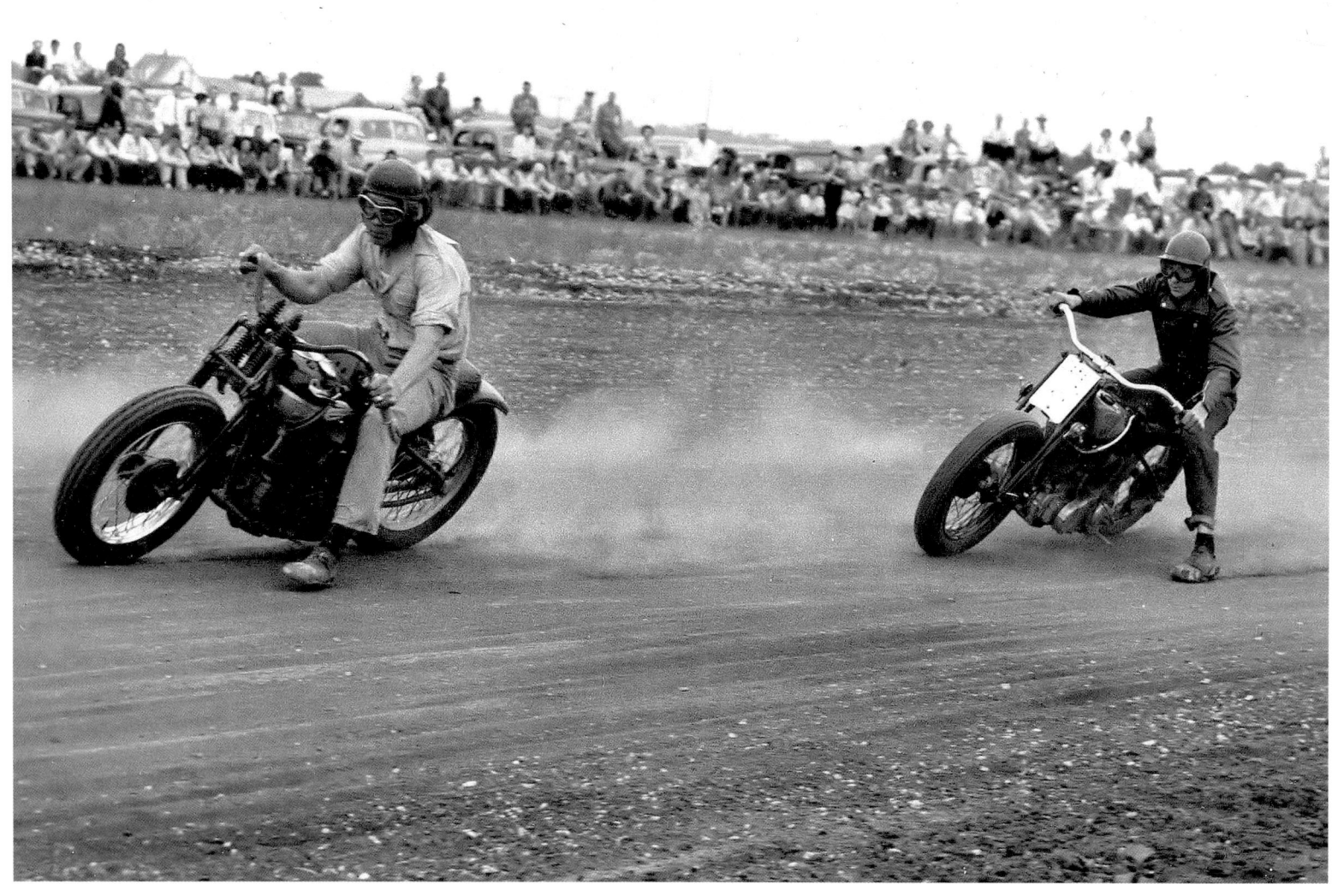

ABOVE: Motorcycle racing also became popular at dirt tracks around North Texas. Early 1940s.

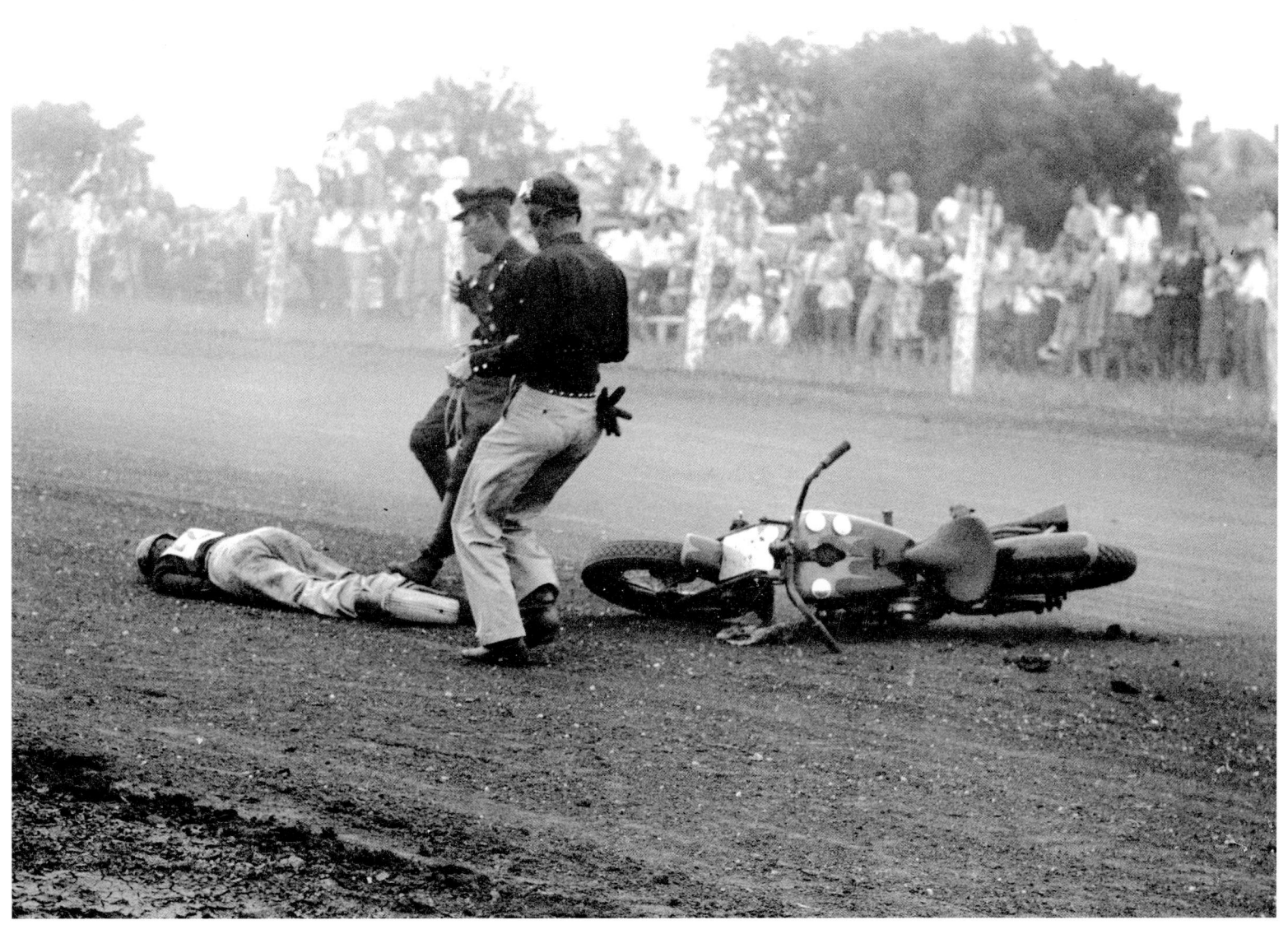

ABOVE: A fallen rider lies injured on the track after accident. Early 1940s.

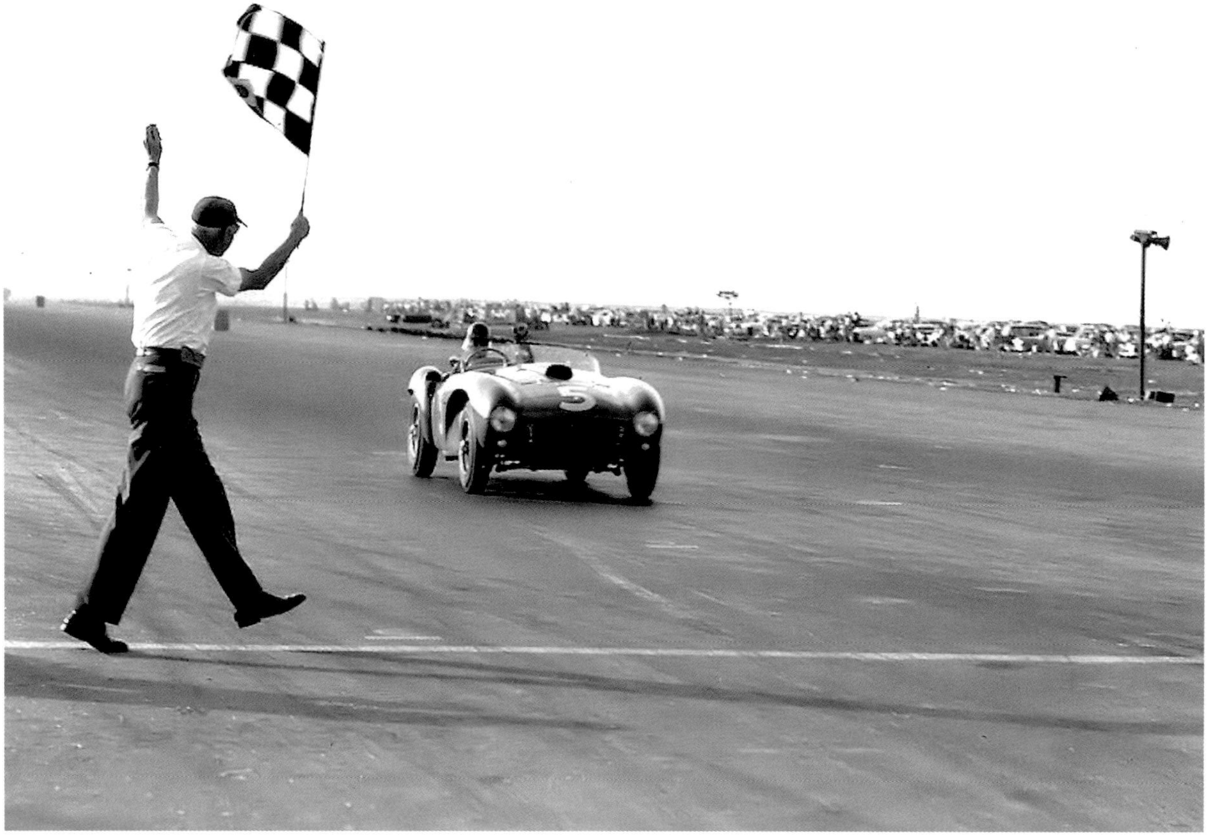

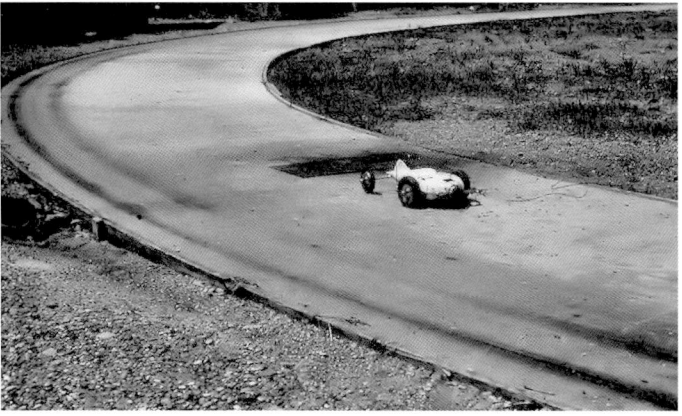

ABOVE: Overall race winner at Bergstrom's March 1954 Lone Star National Sports Car Race, "Gentleman" Jim Kimberly heads to the checkered flag. Kimberly came away that weekend as the overall winner. That year, he and his 375MM Spider Ferrari had one of the best seasons in SCCA history for a sportsman racer, with seventeen class victories in twenty races, and sixteen overall wins! His restored "Kimberly red" #5 sold for $9,075,000 at RM's 2013 Monterey auction. March 1954.

LEFT: At the circular track at Fair Park, the cars were tethered by wire to a metal pole in the middle. An owner would set his car down and hook the wire to it; then, pushing it for a few feet (using a push stick), the car would take off when it fired, racing around the track. Obviously, the death knell for this form of motorsport happened when remote control devices were developed and made their way into the hobbyist's world. 1949.

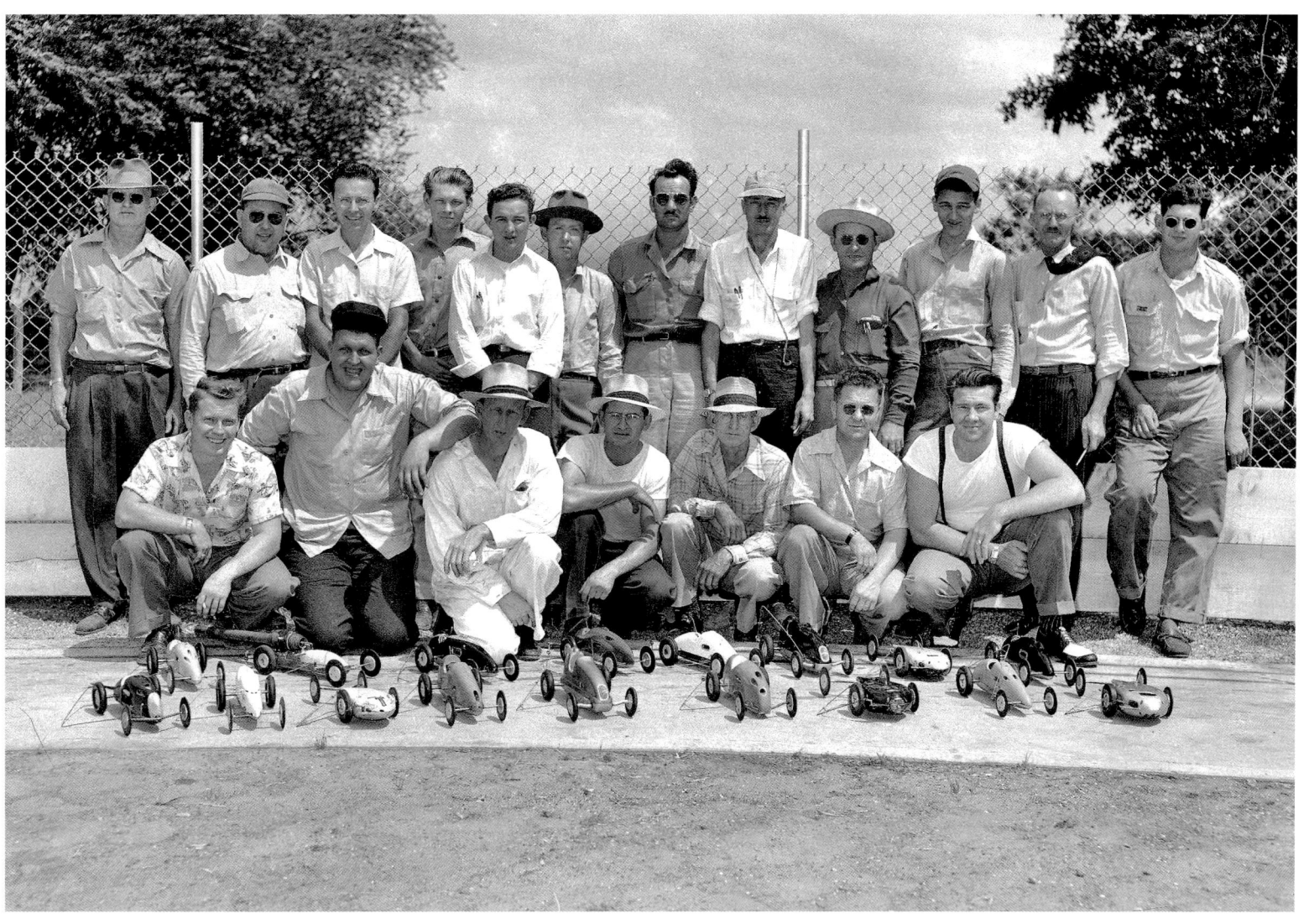

ABOVE: The 1948 spring meeting of the Dallas Model Race Car Club. Members are pictured here along with their tether cars at the dedicated track at Fair Park. 1948.

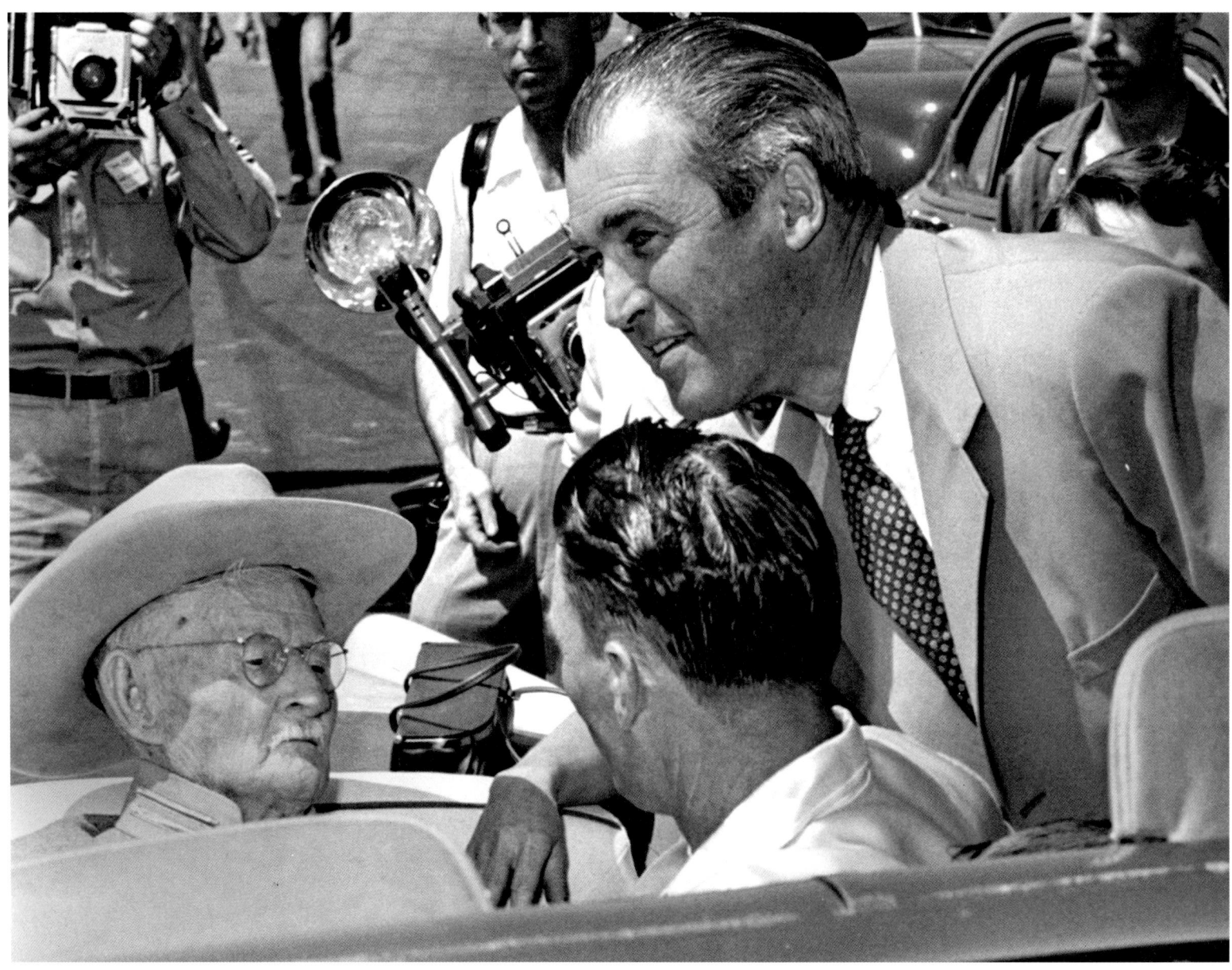

ABOVE: Race Grand Marshal Jimmy Stewart leaning over to talk with the event's special guest, Civil War veteran Walter Williams. Two warriors that fought, one in the air and the other on land, eighty years apart. 1954.

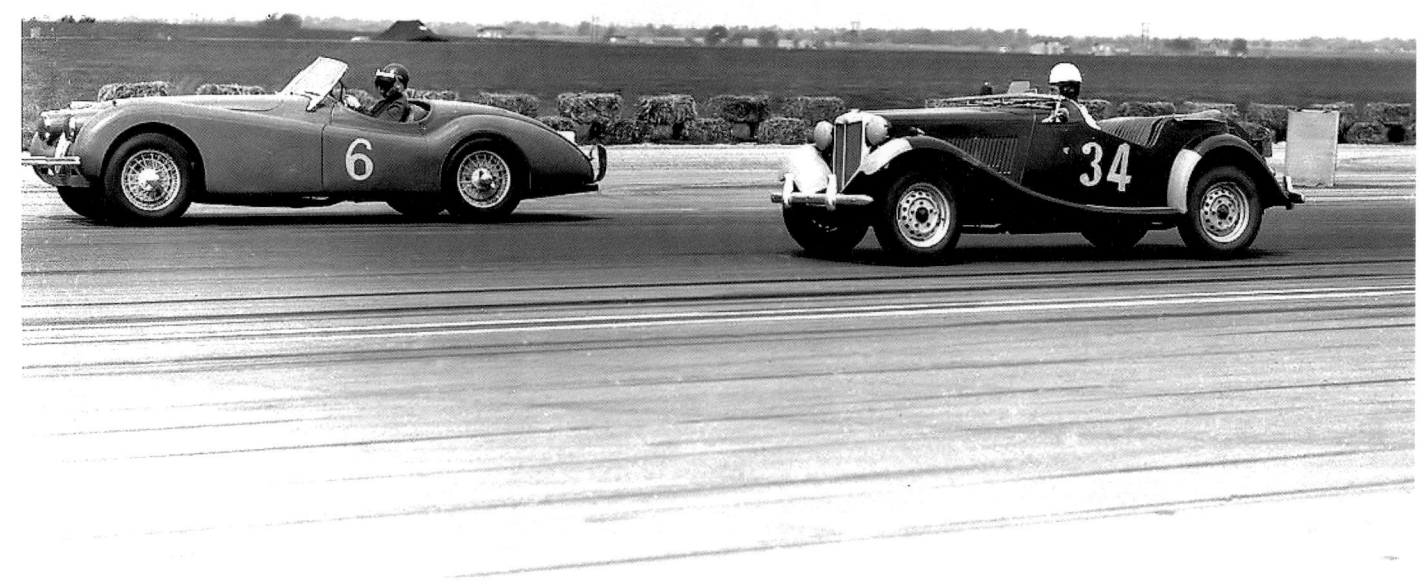

ABOVE: Jaguar XK-120 and an MG-TD at speed. March 1954.

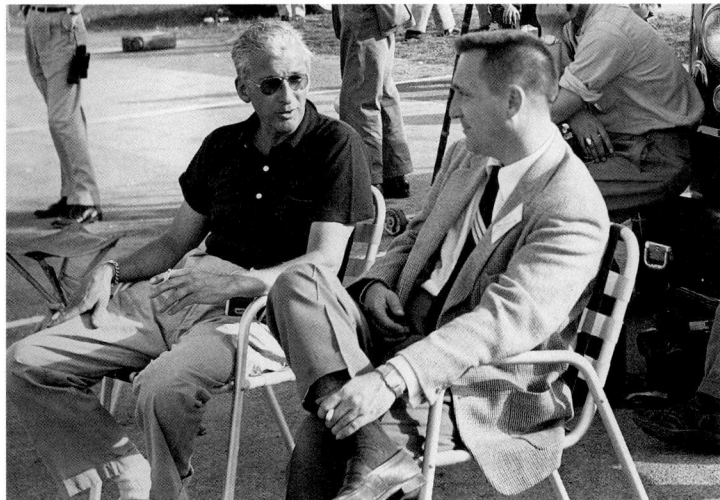

LEFT: Overall race winner, sportsman, past president of the Sports Car Club of America, socialite and heir to the Kimberly-Clark fortune (think Kleenex), "Gentleman" Jim Kimberly (dark shirt). An MIT graduate who wore a gold earring in the '50s, Kimberly was married to a young woman forty-two years his junior named Jacqueline. In the 1980s, the two became involved in the highly publicized divorce scandal of publishing heir Peter Pulitzer and his wife Roxanne that resulted in seemingly never-ending stories in the press, magazine articles, and a book—including a TV movie starring Courtney Cox as Roxanne. March 1954.

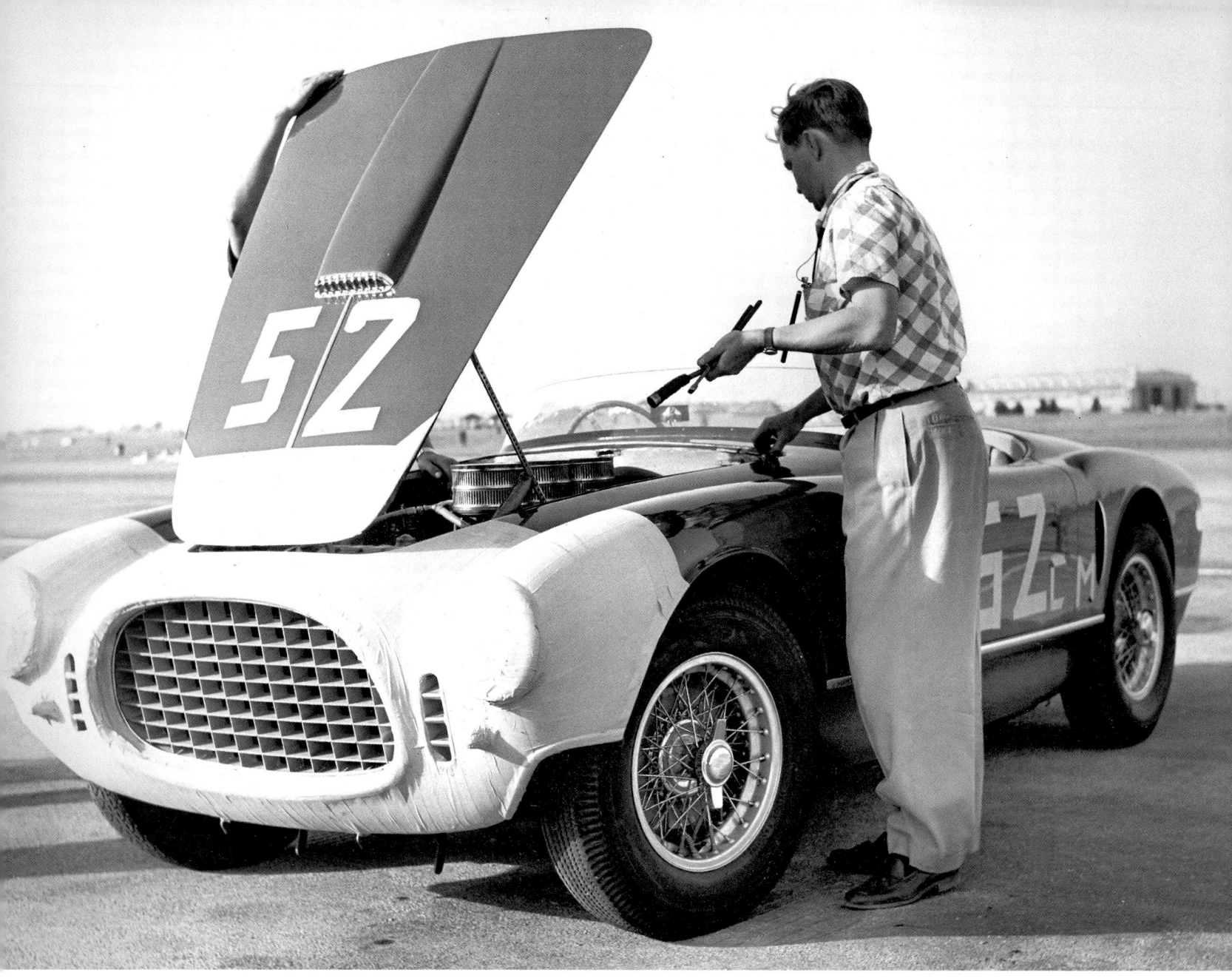

ABOVE: William Jarnigan tuning his Ferrari. March 1954.

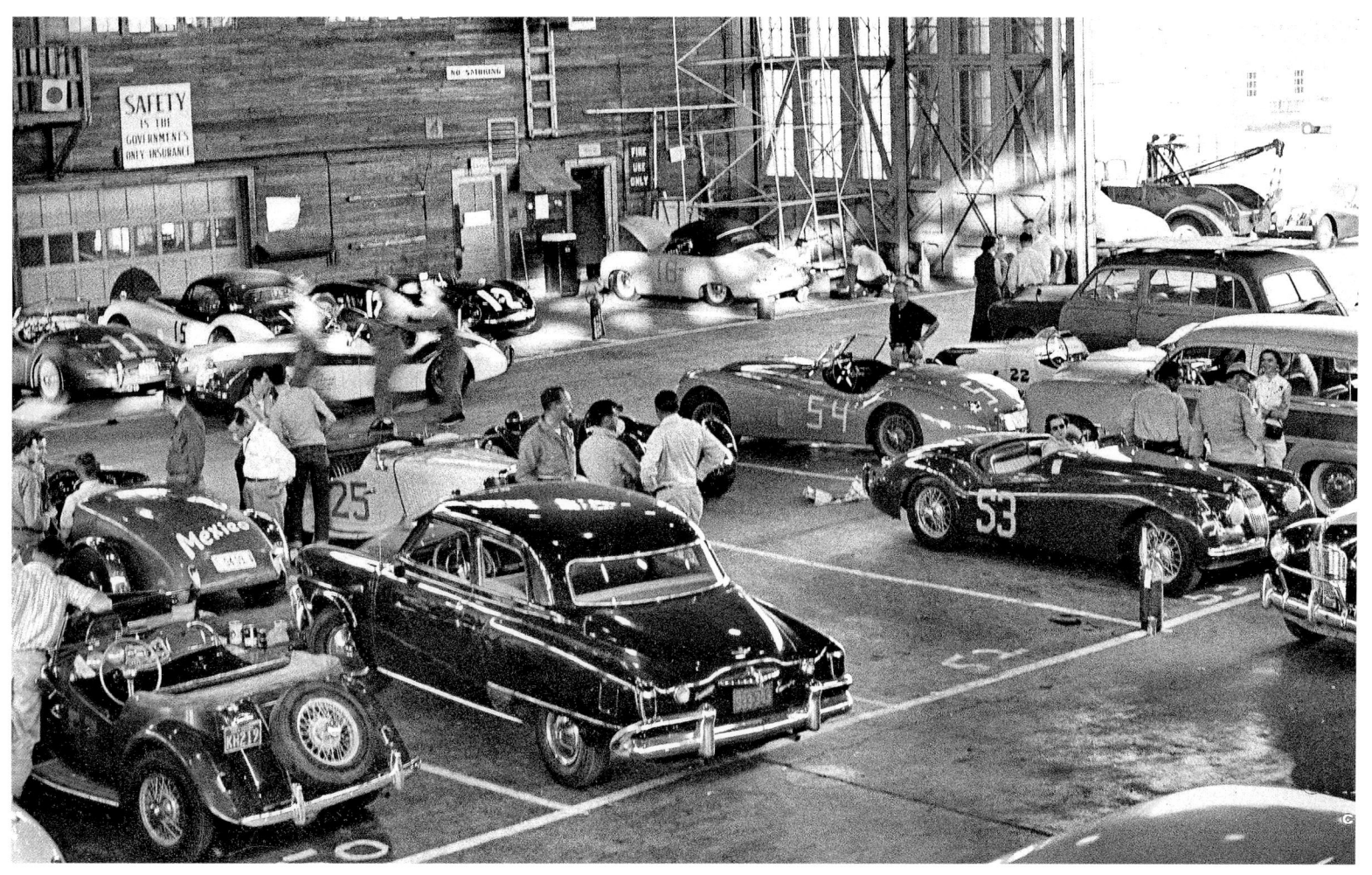

ABOVE: Pit area was inside one of the giant hangars. March 1954.

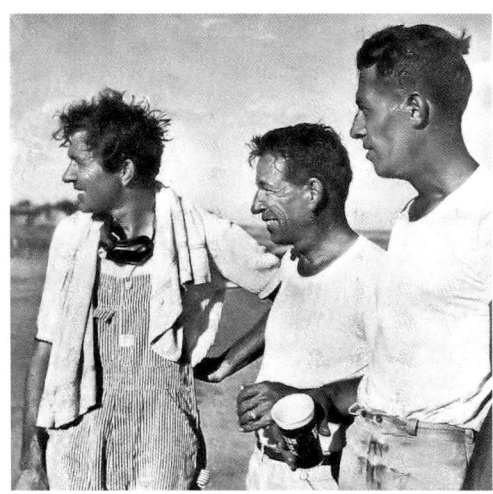

ABOVE: Carroll Shelby, Lorin McMullen, and Dr. Harold Fenner at a race at Eagle Mountain Air National Guard Base in Fort Worth. Carroll took the big "A" win driving Roy Cherryholmes's C-type Jaguar. Carroll was a longtime family friend going back to the very early fifties when he started racing, and Dad was the Texas Region photographer for the SCCA. After Dad died, Carroll would come by occasionally and take me out for a hamburger at Goff's, or I'd come home with a model from a local hobby shop. He even took me to see Elvis's first movie, *Love Me Tender*, at the Inwood Theater in 1956. We had great memories and stayed in touch over the years. 1954.

RIGHT: Carroll Shelby during the trophy presentation after a race at Eagle Mountain, the last race I got to help Dad shoot before his fatal car wreck. Carroll was one of the greatest race drivers and designers ever to come out of the USA. He grew up in Dallas and went to Sunset High. He founded Shelby American, which produced the Cobra sports car, and his relationship with Ford led to the Shelby Mustang. He won the twenty-four hours of LeMans with an American-built car for the first time, driving a Ford GT-40. In a recent movie, *Ford v Ferrari*, actor Matt Damon portrayed Carroll. His logo, Carroll Shelby in script w/the black hat, is known around the world. Besides his car and racing empire, in 1967, along with Dallas's Frank X. Tolbert, he was one of the founders of the famous and annual Terlingua Chili Cookoff, which led to a little Dallas-based sideline in the food business for him with "Carroll Shelby's Original Texas Brand Chili Kit." August 1954.

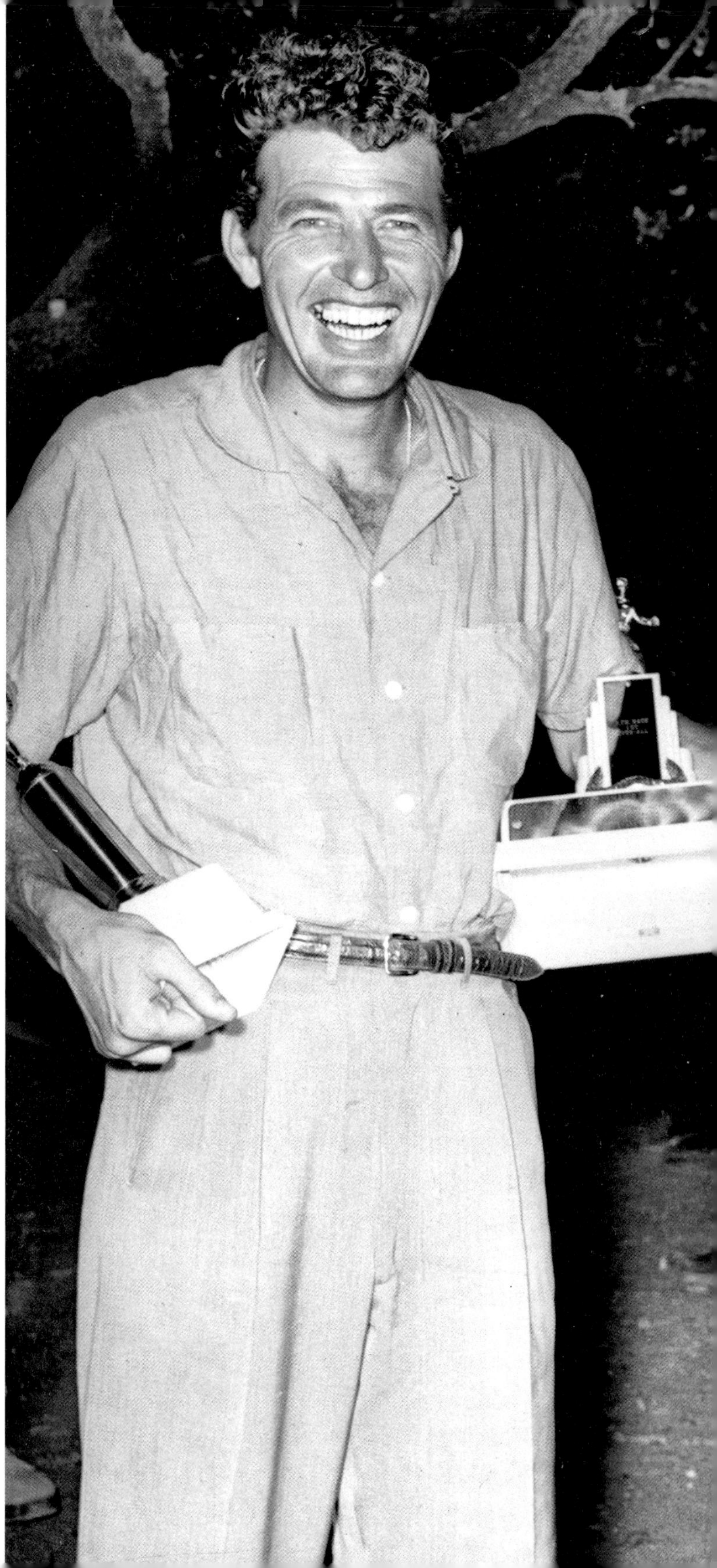

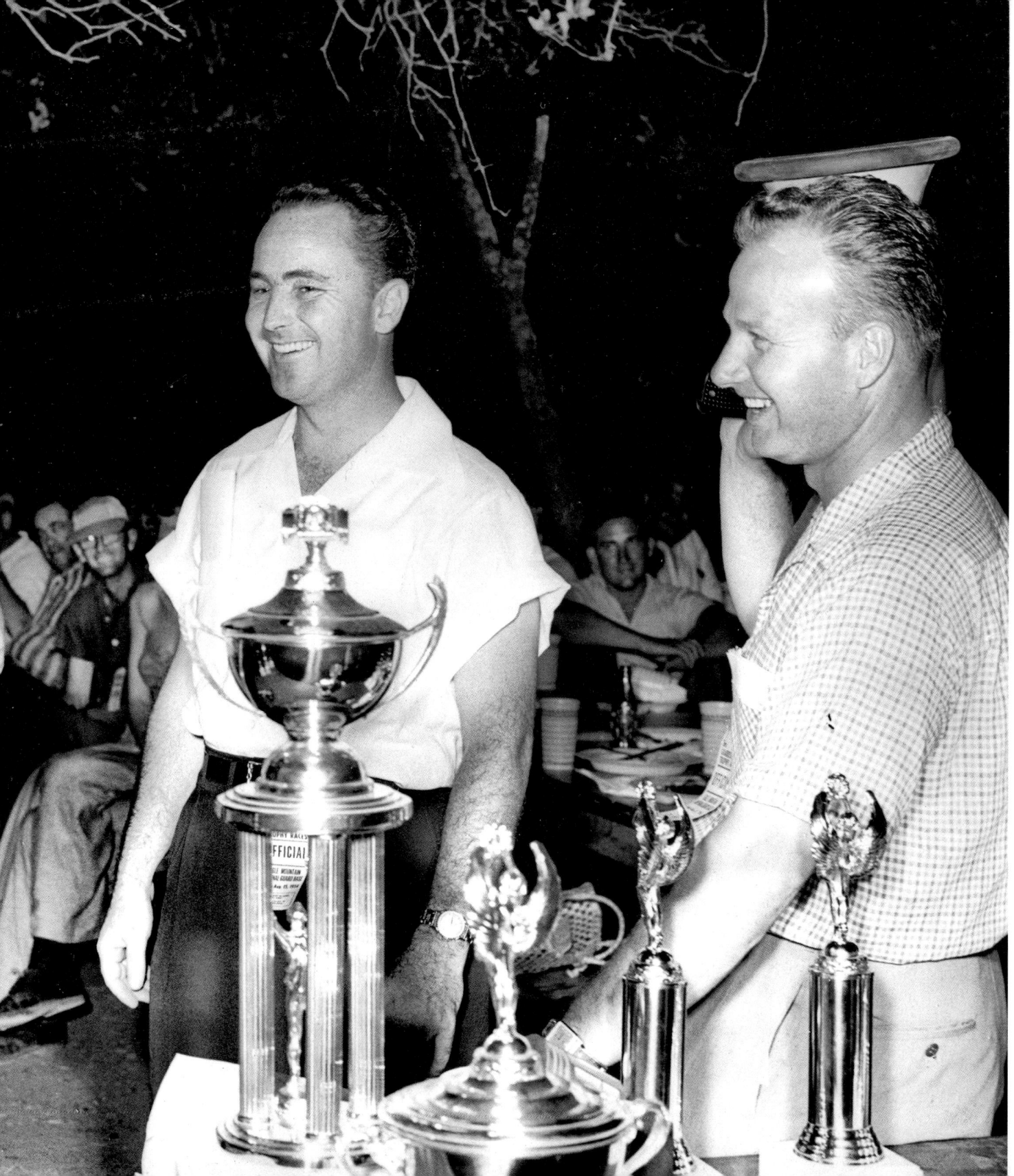

Family & Friends

———

OPPOSITE: My paternal grandparents,
Clarence and Esther Miller. 1951.

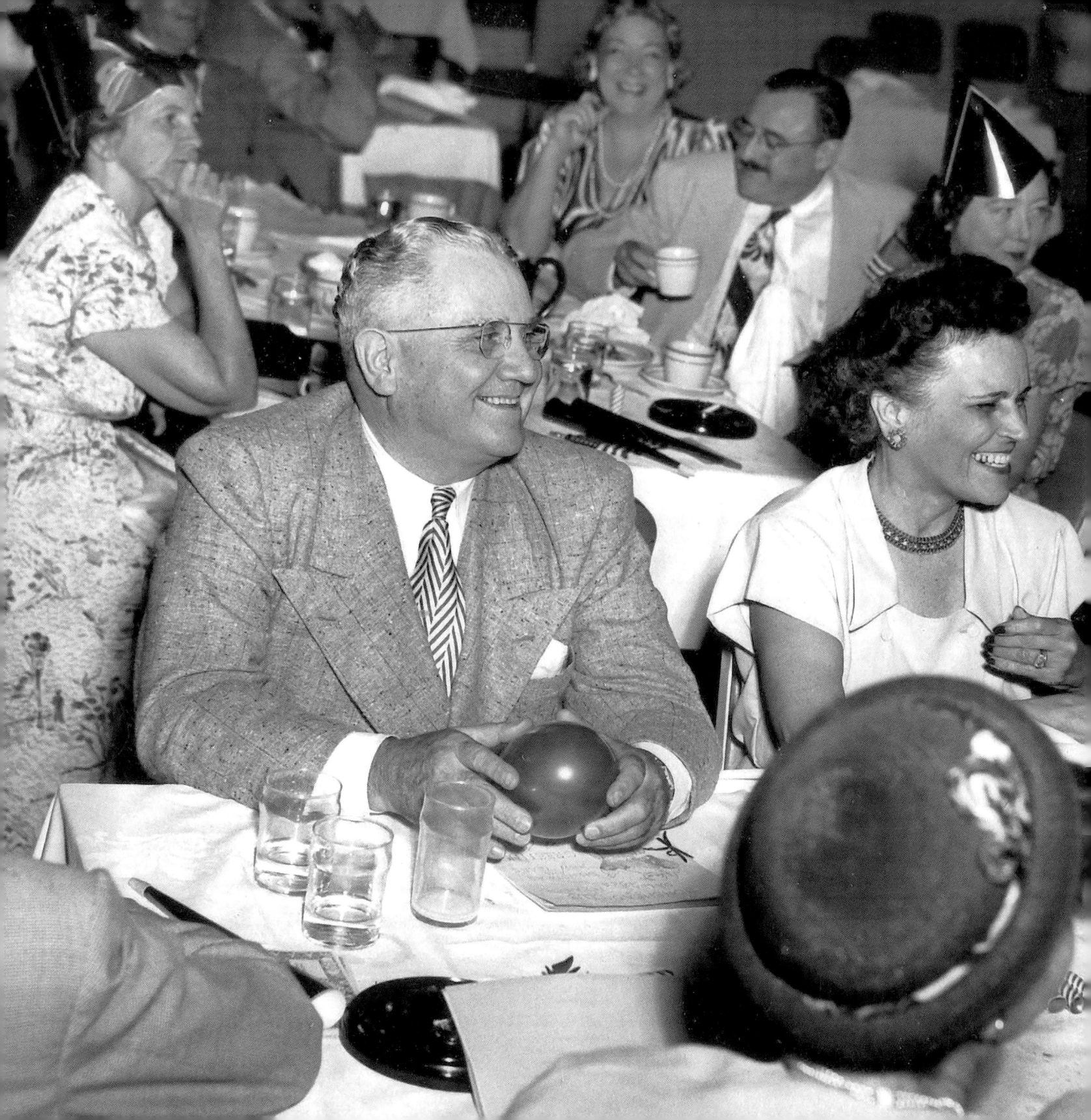

Usually some of the best and most endearing images from any photographer will be those taken of his or her own family and that family's close friends. I feel particularly fortunate that Dad's nice and sharp photographs of family and a few friends have survived to pass along to future generations and their families. I would be remiss had I not included a few of them in this book.

I'm very happy to share images of our family and friends with you here.

——————

RIGHT: When Dad took this, my granddad Clarence ("Pop" to us) had just taken me to a museum in New Orleans where I had gotten to see my first full-sized dinosaur skeleton. Our family was actually in the Big Easy to cheer on Pop's horse in the annual New Orleans Classic Stakes Thoroughbred Race at the Fair Grounds Race Course. 1947.

OPPOSITE: My mother was not a big person but was able to wield that big Speed Graphic large format camera herself on occasion. Here are Burnie, Alex, me (having a conversation with our Pekingese), and Dad on the front porch. 1954.

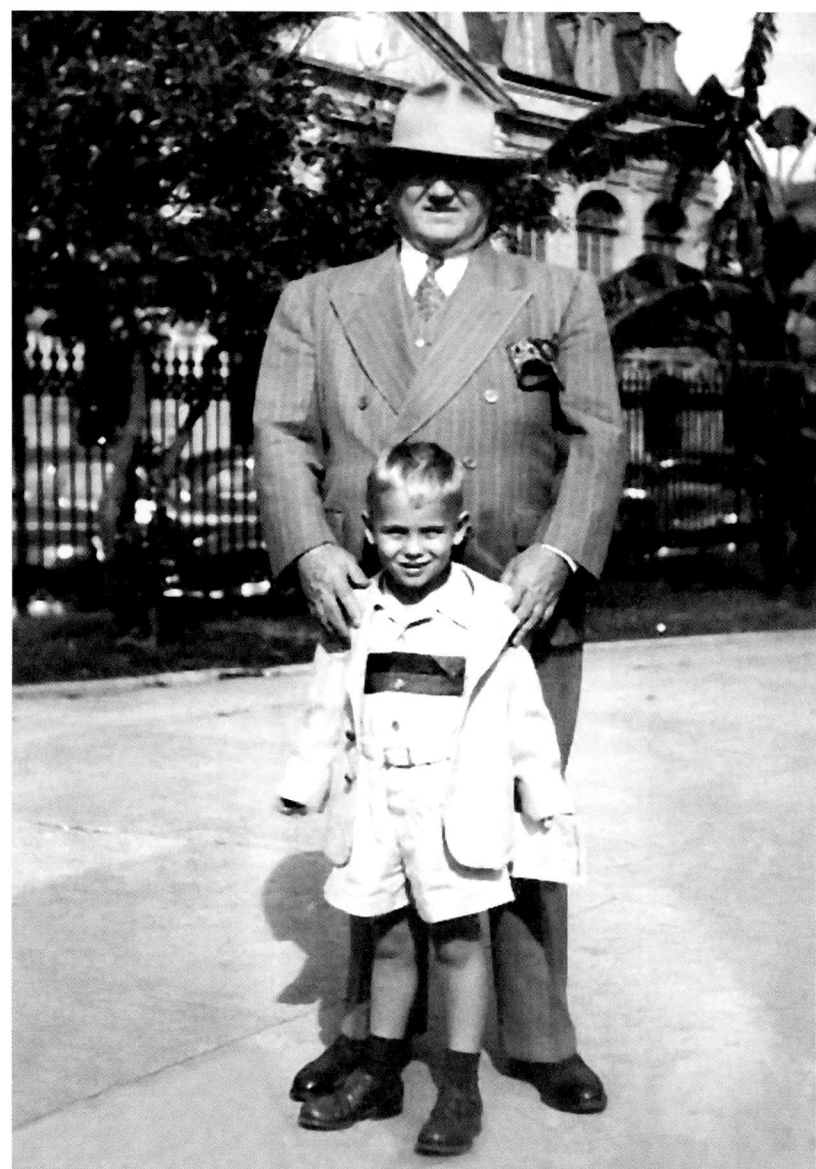

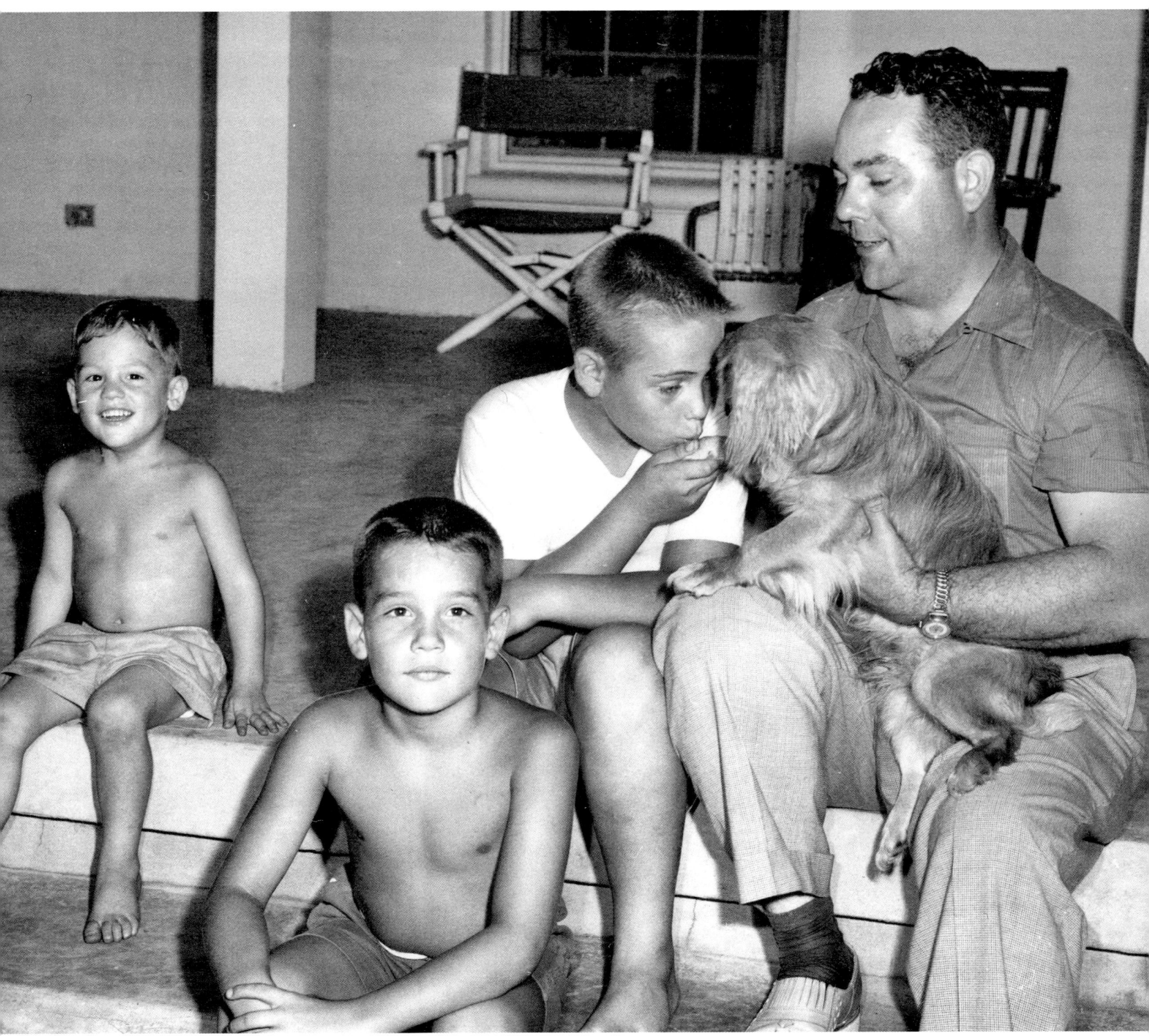

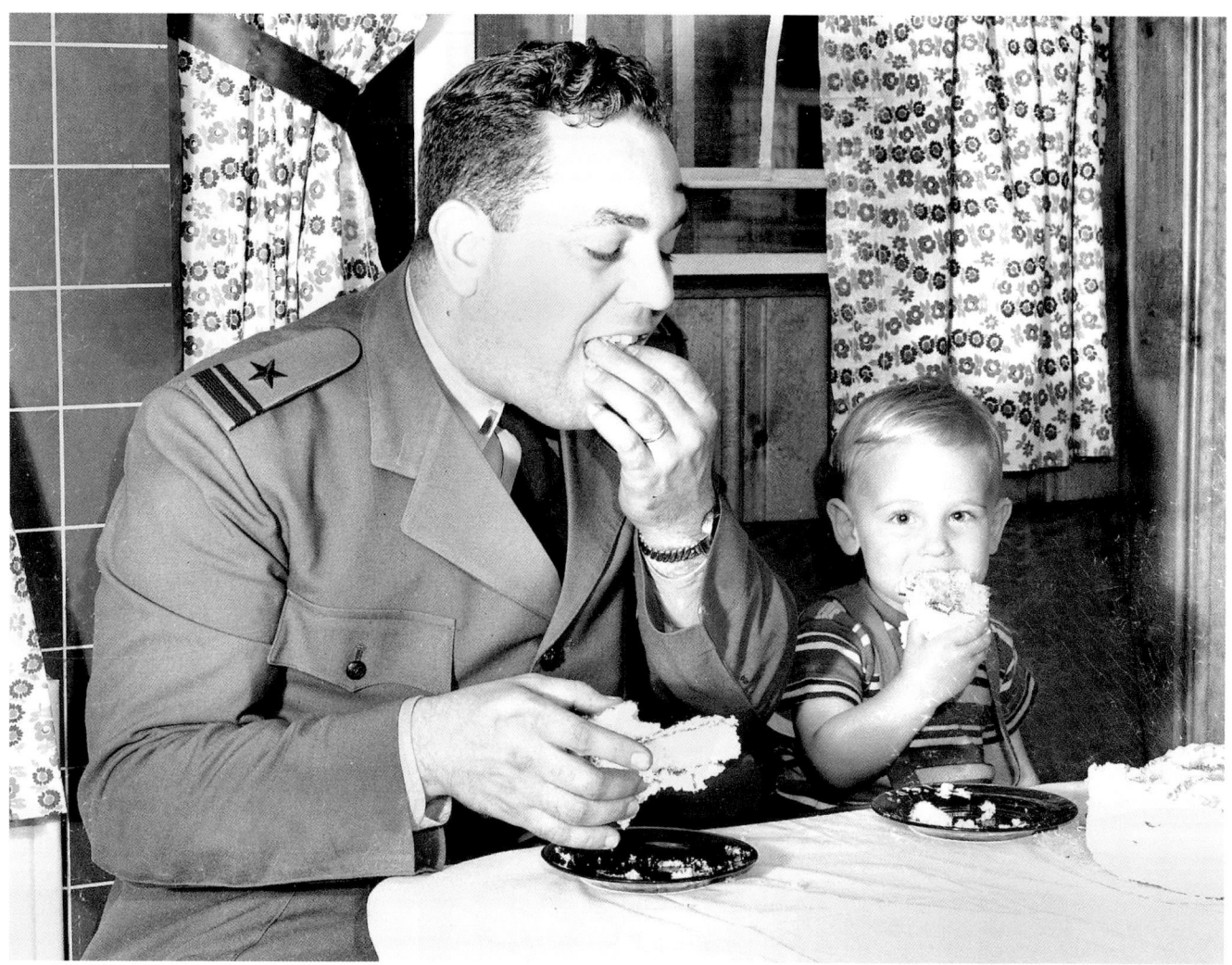

ABOVE: Another photo with Mom behind the camera. I was sharing a piece of cake with Dad as we celebrated my second birthday. This was a month after the end of the war in Europe, and a little over two months later Japan would announce its surrender. 1945.

OPPOSITE: We were all dressed up and going out for a day of taking pictures. Mom with her Super Ikonta, my brother Alex, and I'm holding my early Kodak Brownie (pre-Hawkeye version). Dad, behind the camera, with his 4 x 5 Speed Graphic. 1950.

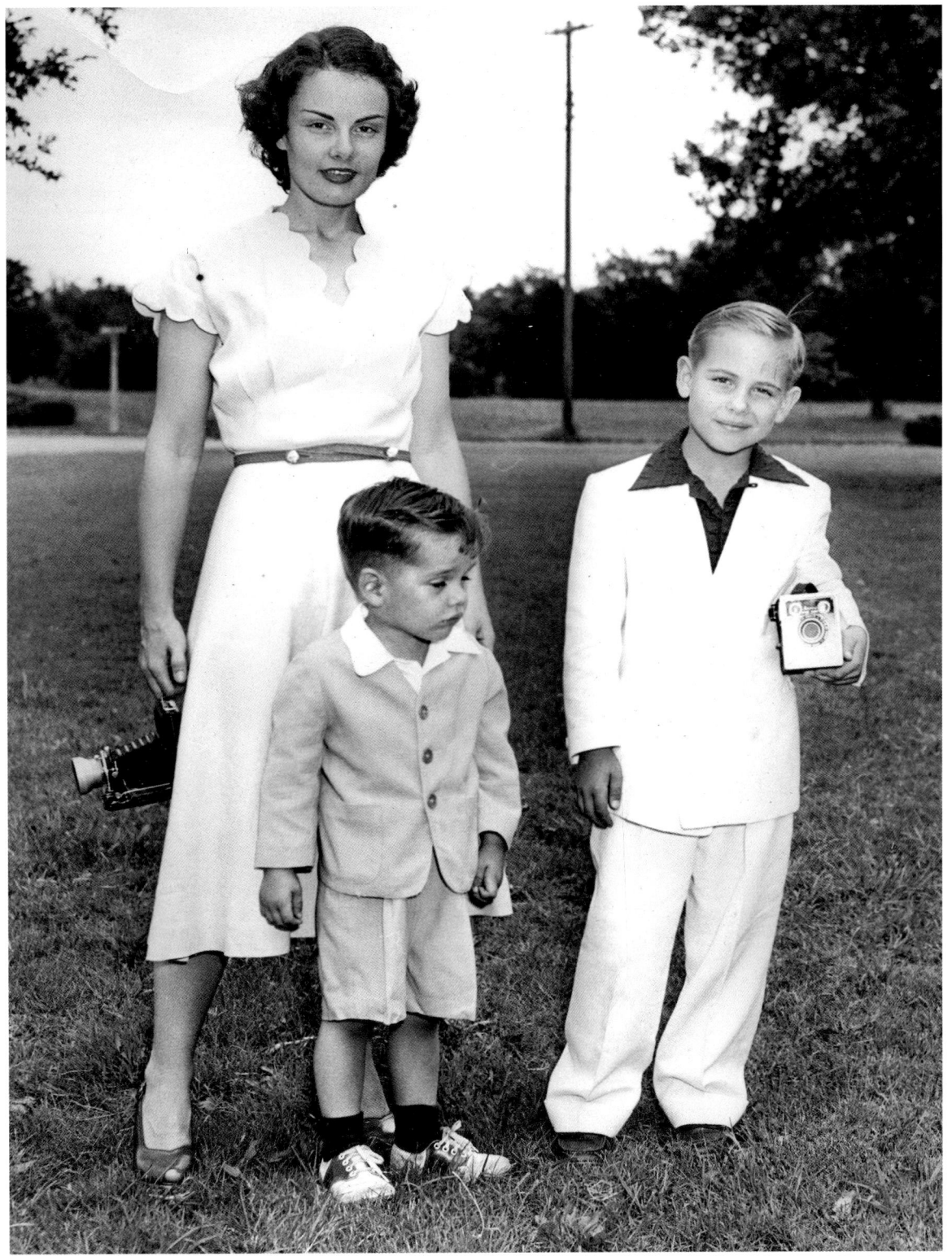

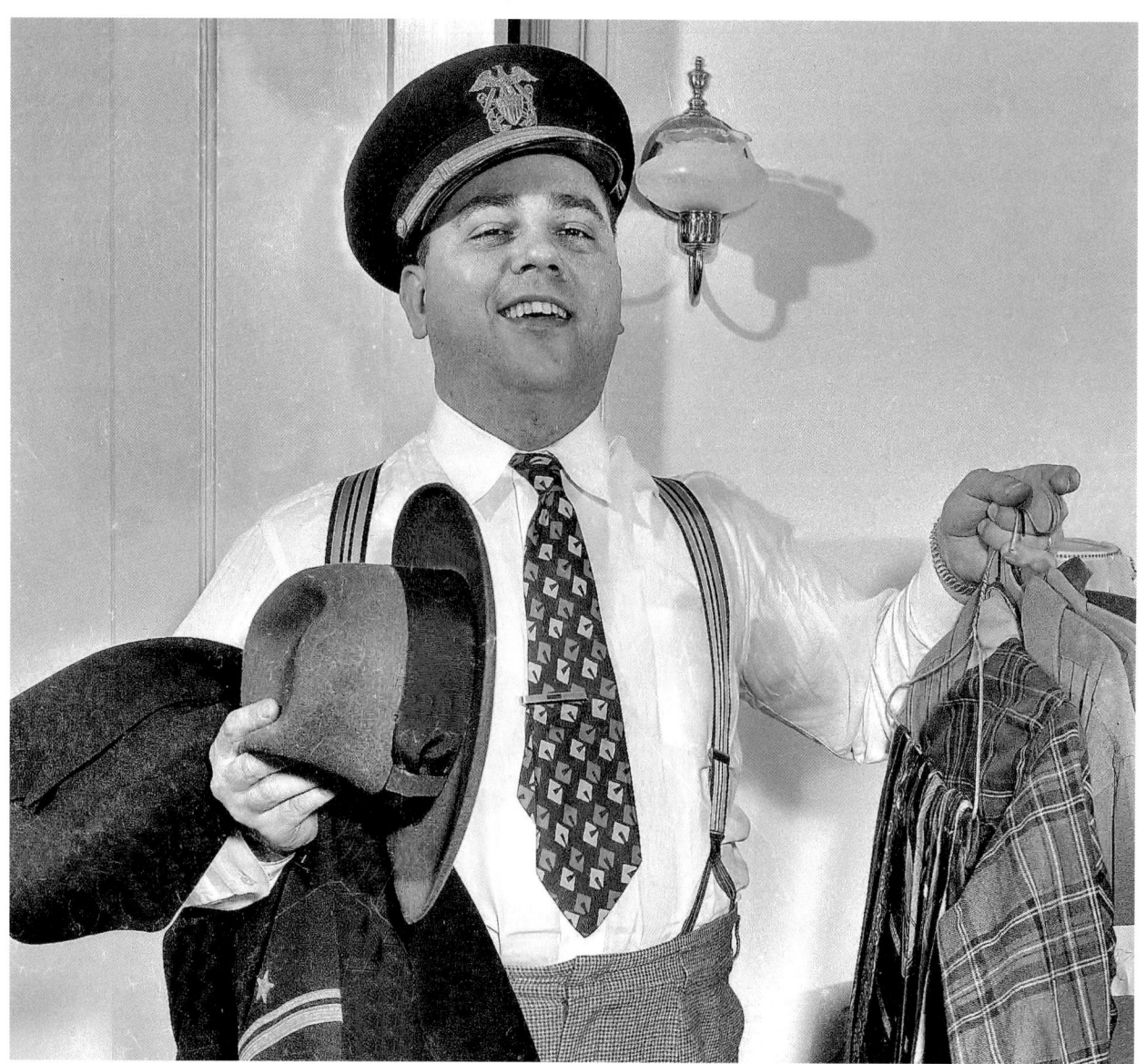

ABOVE: Dad beginning the transition from life as a naval officer aboard the USS *Crosby* back to that as a normal citizen on dry land (even though he would spend a few years as a naval reservist). I was with him in 1952 when he read a letter from the navy offering him a jump in rank if he would re-enlist. With several years of active duty followed by a stint in the reserves behind him, his third son only a year old, and in the middle of building a new home, I remember him saying something like, "Hell no! I think I've done my time!" 1947.

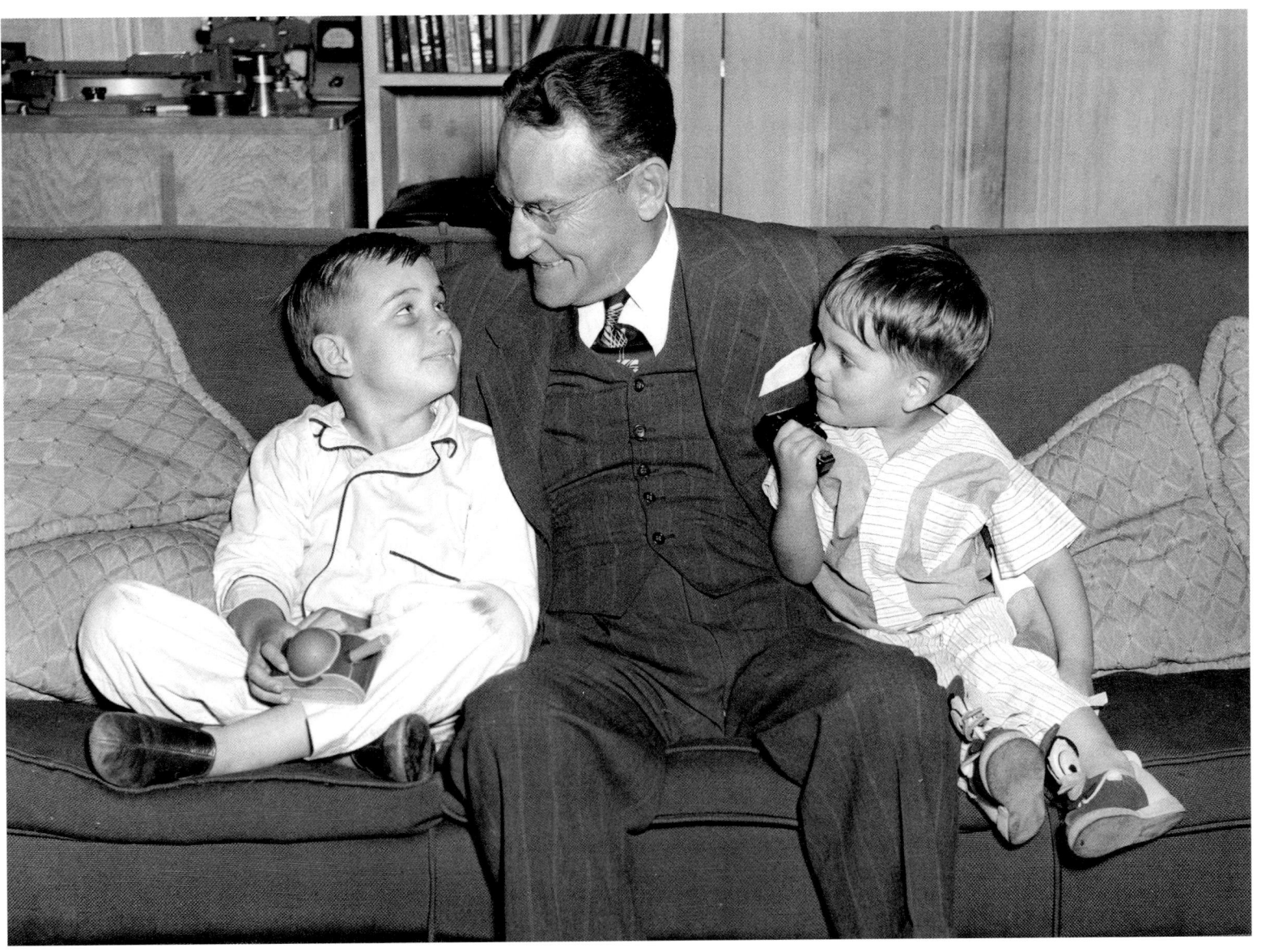

ABOVE: Me with my younger brother Alex with Ralf Burns, our maternal grandfather. He could have had a great career in baseball, but World War I stepped in, and he never pursued it afterwards. 1949.

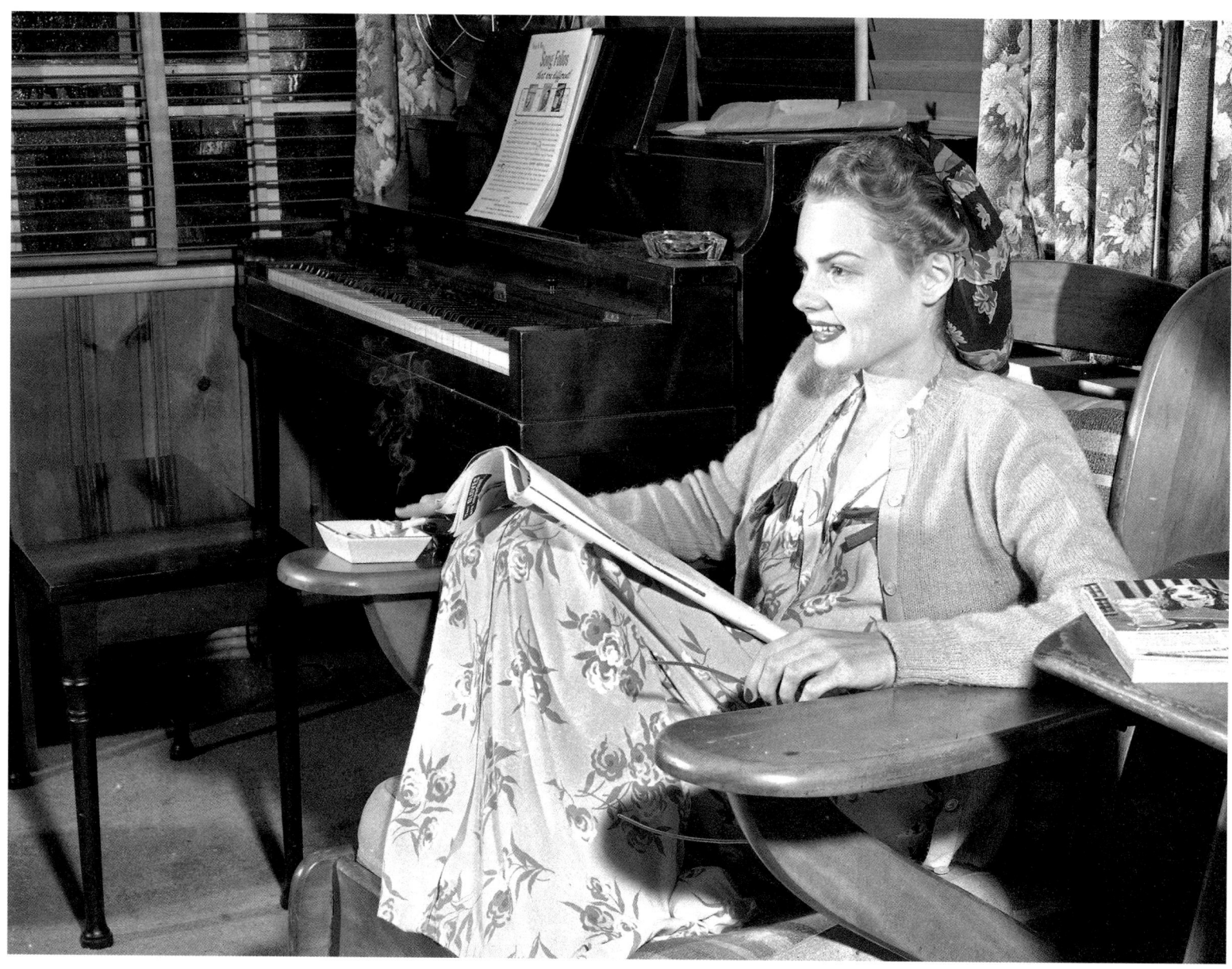

ABOVE: Our mother,
Martha Burns Miller. 1946.

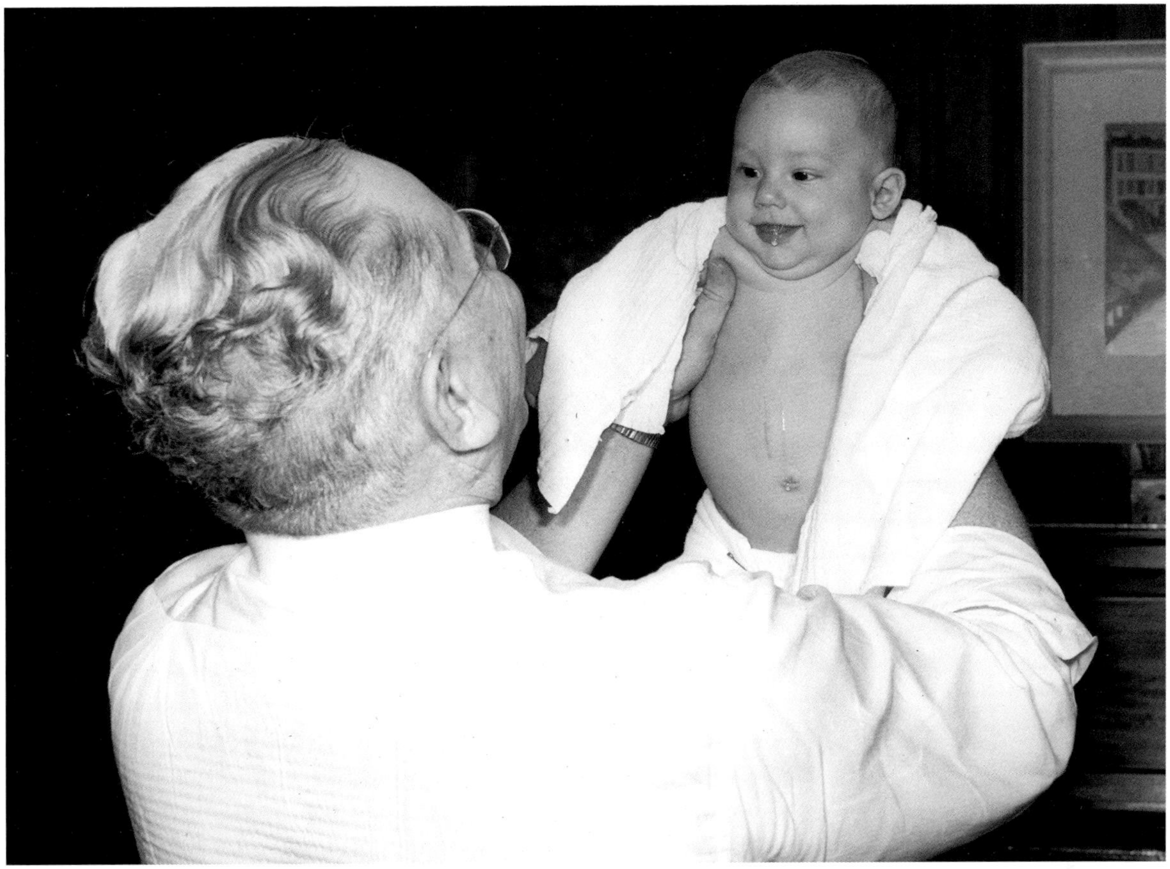

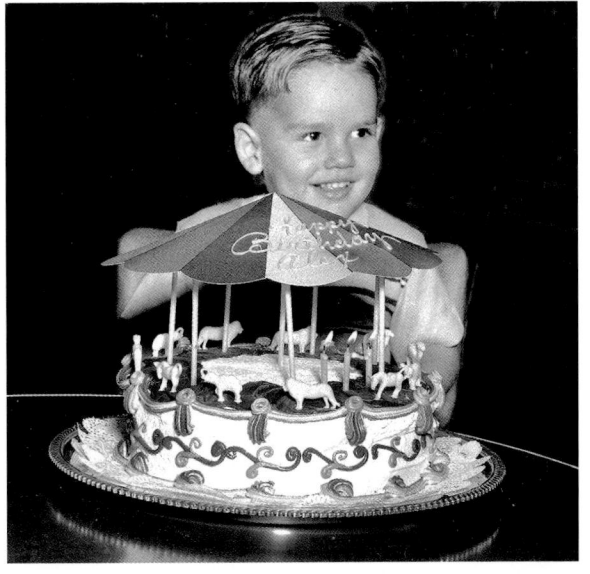

ABOVE: My paternal grandfather, Clarence Miller, with my youngest brother, Burnie. 1951.

LEFT: Alex on his third birthday. We lost him due to a diving accident in 1974. 1950.

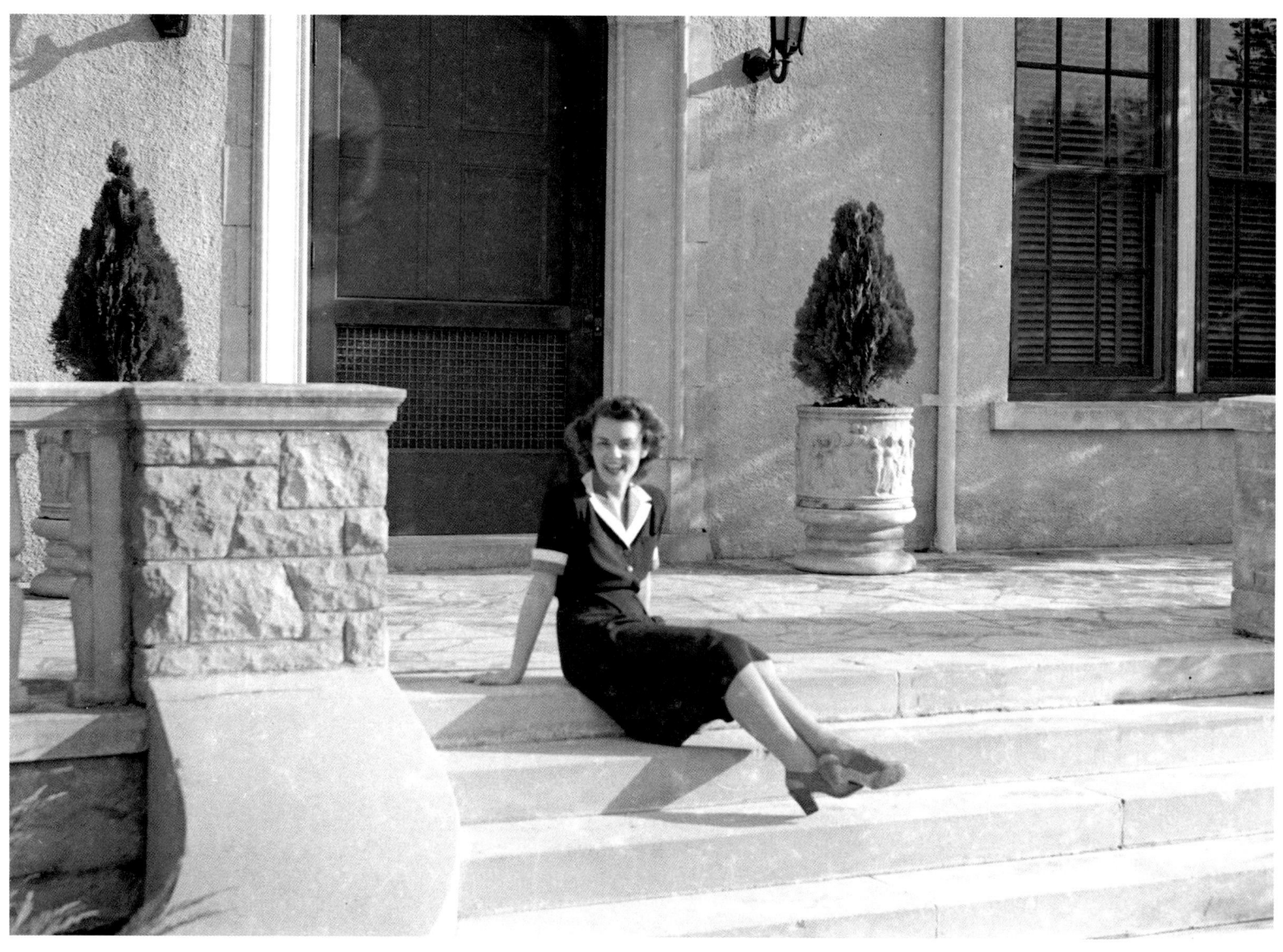

ABOVE: Mom on the front porch of my grandparent's home at 5112 Swiss Avenue in Dallas. 1941.

OPPOSITE: Me sitting, Alex standing, my youngest little brother, Burnie, and Mom on Christmas. 1951.

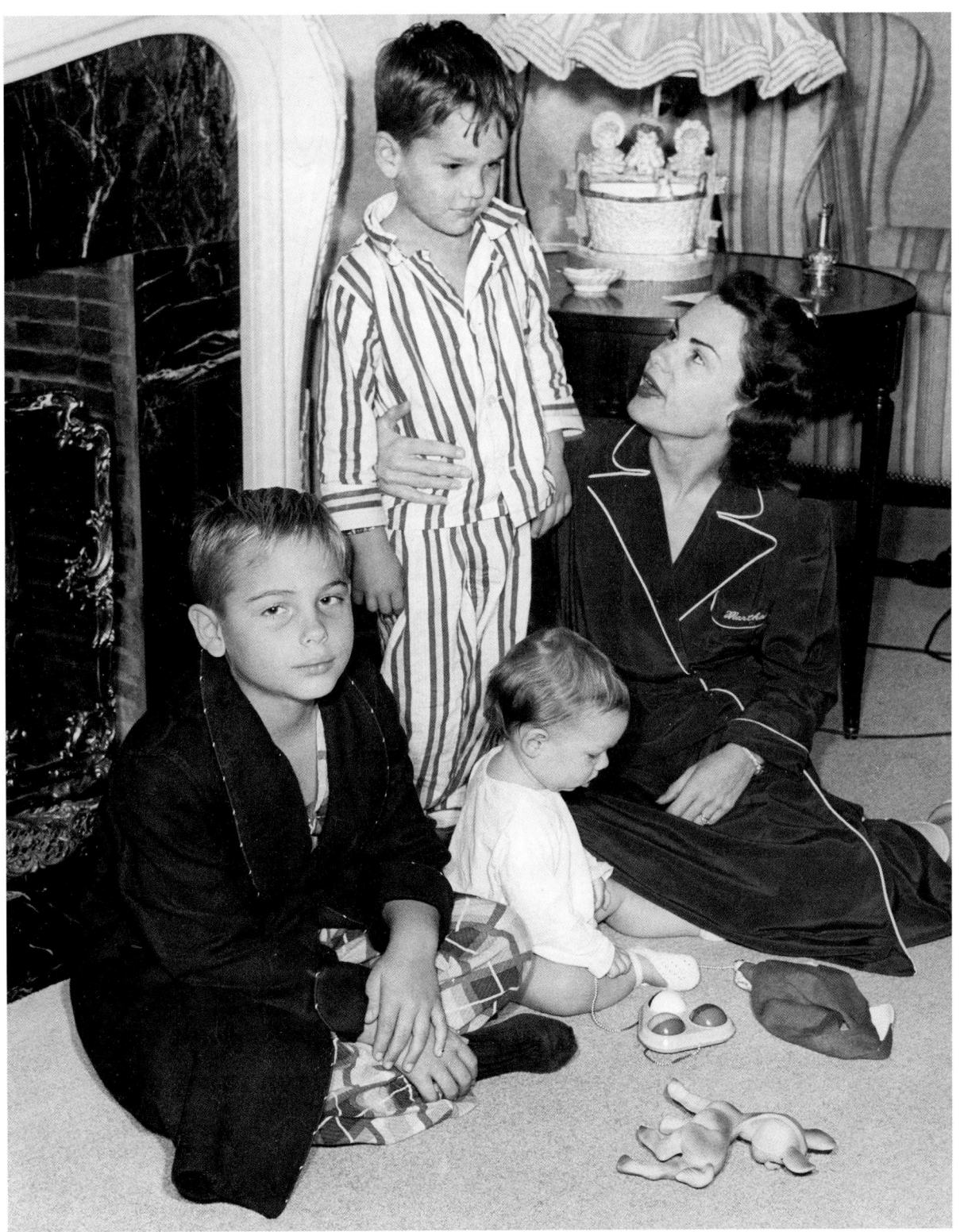

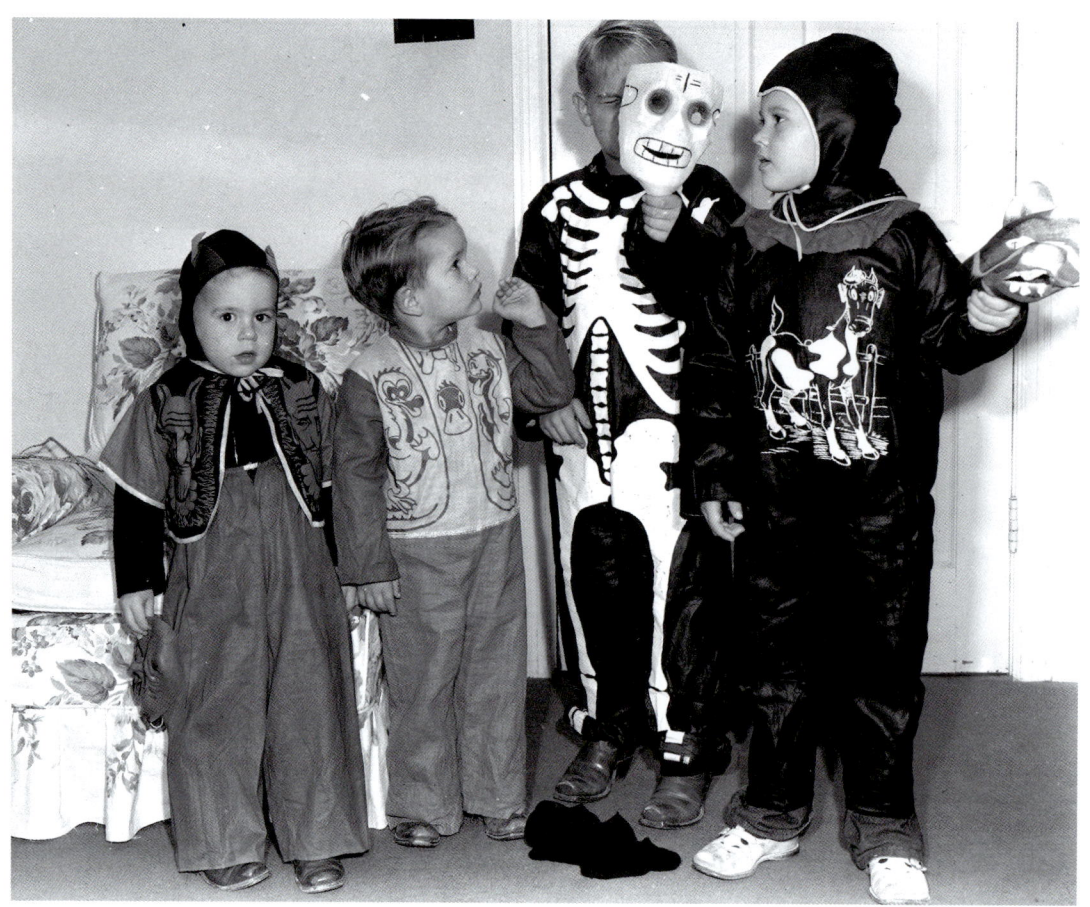

ABOVE: We always dressed up and had fun at Halloween. Younger brother Alex, second from left, and me behind the mask with two other kids from the neighborhood. 1949.

RIGHT: My great-grandparents, Jacob and Lena Burns, with their granddaughter, my nineteen-year-old future mother. They raised her after her mother died and her dad, Ralf, was in Wyoming working in the oilfields. Lena and J.A. felt compelled to come down from Nowata, Oklahoma, to check out this young fellow, Connell Miller, who was courting their precious granddaughter. Fortunately, they approved! 1940.

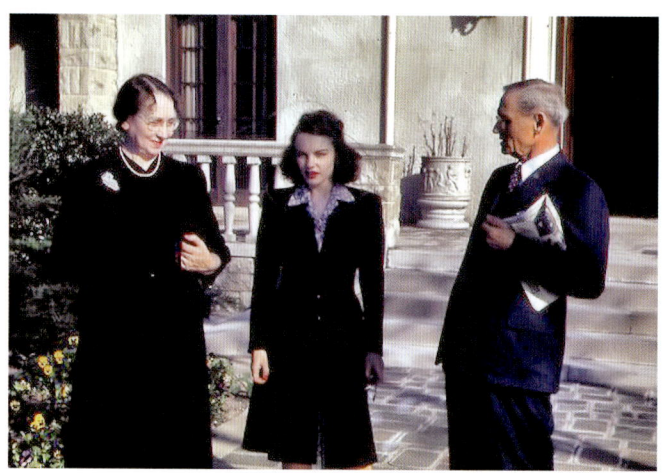

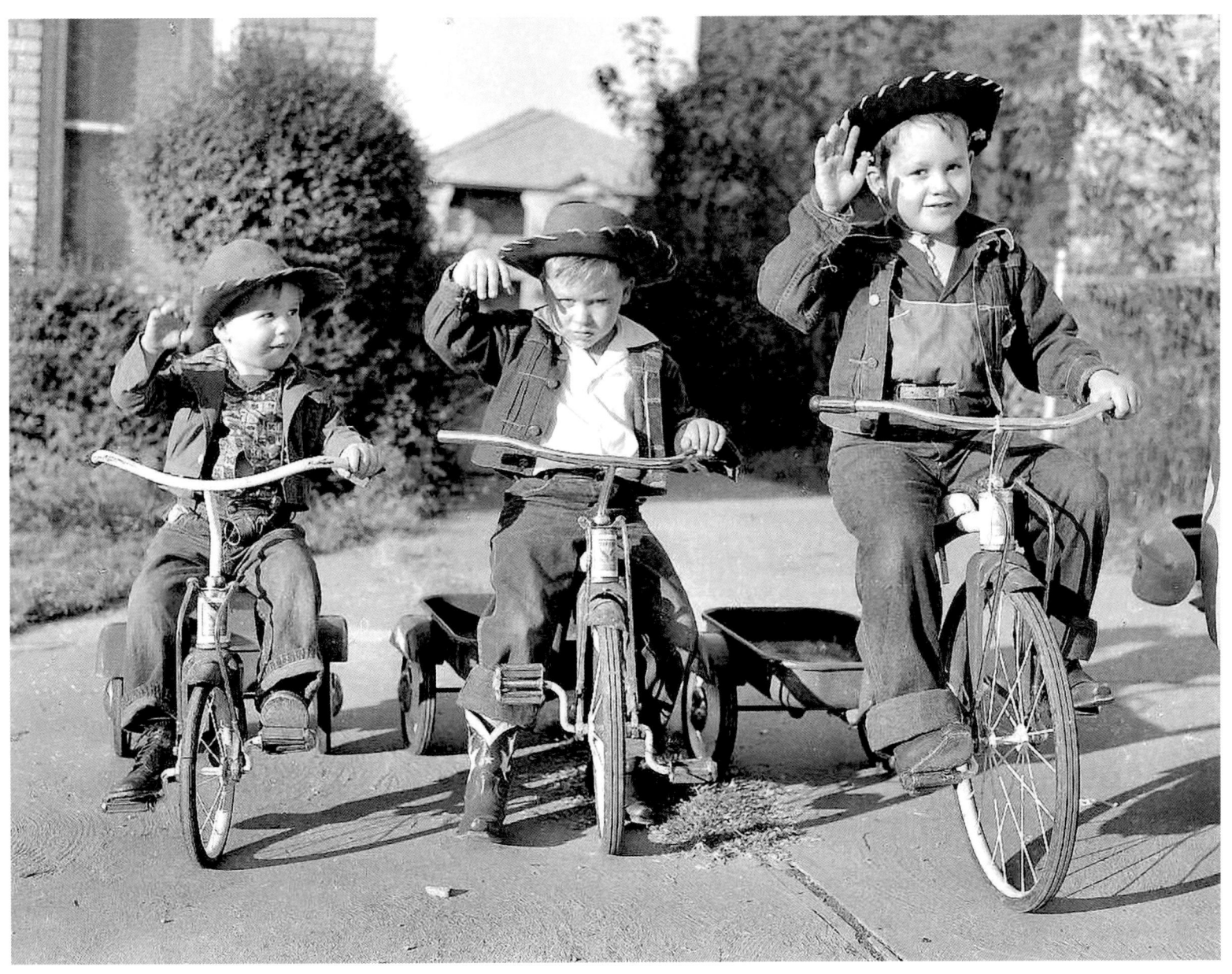

ABOVE: No, it's not the Pep Boys—Manny, Moe, and Jack—those are my three cousins, Donny, Randy, and Ed roaming their Highland Park neighborhood on a trio of tricycles. 1949.

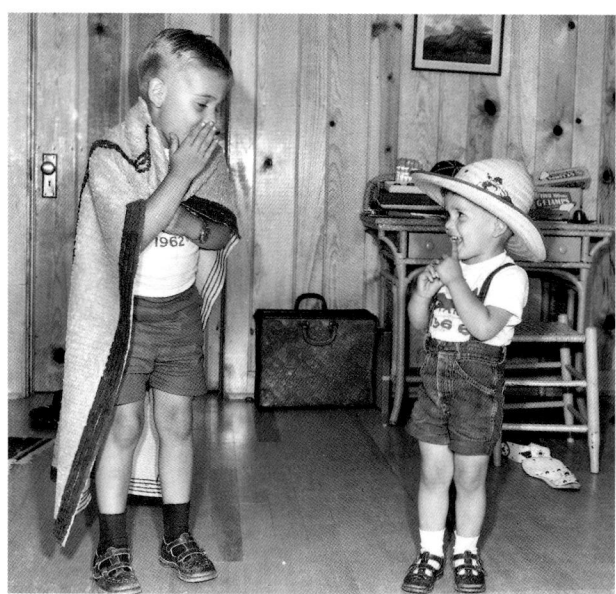

ABOVE: Wearing a cape and whispering to Alex something about my superpowers! I have no idea what the "1962" on my T-shirt is all about (I was actually a sophomore in college in '62). Photo taken in Ruidoso, New Mexico. 1949.

OPPOSITE: Photo used to advertise our family's company, Texas Textile Mills. We sponsored the "Tex-Tex Mill Boys" weekly Western swing broadcasts on WFAA Radio in Dallas. That is my eighteen-year-old father in back with the accordion and my uncle, Bryan Miller (inset photo), the show's regular announcer. I've never heard if they were a threat to Bob Wills and His Texas Playboys or Milton Brown and His Musical Brownies. 1936.

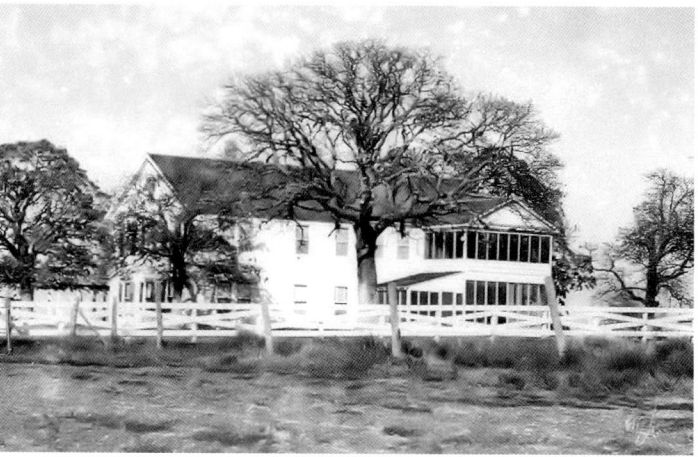

ABOVE: In the 1920s or early 1930s, my grandfather bought 1200 acres of land north of Dallas and near Lewisville. He told the story that when he obtained it, there were a couple of small ramshackle structures on it with a few artifacts in them that indicated it at one time had been a hideout for Sam Bass, notorious Texas outlaw. He had completely cleared everything off the land but told the family he later regretted destroying whatever he found there that might have been classified as having some historical value.

He developed it as a ranch at which to raise his racehorses, some cattle and a few crops. When Dad and his brother Giles were in high school and then college in the late thirties, it was also a great place for them to bring out their friends, girlfriends, and fellow classmates for parties and cookouts, riding horses and boating, since we had a quarter-mile of shoreline with a private dock on Lake Dallas.

I spent many a fun weekend there with my folks, riding my horse, shooting guns (Dad built a large backstop for us), and fishing. When "Pop" Miller passed away on Christmas Eve in 1952, his horses were sold as well as the ranch. It is now a housing development with no semblance of the ranching operation it once was. This was the main ranch house at Crescent Oaks. It was big but not fancy and could house my grandparents, my uncle and his family, and our family all at once. 1950.

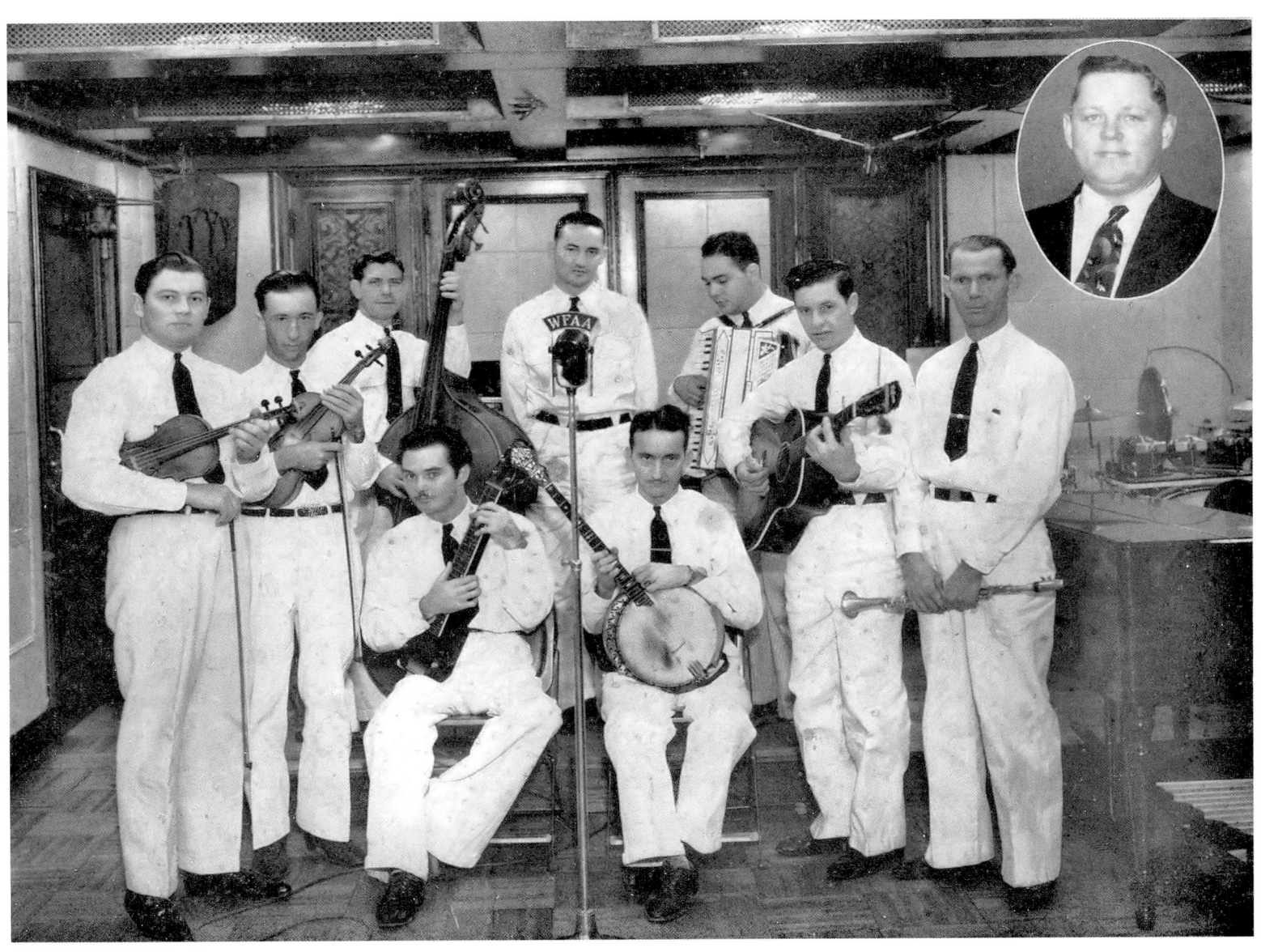

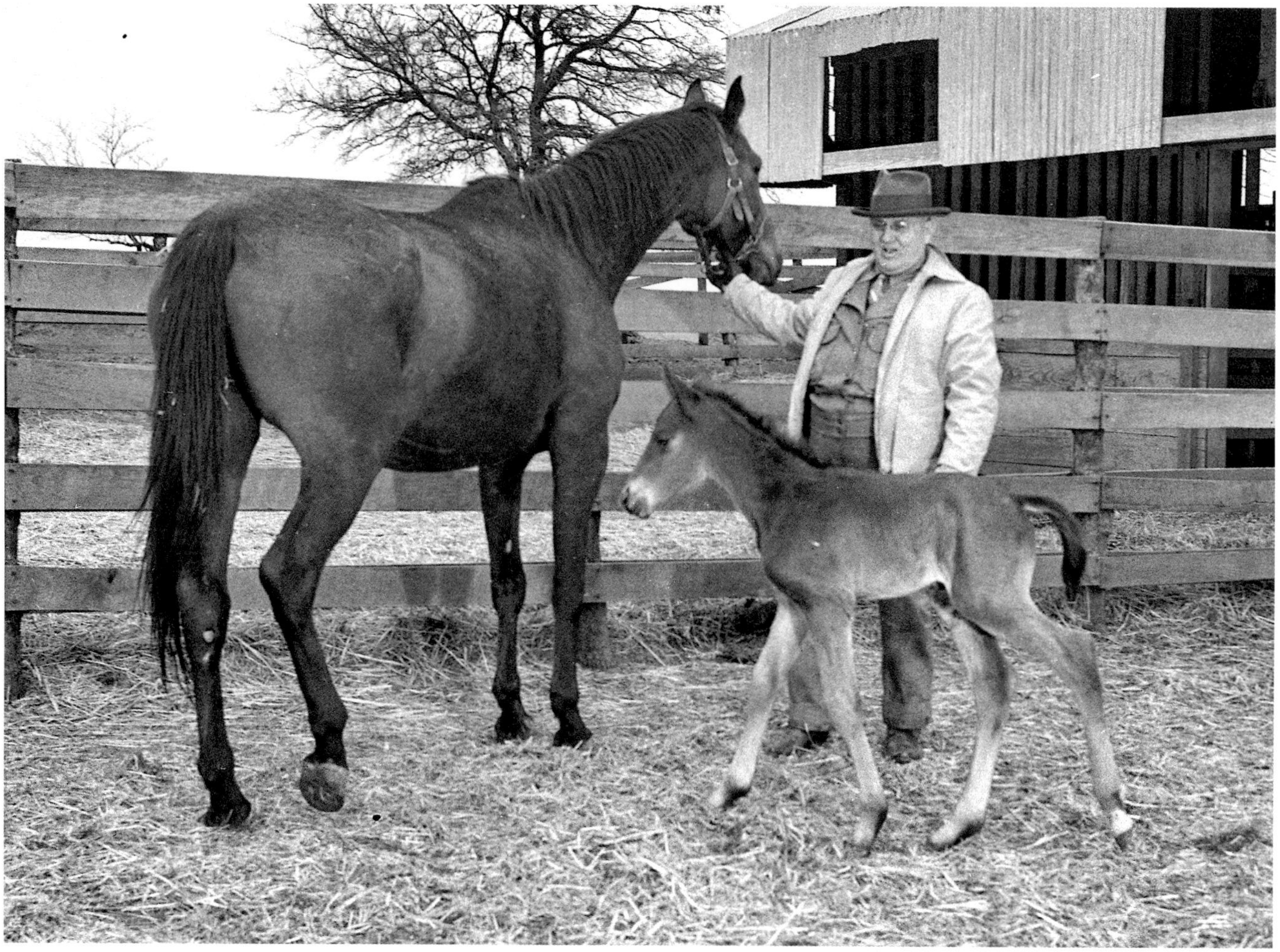

ABOVE: My grandparents lived close to downtown Dallas but loved spending weekends at their ranch and riding horses. 1940s.

LEFT: A horse trainer in a sulky. 1939.

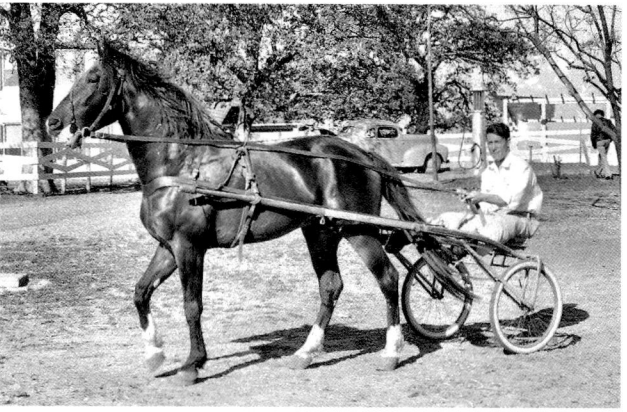

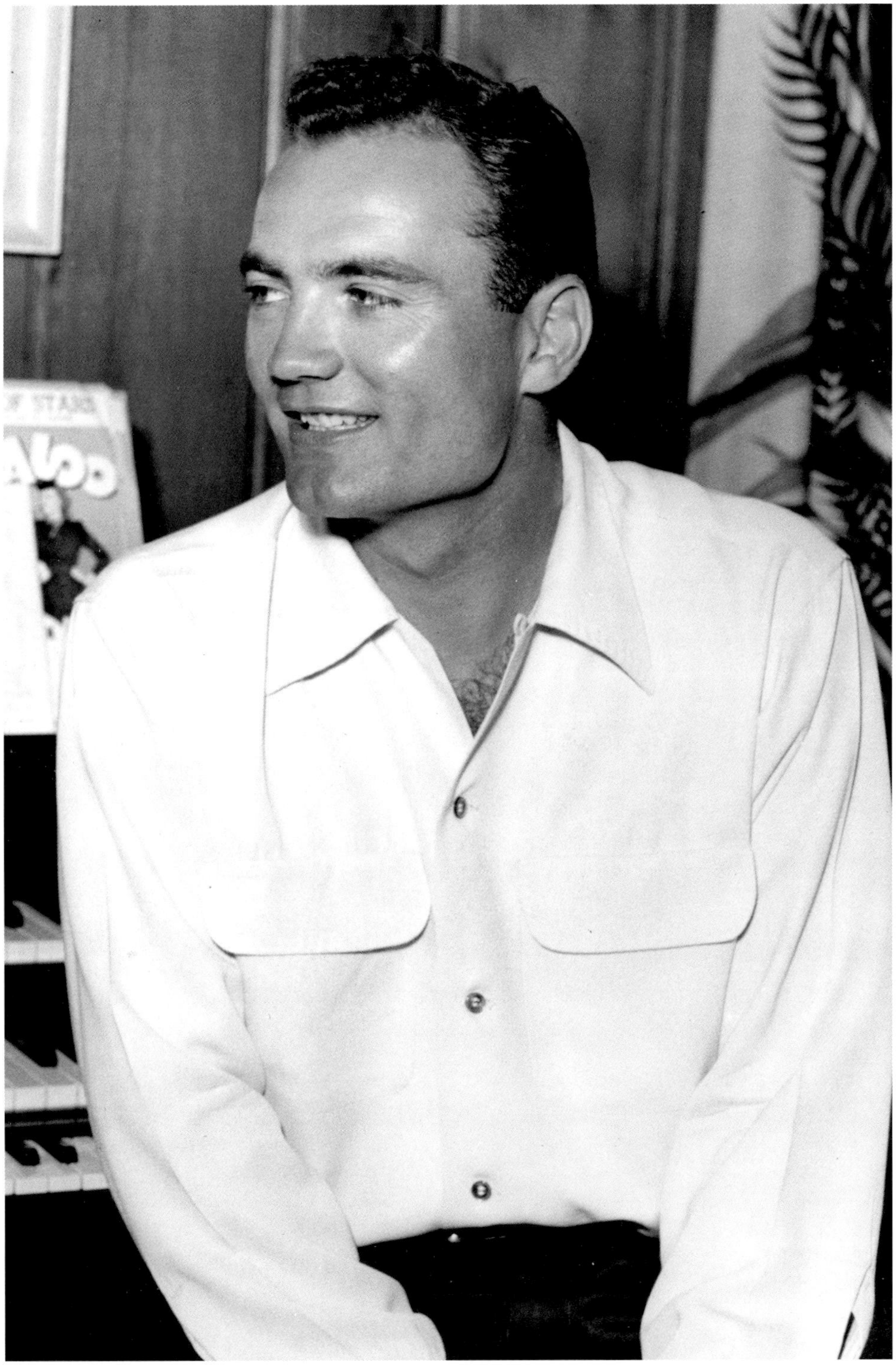

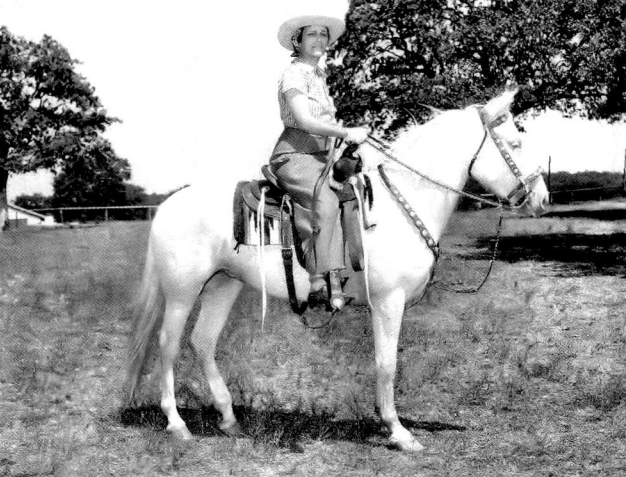

ABOVE: Queen of the ranch, my grandmother, Esther Miller. 1948.

LEFT: Dr. Sylvester Lee Rains was a longtime educator in Dallas and later Tyler. He established and became director of the Research and Evaluation Center for Learning, a cooperative effort between the school district and the Department of Pediatrics at the University of Texas Medical School, for the study of learning and learning disabilities. During the summer in the early 1950s, he and Doug Conner taught swimming and diving at the Dallas Country Club pool. 1954.

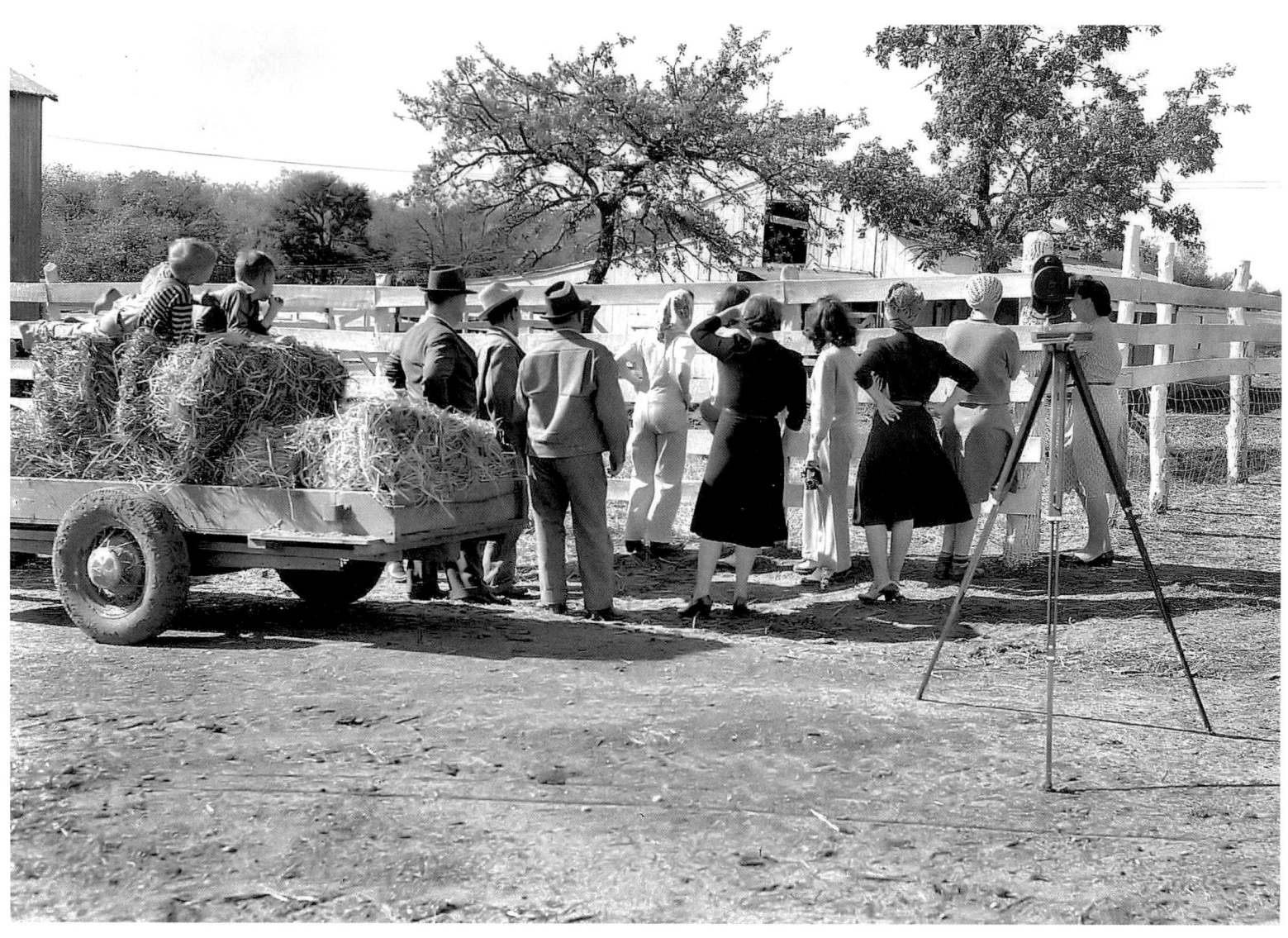

ABOVE: Dad shot this during the auction of my grandfather's racehorses—sad day. 1953.

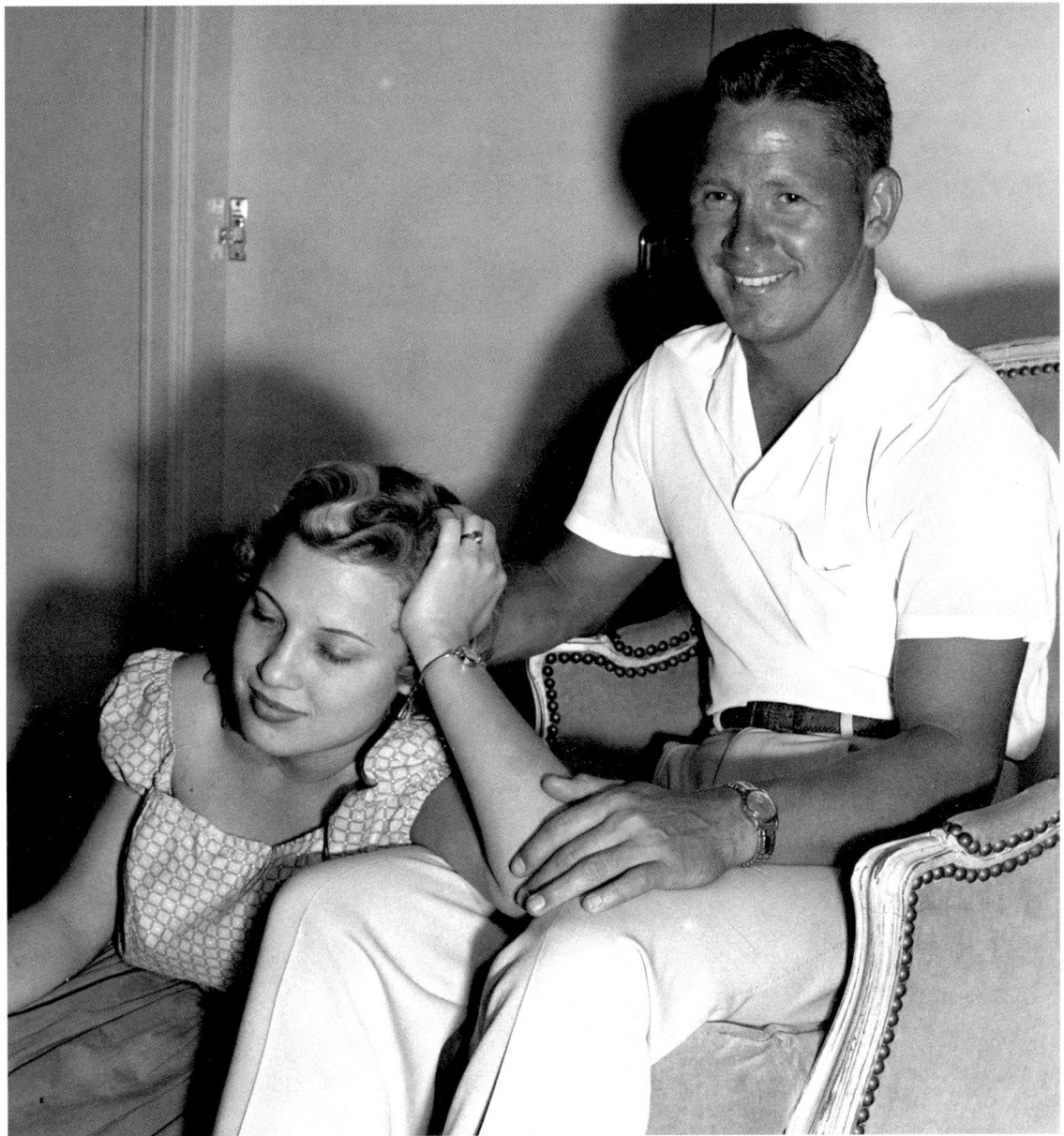

ABOVE: J. Douglas Conner and his wife, Gail. He was registrar and director of admissions at SMU from 1953 to 1966 and was swimming coach at Highland Park High School. During the summer, Doug and his buddy, Sylvester Rains, also gave swim and diving lessons to youngsters at the Dallas Country Club's pool. In 1966, after receiving his doctorate in education psychology from North Texas State University (now the University of North Texas), Dr. Conner went to Washington, DC, to become the first executive director of the American Association of Collegiate Registrars and Admissions Officers. 1954.

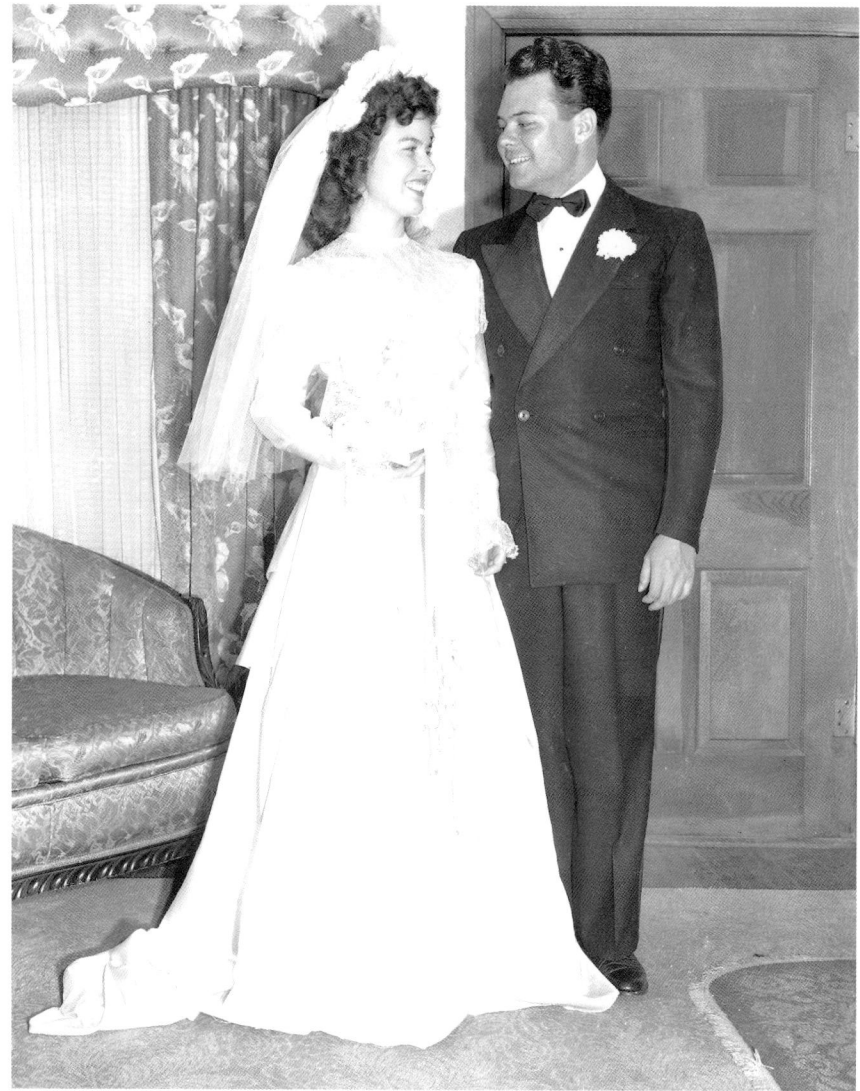

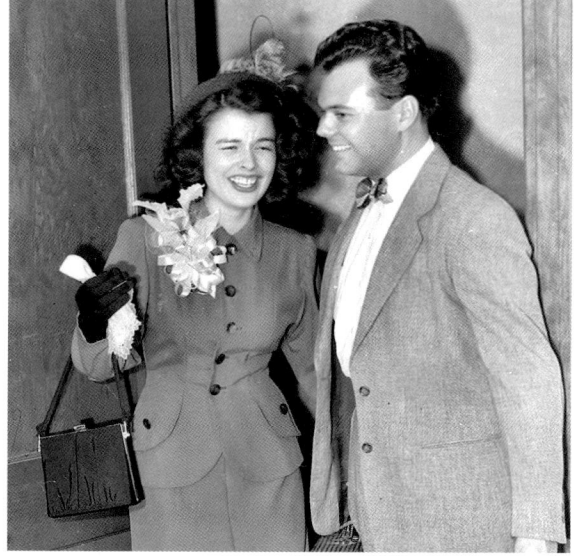

ABOVE: The just-married couple, Mr. and Mrs. Widener, have changed and are leaving for their honeymoon. 1949.

ABOVE: Nuptials between James F. Widener and Betty Grace Bell. The only wedding I am aware of that Dad shot. 1949.

OPPOSITE: James Widener and Dad were fraternity brothers at SMU. Jim and Betty would visit us occasionally, and one time Dad asked her to pose for a glamour-type photo. Here it is from that shoot. Betty was in her nineties and living in Nevada when she passed away in 2024. In 2023, when looking at that shot and noticing she was holding a cigarette, she laughed and said that it was just a prop Dad gave her and that she actually did not smoke. 1949.

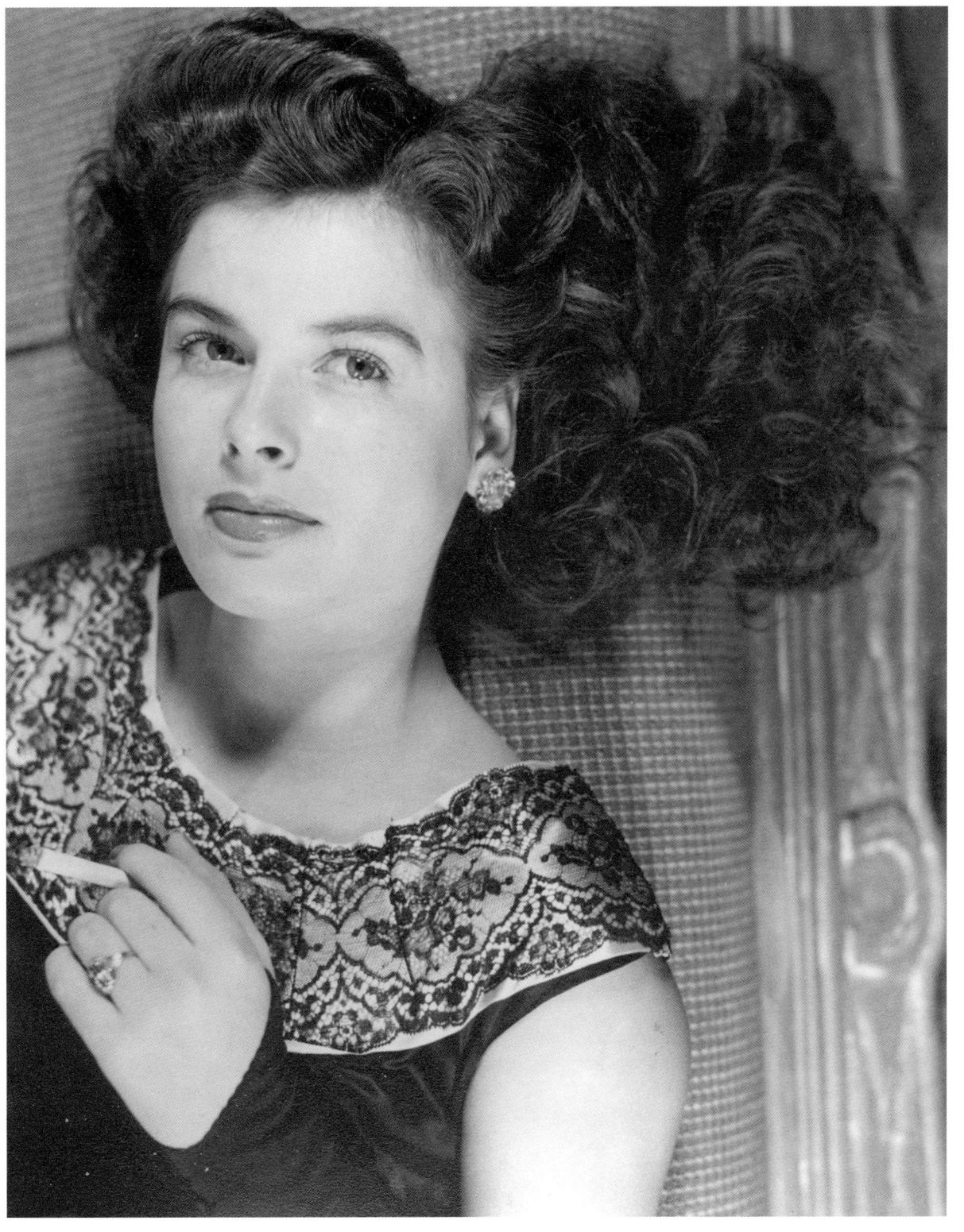

ABOUT THE AUTHOR

Connell R. Miller Jr. is a photographer, artist, musician, and writer living in Bella Vista, Arkansas, with his wife Judy and Tanzie, their Havanese/Bichon mix. Born and raised in Dallas, he has also lived in Fort Worth and Odessa and is a sixth-generation Texan, with roots that include his great-great-great-grandfather Sampson Connell, Sam Houston's Wagonmaster, who delivered the last load of supplies to the ill-fated Alamo and fought alongside Houston at San Jacinto.

Connell has written articles for *D Magazine*, *Texas Monthly*, and *Hot Rod Magazine* and has just finished his first novel. He keeps in touch with old friends in Texas through social media and makes regular phone calls and emails to a Dallas-based hospitality group for which he does consulting.